The Modern Middle East

A HISTORY

Second Edition

James L. Gelvin
University of California, Los Angeles

New York   Oxford
Oxford University Press
2008

Oxford University Press, Inc., publishes works that further Oxford University's
objective of excellence in research, scholarship, and education.

Oxford   New York
Auckland   Cape Town   Dar es Salaam   Hong Kong   Karachi
Kuala Lumpur   Madrid   Melbourne   Mexico City   Nairobi
New Delhi   Shanghai   Taipei   Toronto

With offices in
Argentina   Austria Brazil   Chile   Czech Republic   France   Greece
Guatemala   Hungary   Italy   Japan   Poland   Portugal   Singapore
South Korea   Switzerland   Thailand   Turkey   Ukraine   Vietnam

Copyright © 2008 by Oxford University Press, Inc.

Published by Oxford University Press, Inc.
198 Madison Avenue, New York, New York, 10016
http://www.oup.com

Oxford is a registered trademark of Oxford University Press

Library of Congress Cataloging-in-Publication Data
Gelvin, James L., 1951–
   The modern Middle East : a history / by James L. Gelvin. — 2nd ed.
      p. cm.
   Includes index.
   ISBN 978-0-19-532758-8 — ISBN 978-0-19-532759-5   1. Middle East—
History. 2. Nationalism—Middle East. 3. Secularism—Middle East.
4. Islam and politics—Middle East. I. Title.
   DS62.4.G37 2007
   956—dc22   2007001617

Printing number: 9 8 7 6 5 4 3 2 1

Printed in the United States of America
on acid-free paper

Contents

Vignettes and Maps

Vignettes

Maps

Acknowledgments

Every book is a group effort, mine no less than anyone else's. I would therefore like to use this space to thank those whose assistance has been invaluable to me. First off, there are my former professors, particularly J. C. Hurewitz at Columbia and Zachary Lockman at Harvard, who showed me how it should be done. As the old saying goes, we stand on the shoulders of giants. Others gave direct encouragement, argued, offered advice and solace, and pointed out missteps: Najwa Al-Qattan, David Dean Commins, Michael Cooperson, Howard Eissenstat, Katherine E. Fleming, Carol Hakim, Dina Rizk Khoury, Roya Klaidman, Ussama Makdisi, Karla Mallette, Chase Robinson, and Stefan Weber. Special thanks go to William L. Cleveland, a true gentleman and friend, and to Teo Ruiz at UCLA and Helen Sader at the American University of Beirut, who provided me with the time and support necessary to write this book. T. M. Rollins of the Teaching Company inspired me to begin this project, Bruce D. Borland took an early interest in the manuscript and sold Oxford University Press on the idea, and Peter Coveney, my initial editor at Oxford University Press, saw the first edition of this book through to publication, with the assistance of his committed staff. Many of the photographs in this book came from the private collection of Wolf-Dieter Lemke of the Orient-Institut der Deutschen Morgenländischen Gesellschaft in Beirut and the Fondation Arabe pour l'image, also in Beirut. I am grateful to Sara Scalenghe for apprising me of the latter resource, and Tamara Sawiya for walking me through its extensive collection.

Finally, there are the students I taught at Harvard University, Boston College, Massachusetts Institute of Technology, the University of California, Los Angeles, and the American University of Beirut who, over the years, forced me to distill the narrative and rethink many of the issues raised in this book. It is to them that I dedicate it.

A Note on Transliteration

In this book I have tried to keep the number of foreign words—particularly words borrowed from the Arabic, Persian, and Turkish—to a minimum. To a large degree I think I have succeeded, although, to paraphrase Sigmund Freud, sometimes a *timar* is just a *timar*. Although Arabic in particular contains sounds that do not exist in English (and vice versa), most words readers will confront should pose no problems in terms of pronunciation.

There are two sounds, however, that are represented in English by symbols that will appear strange to the average reader: the *hamza* (represented by ') and the *ayn* (represented by '). The hamza designates what linguists call a glottal stop, the sort of sound one associates with Cockney English, as in " ' allo, guvner!" Thus, when used in the middle of a word, it indicates a breaking off, then a resumption of sound. The *ayn* is a sound produced when the muscles of the throat are constricted as a vowel is pronounced. While it may be difficult for someone who does not speak Arabic to hear the difference between *'amal* and *amal*, for example, the absence of the *ayn* in the latter word alters its meaning significantly, transforming "work" into "hope."

Introduction

9/11
in Historical
Perspective

On 11 September 2001, two hijacked planes crashed into the World Trade Center in New York City, killing 2,752 people. Another plane crashed into the Pentagon Building in Washington, D.C., killing 189. A fourth, possibly headed for the White House or the Capitol, crashed in rural Pennsylvania, killing all aboard.

Soon thereafter, President George W. Bush declared a global war on terror, targeting the mastermind of the crime, Osama bin Laden. American troops entered Afghanistan to destroy bin Laden's support network and associates there and to kill or capture bin Laden. They deposed the government of Afghanistan, which was controlled by a militant Islamic group, the Taliban, and hunted operatives of al-Qaeda, bin Laden's terrorist organization, which had found sanctuary in that country. In the spring of 2003, the United States opened up a new front in the war on terror—Iraq. Although no substantive links between bin Laden or al-Qaeda and the government of Iraq have ever been established, one of the oft-repeated rationales for going to war in Iraq has been, in the words of George W. Bush, that it is "better to fight the terrorists over there than over here." The statistics from the war on terror are grim. As of this writing, over three thousand American soldiers have been killed in Iraq and Afghanistan; estimates of Afghan civilian and noncivilian casualties run between twenty and fifty thousand; and estimates of Iraqi civilian casualties range from fifty to one hundred thousand. The Government Accounting Office has put the cost to the American taxpayer of the war on terror so far at $438 billion. At the moment, bin Laden remains at large.

As anyone who watches the news or reads a newspaper knows, this is a period of extraordinary turmoil in the Middle East. Those policy makers who had argued for the overthrow of the government of Iraq believed that the invasion would be a cakewalk and that the United States could quickly transform Iraq into a regional model of democracy. The facts tell a different story: Presently, mounting sectarian conflict in Iraq threatens to tear apart the fabric of Iraqi society, and Iraq teeters on the brink of all-out civil war. After its initial rout, the Taliban has regrouped and battles rival warlords and NATO troops for power. It also battles for control of the 92 percent of the world's supply of illicit opium now produced in Afghanistan, which it and its warlord adversaries use to finance their military operations. In 1993, Israelis and Palestinians agreed to hammer out their differences through face-to-face diplomacy. When that diplomacy failed, the Israeli government decided that it might end the fifty-year Israeli-Palestinian conflict by constructing a wall (literally) between Israelis and Palestinians, withdrawing from some occupied land, and setting Israel's boundaries unilaterally. By the summer of 2006, tensions between Israel and popular Islamic groups to both the north and south escalated into all-out war. It soon became apparent that neither a negotiated settlement nor an imposed one would be imminent. After eight years under a reformist government that promised democratization at home and moderation in international affairs, Iranians elected a government which resurrected the slogans from the revolutionary era, pursued nuclear weapons in defiance of the international community, and began projecting Iranian influence throughout the region. And far from being the panacea for American woes in the region, elections, such as those held in Palestine, Lebanon, Iraq, and Egypt, have only demonstrated the popular appeal of Islamic parties. How are these phenomena to be explained?

The argument of this book is twofold: First, the only way to understand contemporary events is to understand the history of the region that has become the focus of so much attention. Specifically, this book argues that recent events cannot be understood unless one understands the social, economic, cultural, and political evolution of the Middle East, particularly during the modern period—the period that began in the eighteenth century but has roots that stretch back as far back as the sixteenth. Second, this book contends that the Middle East does not stand outside global history, that the social, economic, cultural, and political evolution of the region parallels (but does not necessarily duplicate) developments in other regions of the world, and that therefore events in the Middle East cannot fully be understood unless placed within their international context. To put it another way, historians specializing in the Middle East certainly have a story to tell, but it is a global story told in a local vernacular.

Although these two propositions would appear to be self-evident, a number of scholars, politicians, and pundits have offered alternative explanations for contemporary events. Some have conjured up something they call an "Islamic civilization," whose main characteristic seems to be an implacable hatred toward the West and modernity. Perhaps the most famous advocate of this position is Samuel P. Huntington, a professor of government at Harvard University. According to Huntington, the world is divided into a number of distinct civilizations which are irreconcilable because they hold to entirely different value systems. Islamic civilization, Huntington asserts, is particularly dangerous because of its propensity for violence (Islam, in Huntington's words, has "bloody borders"). For Huntington and his disciples, the dramatic events of 11 September offer proof positive that Western and Islamic civilizations are doomed to engage in a fight to the death.

Huntington's "clash of civilizations" thesis is open to criticism on a number of grounds. First, Huntington fails to take into account the diversity of the Islamic world. There are, after all, numerous ways Muslims practice their Islam, and there are numerous cultures with which Islam has interacted. This brings us to the second problem with Huntington's thesis: Cultures are not billiard balls that bounce off each other when they come into contact. Throughout history, cultures have borrowed from and influenced each other. During the Middle Ages, for example, Arab philosophers kept alive ancient Greek texts that later provided the foundation for the European Renaissance. Interactions such as this make one despair of ever drawing distinct boundaries for any "culture" or "civilization"—which is why many scholars have abandoned those concepts entirely. Finally, Huntington's thesis is ahistorical. For Huntington and his disciples, the values of Islamic civilization are unchanging and are spelled out in the foundational texts of Islam (such as the Qur'an). But why are we to assume that the meaning and social function of Islam have not changed over time as circumstances have changed? Why are we to assume that a Muslim of the twenty-first century would approach those foundational texts in the same way as a Muslim of the seventh century?

One of the more interesting critiques of Huntington's thesis has come, believe it or not, from the administration of George W. Bush and its supporters. As Bush himself has stated on a number of occasions, America's problem is not with Islam per se. If that were the case, America's purported goal of exporting to the Middle East democracy and freedom—two values the administration maintains are universal—would be futile. Instead, Bush and his supporters have asserted that America's problem is with a radical interpretation of Islam (or what Bush and his supporters have unfortunately labeled "Islamo-fascism"). The real Islam, they publicly contend, is a religion of peace. If only moderate Muslim leaders would step up to the plate, they argue, if only those leaders would wrest control of the hearts and minds of the "Arab street" from the radicals who have hijacked Islam, democracy would spread among benighted Muslims and terrorism aimed at Americans and others would cease.

Of course, a number of Muslim leaders *have* stepped up to the plate. Some have disputed the authority of self-appointed religious experts from the radical fringes to make pronouncements on religious matters (Osama bin Laden, for example, did not learn much theology as an economics major in college). Along with some academic scholars of Islam, these leaders also challenge the radicals' argument that their interpretation of Islam is the one true interpretation of Islam. Take the concept of *jihad*—a concept central to bin Laden's pronouncements. bin Laden and his ilk claim that jihad connotes an armed struggle—a holy war, if you will—against the enemies of Islam. They also claim that it is the duty of each and every Muslim to wage jihad. More mainstream Muslim scholars and scholars of Islam cast doubt on both these arguments. For much of Islamic history, these scholars assert, jihad was not an individual duty; rather, it was a community responsibility. In other words, the duty to defend Islam has traditionally been borne by the proper authorities—such as states—and not by anyone old enough to carry an AK-47 or strap on a bomb. Furthermore, they argue, jihad has had multiple meanings throughout history. For many, it has meant something akin to self-discipline. They derive this interpretation from a statement attributed to the prophet Muhammad himself. Upon returning one day from battle, Muhammad reportedly said to one of his companions, "We return from the lesser jihad [battle] to the greater jihad [usually interpreted as a spiritual struggle or even common labor]." In light of such arguments, one might ask why the radical message resonates at all.

But resonate it does—even among those in the Middle East who abhor bin Laden and his tactics and who crave for themselves more open political systems or the creature comforts enjoyed by Westerners. It is here that the argument advanced by the Bush administration and its supporters breaks down. What the proponents of current American policy in the region have failed to understand is that it is impossible to separate the message from the messenger. Although Americans and Europeans like to think of themselves as the heirs to the Enlightenment traditions of democracy and tolerance, many in the Middle East have experienced otherwise at Western hands. What they see is that after centuries of European imperialism, the United States has simply picked up where the Europeans left off. While the United States proclaims its benevolent intentions, many in the region see the opposite in America's occupation of Iraq and support for Israel. While the United States declares its goal in the region to be the spread of democracy, many in the Middle East remember the American role in overthrowing a democratically elected government of Iran in 1953 and, more recently, America's boycott of a democratically elected government of the Palestinian Authority. And while American leaders weep crocodile tears over human rights, many in the region have paid a high price for America's support of every king and tinhorn dictator from Egypt to Saudi Arabia to Pakistan whose friendship furthers American interests. Little wonder, then, that so many in the Middle East treat America's assurances of goodwill with skepticism.

There are other factors that have contributed to that skepticism as well. Beginning in the 1960s, the Middle East has been hit by a number of debilitating shocks. First, the populist regimes of the 1950s and 1960s—like the regime of Gamal 'Abd al-Nasser in Egypt—which had seemed to promise so much for so many ended up by delivering so little. This was partly caused by their own authoritarian tendencies and the inefficiencies of centralized economic planning, which these regimes encouraged. But just as important, one must count the pressures put on those regimes by the United States, which, during the cold war, viewed them as real or potential Soviet pawns in the high stakes "game of nations" (as one cold warrior called it). Then came the "oil revolution" of the 1970s, a revolution that was sparked by a nearly 400 percent increase in oil prices in 1973–1974. The oil revolution promised to transform social and economic relations of the region. Instead, the oil revolution consolidated the position of America and America's conservative allies in the Middle East, increased the despotic capabilities of governments in the region, and widened the gulf between rich and poor, both within and among the nations of the region. It also opened up the region to the worst consumerist and free market dogmas and brought little in the way of social transformation. Ironically, one of the few accomplishments of the oil revolution was to provide financial support for the bin Laden family. And then the oil bubble popped anyway, leaving broken promises in its wake.

This is not to say that the inhabitants of the Middle East have been passive observers of events. During the period from the 1950s through the 1970s, many in the region looked to secular national liberation movements (like the F.L.N. in Algeria or the Palestine Liberation Organization [PLO]) or nationalist movements (such as those that have represented Arab, Egyptian, Turkish, etc., national aspirations) to challenge Western intrusion, social and political inequity, and economic backwardness. Many still do. But by the late 1970s, secular national liberation and nationalist movements began losing popular support to mass-based Islamic movements for a number of reasons. First, in all too many places in the region, the reputations of secular nationalist regimes had been marred by corruption, inefficiency, and brutality. Islamic movements have offered the beleaguered inhabitants of the Middle East an alternative. Second, during the late 1970s, the United States and international financial institutions not only began preaching the gospel of economic liberalization, they began pressuring increasingly destitute secular nationalist regimes to abandon responsibilities they had assumed in earlier decades. Islamic movements, financed in part by newly enriched oil-exporting states like Saudi Arabia, eagerly stepped into the breach. Groups such as the Muslim Brotherhood of Egypt, Hizbullah, and Hamas built loyal constituencies by providing the medical, educational, and welfare assistance that states in the region could not or would no longer provide. Furthermore, every success scored by one or another Islamic movement provided encouragement to imitators across national boundaries, much as the Algerian Revolution and Nasser had done in earlier decades. After the revolution in Iran, Hizbullah emerged in Lebanon; after Hizbullah emerged in Lebanon, Hamas began its meteoric rise in Palestine. Finally, it did not hurt that Islamic groups addressed popular expectations in a language that seemed more "genuine," more "authentically Middle Eastern," than the secular nationalist language of the regimes they have opposed.

Nevertheless, the highly touted "return of Islam" (as some call it) cannot be used as Exhibit A to prove the Islamic world's natural aversion to modernity, as Huntington and his disciples have done. Just the opposite: Islamic movements are thoroughly modern. They are thoroughly modern, first of all, because they were generated by twentieth-century conditions. For example, Islamic movements are, for the most part, urban movements. They would have been impossible without the enormous growth of urban concentrations in the region—a relatively recent development in Middle Eastern *modernity* ✗

history. These urban concentrations have provided Islamic movements with a prime recruitment ground for an endless stream of underemployed and disaffected activists and supporters. Islamic movements must also be considered modern because they have adopted organizational and operational strategies followed by comparable twentieth- and twenty-first century mass movements, and because they address twentieth- and twenty-first century expectations, such as the expectation that social justice and social welfare are fundamental rights to be enjoyed by all and ensuring those rights should be a primary responsibility of every political system.

The problem is that we are so blinded by associating modernity with the particular historical evolution of the West that we are unable to understand that these movements are offering alternative approaches to modernity. More precisely, the twin towers upon which the modern age rests are an integrated and global economic system and a world system of nation-states. Islamic movements do not offer an alternative to these systems. Indeed, when they do offer a program, they end up—consciously or not—inserting that program within the current economic and state systems. No "Islamic economic system" has been presented or even devised, in spite of all the rhetoric about an "Islamic Third Way." No alternative to the state system has been presented or devised either: Hamas fights for the liberation of Palestine, Hizbullah for the sovereignty of Lebanon. Even the Taliban called the country it once ruled "The Islamic Emirate of Afghanistan." By using the term "Islamic," the Taliban acknowledged that yes, Afghanistan is part of an Islamic cultural sphere. On the other hand, the use of the term "emirate" indicates that the Taliban was claiming for Afghanistan sovereignty within the international state system. The Taliban even sought to represent its "emirate" in the United Nations (it never got to do so).

If it is hard to imagine bin Laden seeking a seat at the United Nations, it is because al-Qaeda represents a totally different type of movement from those we have been discussing. True, al-Qaeda, like Hamas and Hizbullah, for example, communicates its message in an Islamic idiom. And true, this idiom often acts as a road map demarcating proscribed and prescribed tactics and strategies for all three movements. But that is where the similarities end. Unlike Hamas or Hizbullah, al-Qaeda has not organized a mass-based political machine, nor has it built a network of social welfare organizations. As a matter of fact, besides its single-minded focus on jihad, al-Qaeda has no program. While Hamas and Hizbullah wage campaigns of national liberation, al-Qaeda identifies with no particular national struggle. Instead, in their taped messages, spokesmen for al-Qaeda merely allude to the struggles of Palestinians, Bosnians, Chechens, and others (when they remember) to represent the cause of aggrieved Muslims everywhere. While Hamas and Hizbullah have committed horrific acts of violence to achieve specific political goals, the violence used by al-Qaeda is not related to any clear political objective. And while Hamas won the right to lead the Palestinian Authority, and while Hizbullah has similarly won seats in the Lebanese parliament and even cabinet positions in the Lebanese government, it is unthinkable that al-Qaeda, for all its denunciations of impious governments in the region, would take over a government by *coup d'etat*, revolution, or (God forbid) electoral campaign and perform the mundane day-to-day tasks associated with running a modern state.

The preference of the leaders and adherents of al-Qaeda for action over ideology, their single-minded focus on resistance, their lack of programmatic goals, their pursuit of violence for its own sake, their use of a highly decentralized structure built upon semi-autonomous cells—all these factors align al-Qaeda with a type of movement that historically has had nothing to do with Islam at all: anarchism. Like other anarchist movements, al-Qaeda is reactive. It focuses solely on resisting what it considers to be an intrusive alien order and preserving a culture and lifestyle and the homeland of that culture and lifestyle its members believe to be under attack. Unlike other movements whose discourse it shares, al-Qaeda does not operate as a cog within the international state and economic systems. Rather, it wars on those systems.

The world is currently experiencing its second wave of anarchist-style rebellion. Anarchism first appeared during the second half of the nineteenth century, when the modern state and industrial capitalism were spreading throughout the world and replacing previous forms of political and economic organization. The ability of the modern state and industrial capitalism to pervade almost every aspect of social, political, and economic life sparked a defensive reaction—anarchism. Anarchism virtually disappeared with the triumph of the welfare state in the second quarter of the twentieth century. The recent reappearance of anarchist movements (al-Qaeda is just one among many) is directly related to three factors. First, there is the transformation of the international system, both in terms of institutions and guiding principles. Gone are the days when nation-states could set their policies and goals themselves, independent of the strictures of the International Monetary Fund, the World Trade Organization, and the ideology of free trade and open markets. The transformation of international institutions and their guiding principles has not only had economic effects, it has fed fears throughout the world that the internationalization of alien (American or Western) cultural norms and values will have a toxic effect on local norms and values. The second reason for the reappearance of anarchist movements is related to the first: the crisis of the welfare state, which began in the last quarter of the twentieth century in large part as a result of the transformation of the international system. As the social compact that had united citizens with their governments came under strain or dissolved, it was only natural that some of those citizens would respond with rage at both the system they hold responsible for their plight and the sponsors and foreign and domestic beneficiaries of that system. Finally, there is the post-cold war fear that the unrivaled economic and military power of the United States would only fuel its previously restrained imperial ambitions. Needless to say, those fears have not been allayed by recent events.

The anarchist response to the transformation of the international system, the crisis of the welfare state, and the fear of unchecked American power has not been limited to the Middle East. It was not an "Islamo-fascist," after all, who burned down a McDonald's in France, nor are "Islamo-fascists" well-represented at protest rallies held whenever representatives to the World Trade Organization meet. Nor has the only response to the new international dispensation been anarchism, as the recent resurgence of "neo-populism" in Venezuela, Peru, Bolivia, and other places in Latin America demonstrates. Nevertheless, there is a twofold lesson to be drawn from situating al-Qaeda within the framework I have outlined. First, lumping together organizations as diverse as Hamas and al-Qaeda under the label "terrorist" or "Islamo-fascist" is as unhelpful as blaming 9/11 on an Islamic civilization that rejects modernity. Second, the emergence of al-Qaeda and the events of 11 September should not be viewed as some inexplicable "Islamic thing," nor as the result of mere happenstance. It is, as stated above, part of a global story told in a local vernacular. It is to the rest of that story we now turn.

Part 1

THE ADVENT OF THE
MODERN AGE

This book is about the *modern* Middle East. The underlying argument of this book is that the eighteenth century marked a new phase in the evolution of world history. As stated in the introduction, two important characteristics distinguish modern history: a world economy unlike any that had existed before and a world system of nation-states. On the one hand, the modern period marks the emergence of an integrated world market, binding together nations in a global division of labor. On the other hand, during the modern period a new form of political association—the nation-state—appears on the world stage for the first time, spreads, and achieves primacy worldwide. These twin systems have affected economic, social, cultural, and political life everywhere in ways that were unprecedented in world history.

Neither the world economy nor the world system of nation-states appeared overnight. Both needed an incubation period, during which they could be refined and expand throughout the globe. This incubation period took place during a era called by historians the "early modern" period, which lasted from about the beginning of the sixteenth century through the first half of the eighteenth century. Thus, to understand the modern history of the Middle East or any other region, it is necessary first to understand its roots in the early modern period.

Three events occurred in the first decades of the sixteenth century that would redefine the Middle East forever. Only one of these events actually occurred in the Middle East. The other two occurred far away from the Middle East, but would define the global environment in which the Middle East would evolve.

The first event that took place at the dawn of the early modern period was the emergence of large-scale and long-lived empires in the Middle East and beyond. Three such empires emerged during this period. The largest and longest-lived of these great empires was the Ottoman Empire. The Ottoman Empire survived for more than four centuries until it was finally dismantled at the end of World War I in 1918. The Ottoman Empire provides us with a direct link from the early modern period through the modern period.

At its height, the Ottoman Empire governed a huge expanse of territory, not only in the Middle East, but in North Africa and Southeastern Europe—Greece, Hungary, the Balkans, Romania, Bulgaria—as well. Indeed, there is reason for the famous quip by the nineteenth-century Austrian statesman Prince Klemens von Metternich that "Asia begins at the eastern gate of Vienna." The Ottomans, in fact, had laid siege to Vienna itself twice, the first time in 1529, the second in 1683. No wonder, then, that an English historian writing in the beginning of the seventeenth century called the Ottoman Empire, "the present terror of the world."

The second empire to emerge at the beginning of the sixteenth century was the Safavid Empire. The Safavid Empire was centered in Persia but at its height included territories that stretched from the Caucasus mountains in the north to eastern Iraq. The Safavid Empire lasted from 1501 to 1722, when it was overthrown by an invading army from Afghanistan. After a disastrous interregnum period, most noted for bringing Persia incessant war, depopulation, deurbanization, and intermittent famine, another Turkic dynasty took over from the Safavids. This was the Qajar Dynasty, which ruled from 1796 to 1925. Although the Safavid dynasty itself lasted only half as long as the Ottoman Empire, its significance lies in its twofold legacy: The Safavid Empire established a state whose boundaries roughly coincided with the boundaries of present-day Iran and, under the Safavids, the population of Persia became adherents of the Shi'i branch of Islam.

One other Muslim empire emerged during this period, which bears mentioning even though its history lies outside the scope of this book: the Mughal Empire of India. Founded in 1526, the Mughal Empire stretched, at its height, from Afghanistan in the north three-quarters of the way down the Indian subcontinent. The Mughal Empire ran afoul of British imperialism and, in 1858, was ousted by the British, who then made India into a British colony. The Mughal Empire resembled the Ottoman and Safavid empires in many ways: Like the other empires, it was founded by a people from Central Asia (the first Mughal emperor, Babar, claimed descent from the half-Mongol, half-Turkish conqueror, Tamerlaine) and it shared political and economic structures and intellectual traditions with the Ottomans and Safavids. Unfortunately, the Mughal Empire lies outside the artificial boundaries we set for ourselves in writing the history of the modern Middle East. Its history is instead commonly addressed by historians who focus on another artificial geographical division, historians of India.

The second event that occurred at the dawn of the early modern period was the commercial revolution in Europe. During the early sixteenth century, trade among Europeans, on the one hand, and between Europe and other parts of the world, on the other, began to increase dramatically. A variety of factors encouraged the commercial revolution: technological breakthroughs, such as the use of the compass and adjustable sails and multiple masts on ships; new institutions for organizing trade and banking; the introduction of new crops—from tomatoes and potatoes to tobacco—from the New World; the introduction of massive quantities of New World gold and silver into Europe; and the establishment of overseas colonies, from the Persian Gulf to the newly discovered Americas. According to many historians, the commercial revolution set off a chain of events that would culminate in the establishment of the modern world economy. The impact of the commercial revolution on the Middle East is the topic of the Chapter 3.

The final event that took place at the dawn of the early modern era was the Protestant Reformation. The Protestant Reformation is commonly dated from 1517, when Martin Luther nailed his ninety-five theses on the door of the Wittenburg Cathedral in present-day Germany. Luther's theses both protested various policies and doctrines of the Roman Catholic Church and advocated new ones. The Protestant Reformation split Europe into separate Protestant and Catholic kingdoms and principalities, thereby ending the idea of a universal Christian state. It culminated in a series of religious wars during the sixteenth and seventeenth centuries. The Europe that emerged from these wars was very different from the Europe that entered them. As a result of the religious wars, Europe divided into highly competitive and sometimes highly efficient political units. European history became marked by attempts of these states to gain advantage or achieve a balance among themselves. In effect, then, modern nation-states and the nation-state system might be traced to the Protestant Reformation. The spread of the modern state system would have a profound effect on the Middle East.

Of course, the ways in which the three aforementioned events affected the Middle East were to a large extent determined by their interaction with existing social structures, economic arrangements, and cultural norms. Thus, to understand the impact of this period on the Middle East we have to understand the legacy of the earlier history of the region. That is where Part I of this book begins.

The Middle East in Late Antiquity

Elevation (meters)

0–200
200–500
500–1,000
1,000–2,000
2,000–3,000
3,000–4,000

BYZANTINE EMPIRE

SASANIAN EMPIRE

Constantinople

BLACK SEA

Caucasus Mountains

CASPIAN SEA

Taurus Mountains

MEDITERRANEAN SEA

EGYPT

Nile R.

LEVANT

Damascus

MESOPOTAMIA

Ctesiphon

PERSIA

PERSIAN GULF

Medina

Mecca

ARABIAN PENINSULA

RED SEA

ARABIAN SEA

0   500   1000 km

One

From Late Antiquity to the Dawn of a New Age

That which can be called the Islamic "core area"—the area of the first Islamic conquests—is the area that stretches from the Nile River in the west to the Oxus River in the east. The Islamic core area consists of five parts. First, there is the area called the Levant. The word Levant is derived from the French word *lever*, to rise, as the sun does in the east. Accordingly, the Levant is the area that stretches from the eastern Mediterranean coast as far west as the Euphrates River—the eastern Arab world. In the north, the Levant extends to the Taurus mountains in the Anatolian peninsula (the site of present-day Turkey); in the south, it extends to the northern border of the Arabian peninsula.

To the south of the Levant lie Egypt and the Arabian peninsula. To the east lie Mesopotamia and Iran. The name Mesopotamia is derived from the Greek words meaning "middle of the rivers," much as the word hippopotamus is derived from the Greek words meaning "river horse." The term Mesopotamia refers not only to the territory between the Tigris and Euphrates Rivers, but to the areas immediately surrounding the two rivers as well. Iran is the name given to the territory that was once called Persia. In 1935, the shah (ruler) of Persia decreed that foreigners should use the word Iran, a word of ancient pedigree, when referring to his country. The story goes that the shah was so enamored of the racial theories popularized by Adolph Hitler that, at the suggestion of the Persian embassy in Berlin, he had the name Persia changed in diplomatic parlance to Iran to illustrate the "Aryan" roots of his nation. Needless to say, the name has stuck, and even the contemporary rulers of the country refer to their state as the Islamic Republic of Iran.

If you look closely at a map of the core area, you will see at the center a plain surrounded on all sides by mountains, deserts, and plateaus: to the north, in Anatolia, the Taurus Mountains; to the west, a range of mountains that divides the central plain from the coastal plain and the Mediterranean Sea; to the east, the Iranian plateau and the Zagros Mountains; and to the south, the Arabian desert. The plain has been both prize and passageway for conquerors from both the east and the west for millennia.

Islam arose in an era known as Late Antiquity, a period that began in the fourth century and ended in the seventh. At the end of the sixth century, two empires contended for control of the central plain. To the west of the central plain lay the Roman Empire, also known as the Eastern Roman Empire or the Byzantine Empire. Its capital was Constantinople, a city built on the site of a previously existing village, Byzantium (hence, the name Byzantine Empire). It is now called Istanbul. Constantinople was founded by Emperor Constantine in A.D. 324. Toward the end of that same century, the Roman Empire was divided into two administrative parts, with capitals at Rome and Constantinople. With the fall of the Western Roman Empire in 476, Constantinople was, in effect, the sole capital of the Roman Empire. For most of Late Antiquity, the emperors ruling from Constantinople held sway over the Anatolian peninsula, the western Levant, and Egypt.

The Sasanian Empire lay to the east of the central plain. The Sasanian Empire had been founded in the early third century and lasted until the year 651. For most of its history, the Sasanian Empire actually controlled an area larger than contemporary Iran, incorporating parts of the old Soviet Union, Afghanistan, Pakistan, and Iraq. As a matter of fact, the Sasanian capital was Ctesiphon, in what is now Iraq, not far from present-day Baghdad.

Ancient empires were not like the nation-states we know. Imperial governments were mainly concerned with collecting taxes and tribute from their populations, expanding the territory from which they might collect taxes and tribute, and maintaining order in their empires to make that tax and tribute collection possible. Imperial governments did not attempt to impose a single language or ideology or culture on their populations. Nor did they much care that the peoples who lived in them were of different ethnic backgrounds. Thus, although the state language of the Roman Empire in Late Antiquity was Greek and the state religion was Orthodox Christianity, the empire included diverse peoples—Greeks, Latins, Semites, and others—who spoke a variety of vernacular languages and practiced a variety of religions. These included non-Orthodox Christianity, Judaism, Greco-Roman paganism, and local cults. Likewise, the Sasanian Empire housed a variety of ethnic groups that spoke a variety of languages. Although the empire was governed by a Persian ruling class that spoke a language called Pahlavi (the forerunner of modern Persian), Kurds (mainly in the mountains), Aramaic-speaking Arabs (mainly in Iraq), and a variety of other peoples inhabited the empire. The Sasanian Empire sponsored a state religion, Zoroastrianism. Nevertheless, in many of the most densely inhabited places such as Iraq, Christianity overshadowed the official religion.

During the sixth century, energetic leaders in both the Sasanian and Roman empires sought to centralize control and expand their territories. The wars they fought against each other were fought mainly in the Middle East. In A.D. 602, the Sasanian emperor Chosroes II launched an offensive against the Roman Empire and conquered as far west as Syria and Egypt. He even laid siege to Constantinople before the Roman Emperor, Heraclius, counterattacked. The war was devastating for both sides: the Sasanian Empire was, in effect, destroyed by the costs of incessant campaigning and by the loss of Iraq, which had provided more revenue than any other province. The Roman Empire survived, but in truncated and weakened form. Both empires were thus vulnerable to a challenge from the south.

Islamic history begins in A.D. 622, when the prophet Muhammad fled to the western Arabian town of Medina from his hometown of Mecca, also in western Arabia. Muhammad was a merchant. According to Muslims, at the age of about forty he started receiving revelations from God brought by the archangel Gabriel. Persecuted in Mecca, Muhammad established the first lasting Islamic community in Medina. It is significant that, whereas Christians use the birth of Christ as the starting point of their calendar (A.D. 1), Muslims use the formation of the first Islamic community as the starting point of theirs: 1 A.H. (which stands for "after *hijra*," i.e., the year of Muhammad's migration) is, in the Christian calendar, A.D. 622. The notion of the community of believers is important in Islam, and the first community established by Muhammad is particularly important because, as we shall see later, it has provided many with a model for the ideal Islamic community.

Over the course of the next ten years, Muhammad's community continued to grow. By the time of Muhammad's death, much of the Arabian peninsula had joined or was affiliated with the Islamic community of Medina.

The period following Muhammad's death was one of vast Islamic expansion. Within a hundred years of Muhammad's death, Arab/Muslim armies had conquered all of Persia, Mesopotamia, Egypt, and the Levant. They had pushed back the frontier of the Byzantine Empire in the north, had traversed North Africa, and had crossed the Mediterranean. There is still a trace of this crossing in the name of the island between North Africa and Spain— Gibraltar—derived from the words *jabal Tariq*, the mountain of Tariq, the general who led the Muslim armies into Spain. In 732 a Muslim army even launched a foray into the territory that is now France, but was turned back. The Islamic conquests were followed by settlement of Arabs throughout the conquered territories. Different historians have given various reasons for the expansion of Arab settlement: some claim it was the lure of booty or military pay, others religious or warrior zeal.

During the first century of Islamic history, the Islamic community was united in a single empire. Over time, most of the population of the empire converted to Islam. This did not occur overnight, nor did it occur at the same rate in every territory. Using as evidence the adoption of Arab/Muslim names—Persian children who would have once been named Ardeshir were now bearing the name Muhammad—historians have estimated that one hundred years after the Muslim conquests only about 8 percent of the Persian population was Muslim. By the tenth century, from 70 to 80 percent of the Persian population was Muslim. The rates of conversion were probably faster in Iraq and slower in Egypt. With the exception of Persia, most of the population of the core area adopted Arabic as their language.

Three other aspects of the early period of Islam are important for understanding the subsequent history of the region. First, after the death of

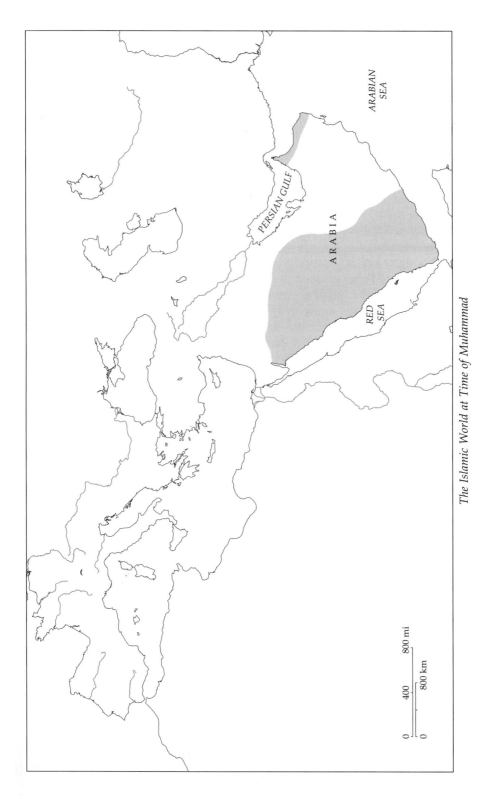

PERSIAN GULF

ARABIAN
SEA

ARABIA

RED
SEA

0   400   800 mi

0   800 km

The Islamic World at Time of Muhammad

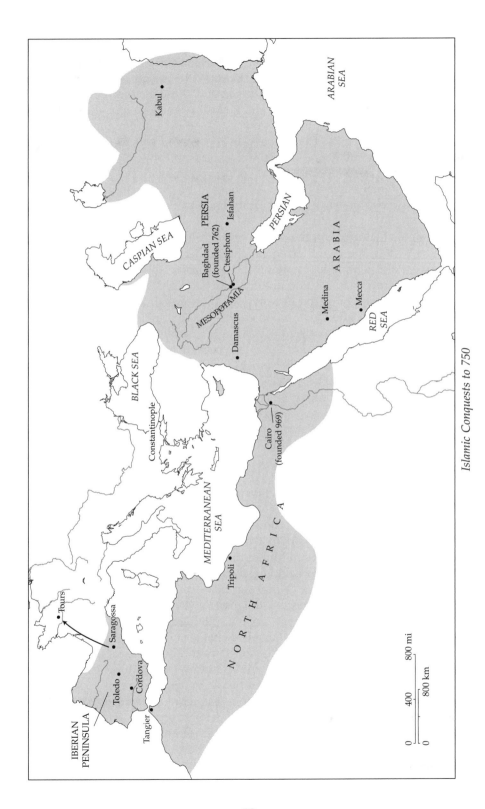

Islamic Conquests to 750

IBERIAN PENINSULA

Toledo
Córdova
Tangier
Saragossa
Tours

NORTH AFRICA

Tripoli

MEDITERRANEAN SEA

Constantinople

BLACK SEA

CASPIAN SEA

Cairo
(founded 969)

Damascus

MESOPOTAMIA

Baghdad
(founded 762)
Ctesiphon
Isfahan

PERSIA

Kabul

RED SEA

PERSIAN

ARABIA

Medina
Mecca

ARABIAN SEA

0   400   800 mi
0   800 km

Muhammad, there was the question of whether or not there should be a leader of the Islamic community and, if so, who that leader should be. Prominent members of the community gathered and chose the first caliph; that is, the first successor to Muhammad. Unlike Muhammad, caliphs did not have a special religious role. Muhammad was, according to Islam, the "seal" (the last) of God's prophets. The function of the caliphs was to protect the interests of the community. Questions of religion and religious law remained in the hands of religious scholars called ulama (singular: ʿalim). They still do. Since 1924, when the last caliph was deposed by the modernizing government of Turkey, the Islamic community has functioned quite well without a caliph.

During its history, both the nature of the caliphate and its seat of power varied. At first, the caliph acted much like a tribal leader. He was "first among equals" who relied more on his persuasive abilities than on his coercive abilities to lead the community. Later, caliphs adopted much of the pomp and ceremony of the Byzantine and Sasanian courts, and even assumed the title "shadow of God on earth," a title originally used by Sasanian shahs. Over time, as caliphs increasingly lost political and military control to local princes, the role of the caliph became more and more symbolic.

The first four caliphs ruled from Medina. Their immediate successors ruled from Damascus. This was a logical development because the city lay on major trade routes linking Arabia with the north and Byzantine territories and provided caliphs with access to reserves of warriors from Arabia. As the center of gravity of Islamic territories shifted to the east, and as more and more non-Arabs converted to Islam, the caliphs ruled from Iraq. As a matter of fact, the city of Baghdad was originally built as the administrative capital of the caliphate.

The second aspect of the early Islamic period that would have ramifications for later history was one of several splits in the Islamic community. The split was originally over who would act as successor to Muhammad. Some in the community thought that ʿAli, Muhammad's son-in-law and cousin, should have succeeded Muhammad. They became known as the partisans of ʿAli, or shiʿat ʿAli, and later just Shiʿis. Most of the Islamic community followed the choice of a group of leading notables, acquiring the name Sunnis (from the phrase "the people of [Muhammad's] example [sunna] and community"). Over time, the split hardened as each community developed its own traditions and sets of beliefs. Today, Shiʿis form a majority of the population in several of the states this book discusses: Iran, Iraq, and Lebanon. Sunnis are predominant in Turkey and, with the exception of Iraq and Lebanon, most of the rest of the Arab world.

One aspect of Shiʿism merits further explanation. At its inception Shiʿism was an opposition party. During the early Islamic period, various Shiʿi sects arose that were united by a fundamental set of beliefs, even though they had political differences. At the center of these beliefs was the notion that the imam, the leader of the community, should be chosen from the house of ʿAli, Muhammad's closest male relative. Over time, the Shiʿi tendency adopted three other beliefs as well. First, Shiʿis came to believe that the imam alone was the community's teacher and religious leader. Furthermore, they believed that the imam had a special, esoteric (hidden) knowledge. This contrasted with the view of the Sunnis that proper Islamic belief was preserved by the community as a whole. Finally, Shi'is came to believe that the next imam had to be designated by the previous imam.

The line of imams continued without interruption from 'Ali through six generations. The sixth imam named his son Isma'il as his successor. But Isma'il died before his father, and so his father selected his second son, Musa, to succeed him. For some Shi'is, this could not be: after all, the imam had secret knowledge and so the father must have foreseen Isma'il's absence. These Shi'is thus believed that Isma'il was not really dead, but instead had gone into what is called "occultation." In other words, Isma'il was around, they just did not know where. At the end of time he would return and establish justice and equity on earth. Because Isma'il was to have been the seventh imam, these Shi'is were sometimes called Isma'ilis. The contemporary Isma'ili community in India, which is under the spiritual leadership of the Agha Khan, are their descendants.

Other Shi'is, however, acknowledged the 'Alid line as it ran through Isma'il's brother's son, Musa. But after the eleventh imam died without apparent heirs, they faced a problem similar to the one they had faced earlier. They came up with a solution similar to the solution at which the Isma'ilis had arrived. They believed that the eleventh imam had had a son, but that he was in occultation. These Shi'is came to be known as Twelvers, because they awaited the return of the twelfth imam. These are the Shi'is who are predominant in Lebanon, Iraq, and parts of the Gulf today—and, of course, the home of the largest Twelver Shi'i community today, Iran. The idea of occultation raised two issues that would be of crucial importance to the Shi'i community in the future: Who should govern the community until the reemergence of the hidden imam and how the community should organize its affairs in the meantime.

The final aspect of the early period of Islam that is important for understanding later developments stems from the fact that the number of Arab conquerors was small in comparison with the number of those conquered. This disparity naturally created difficulties for the conquerors. The caliphs attempted to resolve these difficulties by borrowing administrative techniques from the Sasanians and Byzantines. For the most part, the conquerors allowed the inhabitants of the territories they administered to retain their landed property and to maintain local governance. "Peoples of the book"— a category that included Christians and Jews—were, at least in theory, accorded the status of protected minorities and were allowed to continue practicing their religions. Pagans (polytheists) whom Muslims encountered were not so lucky, and Hindu parents on the Indian subcontinent still spook their children with stories of the eleventh-century Muslim conqueror Mahmud of Ghazna, whose plundering expeditions into India included wholesale massacres. To prevent the conquering Arab/Muslims from being swallowed up by a much larger local population, Muslim generals in Egypt and Iraq often housed their armies and administrators in settlements outside towns. These

From Nadir to Zenith

Benjamin Disraeli, the first (and only) Jewish prime minister of Great Britain, once dressed down an anti-Semitic detractor by reminding him that when his adversary's ancestors were swinging from trees, Disraeli's ancestors were priests in the temple of Solomon. A similar relationship held between the peoples of the Middle East and Europe during the Middle Ages. While Europe was dominated by unversed men with axes, the caliphate was a world center for scientific inquiry and cultural enrichment. Through encounters in Spain, the Mediterranean, and, during the Crusades, the Middle East, Arabs introduced Europeans to a variety of ideas as well as foods and wares associated with the good life. Many of the Arab contributions to the societies of Europe can be traced through etymology—the study of the origin and development of words. It can be assumed that the introduction of words from Arabic occurred simultaneously with the introduction of ideas and commodities from the Middle East. Some of the following common English words originated in Arabic; others originated in ancient Greek, Persian, and Sanskrit—languages largely unknown in Europe—and were transmitted to English through Arabic:

admiral	alkali	atlas	camphor
adobe	almanac	aubergine	candy
albatross	amber	average	caper
alchemy	amulet	azimuth	carat
alcohol	aniline	azure	caraway
alcove	antimony	borax	carmine
alembic	apricot	cable	carob
alfalfa	arsenal	caliber	check
algebra	artichoke	camel	checkmate
algorithm	assassin	camise	cipher

settlements were called *amsar* (singular: *misr*), from which we get the Arabic name for Egypt (Misr). The custom of allowing local control would continue through Ottoman times.

Islam continued to spread long after the period of the first conquests. For example, it was not until the beginning of the sixteenth century that Islam became firmly established in Indonesia, today the most populous Muslim state. Nevertheless, at the beginning of the tenth century, the core area of the Islamic world began to fragment politically. Part of the reason for this political fragmentation was that the Islamic world was subjected to invasion from the outside.

A variety of groups came into the Middle East: crusaders from the West, Mongols from the Far East, and Mongol wannabes (like the legendary Tamerlaine) from Inner Asia. While most Westerners know about the Cru-

coffee	ghoul	mocha	sine
cork	giraffe	mohair	sirocco
cornea	gypsum	monsoon	soda
cotton	hashish	mummy	sofa
crimson	hazard	mufti	sugar
crocus	henna	muslin	syrup
cumin	jar	nadir	tabby
damask	lacquer	orange	talc
drub	lemon	popinjay	talisman
elixir	lilac	racket	tamarind
gala	lime	safari	tariff
garble	lute	saffron	tarragon
gauze	macabre	satin	zenith
gazelle	magazine	sequin	zero
genie	massacre	sherbet	zircon
gerbil	mattress	sheriff	

Some words—like coffee, jar, and gazelle—were simply borrowed from Arabic. Others bear more colorful histories. Tabby comes from a street in Baghdad noted for its striped cloth. Assassin comes from hashish, which, according to legend, a Shiʿi group called the "hashishun" purportedly smoked before going out to kill Crusaders. Racket (as in tennis racket) is derived from the Arabic word for the palm of the hand—the original racket. Gala—as in a gala occasion—comes from the Arabic for a robe of honor or investing with a robe of honor. Satin refers to the city in China to which Arab merchants went to trade for the cloth. And checkmate comes from a Persian/Arabic phrase meaning the king (*shah*) is dead (*mat*). As chess aficionados know, a match ends with the trapping (and implied elimination) of the opponent's king.

sades, most of these military campaigns failed miserably. In fact, the Crusades might actually be considered a sideshow to the main event: invasions from the north and east. For example, the devastation wrought by the Mongols in the Middle East was enormous. According to contemporary accounts, between two hundred thousand and eight hundred thousand people died during the sack of Baghdad. Another city, Nishapur, one of the centers of learning in Persia, never recovered from the command of a Mongol general that "not even cats and dogs should be left alive." But the Mongol invasions brought more than doom and gloom to the Middle East. Just as the Crusades exposed Europeans to the culture and products of their eastern neighbors, the Mongol invasions and subsequent "pax Mongolica" (Mongol peace) exposed the inhabitants of the Middle East to their eastern neighbors as well. The Mongol invasions introduced Middle Easterners to new forms of cultural expression, such as miniature painting and Far Eastern motifs still found in Middle Eastern carpets, and Middle Easterners were quick to take advantage of newly opened trade routes linking the eastern Mediterranean with China—as was Marco Polo, who travelled along the famed silk route on his journey from Venice to Cathay.

In spite of all this, it might be argued that the groups that had the most lasting impact on the Middle East were, in fact, Turkish-speaking peoples from Central Asia. Turkic peoples entered the lands of Islam in two ways. In the tenth century, bought or captured Turks were brought into Islamic lands to be used as imperial guards for caliphs or slave soldiers for local warlords. These military slaves were known as mamluks (those who were owned). Caliphs and local warlords found mamluk warriors useful because they had no connections to any group in the region except their masters. It was therefore assumed that they would be entirely dependent on—and loyal to—those masters. Nevertheless, since mamluk armies often held the balance of power, they were known to seize it. For example, in 1250 slave soldiers of a local dynasty in Cairo pushed aside their former masters and began to rule in their own right. Replenishing their ranks with new mamluks, often from the Caucasus, they ruled independently until 1517 and continued to exercise power in Egypt until the beginning of the nineteenth century. We shall thus meet up with the Egyptian mamluks again later in our story.

Starting in about the eleventh century, entire Turkic tribes began migrating from the Central Asian steppes into the Middle East. Tribes might be defined as groups of people who claim descent from a common ancestor, whether or not they are in reality related to that common ancestor or even to each other. The Turkic tribes that entered the region were, for the most part, pastoralists (think sheep and goats). No one knows for sure why they began migrating south and west. Some historians cite population pressures in their original homelands. Others cite climatic changes that affected all of Eurasia, a strengthening of the Chinese Empire, or the fact that the Middle East was a center of a flourishing civilization whose wealth would naturally attract the attention of outsiders: After all, how are you going to keep them down on the steppe after they've seen Baghdad?

In any case, the Turks who came in were dazzled by the superior civilization of Islam. For their part, many inhabitants of the Middle East had nothing but contempt for these uncouth tribesman and sheepherders. The great tenth-century Arab historian al-Mas'udi wrote of the Turks as follows:

> Because of their distance from the circuit of the sun when it rises and sets, there is much snow among the Turks, and cold and damp have conquered their habitations; their bodies are slack and thick, and their backbones and neckbones so supple that they can shoot their arrows as they turn and flee. Their joints form hollows because they have so much flesh; their faces are round and their eyes small because the warmth concentrates in their faces while the cold takes possession of their bodies. Those who dwell sixty miles beyond this latitude are Gog and Magog. They are in the sixth climate and are reckoned among the beasts.

The most powerful Turkic tribes that entered the Middle East took control of a given area and established principalities. There they adopted many of the local customs, including Islam. Some of these Turkish states covered large expanses of territory: The state established by a tribe called the Seljuks, for example, stretched from eastern Iran to Syria. Nevertheless, these Turkish states were, for the most part, short-lived. Not only was the size of tribes small in comparison to the populations they sought to control (there were only ten to fifteen thousand Seljuks, for example), illiterate tribesmen are inherently better at conquest than at rule. There is the story of how one (apparently feisty) Chinese scholar chided a Mongol leader: "An empire can be conquered on horseback, but it cannot be governed on horseback." (We have no record as to how the Mongol leader took this criticism.) In addition, tribes are notoriously unruly, constantly dividing and reconstituting themselves and constantly warring on each other. As a result, the boundaries of the tribal states were continuously in flux. Often, there was no permanent site of government. Instead, the capital was often situated wherever the army was camped. Hence, there could be no self-perpetuating bureaucracy to maintain the authority of the state over time. Thus it is that few readers of this book have ever heard of the Ghaznavids and Ghurids, the Saffarids and Samanids, and the Akkoyunlu and Karakoyunlu—the so-called white sheep and black sheep tribal confederations. All these tribes established states in the Middle East between the tenth and the fifteenth centuries.

Two states that emerged at the beginning of the sixteenth century did leave a more lasting mark on the region, however: the Ottoman and Safavid empires. The Ottoman Empire began as many other Turkish states had begun. The Ottomans traced their history back to a legendary founder, Osman. Hence, their Turkish name: Osmanlis. Osman lived in the thirteenth century on the northwestern tip of Anatolia. According to legend, Osman was divinely chosen to found a great empire. While a guest of a respected Muslim preacher, the story goes, Osman went to bed and had a dream:

> A moon arose from the holy man's breast and came to sink in Osman's breast. A tree then sprouted from his navel, and its shade compassed the world. Beneath this shade there were mountains, and streams flowed forth from the foot of each mountain. Some people drank from these running waters, others watered gardens, while yet others caused fountains to flow.

According to the legend, when Osman awoke he told the story to the preacher. The preacher told him, "Osman, my son, congratulations for the imperial office bestowed upon you and your descendants by God, and take my daughter to be your wife." Apparently, Osman did so.

Sagas report that Osman was a leader of a band of warriors known as ghazis. Much of Anatolia at this time was a lawless frontier, sort of like the Wild West. The only law in town was the Byzantine Empire, which, by the thirteenth century, was a mere shadow of its former splendor. Ghazis made their living by plundering the wealth of their neighbors. Most ghazi principalities therefore consisted of little more than gangs of bandits. But the principality founded by Osman was different: Because it bordered on the Byzantine territories, Osman's state had more to loot and therefore attracted increasing numbers of ghazis. Because increasing numbers of ghazis led to increasing wealth, Osman's state could also attract artisans, merchants, religious scholars—all the elements necessary to establish a real state. Even peasants were attracted to the Ottoman state: Under the Byzantines, peasants had been serfs, that is, the property of their lords. The Ottomans never introduced serfdom into their domains. The Ottoman peasantry was not property, nor was it legally bound to the land.

The descendants of Osman began their conquests in the far west of Anatolia and in the Balkans, the mountainous territory of southeastern Europe. By the 1350s the Ottomans had a permanent foothold in Europe. In 1389, they defeated a coalition of Serbs, Hungarians, and Bulgarians at the Battle of Kosovo. Less than a hundred years later, the Ottomans finished off the Byzantine Empire by conquering Constantinople. For the next seventy years, they consolidated their position in Anatolia and the Balkans.

In the meantime, a threat to Ottoman power was arising to the east. During the first half of the fifteenth century, a band of Turkish pastoralists who lived in northern Persia gave their allegiance to another legendary figure, Safi al-Din, for whom the Safavid dynasty is named. Safi al-Din was the leader of a sufi order, that is, the leader of one of a variety of popular, often mystical Islamic movements. The followers of Safi al-Din were distinguished by their distinctive red headdress and, as a result, were called Qizilbash (red head) by the Ottomans.

Qizilbash missionaries spread throughout eastern Anatolia and northern Persia. By 1501, the Safavid leader Isma'il, who claimed to be a descendant of Safi al-Din, entered the northern Persian city of Tabriz and proclaimed himself shah. He was fourteen at the time, putting Alexander the Great, who took his throne at the ripe old age of twenty, to shame. Within ten years all Persia was under Isma'il's control. Soon thereafter, Shah Isma'il proclaimed Shi'ism to be the official religion of his realm and imported Shi'i religious scholars from Lebanon and the Persian Gulf island of Bahrain to spread Shi'i doctrines.

The establishment of an expansionist Shi'i state on their borders was a strategic threat to the Ottomans. Ottoman sultans were fond of quoting the thirteenth-century Persian poet Sa'di, who wrote: "ten dervishes can sleep in one blanket, but two kings cannot be contained on a continent." War soon erupted between the two states and, in 1514, at the Battle of Chaldiran, Ottoman gunners overwhelmed the Safavid cavalry and pushed back the Safavid army. In the wake of the battle, a border was established between the Safavid and Ottoman Empires that roughly corresponds to the present-day border between the Republic of Turkey and the Islamic Republic of Iran. Perhaps even more important, to protect the southern flank of their new domains, the Ottomans began their conquest of the Arab Middle East. They did not stop until they reached the Iraqi-Persian border in the east, the Arabian peninsula in the south, and the borders of Morocco in North Africa in the west.

Two

Gunpowder Empires

Previous to the Ottomans and Safavids, Turkic and Mongolian rulers brought to the Middle East a new form of state that historians often refer to as the "military-patronage state." Numerous military-patronage states existed in the post-Turkic, post-Mongol Middle East. Nevertheless, they all shared three essential characteristics. First, military-patronage states were, like the name suggests, essentially military. At the head of society was a chief military leader who would rely on subleaders for local governance. Society was divided into two "classes": a ruling military class, which performed military and other services for the rulers, and the remainder of the population, which produced taxable surplus. The second characteristic of military-patronage states was that nearly all economic resources belonged to the chief military family or families. The ruling family or families could and did redistribute these resources as they wished. They often did so, in return for the aforementioned services rendered by subchiefs or local notables; hence, the "patronage" in the "military-patronage state." Finally, the laws of military-patronage states combined dynastic law, local customs, and Islamic law (*shari'a*).

As mentioned, the military-patronage states that arose before the Ottomans and Safavids were naturally unstable. While the family of a military or tribal chieftain might carve out such a state, it was dependent on other military leaders to control local areas. These leaders, often other tribal leaders, had little loyalty to the dynasties they were supposed to support. Furthermore, because the territory governed by a military or tribal chieftain was frequently large, it was difficult to rule. After all, military chieftains had none of the advantages of modern communications or transportation. Turkic and Mongolian chiefs therefore frequently divided their territories among their sons, thus splitting up empires after a single generation. Finally, the boundaries of the states were constantly in flux and were defined by incessant warfare. And because there was rarely a permanent site of government in such a state, no permanent bureaucracy could be established to maintain the authority of the state over time.

The instability inherent to military-patronage states was ended by the introduction of a new technology into the Middle East: gunpowder. Gunpowder weapons were a technological marvel and they gave their user an extraordinary advantage in warfare. But gunpowder weapons were expensive and required a certain level of trade and industrial development to produce. Those dynasts who could harness gunpowder weapons could do a number of things that rival military chieftains had difficulty doing: they could subdue tribes and less technologically advanced military chiefs, they could protect their realms against invasion from other dynasts, they could build stable bureaucracies to collect revenue, and they could provide security for agriculture. This last factor was key: after all, in the early modern period almost all state revenues were derived from agriculture or pastoralism. Commerce, on the other hand, did not actually produce wealth, it merely rearranged it.

The Ottoman Empire was the first of the two empires to harness gunpowder. Some historians claim that the Ottomans first learned of gunpowder weapons from renegade Christians and used them, to devastating effect, to win the Battle of Kosovo in 1389. The Ottomans certainly used gunpowder weapons effectively during their siege of Constantinople—a siege that finished off the last remnants of the fifteen-hundred-year-old Roman Empire. Historian Edward Gibbon describes the final days of Constantinople in his famous *Decline and Fall of the Roman Empire* as follows:

> After a siege of forty days the fate of Constantinople could no longer be averted. The diminutive garrison was exhausted: the fortifications, which had stood for ages against hostile violence, were dismantled on all sides by the Ottoman cannon; many breaches were opened, and near the gate of St. Romanus four towers had been levelled with the ground. . . . From the lines, the galleys, and the bridge, the Ottoman artillery thundered on all sides; and the camp and city, the Greeks and the Turks, were involved in a cloud of smoke, which could only be dispelled by the final deliverance or destruction of the Roman Empire. The single combats of the heroes of history or fable amuse our fancy and engage our affections: the skilful evolutions of war may inform the mind, and improve a necessary, though pernicious science. But in the uniform and odious pictures of a general assault, all is blood, and horror, and confusion.

The Ottomans again used gunpowder weapons against the Safavids at the Battle of Chaldiran. Learning from their mistakes, the Safavids adopted the weapons soon thereafter.

It is interesting to note that the Ottoman conquest of Constantinople took place in 1453, the same year that the Hundred Years' War (which, in fact, lasted 116 years) ended. The group that turned the tide in that war and forced the British invaders to withdraw from all but a small foothold on the European continent was the Burgundians, the most advanced cannon makers in Europe. As of at least 1453, then, the use of gunpowder weapons had become essential for the survival of states. It also affected the internal dynamics of states.

Harnessing gunpowder weapons enabled the Ottoman and Safavid empires to adopt important features of the military-patronage model while at the same time avoiding many of the problems of their predecessors. Just as a military chief stood at the head of previous military-patronage states, at the top of Ottoman society was the sultan, a member of the house of Osman. At the top of Safavid society was the shah, a descendent of Isma'il. But, unlike their predecessors, the sultans and shahs did not divide their lands among their sons. They did not have to: Gunpowder weapons gave them the ability to establish a central government whose reach, when applied, could be felt throughout a vast empire.

While sultans and shahs remained at the center of imperial governments throughout the Ottoman and Safavid eras, the function each played in governance evolved over time. During the initial stages of conquest, the sultans and shahs were warriors-in-chief. They led campaigns of conquest and even met each other on the field of battle. When the two empires reached the limits of their expansion—which some historians place as early as the seventeenth century—the role of warrior-in-chief was no longer necessary. In fact, because continuous military campaigning brought no new sources of revenue and few other benefits to their empires, it could be downright detrimental. Sultans and shahs thus became less warriors-in-chief than ceremonial icons at the center of a well-oiled bureaucracy. The fact that they withdrew from public view, emerging for infrequent but spectacular religious or dynastic events, only enhanced their iconic status and the ability of the bureaucracy to function without disruption.

Historians used to look at the loss of a warrior ethos among the leaders of the Ottoman and Safavid empires and call it "decline." It was not decline so much as a shift in the function of the sultan or shah. As a matter of fact, it might be argued that after states get established and stabilized, the more a leader interferes with the day-to-day running of an empire the more trouble he will create. Think of how fortunate Americans are that many United States presidents in recent times have not been quite "on top of things." On the other hand, one of the reasons for the longevity of the Ottoman and Safavid/Qajar empires was that these empires could and did respond to changing circumstances. Thus, during the nineteenth century sultans and shahs once again sought to reassert themselves against an entrenched bureaucracy that opposed their plans to restructure their empires along the lines of European nation-states.

Other factors link the Ottoman and Safavid empires to the military-patronage model as well. Both empires divided their populations into two categories (military and nonmilitary), much as their predecessors had done. Very often, the members of the military class were considered property of the sultan or shah. The Ottomans recruited potential soldiers and bureaucrats from among the children of their Balkan Christian subjects. This process of recruitment (*devshirme*) remains a sore spot in Balkan historiography: While many contemporary Turks prefer to look at the process of recruitment as purely voluntary, the word "kidnapping" is not unknown in histories written by Greek scholars. Although Islamic tradition forbade what was, in effect, the enslavement of Christians or, indeed, any of the peoples of the book, the Ottomans were able to get around this injunction with an extraordinarily creative legal maneuver. Ottoman jurists argued that Balkan Christians were different from Christians encountered by Muslims previously. Balkan Christians, they argued, had converted to Christianity after

The Battle of Kosovo

In his famous essay, "What Is a Nation?" nineteenth-century French philosopher Ernest Renan wrote, "Where national memories are concerned, griefs are of more value than triumphs, for they impose duties, and require a common effort." No grief is more important to the Serbian national myth than the defeat inflicted on the Serbian leader Tsar Lazar by the Ottomans at the Battle of Kosovo in 1389. For Serbs, the memory of the battle was sustained through time by a tradition of epic poetry. One such poem, "Musitch Stefan," recounts Tsar Lazar's admonition to his followers on the eve of battle as follows:

> Whoso is a Serb, from Serbian mother,
> Who has Serbian blood and Serbian lineage,
> And comes not to battle, to Kosovo,
>
> May there never to his heart be granted
> Children, neither yet a maid or man-child.
> Underneath his hands shall nothing prosper,
> Neither vineyards nor the silver wheat fields,
> And from him shall misery be oozing
> Till his name and race die out and perish.

the advent of Islam, not before, and therefore should have known better when choosing their religious preference. Regardless of the legalities, these recruits underwent rigorous training, by the end of which they converted to Islam. Some recruits remained soldiers, entering the elite Ottoman infantry as janissaries. Others were siphoned off into the bureaucracy, where they could become scribes or even governors of provinces. In other words, former Christian subjects of the Ottoman Empire might rise to high imperial positions.

A similar process took place in the Safavid Empire. To break the power of the Qizilbash and strengthen the central government, Shah Abbas (r. 1588–1629) imported slaves from the Caucasus: Georgians, Armenians, Circassians, and so on. In one year alone (1616), his armies brought 130,000 Georgians back to Persia. In Persia, these slaves were called *ghilman* (singular: *ghulam*). Shah Abbas not only used these slaves in the bureaucracy and royal household, he made them into a forty-thousand-man standing army equipped with firearms. As in the Ottoman Empire, some were able to rise to high rank in Persia. By the end of Shah Abbas's reign, about half of the provincial governors were ghilman.

Overall, the use of slaves offered sultans and shahs a way out of perhaps the most serious problem of military-patronage states: their tendency to fragment. Sultans and shahs created an army and bureaucracy loyal to the cen-

After the emergence of Serbian nationalism in the nineteenth century, Kosovo came to be regarded by many Serbs as "our Jerusalem." Unfortunately for Serb nationalists, during the late seventeenth and early eighteenth centuries much of the ethnically Serbian population of the region had left and had been replaced by Albanian Muslims. In the aftermath of World War I, Serbia became a province of Yugoslavia, a state established as a homeland for southern Slavs. Because of its distinct history and ethnic composition, the Yugoslav government granted Kosovo autonomous status within the province of Serbia in 1974. Soon after the Serbian nationalist Slobodan Milosevic became leader of Yugoslavia in 1987, he revoked Kosovar autonomy, sparking resistance and calls for Kosovar independence. With the breakup of Yugoslavia in 1991, Milosevic began a campaign to end this resistance and, more ominously, "protect" the ethnic Serbian population of the region by driving ethnic Albanians from their homes. In the resulting "ethnic cleansing," upwards of five thousand ethnic Albanian Kosovars were killed and nine hundred thousand displaced. Ethnic cleansing only ended after a NATO bombing campaign forced Milosevic to relent. Throughout it all, Milosevic exploited the potent symbol of the original battle. Standing on the battlefield, he exhorted Serbs to stand united: "The Kosovo heroism has been inspiring our creativity for six centuries and has been feeding our pride and does not allow us to forget that at one time we were an army, great, brave, and proud, one of the few that remained undefeated when losing."

tral government alone. This enabled them to break the power of local warlords and potentates.

Two other aspects of the Ottoman and Safavid system link them with their predecessors. Like the rulers of previous military-patronage states, the ruling dynasties of the Ottoman and Safavid empires laid claim to the most important economic resource: land. Under this system, called prebendalism, land was considered to be the possession of the ruling dynasty, and the peasants who lived on the land enjoyed a number of freedoms. Peasants had the right to live on, work, and consume the fruits of their lands, in exchange for which they surrendered much of the surplus of their harvests in the form of taxes. But they did not own the lands they worked as "freehold" and could not sell them.

Sometimes, the Ottomans and Safavids bestowed on military leaders, governors, and local notables the right to keep the profits from parcels of land. In exchange, these select individuals had to provide military or administrative services. In the Ottoman Empire, these land grants were called *timars*, in the Safavid Empire *tiyul*.

Unfortunately, the Ottoman and Safavid empires were early modern empires that attempted to govern huge expanses of land. The imperial governments were therefore not particularly adept at collecting revenues, especially revenues from far-flung provinces. This was not a problem of these empires alone: All early modern empires, from Europe to East Asia, were in the same boat. Different empires attempted to resolve this difficulty in various ways. Over time, to help with the collection of taxes, both the Ottoman and Safavid empires auctioned off the right to collect profits from plots of land for a specified period of time to enterprising notables, merchants, civil servants, and the like. This arrangement was known as tax farming. Historians dispute whether this system was beneficial or detrimental to imperial governance. Some assert that tax farming, combined with imperial inefficiency and the increasing length of time tax farmers were allowed to maintain control of the revenues from their lands, alienated land and revenue from the central government. Others claim just the opposite. The latter assert that tax farming was actually a novel solution to a problem faced by all early modern empires and, in fact, might have been the best that an early modern empire could hope to do in order to collect revenues, tap into privately-held wealth, and thereby give local elites a stake in the imperial system.

To expand the wealth of the central government or ruler, and to direct economic resources into vital areas, such as important cities, the Ottoman and Safavid governments sometimes created government monopolies over agricultural and industrial products. For example, because silk was the largest Persian export, Shah Abbas established a silk monopoly. He took one third of all silk produced in Persia as tax, and paid the producers a fixed rate for the remainder. The Ottoman and Safavid governments also encouraged the formation of guilds. Guilds consisted of all practitioners of a given industry—from apprentices to master craftsmen—in a given city or region. There were guilds for those involved in metalwork, textiles, building, baking, transport, and even entertainment. Government sponsorship of guilds enabled the Ottomans and Safavids to regulate prices and help gather taxes. The government assigned each guild a certain amount of taxes that were to be collected from its members; the masters of each guild divided responsibility for its payment.

Finally, like earlier military-patronage states, law in the Ottoman and Safavid empires was derived from a combination of Islamic and dynastic law. This brings us to an important aspect of both empires: the role of religion.

Both the Ottoman and Safavid empires used religion to legitimate their rule. In the case of the Ottomans, it was Sunni Islam; in the case of the Safavids, it was Shi'i Islam. Again, putting religion to use in this way was not unique to the Islamic world: Henry VIII of England, for example, established his own church (which most kings and queens of England have headed ever since) and other European monarchs claimed that they had a divine right to rule. In the early modern world, dynasties throughout Eurasia used religion to legitimate their rule in one of two ways. Sometimes, dynasties presented themselves as protectors of religion. The Ottoman sultans occasionally asserted their role as caliph, took part in religious ritual, sought legitimacy as protectors of Mecca and Medina, appointed judges in the Muslim courts, and sponsored religious endowments. Since making the trip to

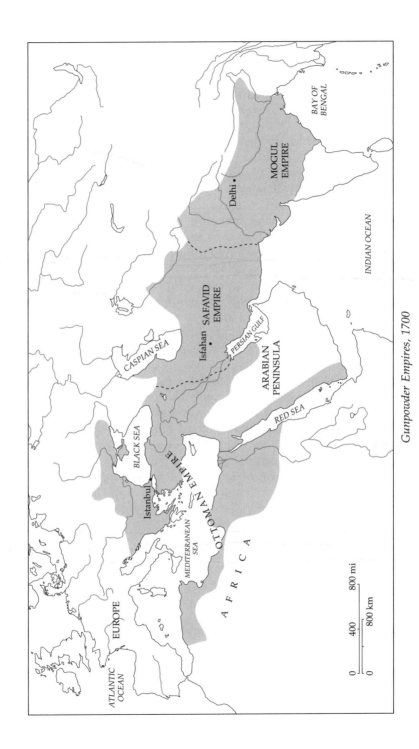

Gunpowder Empires, 1700

Mecca and Medina (*hajj*) was a requirement for all Muslims who could do so, sultans even organized the hajj caravan from Istanbul to the Arabian holy cities. Each sultan took his religious responsibilities more or less seriously. Suleiman the Magnificent (1520–1566), for example, attempted to demonstrate his religiosity by reconstructing and refurbishing Jerusalem, the third holiest city in Islam. He rebuilt the walls of the city (which exist to this day), and constructed aqueducts, fountains, hospitals, and schools there. Likewise, the Safavids claimed to be the protectors of Shiʿi Islam. In some cases, they went even further: They attempted to fit themselves into the Shiʿi narrative of history. For example, at various times, according to different sources, Shah Ismaʿil represented himself as a descendent of ʿAli, a representative of the hidden imam, the hidden imam, ʿAli, or even God.

As had been the case earlier, religious minorities were allowed to organize many of their own affairs, including education, social services, charities, and law. Later—it is not known exactly when but probably varied from community to community—each minority religious community in the Ottoman Empire was represented in Istanbul by a religious dignitary from the sect. Each religious community came to be known as a *millet*, and this system of organizing the relationship between the state and religious communities came to be known as the millet system.

Before we can leave the discussion of the institutions of the Ottoman and Safavid empires, it is necessary to emphasize two points. What has so far been presented has been the ideal, which likely differed from the way things actually worked. Unfortunately, historians are forced to work mainly from official texts—which is like reading the *Federalist Papers* to understand how the United States government actually operates. Second, both the Ottoman and Safavid empires began as early modern empires. Their ability to control events and territory waxed and waned over time. In the past, historians assumed that direct political control was a sign of imperial strength, while lack of direct political control was a sign of decline. We know better now: The Ottoman Empire lasted more than four hundred years. The Safavid Empire lasted more than two hundred. Each empire was either very lucky or was able to adapt. At times, adaptation demanded decentralization. As we shall see, during the eighteenth century the power of local warlords was greater than the power of the central government to control them. These local warlords, such as Dhahir al-ʿUmar and Ahmad Jazzar in Palestine and ʿAli Bey al-Kabir and Mehmet Ali (Muhammad ʿAli) in Egypt, were able to take control of tracts of territory that were sometimes huge. We also will see that, by applying techniques of political organization associated with modern states, the Ottoman Empire was able to reassert central control, albeit over a geographically diminished empire. The Safavids were not so lucky: The power of the central administration began to decline following the death of Abbas the Great, and the Safavid dynasty was overthrown by Afghans in 1722.

Three

The Middle East and the Modern World System

The great University of Chicago historian Marshall G. S. Hodgson once wrote that if a visitor from Mars had come to earth during the sixteenth century, he would have taken a look at the political, military, and cultural power of the Middle Eastern gunpowder empires and concluded that the entire world would shortly become Muslim. These empires not only ruled vast territories, they seemed to have resolved many of the problems of governance that had frustrated their predecessors. Yet, by the seventeenth century, Middle Eastern gunpowder empires were in deep crisis. In all fairness, these empires were not the only states in crisis at this time: States from Britain and France to China also entered into periods of difficulty. The problems these empires faced were so similar that historians even have a term for what was going on: the "crisis of the seventeenth century." Britain, France, China, and the Ottoman and Safavid empires all experienced the same problem: the inability of imperial governments to maintain their authority within their territories. Civil and religious wars wracked France and Britain. In China, the seventeenth century was marked by peasant insurrection and the collapse of the Ming Dynasty, which had ruled for almost three hundred years. The imperial Ottoman government faced popular rebellions, military revolts, and the appearance of warlords who challenged the central government from Anatolia in the north to Baghdad in the east and Yemen and Egypt in the south. The Safavid Empire was so weakened by numerous calamities that in 1722 it became easy prey for invaders from the north.

While there were probably multiple causes for the crisis of the seventeenth century, many historians have emphasized the role played by the general rise in prices that struck almost all of the Eurasian continent. Some have called this the "great inflation"; others, the "price revolution." Historians argue that inflation is the key to the crisis because the imperial governments that ruled in Europe and Asia at that time were, unlike the states that had preceded them, particularly dependent on a cash economy. There were two reasons for this. First, governments throughout Eurasia had attempted to displace the warlords and tame the aristocracies that had provided services to the crown by building armies and bureaucracies loyal to the central government alone. Building these armies and bureaucracies was expensive, and soldiers and bureaucrats had to be paid. Inflation raised the costs of maintaining them in the manner to which they had grown accustomed. Imperial states were, it appears, always short of money.

In addition, as newly centralized empires reached the limits of their expansion, rulers had to find new ways to legitimate their rule. As we have seen, the sultans and shahs of the Ottoman and Safavid empires could no longer claim a right to rule based on their position as warrior-in-chief or even on their personal magnetism or charisma. Imperial governments now entered a phase of their history that the great German sociologist Max Weber called the "routinization of charisma." This was a period in which rulers and bureaucrats had to focus on the mundane problems of running the day-to-day affairs of state. No longer riding at the head of armies, emperors, sultans, and shahs had to find new means to represent their authority to their subjects and outsiders alike. Many did so by building sumptuous palaces and capital cities or by staging elaborate ceremonials that displayed the splendor of their court. This was, after all, the era of Louis XIV of France (r. 1661–1715), the "Sun King," from whose magnificent court in Versailles power radiated. In a similar vein, a British traveler recorded the effect that Shah Abbas's capital city of Isfahan had on both Persians and foreigners:

> The City has no need of Walls, where so many Marble Mountains stand as a Guard, or Bulwark of Defence. . . . The Circumference of the Body of the City I guess may measure Seven Miles; but if the dispersed Gardens and Seats of the Great Men, with the Palace Royal be brought into that Computation, we must allow it as many Pharsangs. . . . Its Founder (or at least, Adorner) *Shaw Abas* the Great, advisedly chose it for his Imperial Throne, that thence he might more readily disperse his Mandates to any suffering Part assaulted by the bold Incursions of his Enemies; irradiating like the Sun in the Firmament all within the Sphere of this Government: So that while the utmost of his Dominions are seasonably supplied with the comfortable Warmth of his Protection, he safely resides within, invulnerable.

Shah Abbas once proclaimed, "To know Isfahan is to know half the world." Such splendor cost money.

Historians do not really know what sparked the inflation that led to the crisis of the seventeenth century. There are three main theories. Some historians claim inflation was caused primarily by demographic expansion. During the sixteenth century, they argue, the Eurasian continent experienced rapid population growth. It is estimated that during the sixteenth century alone, the population of Syria, Egypt, and Anatolia, for example, increased by 40 percent. Again, we are not really sure why this might have been the case. Some claim that the centralized states were able to provide better security for agriculturists than their predecessors had, and with better security came more agricultural production and population increase. Others maintain that the population of Eurasia naturally expanded in the aftermath of the Black Death that had devastated Eurasia during the fourteenth century or that populations were better able to control the spread of infectious diseases. Whatever the reason, historians argue that increase in population put tremendous pressure on

Painting of the Safavid shah Suleiman and his courtiers by the Persian artist Ali Quli Jabbar, ca. 1660s or 1670s. Notice the Dutch supplicant to the shah's left. (From: Layla S. Diba and Maryam Ekhtiar, eds., Royal Persian Paintings: The Qajar Epoch, 1785–1925 (Brooklyn: Brooklyn Museum of Art in association with I.B. Taurus, 1998), p. 120.)

available resources and sparked an inflation as demand for goods began to exceed supply. They point to the fact that the crisis only began to abate after population growth stagnated during the seventeenth century.

Other historians argue that the unusual dependence of states on cash was reason enough for the inflation. States spent an enormous amount of money to sustain their employees. In Persia, for example, an estimated 38 percent of the state's expenditures went to the army. Another 41 percent went to the imperial harem, the royal family, and royal attendants. States competed with the private sector for resources, and this drove up prices. States frequently compounded their problems by debasing their currencies to meet their payrolls. This meant that they often mixed the gold or silver of their currencies with baser metals and attempted to pass these new currencies off as the real thing. Because debased currency was worth less, prices rose and government employees demanded higher salaries.

It seems obvious to us now that the debasement of currencies would inevitably lead to a vicious cycle: Debasement would induce price increases, which, in turn, would encourage shortsighted governments to undertake further debasement. But during the early modern period, notions of economics, where they existed at all, were even cruder than they are today. Sometimes, this guilelessness led to absurd consequences: Spain, for example, went bankrupt twice during the sixteenth century, first in 1557, then again in 1575. In the second instance, when King Philip II of Spain found himself overwhelmed by creditors, he simply called together church leaders who told him what he wanted to hear: Since usury (the charging of interest) was a sin, he was under no obligation to pay back his creditors. The king, finding within himself a wellspring of piety of which he had previously been unaware, obeyed. Spain was not alone in its folly: In the first half of the sixteenth century, the Netherlands, Portugal, and France, like Spain, spent almost twice as much to extract wealth from the New World and to make war on each other so that they might extract wealth from the New World than they actually wrested from the Americas.

This brings us to the third possible reason for the inflation of the sixteenth century: the Spanish conquest of the New World. When they arrived in Peru and Mexico, Spanish conquistadors found tons of precious metals in the Inca and Aztec empires. Huge amounts of gold and particularly silver flooded first into Europe, then into Asia. Wherever the precious metals hit, prices went up. In the six decades between the conquest of Mexico and Peru and 1575, prices in Western Europe increased between 300 and 400 percent. Historians, using the sudden increases in bread prices as their measure, have even timed the journey of precious metals from west to east: first Cadiz, then Paris, then Muscovy, then Istanbul and Delhi, then Beijing. Thus, in 1660 a European trader compared Persia to a huge caravansary—a stopping place and trading center for caravans—with a gate in the west and a gate in the east. Coins, he explained, entered Safavid domains from the Ottoman Empire in the west, circulated in Persia, driving up prices, and finally exited through the eastern gate of Persia to India.

While some historians remain skeptical about the circulation of New World gold and silver to points as far away as the Middle and Far East, others point out that even if the precious metals did not actually reach that far, the looting of the New World had momentous effects on economies throughout Eurasia. They argue that new stocks of precious metals increased the velocity of trade, first among the states of Western Europe, then between the states of Western Europe and the rest of the continent. According to economists, an increased velocity of trade naturally increases inflation. Even if we do not wish to take economists at their word, the arrival of new stocks of precious metals into Europe and the resulting inflation certainly did produce dramatic effects throughout Eurasia. It is well known, for example, that the imperial Ottoman government was unable to halt the smuggling of huge amounts of such commodities as wood, metals, wheat, raw silk, and wool out of the Ottoman Empire and into Europe, where they fetched higher prices. This smuggling denied the Ottoman government precious customs revenues and inhibited its ability to buy social peace: After all, without an adequate supply of basic commodities, the imperial government could not guarantee that its cities would be adequately provisioned. At the same time, the smuggling denied to Ottoman artisans the raw materials they needed to produce their wares and weakened the guilds that had been established in part to protect their members.

Whatever the role of the Spanish silver, most historians agree that sometime during the sixteenth century the world economy began to undergo a revolutionary change. Among the historians who pioneered the research into this change were those who advocated something called "world systems analysis." In its most abstract form, world systems analysis runs something like this:

From the beginning of recorded time through the beginning of the sixteenth century, much of the world had been divided into what might be called "world empires." Taken together, these world empires made up what world systems analysts call the "system of world empires." The system of world empires had four characteristics. First, it was possible for several world empires to exist at the same time. For example, the early Ottoman Empire existed at the same time as did the Safavid, Habsburg (Austrian), and Chinese empires. Second, world empires spread through military conquest or the threat of military conquest. In other words, a world empire was no larger than the territory from which an imperial government might be able to extract taxes or tribute. In addition, each world empire provided for most of its economic needs independent of other world empires. Trade did take place, of course, and this trade was not just in luxury items. As a matter of fact, trade often involved bulk items such as cereals or wood. But in the system of world empires the economies of the trading partners were roughly equivalent and no economy was more "advanced" or dominated another. This is a far cry from the relationship among trading nations today, as we shall see. And this brings us to the final characteristic of the system of world empires: Each world empire was roughly equivalent to any nearby empire that existed at the same time. For example, no empire was technologically superior to any other, nor was any empire organized in a manner that gave it a particular advantage over any other. This stands to reason: If an empire fell behind economically or technologically, it would fall prey to its competitors.

Beginning about 1500, the system of world empires began to change into what is called the "modern world system" or "modern world economy." This change did not occur overnight—it required several centuries to complete. The crisis of the seventeenth century, described at the beginning of this chapter, might be seen as the birth pangs of the modern world system. (As we shall see, the strategies employed by rulers to address that crisis would, in many cases, come to define the future position of their states in that system.) Judging by the effects of the Depression of 1873, which affected every inhabited continent on the globe, we can say with assurance that by at least that year the modern world economy was in place. It has been with us ever since.

Like the system of world empires, the modern world economy possesses a number of distinguishing characteristics. Unlike the system of world empires, which was, for the most part, politically and economically fragmented, the modern world economy is politically fragmented but economically united. In other words, rather than consisting of independent empires that provided for most of their own needs, the independent states that make up the modern world economy participate in a single, integrated global economic system—a single market, if you will. Furthermore, while world empires spread their influence solely through conquest or the threat of conquest, the modern world system spread its influence by bringing outlying districts into a single economic structure. This has occurred through conquest as well, of course, but it also has occurred through the pull of the international market. Since the sixteenth century, agricultural producers throughout the world have discovered that they might profit more from producing goods for the international marketplace than from producing merely for their own consumption. Where agriculturalists themselves did not take the initiative, governments often encouraged the transition in order to accumulate more revenue. Finally, while the system of world empires consisted of roughly equivalent states, some states in the world economy were more technologically and economically "advanced" than others and benefited more than others from the global marketplace. In effect, there are winners and losers in the modern world economy.

At first, Western European states acted as the engine that drove the modern world economy. These states brought other parts of the globe into the world market they dominated, but in a subordinate role. Thus, while states in Western Europe produced manufactured goods that they exported internationally, other parts of the globe bought the products produced in Western European factories and, in turn, produced the raw materials that fed those factories. As a result, the world economy came to be divided into distinct units: a developed core (first, states in Western Europe, then states in Western Europe and North America, then states in Western Europe, North America, and Japan) and what is called the periphery; that is, states at a lower technological and economic level. Some analysts have created a middle category, the semiperiphery, which includes states that share attributes with both core and periphery. The boundaries of the modern world economy expanded for centuries until it encompassed the entire globe. This process, which had an important effect on the Middle East, is known as integration and peripheralization.

Because states in Western Europe functioned as the core of the modern world economy at its inception, the modern world economy spread to outlying regions of the globe during periods in which the European economy expanded. One such period took place in the early nineteenth century, during the relatively peaceful years that followed the Napoleonic Wars. Not coincidentally, this is the period we associate with the industrial revolution. It was during this period that much of the Ottoman Empire became integrated into the modern world economy. Points further east—Iraq and Persia—had to wait until the second half of the nineteenth century.

To understand how the Middle East was integrated into the world economy in the status of periphery, we must go back to the sixteenth century. At their inception, both the Ottoman and Safavid empires stabilized and induced an expansion of the Middle Eastern economy. The Ottomans and

Safavids, like all successful empire builders, encouraged economic self-sufficiency. They did this in a host of ways: by extending rural security, repairing and building infrastructure, making tax collection more efficient and less harsh, removing barriers to intraregional trade, establishing government monopolies, ensuring that their principal cities received provisions, regulating labor practices in those cities, and ending piracy on the seas. In addition, because of their central location, the Ottoman and Safavid empires controlled and profited from most of the spice trade between the East Indies and Europe. They also controlled much of the trade in luxury items such as silk: during the seventeenth century, two-thirds of Persian silk went to Europe. When the Portuguese attempted to horn in on the profitable India Ocean trade by establishing themselves in Aden (in contemporary Yemen) in 1513, the Ottomans swatted them away a quarter century later. While the world of uncontested and uncontestable European military supremacy might have been looming on the horizon, it had not yet arrived.

During the seventeenth and eighteenth centuries, there was a definite shift in the balance of power between Europe and the Ottoman and Safavid empires. This came about in the wake of the commercial revolution in Europe, which had begun in the sixteenth century. As mentioned earlier, there were many aspects to this revolution, some of which spawned it, others that were spawned by it and further encouraged its progress. The commercial revolution was a period in which new technologies of direct benefit to trade were invented and applied. Alongside these technological breakthroughs were breakthroughs in finance and the organization of trade—joint stock companies, insurance, banking—which allowed participants to increase their profits and spread risk among investors. Technological and institutional breakthroughs enabled Europeans not only to embark on voyages of discovery but to exploit them to the fullest. In 1497, Vasco da Gama discovered the Cape Route, which allowed Europeans to reach India and the Spice Islands (present-day Indonesia) by heading south around Africa's Cape of Good Hope, that is, entirely by sea. This enabled European merchants to bypass the Ottoman and Safavid empires and monopolize long-distance trade. As a result, the Ottoman and Safavid governments lost vital customs revenues, and merchants from those empires lost access to the spice trade to their European competitors.

About two decades after Vasco da Gama's discovery, the Spanish conquered Peru and Mexico, flooding Eurasia with tons of precious metals. Over time, all of Eurasia came to be divided into different economic zones in which prices varied widely. Where the precious metals had hit, prices were high; where they had not, prices remained at their usual levels. The division of Eurasia into different economic zones opened up new possibilities for trade. It also affected the social organization of the various zones differently. For example, since the price of grain was initially higher in Western Europe than in Eastern Europe, Eastern European nobles could increase their wealth by expanding their production of grain and selling that grain in the west. Eastern European nobles thus did everything they could to extend their control

Coffee

During the sixteenth century, the European table was enriched with a multiplicity of foods introduced from the New World, including corn (maize), potatoes, yams, peanuts, squash, chili peppers, tomatoes, pumpkins, chocolate, and
manioc (tapioca). Between meals, Europeans could, for the first time, sit down
with a pipe of tobacco (also introduced from the New World) or chew gum made
from chicle—hence "Chiclets"—likewise a New World import. This was one side
of what is called the "Columbian exchange." (In return, the inhabitants of the
Americas got cattle, pigs, horses, German measles, and smallpox.)

One commodity, however, made the trip from another direction: Coffee, introduced into Europe about a century after the previously cited items, originated in the Middle East.

The history of coffee is enshrouded in legend. There is, for example, the tale
of its origins: The story goes that coffee was first discovered in the ninth century when an Ethiopian goat herder noticed his goats got a bit frisky after they
ate the berries of a local shrub. After sampling the berries himself, he, too, experienced the same effect, as did those who undertook coffee cultivation in
Arabia when it was brought there three centuries later. There is the story of
the first coffeehouse in Vienna: The emperor asked the man who acted as a
guide for the Polish cavalry that raised the 1683 siege what he wanted as a reward. Rather than the usual "the hand of your daughter in marriage," he reportedly asked for the bulging sacks he saw in the abandoned Ottoman encampment, thinking they contained gold. In fact, they contained coffee beans.
Thus, the first Viennese coffeehouse. (Strudel and *Linzertorten* would come
later.) Then there is the story of the origin of tipping: In early British coffeehouses, coffeewenches placed cups for coins on each table. On the cups was
inscribed "to insure prompt service"—abbreviated T.I.P.S.

Regardless of the truth of any or all of these stories, early travelers to the Middle East were amazed by coffee and the coffeehouses they found there. One Portuguese traveler, Pedro Teixeira, stopped off in Baghdad in the mid-1580s on his
way to India and reported his first encounter with coffee as follows:

> Amongst other public buildings . . . is a *Casa de Kaoáh* [Teixeira's *kaoáh*
> is borrowed from the Arabic word for coffee, *qahwah*.] Coffee is a veg-
> etable of the size and appearance of little dry beans, brought from Ara-
> bia, prepared and sold in public houses built to that end; wherein all

over land and the peasantry, including binding that peasantry to the land.
The result was what historians of Eastern Europe call the "second serfdom."

The commercial revolution was encouraged further by the rise of new political units in Europe. One such unit was a variation on an old theme: the
merchant republic. Merchant republics had emerged in the Mediterranean
region centuries before the commercial revolution. City-states like Venice
and Genoa were highly efficient because merchants and bankers, not feudal
landlords, controlled the institutions of state. Being at the helm of state, mer-

men who desire it meet to drink it, be they great or mean. They sit in order, and it is brought to them very hot, in porcelain cups holding four of five ounces each. Every man takes his own in his hand, cooling and sipping it. It is black and rather tasteless; and, although some good qualities are ascribed to it, none are proven. Only their custom induces them to meet here for conversation and use this for entertainment; and in order to attract custom there are here pretty boys richly dressed, who serve the coffee and take the money; with music and other diversions. These places are chiefly frequented at night in summer, and by day in winter. . . . There are others like it in the city, and many more throughout Turkey and Persia.

Teixeira was not the only European fascinated by coffee. When coffee was first introduced in Europe, it caused a sensation. Little wonder: Unlike the skeptical Teixeira, most Europeans believed coffee to have the power of an aphrodisiac. In 1732–1734, the composer Johann Sebastian Bach documented the sensation caused by coffee, as well as its purported aphrodisiac powers, in his "Coffee Cantata." In the cantata, a father confronts his daughter as follows:

You wicked child, you disobedient girl,
oh!, when will I get my way;
give up coffee!

To which she replies:

Father, don't be so severe!
If I can't drink
my bowl of coffee three times daily,
then in my torment I will shrivel up
like a piece of roast goat.

After the father promises his daughter to find her a husband if only she would give up coffee, she sings:

If it could only happen soon
that at last, before I go to bed,
instead of coffee
I were to get a proper lover!

(In the end, the ungrateful little vixen gets both a husband and her coffee.)

chants and bankers ensured that the republic's foreign policy would coincide with its trade policy. By the seventeenth century, after the discovery of the Americas had shifted the center of gravity of world trade westward and the importance of the newly emergent Atlantic economy had surpassed the importance of the Mediterranean economy, Britain, France, and the Netherlands eclipsed their Mediterranean rivals. These states possessed two attributes that other European states would seek to emulate. First, like the Mediterranean merchant republics, they possessed a strong central govern-

Slaves, Opium, and the Course of World Trade

The modern world economy began to take shape in the early sixteenth century. Although Spain had access to New World gold and silver, Britain, France, and the Netherlands were soon able to surpass their rival in terms of economic power. And over the course of the next two centuries Britain would eclipse its rivals as well. Along with the institutional changes discussed in this chapter, the ability of the British to dominate international trafficking in a few choice commodities propelled their ascent to the heights of economic power. Among these commodities were slaves and opium.

In 1532, the first boatload of enslaved Africans landed in the New World. This event marks the inauguration of the so-called triangle trade. British merchants, carrying guns, ammunition, and manufactured goods to Africa, traded those goods for slaves, which they then transported to the Caribbean and North America via the infamous "middle passage." There they sold those slaves, and with the proceeds bought sugar, tobacco, and cotton. The triangle trade generated huge profits for British banking houses (and British and North American merchants), enabling Britain to surpass its economic competitors. Britain continued to reap the surpluses from this trade until 1807—the year the British government (and the United States Constitution) declared the slave trade illegal. By that time, a new system for the circulation of commodities and capital was emerging.

Beginning in the early nineteenth century, the British East India Company began selling opium grown in India to China. The company did this to pay for its administrative apparatus in India and to offset its substantial trade imbalance with China. After all, the British had an unslakable thirst for Chinese tea and a boundless appetite for silk and *chinoiserie*, while the "celestial empire" had little use for the products of Britain. Not surprisingly, the Chinese

ment that could maintain domestic order, guarantee commercial credit, and direct a national trade policy. Britain, France, and the Netherlands adopted the doctrine of mercantilism as their trade policy. Mercantilists believed that the more gold a state accumulated, the stronger it would be, and that if states encouraged trade, exported more than they imported, and protected their home industries, they would be able to accumulate more gold. Second, unlike their predecessors, Britain, France, and the Netherlands possessed an integrated internal market that united town and countryside. This ensured the state access to the resources necessary to maintain a high level of economic activity and protect its interests abroad.

In all, beginning in the seventeenth century Britain, France, and the Netherlands were able to dominate and transform the world economic system. Why these states rose to dominance and not others is not entirely government resisted the British attempt to balance accounts by turning China into one large opium den. Twice during the nineteenth century Britain went to war with China—the "opium wars" of 1839–1842 and 1856–1860—to open up the Chinese market to their noxious export and to keep it open. As a result of the wars, the Chinese were forced to accept opium from India and make a number of their ports available for "free trade."

Like the triangle trade system, the India-China trade system that emerged in the wake of the opium wars provided a foundation upon which the world-wide circulation of commodities and capital during the mid-to-late Victorian era would rest. According to economic historian A. J. H. Latham,

> The sale of Bengal opium to China was a great link in the chain of commerce with which Britain had surrounded the world. The chain worked like this: The United Kingdom paid the United States for cotton by bills upon the Bank of England. The Americans took some of those bills to Canton and swapped them for tea. The Chinese exchanged the bills for Indian opium. Some of the bills were remitted to England as profit; others were taken to India to buy additional commodities, as well as to furnish the money remittance of private fortunes in India and the funds for carrying on the Indian government at home.

Besides supporting the global economic environment that the nineteenth-century Middle East economy inhabited, the Victorian-era system for the circulation of commodities and capital affected the region in other ways as well. For example, both the Ottoman Empire and Persia piggy-backed onto the international trade in opium. Soon after the opium wars, the Ottoman Empire became one of the three largest producers of opium in the world (the other two being China and India), and as a result of the availability of opium in Persia, the ranks of drug smokers swelled as never before.

clear. Nor is it clear why this process would have taken place at all. Perhaps it was because these states were better situated to take advantage of the possibilities opened up by the Atlantic economy. Perhaps it had to do with the peculiar nature of that northwestern peninsula of the Eurasian continent where these states were located. On the one hand, Europe was small enough to allow for the rapid diffusion of the technologies and institutional breakthroughs associated with the commercial revolution. On the other hand, it was competitive enough to force states that wished to survive to explore new means of applying those technologies and institutional breakthroughs. Suffice it to say, there were European winners and losers (whatever happened to Spain, much less Venice and Genoa?), and the transformation of the world economy that the winners induced was hardly inevitable.

It was therefore not that the Ottoman and Safavid empires were necessarily doing something wrong that allowed for the emergence of the modern world system with its Western European core. Indeed, these empires did everything that one would have expected them to have done to deal with the crisis of the seventeenth century. Strapped for cash, they curtailed the timar/tiyul systems and increasingly depended on tax farming to make up shortfalls in revenues. As we have seen, this may have resulted in the long-term alienation of resources from the imperial governments. Both governments sold offices in the bureaucracy and even the military to the highest bidder. The Ottoman government allowed members of the elite janissary corps to take jobs and raise families in places where they were stationed, thereby decreasing their incentives to fight wars on the fringes of the empire. Both governments increased taxation, further alienating the peasants whose surplus provided revenue for the state. Both governments debased their currencies, and when this did not resolve their economic woes debased them again. In all, the Ottomans and the Safavids worked within the parameters of a system that had become out of date.

Ultimately, both the Ottoman Empire and Persia were integrated into the world system as periphery. Integration and peripheralization would have a profound effect on the future of the region. Agricultural lands that had once been used for subsistence farming were turned over to the cultivation of cash crops like cotton, opium, and tobacco. By 1880, 20 percent of Persia's exports consisted of opium; on the eve of World War I, cotton comprised 80 percent of Egyptian exports. To facilitate these exports, European and local governments financed and built railroads and expanded ports to handle steamships, in the process changing the face of the region. Throughout the Middle East, a market economy, in which people produced commodities for sale, came to replace local marketplace economies, in which people produced mainly for their own consumption and used whatever surplus was left over to buy those items they could not produce themselves. Land itself became a commodity like any other to be bought and sold, once independent peasants became wage laborers on other peoples' estates, and tribal leaders became landlords while fellow tribespeople worked their lands as tenant laborers. In sum, Europe cultivated a colonial-style trade with Middle Eastern empires, and this relationship affected not only economic relations in the region, but social relations as well.

Four

War, Diplomacy, and the New Global Balance of Power

The last of the three sixteenth-century events that defined the modern world was the Protestant Reformation. From 1517 (the year of Martin Luther's public denunciation of church doctrines and practices) through 1648 (the end of the Thirty Years' War) Europeans engaged in numerous conflicts pitting Catholics against Protestants. The Protestant Reformation ended the dream of a universal Christian empire in Europe. The Peace of Westphalia that ended the Thirty Years' War recognized fixed territorial boundaries among the states of Europe and established the principle that the religion of a state's ruler would be the religion of the state. Europe was now permanently divided into a number of highly competitive sovereign states that sought to defend themselves against each other, gain advantage over their adversaries, and, at times, establish a balance among themselves. In effect, both the modern state and the international political order assembled from those states—the modern state system—might be traced to the Protestant Reformation. We shall discuss the spread of the modern state system to the Middle East in a later chapter. First, however, it is necessary to see how the emergence of modern states in Europe affected the region in other ways.

The Middle East was one of the places where the competition among European states played itself out. In the eastern Mediterranean, this competition came to be known as the "Eastern Question." At first, the Eastern Question involved Britain and France. Over the course of the nineteenth century, it came to include Britain, France, and Russia, then, finally, Britain, France, Russia, and Germany. On the northern frontier of Persia, a related competition pit Great Britain against Russia. This competition was known as the "Great Game," a term popularized by the British writer Rudyard Kipling in his novel *Kim*. Both competitions are the subject of this chapter.

Let us begin by looking at how the Eastern Question evolved. From its founding in the sixteenth century, the Ottoman Empire played a role in the European balance of power. The sixteenth century was the glorious era of Ottoman expansion. The empire pushed forward its borders in southeastern Europe at the expense of the Habsburg Empire, the dominant power in much of central Europe and the Balkans. As mentioned before, the Ottomans even laid siege twice to the Habsburg capital of Vienna. On the seas, the Ottomans fought Venice for naval supremacy in the Mediterranean. By the last quarter of the sixteenth century, the Ottomans had conducted raiding expeditions on the Mediterranean as far west as Italy, and even captured the western Mediterranean port city of Tunis from the Spanish.

To ease their military expansion at the expense of Venice and the Habsburg Empire, the Ottomans made alliances with anti-Habsburg states that were more than anxious to encourage Ottoman diplomatic interference in European affairs. Thus, in 1533 (four years after the first siege of Vienna), the Ottomans sent ten thousand gold pieces to Francis I of France so that he might join with Britain and some German states in an alliance against the Habsburgs.

The Protestant Reformation played a direct role in Ottoman strategies with regard to Europe. The Ottomans viewed the Protestant movement and Protestant states as natural allies in their common struggle against the pretensions of the Catholic Habsburgs. The Ottomans supported Protestant movements because they viewed them as a potential fifth column in Europe, and actually encouraged Calvinist missionaries to propagate their doctrines in the Ottoman-controlled area that is now Hungary and Transylvania (yes, that Transylvania), a region in contemporary Romania. Likewise, Protestant and anti-Habsburg monarchs of Europe were not blind to the strategic value of Ottoman friendship. When Henry VIII of England broke with the Catholic Church and established the Church of England, he confiscated church property. Brass church bells were melted down and the tin they contained found its way to the Ottomans. Tin was an essential ingredient in the manufacture of artillery. It was scarce in the Ottoman Empire but not in the place the ancient Romans had once called the "Tin Islands"—Great Britain.

The Ottomans took the offensive in trade policy as well. In 1569, they granted the first effective capitulations to the French. Capitulations were clauses attached to treaties that granted special economic, commercial, legal, and religious rights and privileges to representatives of foreign powers in the Ottoman Empire. For example, capitulations might grant to European traders the right to establish commercial enclaves in the Ottoman Empire, to construct a church for their exclusive use, to have recourse to the courts of their own nations, or to be exempt from taxes. The granting of capitulations was an important part of the Ottoman diplomatic arsenal. They enabled the Ottomans to gain favor of potential allies in the Christian world. At the same time, capitulations enabled the imperial government to increase customs revenues and obtain goods needed by the empire. Here we see a perfect correspondence between the economic policies of mercantilist states of Europe and those of the Ottoman Empire: Mercantilist states wanted to accumulate gold by exporting more than they imported; the Ottomans were concerned with maintaining stocks of vital commodities for which they were willing to pay. The capitulations provided both with the means to realize their economic strategies.

Since the capitulations encouraged European imports, European merchants and the governments that backed them used the capitulations to bring about the economic penetration of the Ottoman Empire. As a matter of fact, it might be said that during the sixteenth and seventeenth centuries, the capitulations provided *the* means by which Europeans were able to penetrate Ottoman markets. After the French, the Ottomans granted the Dutch, the British, and the Russians capitulatory privileges. Capitulations were not abolished in most of the Ottoman domains until 1914. The end of capitulations in Egypt had to wait until 1937. Well before that time, capitulations had become a major bone of contention between the Ottomans and Europeans, particularly because Ottoman merchants felt they had to operate at a disadvantage when compared to their European counterparts, who could avoid taxes and customs duties.

During the seventeenth century, the nature of Ottoman–European relations began to change. The Ottomans were no longer the unbeatable foe they had once been. In 1656, the Venetians destroyed the Ottoman fleet not far off the coast of Istanbul, and in 1699 the Ottomans were forced out of the territories of contemporary Hungary, Croatia, and parts of Romania by the Habsburg Empire. But worse was yet to come. New, more powerful states supplanted the Habsburgs and Venetians as the main Ottoman adversaries, and as the new Atlantic economy replaced the Mediterranean economy a wider area for conflict between the Ottomans and Europeans emerged.

The Ottomans were thus pushed onto the defensive, and as the eighteenth and nineteenth centuries progressed, the problem faced by European statesmen was no longer how to defend against Ottoman expansion. Instead, the problem became what to do about an increasingly enfeebled Ottoman Empire. Ottoman collapse or retreat from Europe would, after all, have a disruptive effect on the balance of power in Europe. Thus, a series of new questions arose in international affairs. If the Ottoman Empire collapsed, what would become of the territory under its control, particularly the Turkish Straits (the narrow channel connecting the Black Sea with the Mediterranean)? If the Ottomans were pushed out of Europe, what would be the fate of its possessions in the Balkans, such as the territories that are now Greece, Bulgaria, and Serbia? What would be the role of Russia in the European balance of power, and since Russia was the strongest Orthodox Christian state, what would be Russia's relationship with Orthodox Christians in the Ottoman Balkans and Middle East? All these questions were elements of the Eastern Question.

These questions were not posed in a void. Over the course of the eighteenth and nineteenth centuries, three processes forced European statesmen to confront them time after time: the consolidation of the Russian imperial state under Peter the Great (r. 1689–1725) and Catherine the Great (r. 1762–1796) and its relentless drive to the south; the overflow of French/British rivalries into European, Mediterranean, and Indian affairs; and the internal fragmentation of the Ottoman Empire as a result of secessionist movements in the Balkans and attempts by leaders of Egypt to gain

The Siege of Vienna Made Palatable

The second Ottoman siege of Vienna began in July 1683 and lasted for two months. For the inhabitants of the Austrian capital, the experience was horrific. According to one eyewitness account:

> After a Siege of Sixty days, accompanied with a Thousand Difficulties, Sicknesses, Want of Provisions, and great Effusion of Blood, after a Million of Cannon and Musquet Shot, Bombs, Granadoes, and all sorts of Fire Works, which has changed the Face of the fairest and most flourishing City in the World, disfigured and ruined most part of the best Palaces of the same, and chiefly those of the Emperor; and damaged in many places the Beautiful Tower and Church of St. Stephen, with many Sumptuous Buildings. After a Resistance so vigorous, and the Loss of so many brave Officers and Souldiers, whose Valour and Bravery deserve Immortal Glory. After so many Toils endured, so many Watchings and so many Orders so prudently distributed by Count Staremburgh, and so punctually executed by the other Officers. After so many new Retrenchments, Pallizadoes, Parapets, new Ditches in the Ravelins, Bastions, Courtins, and principal Streets and Houses in the Town: Finally, after a Vigorous Defence and a Resistance without parallel, Heaven favourably heard the Prayers and Tears of a Cast-down and Mournful

autonomy for their province. Over the course of two centuries, these processes created crisis after crisis for European and Ottoman diplomats.

During the eighteenth century, Russia became the principal antagonist of the Ottoman Empire. There were two reasons for this. First, the tsars and Orthodox establishment saw Russia as the center of Orthodox Christianity (after the Ottoman capture of Constantinople they called Moscow "the Third Rome") and protector of Orthodox populations outside its borders. Many of those populations lived within the Ottoman Empire. In addition—and probably more important—was the strategic factor that motivated Russian confrontation with the Ottoman Empire. Russia was landlocked for much of the year because freezing temperatures prevented use of its northern harbors. Russian governments therefore coveted the warm-water ports of the Black Sea and Turkish Straits as a commercial and naval outlet to the Mediterranean. Only one thing stood in the way of Russia's Mediterranean ambition: the Ottoman Empire.

Beginning in 1768 Russia and the Ottoman Empire became involved in a series of wars, all of which ended badly for the Ottomans. The first of these wars ended in 1774 with the signing of the Treaty of Kuchuk Kainarja. According to the terms of the treaty the Ottomans ceded to the Russians parts of the Crimean Peninsula, which gave Russia a foothold on the Black Sea.

People, and retorted the Terror on a powerful Enemy, and drove him from the Walls of Vienna.

With all due respect to Count Staremburgh, the decisive factor in forcing the Ottomans to abandon their siege and withdraw their forces was the arrival of a detachment of Polish cavalry under the command of Jan III Sobieski. The Viennese, who shortly before the siege was raised had been contemplating the horrifying consequences of defeat, now reveled in their seemingly miraculous victory. In keeping with the triumphant sentiment, Viennese bakers decided to celebrate the victory by baking their bread in the shape of the Ottoman symbol—the crescent moon—which their customers then symbolically ate. Thus were croissants invented.

There is another story about the culinary effects of the siege of Vienna which, according to most historians, does not stand up to scrutiny. Nevertheless, it is a good story and deserves repeating. According to this story, the Jewish bakers of Vienna decided that they, too, would bake their bread in a celebratory shape. Wishing to memorialize the heroic exploits of Jan III Sobieski's cavalry, the bakers decided to bake their bread in the shape of a stirrup—round, with a hole in its center. The German word for stirrup is *bügel*. Hence, of course, the invention of bagels. (While a good story, most etymologists trace the word "bagel" to the German verb "biegen," "to bend.")

Just as bad, the Russians won freedom of navigation on the sea and the right of their merchant ships to pass through the straits.

With Russia on the Black Sea and, after another war with the Ottomans, Russian influence guaranteed in the Caucasus, the Russians began to put pressure on Persia. In 1801, Russia incorporated the Kingdom of Georgia. Twelve years later, Russia won the exclusive right to have warships on the Caspian Sea. Nevertheless, the Russian drive to the south might have been of minimal concern to other European states, particularly Great Britain, had it not been for the second element of the Eastern Question: the British-French colonial rivalry.

In the eighteenth century the profitability of colonies established by France and Britain over the course of previous centuries declined. Each state sought to consolidate its possessions and frustrate the strategic ambitions of the other. Each state attempted to seize control of the other's colonies. The result was a series of long-forgotten wars, such as the War of the Spanish Succession and the War of the Austrian Succession, that dragged in most European powers and that were fought on several continents at the same time. The most important of these wars was the Seven Years' War (1756–1763), known in the United States as the French and Indian Wars. As a result of the war, France lost to Britain almost all its colonial possessions in North America east of the Mississippi and in India, retaining only a few scattered trading stations.

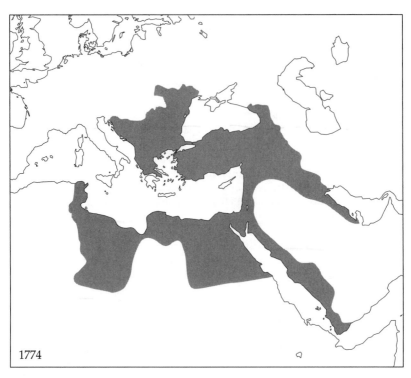

1774

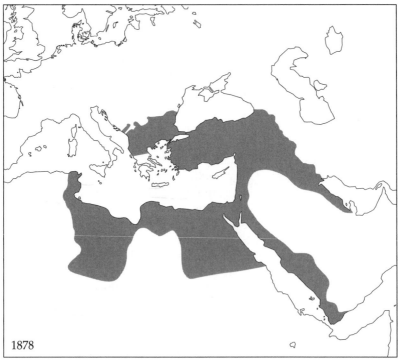

1878

The Ottoman Empire, 1774–1915

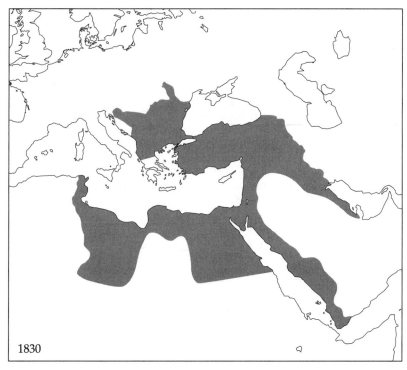

1830

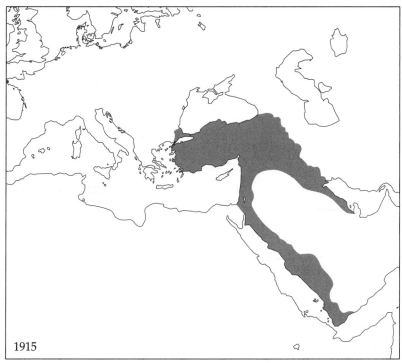

1915

The Seven Years' War thus made Great Britain the dominant European power in India. For the next two centuries, protecting its position in India and protecting the route from Great Britain to India would be a primary concern for British governments.

With the virtual eradication of French power on the subcontinent, the greatest threat to that position came from the north—Russia. Hence, the Great Game, the competition between Russia and Britain for influence in Central Asia and Persia, considered by British strategists the gateway to India. George Nathaniel Curzon, British viceroy of India, wrote in 1892:

> Not content with a spoil that would rob Persia at one sweep of the entire northern half of her dominions, [Russia] turns a longing eye southwards, and yearns for an outlet upon the Persian Gulf and Indian Ocean. The movements . . . along the south and east borders of Khorasan, the activity of her agents in regions far beyond the legitimate radius of an influence restricted to North Persia, her tentative experiments in the direction of Seistan—are susceptible of no other interpretation than a design to shake the influence of Great Britain in South Persia, to dispute the control of the Indian Seas, and to secure the long-sought base for naval operations in the east.

On the other hand, at the end of the Seven Years' War France had few options to obtain raw materials and market finished goods. France lacked control of the seas, had a growing urban population, and had an inadequate food supply. With the Atlantic under British domination, France began to focus on the Mediterranean. Over time, policy makers in France began to look to western North Africa as a site for colonization and to Egypt as a source of grain to overcome their overcrowding and food supply problems.

In 1798, Napoleon Bonaparte, then a general acting under the orders of the French Revolutionary Directorate, invaded Egypt. Some in the directorate had wanted Napoleon to attack Britain, but this seemed too risky to the general. Instead, he landed troops in Egypt to gain access to Egyptian grain and to threaten the British route to India from the Mediterranean. Napoleon did not think that his invasion would create difficulties between France and the Ottoman Empire. Under the latter-day mamluks, Egypt had been virtually independent, and Napoleon claimed he was willing to govern Egypt in the name of the sultan. But the French invasion created economic chaos in the Ottoman Empire. Prices of grain and coffee doubled in Istanbul within the year, and the Ottomans were not fooled by Napoleon's declarations of disinterest. Thus, the Ottomans allied themselves with the British (and the Russians). In the Battle of the Nile, the British destroyed Napoleon's communication lines with France and made Napoleon's position in Egypt risky. The British and Ottomans eventually forced the surrender of the French army in Egypt. By that time, Napoleon had already sailed back to France to seize power there.

The French adventure in Egypt is important for two reasons. The first is the emergence of Mehmet Ali, the leader of an Albanian contingent attached to the Ottoman army that fought the French in Egypt. After the French,

Provoking a Global War

During the eighteenth century, European powers fought a series of wars that were global in scope. For the Middle East, the most significant of these wars was the Seven Years' War (1756–1763), which was fought in Europe, the Mediterranean, the Caribbean, the Pacific, Africa, and North and South America. As a result of the war, the French adopted their "Mediterranean strategy" and Britain, now the undisputed European power in India, came to view the protection of the route to India as its overriding imperial interest.

As in the case of many other momentous conflicts throughout history, a minor incident sparked the Seven Years' War. Worried about French expansion into the Ohio River Valley, Governor Robert Dinwiddie of the British Virginia colony appointed an untested twenty-one-year-old surveyor to lead a detachment of troops to warn the French out of the area. Coming upon a French encampment in an area that is now western Pennsylvania, the Virginians surrounded their adversaries and opened fire. They killed ten of the French party and captured another twenty. The French protested, calling the incident an unprovoked attack on a diplomatic party. After they captured the surveyor, the French even got him to sign a statement in which he called the killing of the leader of the French party "*l'assassinat*," an assassination. Britain and France soon went to war. In the words of British statesman Horace Walpole, "The volley fired by a young Virginian in the backwoods of America set the world on fire." Perhaps the young Virginian panicked. Perhaps he was correct to assume that the French party was a war party. Whatever the case, the young Virginian whose action sparked a global war would later redeem himself to posterity. Now acting in concert with the French, George Washington, as commander-in-chief of the Continental Army, went on to eliminate much of the British empire in North America—an empire built in the wake of his youthful impetuousness.

British, and most other Ottoman troops had left Egypt, Mehmet Ali took advantage of the chaos they had left and assumed power. He and his heirs would rule Egypt, first as Ottoman governors, then, after 1914, as kings. The Mehmet Ali dynasty of Egypt lasted until 1953.

In addition to the emergence of the Mehmet Ali dynasty in Egypt, the French adventure forced Britain to reassess its role in the eastern Mediterranean. Napoleon's invasion of Egypt demonstrated to the British the vulnerability of their communication and supply lines to India. For the most part, British policy would remain one of ensuring the survival, and sometimes the territorial integrity, of the Ottoman state, if only to prevent competition from one or another European power in the eastern Mediterranean.

The occasional deviation notwithstanding, this policy was only reversed with the onset of World War I in 1914.

At the close of the Napoleonic era, the third process mentioned above—the internal fragmentation of the Ottoman Empire—began to redefine the nature of the Eastern Question. For the rest of the nineteenth century, the Eastern Question was concerned with the conflict between the Ottoman government and its Balkan subjects, on the one hand, and between the Ottoman government and its unruly governors in Egypt, on the other. When Balkan nationalists demanded independence, or when Mehmet Ali and his descendants demanded greater autonomy for Egypt, the Ottoman government resisted, as imperial governments are wont to do. Often, European powers stepped into the fray in an attempt to find some solution that would protect the interests of each state while not upsetting the overall balance of power in Europe.

There were several reasons for the rise of Balkan nationalism during the immediate post–Napoleonic period. Most important was the consolidation and spread of the world system of nation-states. Starting in the nineteenth century, the nation-state became the gold standard for political organization worldwide. At the root of any modern nation-state lies the belief that because a given population shares (or can be made to share) certain identifiable characteristics—religion, language, shared history, and so on—it merits an independent existence. Any people that wanted to play in the big leagues of international politics had to join the world system of nation-states and be recognized as the local franchise of the system.

Nationalism emerged in the Balkans during the early nineteenth century for another reason as well. Nationalist movements can only emerge under a proper set of circumstances. The appearance of these circumstances does not guarantee the emergence of nationalist movements; rather, the circumstances form the preconditions without which nationalist movements could not exist. We can identify three such circumstances that enabled the emergence of nationalism in the Balkans. First is the emergence of an intelligentsia that could articulate the doctrines and rationale for nationalist movements. This intelligentsia acts as a mediator between the international community and the population. Such an intelligentsia emerged in the Balkans during the nineteenth century. The second circumstance necessary for the emergence of nationalism is the spread of market relations among a population. Market relations unite the population economically and create a division of labor within proposed national boundaries. It just so happened that there was an enormous economic growth and internal economic differentiation in the Balkans in the wake of the Napoleonic Wars. Finally, there is the presence of a clearly identifiable "other" against which nationalist movements could mobilize. This "other" is anyone who does not share whatever distinguishing characteristics a nationalist movement credits to the nation. In the case of Balkan nationalisms, this "other" was usually the Turkish-speaking Muslim elites who governed them, although in some cases "Greeks" would do.

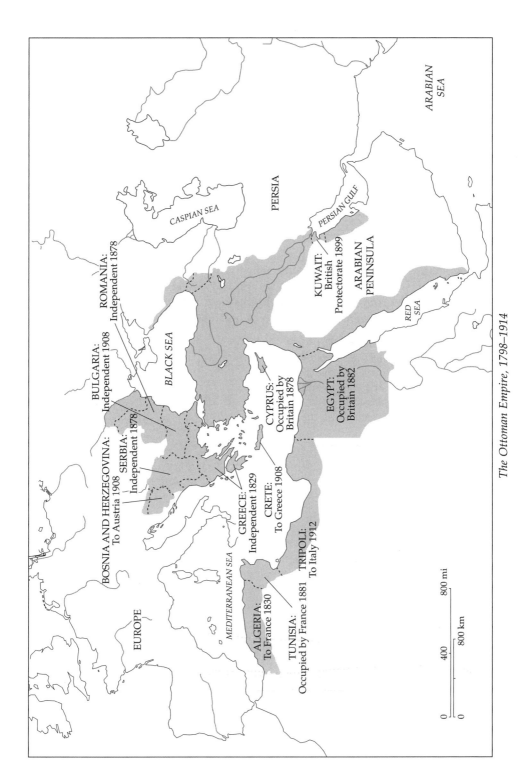

The Ottoman Empire, 1798–1914

BULGARIA:
Independent 1908

ROMANIA:
Independent 1878

KUWAIT:
British
Protectorate 1899

BOSNIA AND HERZEGOVINA:
To Austria 1908

SERBIA:
Independent 1878

CYPRUS:
Occupied by
Britain 1878

EGYPT:
Occupied by
Britain 1882

GREECE:
Independent 1829

CRETE:
To Greece 1908

ALGERIA:
To France 1830

TRIPOLI:
To Italy 1912

TUNISIA:
Occupied by France 1881

EUROPE

PERSIA

ARABIAN
SEA

CASPIAN SEA

PERSIAN GULF

ARABIAN
PENINSULA

RED
SEA

BLACK SEA

MEDITERRANEAN SEA

0   400   800 mi

0   800 km

This is not to say that the Ottoman Empire was an alien power that imposed its presence on preexisting nations of Bulgarians, Greeks, Serbs, and so on. That would be the equivalent of saying that nations are timeless and natural entities rather than entities that are modern and fabricated. While some would argue that the former is the case, most scholars of nationalism working today do not agree. Instead, most would say that once the logic of nationalism is accepted—the oneness of a population on the basis of shared characteristics—those who do not share those characteristics become unabsorbable "others."

The final reason for the emergence of Balkan nationalisms was that these nationalisms were encouraged from the outside. The Russians, for example, wanted allies in the Balkans. If independent states in the region were to emerge from the Ottoman Empire, those states would, more likely than not, want to use Russia as a counterweight to the Ottoman Empire. In return, the Russians would be able to gain their strategic goal. The Russians were not alone in supporting Balkan nationalisms, however. Throughout Europe the cause of Greek independence, for example, became a *cause célèbre*, drawing in a diverse group of liberals and Romantics, including the English poet Lord Byron. He described the struggle of his idealized Greece thus:

> *The isles of Greece, the isles of Greece!*
> *Where burning Sappho loved and sung,*
> *Where grew the arts of war and peace,*
> *Where Delos rose and Phoebus sprung!*
> *Eternal summer gilds them yet,*
> *But all, except their sun, is set. . . .*
>
> *The mountains look on Marathon—*
> *And Marathon looks on to sea;*
>
> *And musing there an hour alone,*
> *I dream'd that Greece might still be free;*
> *For standing on the Persians' grave,*
> *I could not deem myself a slave. . . .*

And William Gladstone, the sometime prime minister of Britain during the last quarter of the nineteenth century, coined the term "unspeakable Turk" in his 1876 pamphlet, "The Bulgarian Horrors and the Question of the East." Gladstone used his pamphlet as a stick to beat his political rival, Benjamin Disraeli, who quite logically seemed more concerned about maintaining Britain's strategic position than about Bulgarian independence.

Thus, starting in the second decade of the nineteenth century a series of revolts took place against Ottoman control in the Balkans. From these revolts, a host of independent states emerged, from Serbia and Greece to Romania and Bulgaria. These states arose at the confluence of three empires: the Ottoman, the Habsburg and the Russian. By the end of the nineteenth century, the Balkans had thus became a tinderbox, arraying nationalist movements against each other, empires against nationalist movements, and empires against each other. The Prussian foreign minister Otto von Bismarck once remarked that a world war would one day be sparked by some "damned fool incident in the Balkans." He was, of course, right.

The Greek revolt of 1821 is particularly important, for it endangered the balance of power in Europe by threatening the very integrity of the Ottoman Empire. To put down the revolt, the Ottomans called on their nominal vassal, Mehmet Ali, who had by this time built the best army in the empire. The Ottomans promised Mehmet Ali control over Syria if he suppressed the revolt. At first Mehmet Ali's army was successful in putting down the insurgents. But when reports reached Europe that Egyptian troops had conducted mass deportations—ethnic cleansing—the great powers intervened. At the Battle of Navarino a combined British/French/Russian fleet destroyed the Egyptian fleet and ultimately forced the Ottoman Empire to accept Greek autonomy, then Greek independence.

Nevertheless, for Mehmet Ali a deal was a deal, and Syria belonged to him. In 1831, his army invaded Syria and then, when the Ottomans protested, it began a march on Istanbul. To save themselves, the Ottomans initially threw themselves into the arms of Russia—an act that naturally worried the British. In response, the British for the first time committed themselves to protecting the integrity of the Ottoman Empire, issuing the following statement:

> His majesty's government attach great importance to the maintenance of the integrity of the Ottoman Empire, considering that state to be a material element in the general balance of power in Europe.

In 1840, the British and Ottomans together forced the Egyptians out of Syria. To ensure that Russian influence over the Ottoman Empire would be limited, the British organized a conference in London that made the concert of European powers—not any single power—the ultimate guarantor of the Ottoman Empire.

Overall, the concert of European powers managed both to protect the interests of the individual European nations in the Ottoman Empire and to diffuse crisis after crisis through diplomacy. Only once during the remainder of the century—during the Crimean War of 1853–1856—did European nations go to war to resolve a dispute involving the Ottoman Empire. But the rise of a united Germany in 1871 disrupted the European balance of power, and thus disrupted the concert of Europe. And the end of the concert of Europe in 1914 heralded the end of the Ottoman Empire. But here we are getting ahead of ourselves.

DOCUMENTS

Draft Treaty of Amity & Commerce between the Ottoman Empire and France, February 1535

> The following commercial agreement between the Ottoman Empire and France was negotiated in 1535. Although never ratified, it demonstrates the sort of privileges sought by European powers in their dealings with the empire.

Be it known to everybody that in the year of Jesus Christ one thousand five hundred and thirty-five, in the month of February, and of Mohammed 941, in the moon of Chaban, Sire Jean de la Forest, privy councilor, and ambassador of the most excellent and most powerful prince Francis, by the grace of God most Christian King of France, accredited to the most powerful and invincible Grand Signior, Sultan Suleiman, Emperor of the Turks, and having discussed with the powerful and magnificent Signior Ibrahim, Serasker of the Sultan, the calamities and disadvantages which are caused by war, and, on the other hand, the good, quiet, and tranquillity derived from peace; and knowing how good it is to prefer the one (peace) to the other (war), each of them guaranteeing the above-mentioned monarchs, their superiors, they have negotiated and agreed upon the following chapters and conventions in the name and on the honor of the said monarchies which are the protectors of their component States and the benefactors of their subjects:

I. They have negotiated, made, and concluded a valid and sure peace and sincere concord in the name of the above Grand Signior and King of France during their lives and for the kingdoms, dominions, provinces, castles, cities, ports, harbors, seas, islands, and all other places they hold and possess at present or may possess in the future, so that all subjects and tributaries of said sovereigns who wish may freely and safely, with their belongings and men, navigate on armed or unarmed ships, travel on land, reside, remain in and return to the ports, cities, and all other places in their respective countries for their trade, and the like shall be done for their merchandise.

II. Likewise, the said subjects and tributaries of the said monarchs shall, respectively be able to buy, sell, exchange, move, and transport by sea and land from one country to the other all kinds of merchandise not prohibited, by paying only the ordinary customs and ancient dues and taxes, to wit, the Turks, in the dominions of the King, shall pay the same as Frenchmen, and the said Frenchmen in the dominions of the Grand Signior shall pay the same as the Turks, without being obliged to pay any other new tribute, impost, or storage due.

III. Likewise, whenever the King shall send to Constantinople or Pera or other places of this Empire a bailiff—just as at present he has a consul at Alexandria—the said bailiff and consul shall be received and maintained in proper authority so that each one of them may in his locality, and without being hindered by any judge, cadi, soubashi, or other, according to his faith and law, hear, judge, and determine all causes, suits, and differences, both civil and criminal, which might arise between merchants and other subjects of the King. . . .

J. C. Hurewitz, *The Middle East and North Africa in World Politics: A Documentary Record*, vol. 1: *European Expansion, 1535–1914* (New Haven, Conn.: Yale University Press, 1975), pp. 2–3.

The Travels of Sir John Chardin into Persia and the East-Indies

Sir John Chardin (1643–1713) was an Anglo-French traveler who began his travels to the East when he was twenty-one years old. In this selection, he describes the rival trade missions to the Ottoman Empire and the inflation-inducing trade in debased coins.

The English drive a great Trade at *Smyrna*, and over all the *Levant*. This Trade is driv'n by a Royal Company settled at *London*; which is Govern'd after a most prudent manner, and therefore cannot fail of success. It has stood almost these hundred Years, being first Confirm'd towards the middle of Queen *Elizabeth's* Raign. A Raign famous for having, among other Things, giv'n Life to several Trading Companies, particularly those of *Hamborough, Russia, Greenland,* the *East-Indies* and *Turkie,* all which remain to this Day. Trade was then in its Infancy; and there is no greater Mark of the Ignorance of those Times, in reference to Countries, though a little remote, then the Association which those Merchants made: for they joyn'd several together in one Body, for mutual Conduct and Assistance. That Company which relates to the Turkish Trade, is of a particular sort: For it is not a Society, where every one puts in a Sum for one General and United Stock: It is a Body which has nothing in Common, but a peculiar Grant and Priviledge to Trade into the *Levant*. It assumes to it self the Name of *The Regulated Company*. None are admitted into it, but Sons of Merchants, or such as have served an Apprenticeship to the Trade, which in *England* is for Seven Years. They give to be admitted into the Society about an Hundred and Twenty Crowns, if under the Age of Twenty Five Years; and double if above that Age. The Company commits to any one single Person their Power, nor the sole Management of their Affairs, but manage their Business among themselves by the Plurality of Voices. So that who has sufficient to drive a Trade that will bear an Imposition of Eight Crowns, has as good a Vote as he that Trades for an Hundred Thousand. This Assembly, thus *Democratical,* sends out Ships, Levies Taxes upon all their Commodities, presents the Ambassador whom the King sends to the *Port,* Elects two Consuls, the one for *Smyrna,* the other for *Aleppo,* and prevents the sending of Goods which are not thought proper for the *Levant*. It consists at present of about Three Hundred Merchants, besides that they bring up in *Turkie* a great number of young Persons well descended, who learn the Trade upon the Place it self. This Trade amounts to about Five or Six Hundred Thousand Pounds yearly, and consists in Cloaths made in *England,* and Silver which they carry as well out of *England,* as out of *Spain, France,* and *Italy*: In exchange of which they bring back Wool, Cotton-Yarn, Galls, Raw Silk and Wov'n, together with some other Commodities of less value. . . .

The Hollanders also drive a great Trade at *Smyrna,* and more than any other Nation of *Europe,* but they have little to do elsewhere; all their Dealing in all the rest of the Cities in the *Levant* amounting to little or nothing. Their principal Profit consists in carrying the *Armenians* and the Goods into *Europe*, and carryin 'em back again. They also make great Advantage of their Money, of which *Turkie* is very full. This money of theirs is made of base Mettle, and notoriously inter-mix'd with Counterfeit pieces. It chiefly consists of Crowns, Half-Crowns, *Testons*, or Eighteen-penny pieces, and pieces of Fifteen *Sous*. The Crowns and Half-Crowns for the most part carry the Dutch Stamp. Which the Turks therefore call *Aslani*, that is to say *Lyons*; in regard of their being mark'd on both sides with the Figure of a Lyon. The Arabians, either out of Ignorance or otherwise, mistaking the Lyon for a Dog, give'em the Name of *Abou-Kelb*, or *Dogs*. The Quarter-Pieces are almost all Counterfeit; or at Best, but Half Silver. However the Turks are so void of Judgment and Understanding, that they esteem this Mony beyond that of *Spain*, which they call *Marsillies*, by reason that the Merchants of *Marseilles* first brought it in great Quantities into *Turkie*. . . .

The French are very numerous in *Smyrna*, and over all the *Levant*, there not being a Port of *Turkie* upon the *Mediterranean* Sea, wherein there are not several. They are for the most part all *Provençalls*. But the Trade which they drive is so inconsiderable, that one Merchant in each Place might dispatch all Business. . . . [T]he *Provençalls* have formerly had in *Turkie* those fortunate Chances and Luckie Opportunities, that it is highly to be wonder'd, that they did not fill their Country with Wealth in that happy Conjuncture. One of those Lucky Seasons began about the Year 1656, and lasted Thirteen Years, during which time they drove a Trade, by which they gain'd Fourscore and Ninety *per. Cent.*

This Trade which was really and truly a great piece of Knavery consisted in these *Five-Sous-Pieces* that have made such a Noise. For the Turks took the first that were brought at Ten Sous apiece; At which rate they held up for some time; tho afterwards they fell to Seven *Sous* and a half. There was no other Money Stirring: all *Turkie* was full of it; neither was there any other Mony to be had; for that the French carri'd all the other Money away. This good Fortune so intoxicated their Senses, that not content with such great Gains, they still thirsted after more; and to that purpose they set themselves to alter their own pieces of *Five Sous*, and made others of the same sort, but of base Mettle, which they Coin'd first at *Dombes*, then at *Orange*, and afterwards at *Avignon*. More then this, they Stampt far worse at *Monaco* and *Florence*: And lastly they made more of the same Stamp in the remote Castles belonging to the *State of Genoa*, and other private places, which were only Copper plated over. The Merchants of *Marseilles*, to utter this Money, brought down the price themselves, and put off their Pieces in payment, and to the Mony-Changers at a lower Rate then the Current Value. The Turks were a long time before they perceiv'd the Cheat that was put upon'em, though so palpable and of so great a Consequence; but so soon as they found it out, they were so incens'd, that they laid most heavy Impositions upon the *French*, using'em no better then Counterfeiters of Money, though the *Dutch* and *Genoeses* had a hand in it as well as they. Therupon they forbid'em to utter any of those Pieces which they call'd *Timmins*, but such as were stamp'd with the real Arms of *France*, which they also brought down and put at Five *Sous* apiece. So that all the *European* Merchants, except the *English*, were loaded at that time with great Quantities of those *Timmins*. Their Warehouses were full, whole Ships Loadings of 'em arriv'd daily, and they began to Coin'em in all parts. But soon after, this Money being cry'd down, several of those Money-Merchants lost all their Gains, and many much more then ever they got.

The *English* were the Procurers of this Decry. For had that Money continu'd Currant, their Trade had been ruin'd, which consisted chiefly in the purchase of Silks. And the reason was, because the *Timmin*-Merchants caus'd an advance to be made upon the price of Silks, not caring what they gave, provided the Sellers would take their Pieces of Five *Sous* in payment. I have seen above Fifty several sorts of Coins of this sort of Money. But the most common sort carri'd on the one side a Womans Head with this *Motto*, *Vera Virtutis Imago*: On the other, the Arms of *France*, with this Impresse, *Currens per totam Asiam*.

There are no People in the World that have been more frequently cheated, or that are more easily gull'd then the *Turks*; as being naturally very dull, and thick-skull'd, and apt to believe any fair Story: Which is the reason that the Christians have impos'd a Thousand Cony-catching-Tricks, and Cheats upon'em. But though you may deceive'em once or twice, yet when their Eyese are op'n, they strike home, and pay ye once for all. And those sort of Impositions which they lay upon Offenders in that Nature, are call'd *Avanies*; which are not always un-just Impositions neither; they being like the Confiscations so frequent in Custom-Houses: Where for the most part the Chief Ministers and their Officers devour the People, while the *Port* winks all thee first time, and only exhorts to Amend-ment. If the Complaints cease, the Offence is stifled; but if the Clamour grow too loud, the *Port* sends to take off the Head of the Party accus'd, and Confiscates his Estate. By which means the People are satisfied, the Treasury is fill'd, Justice is done, and the Example remains to terrifie others.

Sir John Chardin, *The Travels of Sir John Chardin into Persia and the East-Indies*, vol. 1 (London: Moses Pitt, 1686).

The Travels of Sir John Chardin into Persia and the East-Indies

Sir John Chardin traveled to Persia from the Ottoman Empire. Here he describes the steps taken by the Safavid government to deal with famine in Isfahan.

All this while the Dearth encreas'd at *Ispahan*, and the poor people cry'd aloud against the excessive price of it. And indeed there were many causes of this Scarcity. First, the last Harvest did not amount scarce to the half of what they expected; for the Locust had devour'd the Ears. Then the whole Train of the Court was come all together of a sudden to *Ispahan* before they were expected, so that they had tak'n no care to lay in their Stores against Winter. Moreover, at the King's first coming to the Crown, the greatest part of the Officers of the Empire coming to present themselves before Him, and a vast number of pri-vate persons crouding together about business, or for curiosity, the Multitude of Inhabitants was encreas'd to above half as many again, so that of necessity the Price of Provisions must be double in Proportion. But the chief Reason that all things were so dear was the bad appearance of the Harvest at hand, which promis'd no better then the last year. For in regard the Harvests in these Cli-mates are generally reap'd in the Months of *June* and *July*, it is easie to con-jecture in *March* and *April* what the year will produce. And therefore the Corn Merchants perceiving that there would be an infallible scarcity of all sorts of Grain, enhans'd their Prizes, and would not part with what they had, but staid till the Prizes were at the highest, so that the probability of a dearth to come caus'd a present Famine. Lastly, the ill Government was in part a great cause of the scarcity, for that the Laws were not observ'd, and the Magistrates neglected their duty, without fear of being punish'd. And this was the Reason that the *Mochtesek*, or Chief of the Government, receiv'd Bribes of those that sold the necessary Provisions, and therefore to gratifie'em he publish'd every Week the Prizes of things as those people desir'd; that is to say, at an excessive rate, and three quarters higher then in the time of the deceas'd King. For we are to observe, that it is a Custom in *Persia*, that every *Saturday* the Chief Justice sets the Price of all Provisions for the Week following, which the Sellers dare not exceed under great forfeitures. This Knavery then of the Judge of the City Government, who stood in no aw of the superior Government, was the cause that all things were sold at double and treble the Rate they ought to have been.

The People therefore almost starv'd by this Scarcity, redoubl'd their Cries, so that they reach'd the very Gate of the Palace Royal, which mov'd his Majesties Compassion to that degree, that he committed the Affair to *Ali-Kouli-Kaan*, General of all his Forces. Who began his first endeavours of redress with an Act of Generosity and Justice, which made him dreaded by all the Merchants and Corn-sellers. He had commanded one of the most eminent Merchants in *Ispahan* to send him in upon the place, the first day of the Market, two hundred Sacks of Wheat, and not to sell'em at a dearer rate then they were sold the year before. Now the Merchant thought that he expected a Bribe; and therefore upon the Market day, thinking to exempt himself from obedience to his Command he sent him two hundred *Tomans*, which amount to the value of about a thousand *Pistols*. Thereupon the *Generalissimo*, being highly offended, sent for him, and when he came, *Dog as thou art*, said he, *is it thus thous goest about to famish a whole City? For the Affront thou hast done me receive a hundred Drubs upon the soles of thy feet.* Which were paid him at the same instant; and besides, the General condemned him in a Fine of two thousand Crowns; which he took to himself, sending the thousand Pistols to the King.

Presently, he order'd a great Oven to be built in the Royal *Piazza*, and another in the publick *Piazza*, ordering the Criers to proclaim that those Ovens were fixed to bake those alive, that should sell their bread at a rate above the set price, or that should hide up their Corn. There was moreover a fire continually kept in these Ovens, but no body was thrown in; because no body would venture the pain of such a rigorous punishment of his Disobedience.

At the same time he also went himself to visit all the Granaries and Storehouses of Corn and Meal that were in *Ispahan*, and having taken an accompt in Writing of their Number, every Week he commanded the Merchants to send a certain quantity according to the Proportion of what the Store-houses contain'd, and not to sell but at a certain Price, and not to deliver their goods to any but such as brought a Note under his hand. He gave the same Command for Barley: so that almost for a whole years time there was neither Wheat or Barley to be had without a Ticket seal'd with his Signet. All the Bakers went for such a Ticket. And in regard the General knew full well what every one of 'em vented, he would not permit the Baker by vertue of his Ticket to buy any more then what he had occasion for. To that purpose he prohibited the Bakers to sell to any other then those of their own Precinct, nor to sell'em any more then what was needful for their subsistence according to the usual rate of their spending, to the end that the Bakers should not pretend that persons came from abroad to buy their bread, or that those in their Precincts bought more one Week than they did another, and so that the vent could not be always equally proportion'd. And for the Price, he order'd that the *Batman-cha* of Bread (the Royal weight of *Persia*, consisting of eleven pounds three quarters) should be worth an *Abassi*, which makes four Groats.

By this good management he wonderfully eas'd the People, who before paid for eleven pound and three fourths of Bread an *Abassi* and a quarter, or twenty pence; whence it also came to pass, that there was Plenty sufficient. Thus the Complaints and Cries of the People ceas'd. For the Bakers being oblig'd to furnish those in their Precincts with as much bread as they stood in need of, no body was apprehensive of the scarcity, but only that he paid five farthings for that which cost not above four in time of plenty. And to the end that the same rate might continue, he sent to all the Burroughs, Towns, and Villages, from either to nine days journey round about, to send in such a number of Waggon-Loads of Corn and Meal to *Ispahan*, and there to sell it at the net price. By which means there came enough to supply the City for six Months. Moreover, when any considerable Quantity arriv'd, he order'd it to be brought in, as it were, in triumph; the People dancing before with their Instruments of Musick, and the horses being cover'd with Housses, and gingling an infinite number of little Bells, which together with the Acclamations of the Rabble made a strange, confused, and yet pleasing noise.

Some villages there were mutiny'd and refus'd to send in their Corn; but the punishment of the Inhabitants of *Ispahanim-cha* strook a terrour into the rest. For the General had sent to this Place, being a great Town consisting of four thousand Houses, two Leagues distant from *Ispahan*, one of his Officers with a Command from the King to send at the set Price two hundred Sacks of Meal to the Capital City for the present necessity. The Townsmen made answer, 'twas nothing to them if there were such a Famine in the City, for that they had paid all their duties and Impositions for the last Harvest: that they had something else to do then to send their Corn and the Meal to *Ispahan* Market, and that those that wanted might come to them, for that they were not bound to sell but in their own Town. Thereupon the Officer remonstrated to the Principal of the Village that it was the Kings pleasure, and shew'd 'em the Kings Warrant which he had in his hands; to which their answer not being with that becoming reverence which became 'em, the Officer laid his hand upon his Sword, thinking to have frighted 'em into obedience. But the Country fellows not understanding his hard words, fell upon the Officer, beat him almost blind, and tore the Kings Command, crying out, 'twas a Cheat and Counterfeit.

The General highly offended at this Insolence of the Countrymen, gave the King an account of it, who order'd him to inflict such punishment as the Offence deserv'd. Upon which he sent two hundred of his Guards, who Drubb'd to excess the Principal of the Ringleaders. He also set a Fine upon their heads of a hundred thousand Crowns; which was mitigated to a third part, tho after many Petitions and Submissions, with a Present to the General of a thousand Pistols, which was all paid down upon the nail.

Sir John Chardin, *The Travels of Sir John Chardin into Persia and the East-Indies*, vol. 1 (London: Moses Pitt, 1686).

SUGGESTED READINGS

General Works on Middle Eastern History

Beinin, Joel. *Workers and Peasants in the Modern Middle East*. Cambridge, England: Cambridge University Press, 2001. Very readable social history of labor in the modern Middle East.

Burke, Edmund III. *Struggle and Survival in the Modern Middle East*. Berkeley: University of California Press, 1993. Collection of biographies of lives of Middle Easterners—ranging from bedouin and peasants to workers and political activists—from the nineteenth century to the present.

Cleveland, William. *A History of the Modern Middle East*. Boulder, Colo.: Westview Press, 1994. The best comprehensive history of the modern Middle East.

Daly, M. W., ed. *The Cambridge History of Egypt, vol. 2: Modern Egypt from 1517 to the End of the Twentieth Century*. Cambridge, England: Cambridge University Press, 1998. Excellent collection of essays on Egyptian politics, society, and culture from the beginning of the Ottoman period to the present day.

Faroqhi, Suraiya, et al., eds. *An Economic and Social History of the Ottoman Empire, vol. 2: 1600–1900*. Cambridge, England: Cambridge University Press, 1994. Detailed studies of three hundred years of Ottoman life written by top scholars in the field.

Hodgson, Marshall G. S. *The Venture of Islam: Conscience and History in a World Civilization*, 3 vols. Chicago: University of Chicago Press, 1961. Difficult reading, but a must for the serious student of Middle Eastern history.

Hourani, Albert, et al., eds. *The Modern Middle East*. Berkeley: University of California Press, 1993. An important collection of essays on the modern Middle East, most previously published elsewhere.

Keddie, Nikki. *Roots of Revolution: An Interpretive History of Modern Iran*. New Haven, Conn.: Yale University Press, 1981. A readable, old-fashioned narrative history of Iran in the modern period.

Lapidus, Ira M. *A History of Islamic Societies*. Cambridge, England: Cambridge University Press, 1995. Large and comprehensive, covering the entire Muslim world from the time of Muhammad to the present. Lapidus is at his best in earlier periods.

Lewis, Bernard. *The Emergence of Modern Turkey*. New York: Oxford University Press, 2002. Although deeply embedded in modernization theory, Lewis has written a flowing narrative history of Turkey from its Ottoman roots.

Specialized Works

Bozdogan, Sibel, and Kasaba, Resat, eds. *Rethinking Modernity and National Identity in Turkey*. Seattle: University of Washington Press, 1997. Stimulating collection of essays on different perceptions of "the modern" in Turkey.

Brown, Carl. *International Politics and the Middle East: Old Rules, Dangerous Game*. Princeton, N.J.: Princeton University Press, 1984. While the second half of this book deals with the cold war and is a bit dated, the first half provides a well-written synopsis of the relationship of the West and the Middle East during the "long nineteenth century."

Foran, John. "The Long Fall of the Safavid Dynasty: Moving Beyond the Standard Views." *International Journal of Middle East Studies* 24 (1992): 281–304. A unique study that applies world systems analysis to Persia in the seventeenth and eighteenth centuries.

Gaonkar, Dilip Parameshwar. *Alternative Modernities*. Durham, N.C.: Duke University Press, 1999. A collection of essays outlining a useful approach to the problem of modernity.

Hodgson, Marshall G. S. "The Role of Islam in World History" and "The Unity of Later Islamic History." In *Rethinking World History: Essays on Europe, Islam, and World History*, edited by Edmund Burke III, 97–125, 171–206. Berkeley: University of California Press, 1993. Brilliant if densely written essays that put the Middle East and the Islamic world in a global context.

Huntington, Samuel. "The Clash of Civilizations?" *Foreign Affairs* 72 (Summer 1993): 23–49. Influential article attempts to forecast the upcoming conflict between "the West" and "the rest."

Islamoglu-Inan, Huri, ed. *The Ottoman Empire and the World Economy*. New York: Cambridge University Press, 1987. Collection of essays applying world systems theory to the Ottoman Empire.

al-Jabarti, ʿAbd al-Rahman. *Napoleon in Egypt: Al-Jabarti's Chronicle of the French Occupation, 1798*. Translated by Shlomo Moreh. Princeton, N.J.: Markus Wiener, 1993. An eyewitness account of Napoleon's campaign in Egypt, told from the Egyptian point of view.

Kafadar, Cemal. *Between Two Worlds: The Construction of the Ottoman State*. Berkeley: University of California Press, 1995. Accessible work on the history and historiography of Ottoman beginnings.

Kasaba, Resat. *The Ottoman Empire and the World Economy: The Nineteenth Century*. Albany: State University of New York Press, 1988. Examines why the Ottoman Empire became a peripheral part of the world economy in the nineteenth century.

Kunt, Metin, and Woodhead, Christine. *Suleyman the Magnificent and His Age: The Ottoman Empire in the Early Modern World*. London: Longman, 1995. Solid collection of essays on the Ottoman Empire during its purported "golden age."

Said, Edward. *Orientalism*. New York: Pantheon, 1978. This groundbreaking work analyzes the reasons for misperceptions of the Middle East in the West. A useful riposte to Huntington, although written a decade before.

Shannon, Thomas R. *Introduction to the World Systems Perspective*. Boulder, Colo.: Westview Press, 1989. Situates world systems theory in its historical context and analyzes its strengths and weaknesses.

Wright, Lawrence. *The Looming Tower: Al-Qaeda and the Road to 9/11*. New York: Knopf, 2006. Well-written and timely history of the origins and evolution of jihadi Islam.

Part 2

THE QUESTION
OF MODERNITY

This section is about "modernity" and its effects on the Middle East. In 1964, when the United States Supreme Court was considering the question of the censorship of "obscene" materials, Associate Justice Potter Stewart remarked that he could not define pornography but he knew it when he saw it. The same might be said of modernity: Everyone thinks they know it when they see it, but getting a handle on the concept has not been easy.

The term "modernity" has been in the social science vocabulary since the dawn of the social sciences. Beginning in the eighteenth century, European and North American scholars came to believe there were societies that were "civilized"—that is, had reached the stage of modernity—and other societies that had not yet advanced along the path to civilization. Modern societies, they believed, were those that duplicated the European experience: These societies trusted in science, not superstition; secularism, not religion; freedom, not despotism. As far as the social sciences were concerned, European society was complex and dynamic, while "traditional" society was simple and stagnant. Scholars thus assumed that the evolution of European society and the European form of modernity could serve as a model that could be applied universally. They believed that there was a single path to modernity that every nonmodern society had to tread and from which they could not deviate.

This view of modernity had an unusually long run in the social sciences. It was only recently, when social scientists began question-

ing many of the assumptions that had guided them in the past, that
the consensus about modernity broke down. Some voiced skepticism
about some of the fundamental beliefs that had guided the social sciences in the past, such as the belief that there was progress in history or that societies evolve in the same way as biological organisms.
Other social scientists pointed out that those who spoke about the
scientific, secular, and free nature of Western societies were hopelessly naive, particularly because they idealized some aspects of Western society and disregarded others that were not so appealing. Still
others pointed out that applying the European model of modernity
universally was simply another example of European narcissism. After all, most social scientists had little or no acquaintance with societies outside Europe and North America—how could they presume
to generalize about societies of which they had no knowledge?

But, while many social scientists writing today scorn the assumptions of their predecessors, we should be careful not to throw
out the baby with the bathwater. Although historians may disagree
about a definition of modernity, or even the usefulness of such a concept, almost all would agree that the Middle East underwent widespread social, economic, and cultural changes during the nineteenth
century and these changes propelled Middle Eastern societies in an
entirely new direction.

The emergence of the contemporary world economic system, beginning in the sixteenth century, and the emergence of a world system of nation-states, beginning in the eighteenth century, fundamentally transformed the trajectory of world history. The world
defined by these twinned systems is a world that we might call modern. This is not to say that societies were unchanging before the advent of modernity. There was plenty of change. Nor is it to say that
the advent of modernity created a world that was homogeneous. Responses to the emergence of these twinned systems were hardly uniform throughout the world or even within the various states of the
world. The attributes of "French modernity" have been, of course,
different from the attributes of "Chinese modernity" or "Ottoman
modernity." And the attributes of Ottoman modernity were different in Istanbul and Cairo, among rich and poor, town dwellers and
their country cousins. Nevertheless, in the modern world the contemporary economic and state systems defined the parameters in
which every functioning society had to operate.

There were a number of ways in which the modern economic and
state systems came to the Middle East. One way that the spread

of the modern economic system—the process of integration and peripheralization—took place in the region was by the pull of the international market. Throughout the world, farmers, landlords, and merchants began to orient production and trade toward the international market, where there were profits to be made. But integration and peripheralization could not have taken place had there not been an accompanying political process that propelled the spread of the modern world economy. This political process had many dimensions. Sometimes, European states used diplomatic pressure and gunboat diplomacy to open up markets and keep them open. At other times, rulers of states outside Europe actively sought to participate in the new economic order and restructured their economies to do so.

A similar process encouraged the spread of the world system of nation-states. Sometimes, rulers and would-be rulers of states outside Europe copied European methods of governance and imposed them on their domains. They did this because those methods seemed to provide the most effective means to protect themselves and mobilize and harness the energies of their populations. At other times, European states imposed modern state institutions through the direct colonization, occupation, or administration of non-European territories. While the first process—known as "defensive developmentalism"—was more commonly applied than the second in the Middle East, both took place in the region and we are still living with the consequences of each.

Five

Defensive
Developmentalism

As we have seen, the crisis of the seventeenth century had different effects in different regions of the Eurasian continent. Some states connected to the Atlantic economy, such as Britain, the Netherlands, and France, underwent a radical transformation that enabled them to eclipse states such as Spain and the Mediterranean merchant republics. In parts of Eastern Europe, a different transformation took place in the wake of the crisis: the second serfdom. The crisis of the seventeenth century had long-lasting effects in the Middle East as well. Imperial governments stumbled from financial crisis to financial crisis, often seeking cures that were worse than the disease. Warlords asserted themselves against weakened central governments, refused to send taxes or tribute to the imperial capital, and often waged war against representatives of the imperial government and on each other. By the end of the eighteenth century—even before the arrival of Mehmet Ali on the scene—the Ottomans had lost effective control of Egypt. Egypt would remain part of the Ottoman Empire until 1914, but its peculiar history and status within the empire almost demand that we treat it separately from the history of much of the rest of the empire. In Persia, the Safavid dynasty, weakened by tribal insurrection, collapsed under the impact of invasion from Afghanistan. Although the Qajars—a family of Turkish descent—established a dynasty that would rule Persia for a century and a half, their control outside their capital of Tehran was, according to many historians, never particularly impressive. All too often the Qajars had to balance off or bargain with local leaders. They were also at the mercy of the British and Russians who fought out the "Great Game" on their territory.

Middle Eastern sultans, shahs, and local dynasts such as Mehmet Ali were not blind to what was going on. Nor were they blind to the fact that the balance of international power had shifted to the West. Thus, beginning in the early nineteenth century, Ottoman sultans, Persian shahs, and Egyptian dynasts—later accorded the title khedive in acknowledgment of the special status of Egypt in the empire—undertook deliberate policies to reverse the process of fragmentation and to centralize and expand their authority. Their goal was to strengthen their states in the face of internal and external threat and to make their governments more proficient in managing their populations and their resources. This process is known as defensive developmentalism.

Once rulers adopted the policy of defensive developmentalism, the process took on a life of its own. In the abstract, the process of defensive developmentalism followed a number of predictable steps. The first step was military reform. This was a logical choice: In both the Ottoman and Qajar empires leaders understood that they could preserve the independence and unity of their empires only if they were better able to project power internally and protect themselves from foreign aggression. Ottoman sultans and Persian shahs learned from successive military defeats that their military forces were overdue for an overhaul. They therefore sought to borrow recruitment, disciplinary, organizational, tactical, and technological strategies from European states where armies were more professional and effective. This also stood to reason. Military reforms first introduced into France and Prussia around the turn of the nineteenth century diffused throughout Western Europe and Russia, making European armies not only formidable foes but models to be emulated. Mehmet Ali also began his program of defensive developmentalism with military reform, but for a different reason. The power from which he sought to protect his regime was not European, but the Ottoman Empire. Not only did he hope that military reform would help consolidate the position of his family in Egypt, he sought to use a reformed military to strengthen the position of Egypt in the region.

The next steps in the process of defensive developmentalism derive directly from the policy of military reform. To build and support a modern army and defend their territories, Middle Eastern rulers needed to expand the sources of revenues under their control, their ability to coordinate the activities of their populations, and their ability to discipline their populations so that they might act in a manner advantageous to the state. To achieve the first goal, they encouraged the cultivation of cash crops, for example, and tried to restructure tax collection to increase tax revenues. As we shall see, encouraging the cultivation of cash crops may have been penny-wise but turned out to be pound-foolish: To protect their political independence, Middle Eastern rulers were, in effect, mortgaging their future economic independence.

To collect new taxes, man their new armies, and discipline and coordinate the activities of their populations, Middle Eastern rulers needed to eliminate tax farmers and other intermediaries who sapped resources from the state, augment their administrations, introduce uniform legal practice, and educate new administrators and soldiers. They therefore expanded access to education and standardized curricula, promulgated new legal codes, and experimented with centralized economic planning. In sum, the defensive developmentalists sought, and often succeeded in building, a state apparatus capable of penetrating the lives of their populations in ways that could not have been implemented, much less imagined, a hundred years before.

Defensive developmentalism was not without its problems, however. All too often the achievements of defensive developmentalist rulers looked more impressive from the vantage point of their palaces in Istanbul, Tehran, or Cairo than they in fact turned out to be. Sometimes plans carefully worked out in the seat of government met with local resistance. Tax farmers, for example, were rarely enthusiastic about programs designed to speed their elimination. Defensive developmentalist policies also fostered the emergence of a new class of professional soldiers, intellectuals, and bureaucrats who were educated in Western techniques. Members of this new class frequently clashed with those who either had a stake in the old order or who believed that the new ways did more harm than good.

In a way, the old guard was correct to be suspicious of the ambitions of members of the new class. The members of the new class were frequently dissatisfied with their position in society. They were educated, but they held little effective power and were rarely consulted at the highest levels of government. During the latter part of the nineteenth century and early twentieth century, members of this new class led or participated in a series of revolts in an attempt to gain access to the corridors of power. Sometimes these revolts were led by civilians who demanded a greater role in governance. They often framed their complaints in the form of a demand for constitutional rule, which, they assumed, would limit the authority of the sultan or shah and delegate more power to them. Hence, intellectuals and bureaucrats led the agitation for an Ottoman constitution, which was granted in 1876, and members of the two groups played a significant role in the Persian Constitutional Revolution of 1905. At other times, professional military officers took matters into their own hands. During one such revolt, spearheaded by Colonel Ahmad 'Urabi in 1881–1882, the khedive of Egypt felt so threatened that he sought refuge with a British fleet anchored nearby. Another military revolt, led by Turkish army officers in 1908, succeeded in restoring the Ottoman constitution, which had been suspended for thirty years.

Local resistance and the defection of military officers, intellectuals, and bureaucrats were not the only reasons why defensive developmentalist policies might fail. Programs ran afoul of the law of unintended consequences as well. The most famous example of this was the 1858 Ottoman Land Code. The code gave peasants the right to register the lands they were working in their own names as private property. The Ottoman government designed the code to increase accountability for taxation, expand agricultural production, and end tax farming. But peasants were, more often than not, suspicious of the motives of the Ottoman government. They feared that the government made this "gift" of land merely to increase their tax burden and that registration would lead to the conscription of their sons into the Ottoman army. As a result, some fled their land, or signed it over to urban-based notables, or soon lost it because they could not afford the registration fee or because they used it as collateral on loans to usurers. In the process, a law intended for entirely different purposes became the instrument by which peasants were frequently reduced to landless tenant farmers and absentee landowners came to possess huge agricultural estates.

As if these problems were not serious enough, defensive developmentalism repeatedly faced opposition from European states as well. Europeans opposed policies that did not serve their immediate economic or strategic interests. For example, many planners in the Middle East hoped to pay for their new armies or other institutions by fostering industry. European states, on the other hand, opposed two key components that defensive developmentalists thought necessary for industrial development: government monopolies and protective tariffs. The establishment of state monopolies in their territories would have allowed Middle Eastern governments to direct and set prices for raw materials used in government factories without the fear that competition from European merchants would drive prices up or deplete their supply. Protective tariffs would have allowed Middle Eastern governments to prevent European manufacturers from destroying local industry by dumping cheaper European products on their markets. Thus, in 1828 the Russians forced the Persians to agree to a ridiculously low 5 percent tariff on goods imported from Russia. At the dawn of the twentieth century, when Russian merchants were still paying their 5 percent tariffs on Russian exports to Persia, Persian merchants were paying upward of 20 percent on select commodities. Likewise, in 1838, the British forced the Ottomans to sign a treaty abolishing monopolies in their territories and setting the same ridiculously low—5 percent—tariffs on British imports.

Ultimately, the most significant problem with defensive developmentalism in the Middle East was that it was, in a way, counterproductive. For example, to accumulate money to pay for modern armies, rulers expanded the growth of cash crops (cotton, silk, tobacco) that were exported to Europe. They then borrowed money from Europeans to build expensive railroads and modern ports to get those crops to market. Thus, to resist European military expansion, Middle Eastern rulers actually encouraged European economic expansion into, and the further peripheralization of, their domains.

So much for an overview of defensive developmentalism. Let us now turn to the specifics of defensive developmentalism in Egypt, the rest of the Ottoman Empire, and Persia.

The most striking example of defensive developmentalism took place in Egypt under the dynasty established by Mehmet Ali. For Mehmet Ali, military reform was essential to consolidate his control over Egypt and to protect Egypt's near total autonomy in the Ottoman Empire for himself and his descendants. Furthermore, Mehmet Ali wanted to expand the area under his control to ensure the supply of raw materials crucial to Egypt's economy and development and to monopolize east/west trade routes. Under Mehmet Ali, Egyptian expansion took place in three directions. First, Mehmet Ali sent his armies south into the Sudan to obtain gold, slaves, and control of the west bank of the Red Sea. When the Ottomans requested his aid in putting down a revolt in Arabia, Mehmet Ali was eager to comply: An Egyptian presence in Arabia would guarantee Egyptian control over the east bank of the Red Sea and thus the lucrative coffee trade (the importance of western Arabia in the coffee trade can be seen in the name of a port city in

Yemen—Mocha—that is to this day frequently applied to coffee). Finally, in 1831, Mehmet Ali's son, Ibrahim, led an expedition into Syria. As discussed earlier, the Ottomans had promised Mehmet Ali control over Syria (present-day Syria, Lebanon, Jordan, and Palestine, also known as "Greater Syria") if he put down the rebellion in Greece. In reality, Syria was key to Mehmet Ali's plans for the Egyptian economy. Having control of Syria would give Mehmet Ali access to Levantine ports and long-distance trade routes as well as to raw materials such as timber and silk from Mount Lebanon.

While occupying Syria, Ibrahim introduced policies into the region typical of defensive developmentalists: He conscripted Syrians into armies built on the French model, eliminated tax farming and introduced direct taxation, encouraged the cultivation of cash crops that could be sold abroad to earn foreign exchange, oversaw measures to increase security in the countryside, and ordered the construction of public works to expand agricultural revenues, get cash crops to market quickly, and strengthen central control. Egypt continued to occupy Syria for almost a decade. In 1840, the Ottoman government, with British assistance, was able to reassert its control. The price paid by the Ottomans for British assistance was a high one. In 1838, the Ottomans signed the Treaty of Balta Liman with the British—the treaty that forbade monopolies in Turkish territories and set low import tariffs for foreign goods. The treaty thus assured the British continued economic penetration of Ottoman territories, including Egypt.

To support his military adventures abroad, Mehmet Ali undertook new economic policies at home. For example, Mehmet Ali abolished tax farming. He literally destroyed the mamluk tax farmers by inviting them to dinner, killing those who attended, and hunting down the remainder in the provinces of Egypt. Mehmet Ali then confiscated their lands and placed those lands directly under the control of the Egyptian government. He did the same with properties that had been set aside as religious endowments: If the holders of an endowment could not provide the proper documents proving a right to the property, they lost it. Since many religious endowments dated back to the Middle Ages, many holders could not. To eliminate the threat posed by bedouin to settled communities, Mehmet Ali gave them a choice: settle on unused agricultural lands or suffer the same punishment as had the mamluks. Because agriculture was proving to be so profitable anyway, most chose the former.

At the same time, the Egyptian government attempted to control all aspects of agriculture. It encouraged the planting of cash crops, particularly cotton. It set up a government monopoly (abolished, of course, after the Treaty of Balta Liman) that bought cotton from the cultivators and sold it to European agents. It invested in industries associated with cotton, such as ginning and spinning. These changes had important social consequences. Women were put to work in factories spinning and weaving while their husbands were recruited to perform forced labor for the government, such as digging irrigation canals. As a result, government intervention into the economy ended up upsetting established family relations.

Ship passing through the Suez Canal soon after its opening. (From: The Collection of Wolf-Dieter Lemke.)

Mehmet Ali's encouragement of cotton cultivation further integrated Egypt into the world economic system, and Egyptian revenues became directly dependent on the price of cotton in the international marketplace. In 1800, for example, more than 50 percent of Egypt's trade was with the rest of the Ottoman Empire and 14 percent was with Europe. By 1823, these figures were reversed.

Cotton production proved to be both a blessing and a curse for Egypt. During the American Civil War, the Northern blockade of Southern ports cut off Europe's supply of Confederate cotton and drove prices up. This situation dramatically increased Egyptian revenues and dependency on cotton cultivation. Mehmet Ali's successors, anticipating a lasting boom, borrowed heavily from European bankers to finance internal improvements. One such improvement was the Suez Canal, which was opened in 1869. The Suez Canal was not only an engineering marvel, it reduced by half the distance that merchant ships traveled from London to Bombay. The Egyptian government also built prestige projects, such as an opera house in Cairo. After all, every "civilized" country had at least one opera house. When the American Civil War ended in 1865 and American cotton went on the market again, the price of cotton plummeted. Egyptian revenues collapsed. Then the Egyptian economy received a second shock: the international depression of 1873. By 1876 Egyptian debts had reached more than ninety million British pounds, most of which was owed to foreigners. The Egyptian government was forced to declare bankruptcy that same year. European creditors then established a commission to supervise the Egyptian budget and oversee the repayment of Egyptian debt.

It is thus ironic that the policy originally intended to ensure political and economic independence had just the opposite effect. For Egypt, defensive developmentalism led to borrowing, borrowing led to bankruptcy, bankruptcy led to the 'Urabi Revolt in 1881, and the 'Urabi Revolt—which threatened the British position in the eastern Mediterranean and therefore Britain's route to India—led to British occupation in 1882. British occupation continued, in one form or another, until 1956. Well before that time, Egypt had become an economic satellite revolving around a British star. Adding to the irony was the fact that once they occupied Egypt, the British encouraged the continued cultivation of cotton to feed British textile mills. At the same time, they discouraged investment in industries that might compete with those in Britain.

Defensive developmentalism in the remainder of the Ottoman Empire also produced mixed results. Historians commonly divide the attempts at defensive developmentalism in the Ottoman Empire into two periods. They call the first period the period of "liberal reform," or the *tanzimat* period. (*Tanzimat* means "regulations" in Turkish.) Historians often date this period from 1839, but its roots go back further, as we shall see. The *tanzimat* culminated with the announcement of the short-lived Ottoman constitution of 1876. The second period of defensive developmentalism took place during the long rule of Sultan Abdulhamid II, who suspended the Ottoman constitution in 1878 and once again centered imperial governance in the palace. This period is commonly known as the period of "autocratic reform" and lasted until Abdulhamid II was deposed in 1909.

Unfortunately, the terms "liberal" and "autocratic" are a bit misleading. Actually, both periods were autocratic—constitutionalism should not be equated with democracy, after all, merely with the establishment of a written blueprint that would expand the role of "modernizing" intellectuals and bureaucrats in governance. It is true that during the first period bureaucrats and intellectuals made more of a conscious effort to mimic the institutions and ideas of Europe that were then fashionable. Of particular importance to them were the economic and political ideas associated with British Liberalism—individual rights (for society's elites), free market economics, and respect for private property. And it is true that the rhetoric of Abdulhamid II and his political allies drew from Islam, not Liberalism. But while the thin layer of Ottoman Westernizers may have thought it natural to couch their rhetoric in the rhetoric of British Liberalism, few others were convinced. Many embraced the idea of defensive developmentalism but found the principles of Liberalism to be distasteful. Others argued that Liberalism provided an insufficient basis for imperial revival. By the late 1870s, many Ottoman political elites had discovered a new model to emulate: the model provided by political developments in Germany and Italy after each had achieved unification in 1870–1871. This model emphasized governmental activism and change imposed from the top. And, if measured in terms of efficacy, far more development and government expansion took place in the latter period than in the former.

The Ottoman Empire that defensive developmentalists had inherited was hardly capable of swimming with the European sharks. Instead of power being concentrated in Istanbul, the influence of local notables often surpassed the power emanating from the central government. Even in those regions where the state could exercise power, however, it often did not do so, choosing instead to allow the population to organize its own affairs through informal networks. During the nineteenth century, the state not only attempted to curb the powers of local leaders, but also to expand its own authority into areas where government had never before intruded, such as education and social welfare.

Of course, military reform was of primary concern to the nineteenth-century Ottoman sultans. Sultan Selim III (1789–1807) established a new military corps, known as the *nizam-i jedid* (new order), that adopted Western forms of drill and armament. By 1806, the corps included about twenty-four thousand trained soldiers. While Selim III was forced to abdicate by those opposed to his policies, including a jealous janissary corps, one of his successors, Mahmud II (1808–1839) continued his efforts. In what became known as the "Auspicious Incident" (1826) to everyone but the janissaries, Mahmud II used the new corps to wipe out the janissaries in Istanbul and then hunt down remaining janissaries in the provinces. The achievements of Ottoman military reforms were such that they were mimicked in the Egypt of Mehmet Ali.

The creation of an effective army gave Mahmud II and his successors greater leeway in introducing new policies. Over the course of the nineteenth century, the Ottoman government legislated (unsuccessfully, as it turned out) against tax farming, restructured the central bureaucracy along European lines, and established provincial councils based on representative principles. It codified law and extended the authority of secular law. It established schools that took children after Qur'an training and prepared them for Western-style colleges. By the end of the nineteenth century, Istanbul hosted a school to educate bureaucrats, another to "civilize" the children of tribal leaders, and a third to train military officers. In all, by the beginning of the twentieth century more than half a million Ottoman civil servants managed activities commonly associated with modern nation-states, from the administration of hospitals to the construction and maintenance of essential infrastructure.

As in the case of Egypt, the state increasingly assumed responsibility for directing the economy as well. Over the course of the nineteenth century, the Ottoman state backed away from the stranglehold of free trade that had done so much to integrate it into the world economy. The imperial government intervened directly to promote the economic development of the empire. Sometimes, government policy failed miserably. Attempts to establish state-run factories floundered not only because the Ottomans faced Western competition and shortages of skilled workers, but also because the empire suffered from a lack of investment capital. As a result, the state turned instead to programs that were intended to foster private industrial production. By the end of the century, the state had reorganized the guilds, assembled cooperative associations, offered tax breaks to entrepreneurs, set production standards, and raised customs duties. The Ottoman state attempted to attract foreign investment capital by offering concessions for building telegraph lines, railroads, and tramways and for expanding port facilities in Istanbul and Beirut. The Ottoman state attempted to address the international agricultural crisis that began in the 1870s by establishing agricultural schools and issuing credits and seed to impoverished farmers. It even sent out teams of agronomists to the countryside to offer agricultural advice to peasants.

Whatever the efforts of the state, however, the effects of Ottoman defensive developmentalism were uneven. The nineteenth-century Ottoman Empire included Anatolia, the Balkans, parts of North Africa, and the Arab Middle East. The empire was so widespread that it was difficult for the power of the central government to radiate out through the provinces, even with the use of nineteenth-century technologies such as telegraphs and railroads. The diversity of the land and its peoples also obstructed the success of even the best-laid plans. Compare the Ottoman Empire with Egypt, a province that was relatively homogeneous both demographically and geographically. It was far easier for Cairo to dictate economic policy, especially because Egyptian soil and climate allowed it to base its economy on the cultivation and export of a few cash crops, particularly cotton. In contrast, the needs of Lebanese silk producers, as well as the organization of their communities, differed dramatically from those of the cotton producers of nearby Palestine, not to mention those of tobacco cultivators of the Balkans. Ottoman dependence on a variety of cash crops was hardly an effective economic strategy anyway. As in the case of Egypt, the cost of defensive developmentalism combined with the international depression of 1873 eventually led to bankruptcy and to European supervision of Ottoman finances.

Furthermore, as might be expected, the Ottoman government faced resistance to its policies. In addition to the "losers" in the process of defensive developmentalism—janissaries and tax farmers—specific imperial policies were regarded by too many as a threat. Ultimately, defensive developmentalism meant centralization, and centralization threatened the pivotal role played by informal, local networks in Ottoman life. For peasants, the policies of the imperial government threatened to bring about more efficient taxation and conscription. For ulama who were not attached to the central bureaucracy, the policies threatened to bring about a loss of prestige and limit their educational and judicial functions. For local notables, the policies meant loss of power. Because of this local resistance, many of the regulations failed to achieve the intended goals.

One of the most glaring examples of how Ottoman policies yielded unanticipated results had to do with the attempt to adjust the relationship among religious communities. During the *tanzimat*, the Ottoman government issued two decrees that many historians consider to be the cornerstones of the period of "liberal reform": the *Hatt-i Sharif* of Gulhane (1839) and the *Islahat Fermani* (1856). The documents promised all Ottoman subjects "perfect security for life, honor, and property" and religious liberty and equality for the non-Muslim inhabitants of the empire. In other words, the *Hatt-i Sharif* of Gulhane and the *Islahat Fermani* were attempts to promote a notion of Ottoman identity, *osmanlilik*. Henceforth, it was hoped, the empire would consist of a community of equal citizens bound together by an allegiance that transcended their religious allegiances.

For all its good intentions, a policy that attempted to establish equality among Ottoman citizens satisfied few Muslims or Christians. Muslim political and social elites resented a policy that threatened Muslim predominance and that was so obviously European in inspiration (in fact, the *Islahat Fermani* was dictated to the Ottoman government by the British ambassador to Istanbul, Stratford Canning). Muslim elites objected to the fact that the documents seemed to single out Christian communities for special consideration and opened the door to granting them economic and political privileges that Muslims did not enjoy. Many Christians, on the other hand, were not pleased that the notion of equality was applied in such areas as military conscription—a privilege of citizenship most Christians would have just as readily foregone. Their protests once again enabled Christians to avoid military service through the payment of a fee, an option not open to their increasingly resentful Muslim fellow citizens. Other Christians, looking to developments in the Balkans, preferred the path of nationalist separation rather than equality within a predominantly Muslim empire. It is thus ironic that the policy of promising equality to all inhabitants of the empire, regardless of religious affiliation, hardened communal boundaries and precipitated instances of intercommunal violence. In the process, it created the distinctly modern phenomenon of sectarianism all too familiar to observers of the contemporary Middle East.

The Persian experience with defensive developmentalism was different from that of either Egypt or the Ottoman Empire. Historians commonly cite two reasons for this. The first was the nature of Qajar rule. The Qajar dynasty was of recent vintage, having established itself more than two centuries after the founding of the Ottoman Empire. Unlike the Ottoman Empire, it did not build an empire from scratch, but rather on the ruins of the Safavid Empire. An entirely new political order thus did not accompany conquest as it had with the Ottomans. And the ruins upon which the Qajars established their rule were extensive: As a result of the Afghan invasion that finished off Safavid rule, it is estimated that approximately 20 percent of the population of the Safavid Empire died, while the cities of Persia lost upward of two-thirds of their population. The Afghan invasion was hardly the only disaster to strike Persia during the eighteenth century.

Not only was the Qajar dynasty new, relatively untested, and heir to a devastated land, Persia suffered from the ill fortune of being the site on which two stronger powers waged their struggle. Occasionally, Persia did benefit from the presence of rival imperialist powers on its borders. For example, Britain introduced the first telegraph line in Persia during the mid-1860s because it needed fast communications from India to London and Persia happened to be situated in between. And sometimes the British-Russian rivalry itself left its trace on Persia: In 1891, three years after the British established the first modern bank in Persia, the Russians simply had to follow suit. But, for the most part, the "Great Game" blocked the introduction of nineteenth-century technologies and institutions into Persia. Both Britain and Russia discouraged the Persian government from seeking technical assistance or loans from its rival. For example, neither power was enthusiastic about the other building a north-south railroad in Persia for obvious reasons, so that project had to wait until 1927. There is a cruel irony here. For all its evils, in most of the world imperialism fostered institutions and infrastructure, if only to expand the reach of the imperialist power and integrate the colonized into the world economy. In Persia it all too often had the opposite effect.

If the Qajars did suffer from such internal and external challenges, then how were they able to rule for so long? The answer, according to many historians, was that they never quite ruled at all. Historians cite the fact that throughout Qajar history, governors were powerless outside the provincial capitals and local communities were virtually autonomous. The Qajars maintained their position, the argument goes, by balancing off various factions within society: tribe against tribe, province against province, region against region, social class against social class. Qajar rule was minimalist. Unlike the Safavids, the Qajars only intervened in the economy to prevent urban insurrections when prices rose too high or shortages threatened. They also allowed others to run the economy: They auctioned off governorships to the highest bidders, who then farmed out tax collection in districts and cities. They also auctioned off the right to collect customs and mint coins to the highest bidder. By 1850, the Qajars even lost control over the lands that had been granted as *tiyul*. This land became the virtual private property of merchants, ulama, and high officials. Their inability to project power meant that the Qajar shahs could only respond feebly to those religious scholars who resisted the government because it attempted to usurp their legal and educational functions, landowners who were unappreciative of government efforts to streamline tax collection and keep better track of titles to land, and merchants who feared they could not compete in international trade with foreigners backed by their governments.

This is not to say that the Qajar dynasty did not take a stab at defensive developmentalism. In fact, it tried twice, once during the mid–nineteenth century and a second time in the 1870s. Under the direction of two centralizing chief ministers, the government attempted to construct state-run factories, reform the budget, build a modern military based on conscription rather than tribal levies, and build modern educational facilities. Their ef-

Members of the Cossack Brigade posing for photographer. Date unknown. (From: The Collection of Wolf-Dieter Lemke.)

forts failed, with two notable exceptions. The first was the Dar al-Funun, a school founded in 1851 to train military officers and bureaucrats. At its peak at the end of the nineteenth century, the Dar al-Funun admitted roughly 250 students each year. Many of the graduates of the Dar al-Funun chafed at what they considered Qajar despotism and inefficiency. They would later participate in the Constitutional Revolution of 1905. The second institution founded during the brief Persian experiment with defensive developmentalism was the Cossack Brigade, an elite military force led by Russian officers. The brigade, under the leadership of Reza Khan, would overthrow the Qajar dynasty in the wake of World War I. Ironically, then, the two institutions with lasting impact that were founded during the defensive developmentalist periods were two institutions that weakened, then eventually overthrew, the Qajars.

Because of their limited control over the country, the Qajars attempted to generate revenues and hasten development by granting concessions to European financiers and adventurers. That is, the Qajars attempted to encourage "modernization," raise quick cash, or do both by selling select Europeans the right to produce, market, and export a commodity or commodities found in Persia. For example, in 1872 the Persian shah granted to Baron Julius de Reuter, a British subject, the exclusive rights to build streetcars and railroads, extract minerals, establish a national bank, and exploit the national forests in exchange for a modest down payment and the promise of future royalties. Lord Curzon called what came to be known as the Reuter Concession "the most complete and extraordinary surrender of the entire industrial resources of a kingdom into foreign hands that has probably ever been dreamed of, much less accomplished, in history." Because the Reuter Concession met opposition in Persia and was hardly pleasing to the Russians, the shah cancelled it. Reuter retained the right to build the state bank of Persia, which financed the government, and, of course, did not walk away from an indemnity of forty thousand British pounds that the Persian government had to pay. It should not be surprising, therefore, that after the Reuter Concession the Persian government never again granted a concession simply to foster modernization.

But this did not stop the Persian government from granting concessions altogether. In 1890, after bribing the right Persian officials, a British adventurer acquired from the shah the right to control the cultivation, sale, distribution, and export of all Persian tobacco and tobacco products for fifty years—all for an annual payment of fifteen thousand British pounds and a quarter of the anticipated profits. Soon afterward, he sold these rights to the Imperial Tobacco Company of Britain. The announcement of the concession aroused opposition from several layers of Persian society, particularly from merchants. By the time of the Tobacco Concession, merchants were already suffering. With the onset of the Depression of 1873, both trade and the price cash crops fetched on the international market had fallen. In addition, Persian merchants found it difficult to compete with European merchants, who had better organizational and financial backing and who paid lower customs duties. Soon after the government granted the concession, merchants in Tehran, then in other cities, began to protest and urge a boycott of tobacco. They were joined by the leading ulama of Isfahan, where merchant power was concentrated. Although leading ulama in Tehran were tied financially to the court and therefore initially opposed the merchants' actions, they could not stay out of the fray once merchants began to present their case in religious terms and circulate the rumor that the leading cleric had issued a religious ruling banning the consumption of tobacco. The cleric, seeing the strength of the protest, did not disavow it.

Once again, the shah cancelled the concession. Once again there were penalties. This time, the cost of cancellation was 346,000 British pounds. To pay the indemnity, the shah contracted the first foreign loans contracted by a shah of Persia to the tune of 500,000 British pounds. This, of course, created huge deficits for the Persian government, which necessitated more foreign borrowing. But there was another penalty to be paid by the Persian government as well: The popular mobilization against the tobacco concession set a precedent for future mobilizations against the government. In the future, all successful mobilizations would be built on alliances of various social classes united by a broad and vague ideology that often used religious symbols. Of course, none of these mobilizations were religious per se, nor were they actually led by clerics—until, that is, clerics seized control over the Iranian Revolution of 1979. Shi'ism was not a cause of these revolts. To the contrary, like most other revolts, the causes were social and economic. Nevertheless, Shi'ism provided a unifying language and set of symbols, and the involvement of Shi'i clerics would lend legitimacy to revolts in Persia for the next century.

Perhaps the concession that had the most significance for the future of Persia was granted to an Anglo-Australian adventurer, William Knox d'Arcy. In 1901 the Persian government granted d'Arcy the right to "obtain, exploit, develop, render suitable for trade, carry away and sell" petroleum and petroleum products from all of Persia in exchange for forty thousand pounds in cash and stock and 16 percent of its annual profits. The British admiralty, seeking to convert its navy from coal to oil, saw the strategic value of this concession. (When criticized in Parliament for acting against the traditions of the British navy, the vice lord of the admiralty, Winston Churchill, reportedly responded acidly that the only traditions of the British navy were "rum, sodomy, and the lash.") To prevent d'Arcy from selling the concession to the French, the British government bought the concession and created the Anglo-Persian Oil Company. This was the first oil concession granted in the Middle East and provided the model for all others that followed. By 1923, Winston Churchill would claim that the concession had earned Great Britain forty million British pounds, while the concession earned Persia a mere two million.

Overall, then, what were the effects of defensive developmentalism in Egypt, the Ottoman Empire, and Persia? If success in centralization and the spread of governmental authority into previously unregulated areas of society are the criteria, then it is possible to claim that defensive developmentalism succeeded best in Egypt, then the Ottoman Empire, but met with very modest success in Persia. However, the purpose of defensive developmentalism was to defend Middle Eastern states from Western political and economic intrusion, and in this the effort failed. During the nineteenth century, the Ottoman Empire lost most of its Balkan and North African territories, Egypt was subjected to British occupation, and in 1907 Britain and Russia conspired to divide Persia into spheres of influence. Economically, some measures—encouraging the cultivation of cash crops, foreign borrowing, and the construction of networks of communication and transportation—actually facilitated Western economic penetration of the region. Even the establishment of "modern" educational, legal, and governmental structures in the Middle East advanced the integration of the region into the modern world economy. After all, in the wake of Ottoman legal reforms European merchants doing business in Salonika or Alexandria could trust in the fact that they would be subject to a uniform set of regulations that often corresponded to those found in Europe.

But there was another lasting legacy of defensive developmentalism that bears mentioning as well. Even when they misfired, measures taken by defensive developmentalists—conscripting soldiers, standardizing education, nurturing economic development, and even promoting ideologies like *osmanlilik*—had important consequences. Defensive developmentalists engaged their populations in common activities, organized and disciplined

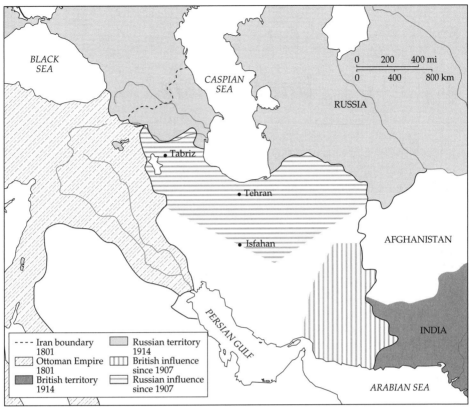

Qajar Persia, 1800–1914

those populations, and spread new conceptions about the role of the state in society and the responsibilities of the state and the populations it governed toward each other. Some defensive developmentalists were, of course, more successful in these endeavors than others. Nevertheless, by transferring the notion of the state first invented in eighteenth-century Europe to the Middle East, defensive developmentalists were instrumental in spreading the principles of the modern state and modern state system to the region.

Six

Imperialism

Defensive developmentalism was not the only means by which the structures of governance and economics associated with the modern period were introduced into the Middle East. There was also imperialism. Historians and political scientists have yet to agree on a definition of imperialism. However, a good starting point is the definition provided by a scholar of the subject, Ronald Robinson. According to Robinson, "Imperialism . . . is a process whereby agents of an expanding society gain inordinate influence or control over the vitals of weaker societies by . . . diplomacy, ideological suasion, conquest and rule, or by planting colonies of its own peoples abroad." One of the key concepts in this definition is contained in the phrase "gain inordinate influence or control over the vitals of weaker societies." This differentiates modern imperialism from the acquisitions-of-land-through-conquest that took place in history prior to the modern period. True, pre-modern conquerors sometimes transformed social and economic relations in the societies they conquered. For example, once free populations might be reduced to slavery. But modern imperialism had a singular and inevitable effect: In the aftermath of the eighteenth-century industrial revolution, imperialism compelled the integration of targeted societies into the modern world economy. In the process, new economic and political structures and new forms of social organization compatible with the modern world economy emerged in those societies, whether as a result of conscious design on the part of imperialist powers or as an unforeseen consequence of their intrusion. In other words, wherever European imperialists set foot, they left behind market economies and the framework for modern states.

Europeans used all the methods identified by Ronald Robinson—diplomacy, ideological suasion, conquest and rule, planting colonies—at one time or another, in one place or another, in the Middle East. For the most part, European imperialism in the Middle East was carried out in two ways: by economic penetration carried out through investments, loans, and the creation of spheres of influence; and by diplomatic coercion, through which Europeans acquired capitulatory rights or forced treaties favorable to their interests on weaker states. The concessions extracted from the Persian government are a good example of the former, the Treaty of Balta Liman an example of the latter.

There were, however, several notable exceptions to this rule that deserve scrutiny. At various times, Europeans colonized, occupied, and imposed special administrative zones in the Middle East. The purpose of this chapter is to look at three such instances.

Algeria: A Settler-Plantation Colony

During the nineteenth century, Algeria was transformed from an Ottoman territory into a French one. Before the French sent their fleet to Algeria in 1830, Algeria had been virtually autonomous within the Ottoman Empire. It was ruled by locally chosen Ottoman governors called deys. For most of the Ottoman period, the main source of local revenue came from piracy. By the end of the eighteenth century, however, Mediterranean piracy had seen better days. Not only had European states become quite adept at projecting their power onto the seas, they had become increasingly intolerant of what was, in effect, an extortion racket practiced by pirates and their North African sponsors.

As revenues from larceny, the ransoming of captives, and the sale of protection to European governments seeking to safeguard their merchants decreased, the authority of the dey and the dey's government weakened. Around the same time, the French adopted their Mediterranean strategy— the same strategy behind Napoleon's expedition to Egypt. As a matter of fact, although dead for almost a decade, Napoleon was in a way responsible for the French invasion and colonization of Algeria as well as the invasion and occupation of Egypt. While in Egypt, French forces bought Algerian grain, and the French debt to Algeria remained a sore spot between the two governments for decades afterward. During one particularly grueling round of negotiations about the debt, the exasperated dey of Algeria hit the French consul with a flyswatter. The French government used the famous "fly-whisk incident" to launch a naval campaign against Algeria. The campaign began with a naval blockade and culminated in the French occupation of the Algerian capital, Algiers, in 1830. In 1848, the French integrated Algeria into France as three French *départements* (provinces). In the eyes of the French government, Algeria was as much a part of France as Paris. It remained so for over one hundred years.

French imperialism in Algeria took a form that was rare in the Middle East. During the period of French rule, a European population settled in Algeria and established a plantation economy. Settlers came to Algeria for both political and economic reasons. The French government used Algeria as a convenient place to dump political dissidents, particularly those who had fought in the French Revolution of 1848 or who had participated in the Paris Commune of 1871. But it would have been impossible to build a settler economy with political dissidents alone. During the nineteenth century, the population of southern Europe grew faster than its resource base, creating widescale impoverishment. Many from the region emigrated abroad, including numerous southern Italians, who came to the United

States. Others—not only French, but Italians and Spanish as well—headed for Algeria.

In addition to impoverished peasants seeking a fresh start beyond the reach of their landlords, workers and artisans from southern Europe were drawn to Algeria by the lure of employment. Prospects for employment were good in Algeria because European capital was attracted to colonial outposts like Algeria during the nineteenth century. Since risk was high and liquidity (the amount of money available locally) low in European colonies, the possibility that European investors would earn a sizable return on their investments was also high. Money flooded into those companies that promoted ventures associated with colonial economies, such as the construction of ports, roads, telegraph lines, and the like. The Algerian rail system dates from 1857—it was constructed at around the same time as the rail system in European France. These projects allowed colonizers to open up new areas of Algeria for cash cropping, speed crops to European markets, and maintain control over far reaches of the countryside. The construction of such projects required skilled and semiskilled workers. By the outbreak of World War I, there were approximately seven hundred thousand European settlers in Algeria—the vast majority of whom had actually been born there. They, rather than the almost five million Muslim inhabitants of the territory, controlled both political and economic institutions.

To accommodate these settlers and attract European capital to Algeria, the French government seized religious endowments, lands owned by the dey, pasture lands used by nomads, and abandoned urban property. Lands previously held by non-European inhabitants of Algeria became the property of European speculators and entrepreneurs who consolidated them into large plantations for the cultivation of crops bound for the export market—grain, cotton (particularly during the American Civil War), tobacco, even flowers. During the 1870s, when the wine industry in France was virtually decimated by a parasite that ate the roots of grapevines, speculators and entrepreneurs with holdings in Algeria began expanding grape cultivation to take advantage of the shortfall. By 1914, one-third of Algerian exports was wine. The expansion of the plantation system squeezed out European settlers with small landholdings. At the same time, plantation owners hired the indigenous inhabitants of Algeria to work for low wages as seasonal laborers on their plantations. Others who had become landless or who owned plots that were too small for subsistence flocked to cities where they became day laborers or joined the ranks of the unemployed. Overall, then, French imperialism in Algeria encouraged the spread of market relations, disrupted rural life, and increased the population of towns and cities.

The integration of Algeria into the French political and economic system had other effects that no French policy maker could have foreseen in 1830. French colonialism resembled other colonialisms inasmuch as the French justified their activities by claiming that they brought civilization to the benighted natives—what the French called their civilizing mission (*mission civilisatrice*). At the same time, however, European settlers and their descendants had access to rights of citizenship that no Muslim Algerian could hope to attain. As we shall discuss in a later chapter, the integration of Algeria into the "civilized world"—what was, in fact, the integration of Algeria into the modern world economic and state systems—made the emergence of Algerian nationalism possible; the differentiation between European French citizens and Algerians on the basis of race or language or religion made the emergence of Algerian nationalism likely.

That likelihood was increased after the outbreak of World War I in 1914. During the war French industrial workers were conscripted into the French army. To take their place, seventy-six thousand Algerians went to metropolitan France to work in factories there. By 1950, their numbers had swelled to over six hundred thousand. Another 173,000 fought in the French army during World War I (about twenty-five thousand died). A number of these Algerians joined trade unions, communist organizations, and emigrant societies that nurtured political activists and introduced them to the latest techniques for political organization and agitation. Beginning in the late 1920s, groups of emigrant workers in France and former emigrant workers in Algeria began to form associations that demanded Algerian independence. Between 1954 and 1962, Algerians, under the leadership of the F.L.N. (*Front de libération nationale*, the National Liberation Front) fought an extremely bloody war for Algerian independence from France—a war in which over one million Algerians died. The F.L.N. rules Algeria to this day. Its rule has hardly been unchallenged, however: In 1992, when the F.L.N. annulled the results of elections it had lost to its Islamist opponents, Algeria once again descended into war.

Although Algeria lies outside the geographic area routinely covered by this book, its history is important for a number of reasons. French administrators trained in Algeria provided expertise for the French in other parts of the Middle East, including Lebanon and Syria, which the French came to control after World War I. (India played a similar role for the British, and many a British administrator in Egypt, Iraq, and elsewhere in the Middle East had cut his teeth in the Indian civil service.) Algeria also provided the model for a second, less successful attempt to implant a settler-plantation colony in the Middle East. Seeking to replicate the Algerian example, the French financier and philanthropist Baron Edmund de Rothschild financed settler-plantation colonies in Palestine beginning in 1882. Rothschild's plan called for European Jews to emigrate to Palestine and establish and oversee plantations for the cultivation of citrus, almonds, and particularly grapes for wine. (Anyone who has drunk Levantine wine can only be thankful that Rothshild's experiment failed, even though he imported administrators who had gained experience in Algeria.) By 1900 Rothschild had lost patience with his experiment and withdrew his support, and within a few years about two-thirds of the Jewish agricultural workers left Palestine. Although Jewish immigration to Palestine would expand over the course of the next century, the attempt to establish a plantation system in Palestine that would integrate Jewish and Arab labor was never attempted again.

Besides providing the model for settler-plantation colonies elsewhere, Algeria provided another model as well. During the 1950s and 1960s, the Algerian independence struggle became both a rallying point and a model for other revolutionary struggles throughout the world. Here's what Malcolm X had to say about Algeria in a speech to an African American audience in 1963:

> The Algerians were revolutionists, they wanted [their] land. France offered to let them be integrated into France. They told France, to hell with France, they wanted some land, not some France. And they engaged in a bloody battle. . . . Revolution is in Asia, revolution is in Africa, and the white man is screaming because he sees revolution in Latin America. How do you think he'll react to you when you learn what a real revolution is?

We shall discuss the sad history of the revolutionary experience in the Middle East in a later chapter.

Egypt: Bankruptcy and Occupation

If Algeria presents an example of imperialism as colonization, Egypt presents a different example of imperialism: imperialism as occupation. While British administrators, under the protective gaze of British soldiers, ran most Egyptian affairs, Egypt never became the site of large-scale population transfer. Nor did Britain officially make Egypt part of its empire, as it did Canada and India. Egypt remained part of the Ottoman Empire until the outbreak of World War I.

The story of how the British ended up in occupation of Egypt begins, once again, with cotton. As we have seen, after the American Civil War the price of cotton collapsed. A second jolt to the cotton market came a few years later with the onset of the Depression of 1873. The Egyptian government, expecting the price of cotton to remain high, had borrowed heavily to finance internal improvements and, on more than one occasion, extravagances. In 1876, unable to pay back its debts, the Egyptian government declared bankruptcy. In response, the British, French, Italian, Austrian, and later the Russian governments came to the aid of their citizens who had invested in Egypt. The European governments set up an agency called the Caisse de la Dette, which oversaw Egyptian finances with an eye toward debt repayment (they would also set up an Ottoman Public Debt Administration for the same purpose in the wake of the Ottoman bankruptcy). The Caisse's administrators took control of over 50 percent of Egyptian revenues. The 1880 Law of Liquidation regularized the debt repayment. According to the law, the Caisse was to direct all net revenue from railroads, the telegraph, and the port of Alexandria to the repayment of Egypt's foreign creditors. The law also granted the Caisse the right to all income derived from customs and import taxes on tobacco and wrested from the government of Egypt control of all tax revenues from four Egyptian provinces. Finally, the Caisse demanded the reinstatement of taxes on land that had previously been exempted. The

Caisse's actions infuriated a cross-section of the Egyptian population, from landowners who found their tax burden suddenly increased, to military officers who suffered as a result of government cutbacks, to religious, commercial, and political elites who found foreign control difficult to stomach.

Many in the military harbored other grievances as well. From the beginning of Ottoman rule through most of the nineteenth century, a Turkish-speaking elite dominated the highest rungs of Egyptian society. This elite, which at the beginning of the nineteenth century numbered no more than ten thousand members, was Ottoman in culture and outlook. Mehmet Ali, it must be remembered, hailed from Ottoman Albania, did not speak Arabic, and acted much like other Ottoman warlords who sought to carve out a privileged role for themselves and their families within the empire, not separate from it. Over the course of the nineteenth century the gap between the ruling elite and the population narrowed. Political and military elites in Egypt increasingly came to speak Arabic and intermarry with the native inhabitants of Egypt. At the same time, those inhabitants came to penetrate the bureaucracy and officer corps of the military, once the exclusive preserve of the Ottoman elites. Nevertheless, the discrimination felt by many in Egyptian society stung, and officers who believed that their rise in the ranks had been blocked because of their background were in a position to do something about it. In 1881, the army under Colonel Ahmad 'Urabi mutinied. The mutiny touched the exposed nerve that foreign interference and social cleavages had created in Egyptian society. 'Urabi forced his way into the government and began preparing to defend Egypt from the assault from Europe that was sure to come.

And come it did. Historians disagree about the precise reasons for the British invasion and occupation of Egypt. Some attribute it to British fears for the Suez Canal. After all, the British felt that the canal was so important for preserving their interests in India that in 1875 they had bought a majority of its shares from an Egyptian government on the verge of bankruptcy. The British also feared for the repayment of the Egyptian debt, 25 percent of which was owned by British investors. They also feared instability in the eastern Mediterranean, particularly since Europeans living in Egypt began sending back exaggerated reports of massacres of Christians. Probably all of these factors led to the British invasion and occupation. The British sent a flotilla to Egypt and established residence there that would last for three quarters of a century.

Once in Egypt, the British exercised control through both military and political means. Although the size of the British occupation forces was small in comparison with the size of the population, its presence provided a reminder to the Egyptians of Britain's power in the territory. The British did not eliminate the Egyptian army, which had been the pride of Egyptian rulers since the time of Mehmet Ali, but they did reduce its size and place British officers in positions of command. At the same time, the British exercised political power through a local administration. Theoretically, of course, the Ottomans still ruled Egypt and invested its khedives. In reality, the most important political figure was the British consul general. The first consul general, Evelyn Baring, the Earl

The British invasion of Egypt in 1882 began with the shelling of the port city of Alexandria. On this page, Alexandria before bombardment. On the facing page, Alexandria after bombardment. (From: University of Chicago Library (left) and Hume Family Collection, The University of Queensland, Australia (right).)

of Cromer (who was, coincidentally, a member of the family that had established the famous Barings bank) replaced anti-British Egyptian ministers with British appointees. His high-handed attitude toward the Egyptians he ruled is reflected in the following passage from his memoirs:

> The European is a close reasoner; his statements of fact are devoid of ambiguity; he is a natural logician, albeit he may not have studied logic; he loves symmetry in all things; he is by nature skeptical and requires proof before he can accept the truth of any proposition; his trained intelligence works like a piece of mechanism. The mind of the Oriental, on the other hand, like his picturesque streets, is eminently wanting in symmetry. His reasoning is of the most slipshod description. Although the ancient Arabs acquired in a somewhat high degree the science of dialectics, the descendants are singularly deficient in the logical faculty. They are often incapable of drawing the most obvious conclusions from any simple premises of which they may admit the truth. Endeavour to elicit a plain statement of facts from an ordinary Egyptian. His explanation will generally be lengthy, and wanting in lucidity.

By 1908, the year Cromer wrote those lines, the British controlled all government ministries but one: the ministry that oversaw religious endowments. Egyptians held only 28 percent of high government posts.

Over the course of their occupation, the British imposed policies in Egypt modeled on their experience at home or in India. At a time when municipal reform was of central concern to reformers in Britain and was just being implemented in India, British administrators in Egypt oversaw the es-

Alexandria after the war.

tablishment of municipal governments with responsibilities for taxation and public services. Five years after the colonial government in the Punjab region of India passed a law to prevent moneylenders from foreclosing on peasant-owned lands, the occupation government of Egypt did the same. As with many of the defensive developmentalist policies of the khedives, however, this law—the so-called Five Feddan Law—had unforeseen effects. The law forbade moneylenders from demanding land as collateral on loans if a peasant's holdings were five feddans or less (a feddan is about an acre). The law was intended to prevent peasants from losing their property to unscrupulous usurers. Instead, moneylenders simply refused to loan money to peasants covered by the law. Lacking money to buy seed, peasants with small plots of land were often worse off than ever.

British occupation had other long-term economic effects as well. The British encouraged the expansion of cotton cultivation to feed their textile mills and constructed infrastructure that would foster not only the cultivation, but the transport and sale of cotton as well. In the period between the onset of the British occupation and the beginning of World War I, almost one million additional acres of land came under cultivation and over four thousand kilometers of track for railroads was lain. At the same time, the British did everything they could to ensure the Egyptians would not establish a textile industry that might compete with their own. When Egyptian businessmen implored Cromer to impose tariffs on imported cloth so that they might establish textile factories free from competition from abroad, Cromer refused, citing the principle of free trade between Britain and its colonies. By the early twentieth century, the lesson that had been brought home to many political and economic elites in Egypt was that Egypt could never achieve full economic development under British rule.

Although the British discouraged investment in Egyptian industry to protect the interests of their manufacturers at home, this was not the only reason they did so. Many British policy makers believed that rapid economic
development in Egypt would undermine the calm in their new acquisition
and threaten their position there. British imperialists of the nineteenth and
twentieth centuries were not alone in thinking that economic development
brings social disruption and social disruption brings rebellion. After the Iranian Revolution of 1978–1979, many scholars in the United States likewise
blamed rapid development under the previous regime for the revolutionary
upsurge. However one-dimensional such reasoning might be, British fears
of turmoil and rebellion in Egypt led to what one economist has called the
asymmetrical development of Egypt. From the beginning of the occupation
through the outbreak of World War I, the Egyptian economy grew, but this
growth could not be maintained because investment in education and industry lagged behind. As a matter of fact, per capita income among Egyptians actually declined over the course of the first half of the twentieth century. Investors—mainly Europeans and "foreigners" (Greeks, Jews, Syrians)
living in Egypt—channeled their money into those areas of the economy that
promised high returns on their investments. These areas were not necessarily ones that would ensure sustained, independent economic development. Egypt got its railways and its urban tramways, for sure, but by the
time of World War I it had only sixty-eight publicly financed schools and
spending on education took up no more than 1 percent of the government's
budget. This was no accident: The British purposely restricted the enrollment in secondary schools and universities to a narrow group that could be
absorbed into the economy. By doing so, they hoped to prevent the growth
of a class of disaffected intellectuals.

The British were only partially successful, however. Disaffected intellectuals would go on to organize the first modern nationalist parties in the
Arab world. As in the case of Algeria, it was the very presence of imperialists that encouraged the emergence of nationalism in Egypt. Building on
the work of their khedival predecessors, the British engaged Egyptians in
common activities and in a common marketplace. In the process, they in-
stilled among Egyptians a sense of national community. At the same time,
the British presence in Egypt provided the population with a clear target
against which to mobilize. Because of this, the Egyptian national movement
followed a trajectory that was different from that followed by nationalisms
in the rest of the Ottoman domains. Over time, that difference would assure the emergence of a distinct Egyptian territorial identity and the dissemination of a national myth that would trace "Egyptianness" backward
to antiquity.

Mount Lebanon: Military and
Political Intervention

European imperialism in the Middle East did not only take the forms of colonization and occupation. European powers also supervised the adminis-

British imperialism in Egypt had long-lasting effects. Fighting imperialism under the pyramids, ca. 1960. (From: Fondation Arabe pour l'image, Beirut.)

trative reorganization of Mount Lebanon and guaranteed its autonomy. European states intervened into the politics of Mount Lebanon to put an end to sectarian—interreligious—conflict that pit Maronite Christians against their Muslim and Druze neighbors. (Maronites are Christians who recognize the Catholic pope's authority but maintain their own traditions. The Druze are a religious sect that branched off from mainstream Islam in the eleventh century. Both groups live in Mount Lebanon.) As discussed earlier, sectarian strife of the sort that took place in Mount Lebanon can be traced to the transformation of Middle Eastern society in the nineteenth century. It was then that the boundaries between Muslim and minority communities began to harden, the social and economic histories of those communities began to diverge, and religious affiliation became the platform from which imperial subjects asserted political claims.

There were both economic and political factors that encouraged the rise of sectarianism in the eastern Mediterranean. During the nineteenth century, as the Ottoman Empire became increasingly integrated into the world economy, the prosperity of the Christian community along the Mediterranean coast increased dramatically. Christian (and Jewish) merchants acted as middlemen in the European trade. They frequently knew European languages, had contacts abroad, and could provide European merchants with information about local conditions. The local consulates of European states often granted these minority merchants special certificates, known as *berat*s. Merchants who obtained *berat*s were covered by the capitulatory agreements between the Ottoman Empire and the state that issued them. In other words, subjects of the sultan who happened to be members of minority groups obtained the same access to the commercial and legal rights the empire had accorded merchants of European states. Because they paid lower customs duties and received tax breaks, they were often more prosperous than their Muslim competitors.

The number of these *beratlis*, as these merchants and other foreign protégés were called, was not insignificant. By the turn of the nineteenth century, the Austrians had granted consular recognition to two hundred thousand Ottoman subjects. Around the same time, the Russians recognized an additional 120,000. Most of those recognized by the Russians were Greeks who shared religious affiliation with the Russians and who were employed by the Russians as "interpreters." Thus, one out of every one hundred Ottoman subjects was accorded the rights of Russian and Austrian citizens. And then there were the British, the French, the Prussians, and even the Americans. Each selected their favorite minority—Maronites for the French, Protestants for the British and Americans—and conferred on them the same privileges that were available to their own citizens.

But economic jealousy alone does not explain why Muslim/minority tensions would rise during the nineteenth century, nor does it explain why it would affect such a relatively isolated area as Mount Lebanon. For that, we must look at the promise of equality of citizenship offered by the *Hatti-i Sharif* of Gulhane and the *Islahat Fermani*, discussed in Chapter 5. Immediately after the announcement of the new Ottoman policy, local notables, clergyman, and even commoners began to assert claims for the political rights promised in the documents. But they asserted those claims in a novel way. Local notables, clergymen, and even commoners knew that they would gain support from European states and concessions from an Ottoman government that was vulnerable to those European states if they presented their claims in the name of one or another downtrodden religious community. By claiming that they were acting to protect the interests of their religious community, they were saying, in effect, that their religious community was a distinct social unit that had interests that differed from the interests of other religious communities. As a result, they made religious communities competitors in the political arena.

The mixture of religious affiliation and political identity had dangerous consequences. It became all too easy for the inhabitants of areas in which several religious communities lived side by side to interpret every indignity or act of exploitation they suffered as an assault on their religious community. And there were all too many leaders or would-be leaders in religious communities ready to exploit the occasion for their own political purposes. Thus, in 1858 a dispute between Maronite peasants and Maronite landlords in Mount Lebanon soon transmuted into a rebellion of Maronite peasants against Druze landlords. The Druze retaliated and the fighting spread. In various places in the eastern Mediterranean, Muslims, angered by the rising economic and political status of Christians, attacked them. In Damascus alone, between five and ten thousand Christians were massacred and European consulates burned. Other massacres took place in Aleppo, Syria, and Nablus, Palestine. To protect their Maronite clients, the French landed a force in Beirut.

In the wake of these events, a conference of European representatives met in Istanbul in 1861 to impose a solution on the Ottoman government. Although the roots of the problem were complex, the European delegates saw it exclusively in religious terms. For them, the violence was the latest manifestation of an age-old problem: Muslim fanatics preying on oppressed non-Muslim communities. As a result, the Europeans stepped in to protect the Christians of Mount Lebanon. They insisted that the Ottomans grant Mount Lebanon autonomy and placed the region under the protection of all European powers acting in concert. Mount Lebanon became a special administrative district, a *mutasarrifiya*, governed by a non-Lebanese Ottoman Christian who was assisted by an elected representative council. That council consisted of four Maronites, three Druze, two members of the Greek Orthodox church, one Greek Catholic, one Sunni Muslim, and one Shiʻi Muslim. This arrangement fixed the connection between politics and religious allegiance and based political representation in Lebanon on the relative size of each religious community.

The arrangement reached in 1861, then amended in 1864, was the historical ancestor of the system of proportional representation that exists in Lebanon to this day. In 1943, the year Lebanon became independent, leading Christian and Muslim politicians in Lebanon reached an informal understanding called the National Pact. The purpose of the pact was to define the political spoils available to each religious community. The pact stipulated that the president, prime minister, and speaker of the lower house of parliament would be a Maronite, a Sunni, and a Shiʻi, respectively, that the lower house would be divided between Christians and Muslims in a ratio of six to five, and that even cabinet posts would be distributed according to a representational formula that until 1990 would be based on the last census taken in Lebanon—the census of 1932. After fifteen years of civil war, the representational formula was amended in 1989. This formula apportioned seats in the lower house of parliament equally between Muslims and Christians—this, at a time when it is estimated that Lebanese Muslims far outnumbered Lebanese Christians.

Sectarianism in the Middle East has not been limited to Lebanon. It has affected much of the region, from Algeria to Iraq. For example, in 1870 the French government issued the Crémieux Decree, which granted French citizenship to the forty thousand Jews of Algeria. Because no such privilege was granted to Algerian Muslims, French policy had the effect of separating and hardening the boundaries between the two communities. Again, the results were disastrous: In 1934, incited by anti-Semitic Nazi propaganda, elements from the Muslim community in the Algerian city of Constantine engaged in anti-Jewish riots, killing about two dozen Jews. In the wake of these riots, most Algerian Jews fled to European France. As elsewhere in the region, European imperialism in Algeria nourished the idea that religious (and ethnic) differences were not only natural, age-old, and unalterable, but that they mattered.

Seven

Wasif Jawhariyyeh and the Great Nineteenth-Century Transformation

By the late nineteenth century, integration and peripheralization, defensive developmentalism, and imperialism had established the ground rules for the subsequent economic, social, and political development of the Middle East. These processes did not operate in a vacuum, however, and when they intruded upon the social, economic, and cultural life of the region the effects were dramatic. New social classes were created while others were destroyed. Urban centers were demolished and reconstructed. The introduction of new agricultural methods, crops, property rights, and markets transformed rural life. The emergence of new groups of cultural producers and consumers and experimentation with novel forms of cultural expression reshaped cultural and political life. Governments and citizens renegotiated their mutual responsibilities.

This chapter looks at these changes through the eyes of a Jerusalem musician by the name of Wasif Jawhariyyeh. Jawhariyyeh left behind voluminous diaries that begin in 1904 and end in 1968. They describe in detail not only his life, but the social and cultural life of Jerusalem. These diaries were recently brought to light and edited by the Palestinian scholar Salim Tamari. This chapter is based on Tamari's work.

Wasif Jawhariyyeh's diaries provide an ideal jumping-off point for understanding life in the Middle East in the late nineteenth and early twentieth centuries for other reasons as well. Jawhariyyeh was not a particularly important individual. This makes his diaries all the more interesting. We have many memoirs from political and cultural elites. These memoirs were written mostly to justify the political activities or to glorify the cultural achievements of their authors for posterity. Jawhariyyeh did not write for either purpose. And while Jawhariyyeh came from a fairly privileged background, his family was hardly at the pinnacle of Jerusalem life. Furthermore, Jawhariyyeh's diaries record daily life at a critical juncture in Jerusalem's history. When Jawhariyyeh began writing his diaries in 1904, Jerusalem was a relative backwater of the Ottoman Empire. As such, the city was a rather late entrant into what might be called the "great nineteenth-century trans-formation," and Jawhariyyeh was a witness to that transformation.

To understand the position of Jerusalem among cities of the Ottoman Em-pire, it is worth comparing it with two other important cities in Palestine at the time: Jaffa and Nablus. Jaffa was a port city that grew in response to in-creased trade with Europe and the introduction of steamships into the Mediterranean. Between 1856 and 1880, the cultivation of citrus fruit shipped through Jaffa quadrupled and the value of Jaffa's exports increased 1,400 percent. The Jaffa orange—an orange that could survive long-distance ship-ment unscathed because of its thick skin—became a major export crop at that time. As Jaffa's importance as an export hub increased, so did the pop-ulation of the city. At the beginning of the nineteenth century, the popula-tion of Jaffa ranged from five hundred to five thousand, depending on the state of the agricultural economy, security in the countryside, and the avail-ability of urban employment for farmers immigrating into the city. By 1912, population had reached fifty thousand. At that time, only about ten thou-sand inhabitants of the city were Jews recently arrived from Europe.

Nablus, on the other hand, was an inland commercial center under the sway of a few merchant families. Because it was dominated by merchants, the city of Nablus was more outward-looking than Jerusalem—it had industries such as soap manufacture and weaving, as well as a greater integration with both the outside world (Greater Syria, Egypt, and Europe) and its immediate hinterland, from which it derived raw materials for its manufactures.

Unlike Nablus, the major industries of Jerusalem were associated with its function as a religious center. Jerusalem catered to pilgrims and the Euro-pean tourist trade that had emerged in the aftermath of the Napoleonic Wars. The city did not have a modern municipal water system until 1901, nor did it have a modern sewage system until about a decade later. The famous Jerusalem clock tower was constructed at the same time as the water sys-tem. The clock tower was an important symbol for the inhabitants of the city in the early twentieth century and an important signpost for historians. For the former, it represented an expanded imperial presence in the city as well as the Ottoman impulse for "modernization." For the latter, it represents what historian E. P. Thompson has called the intersection between "time and work discipline"; that is, for historians the clock tower exemplifies the at-tempt to regulate Jerusalem's labor force and make it submissive to a daily, nine-to-five type of schedule. In 1909, Jerusalem's wagon drivers went on strike to protest increased taxes. The strike shut the city down. Think of it: a modern form of social protest made effective because of the central eco-nomic role played by an antiquated technology.

Wasif Jawhariyyeh begins his diaries as follows:

> I was born on Wednesday morning the fourteenth of January 1897, according
> to the Western calendar, which happened to be the eve of the Orthodox New
> Year. At the moment my father was preparing a tray of knafeh [a sweet] for
> the occasion as was customary then in Eastern Orthodox households. I was

The Jerusalem clock tower. (From: Fondation Arabe pour l'image, Beirut.)

named Wasif after the Damascene Wasif Bey al-Adhem, who was then my father's close friend and the sitting judge in Jerusalem's Criminal Court.

Wasif Jawhariyyeh's father was a prominent member of the Eastern Orthodox community, a member of Jerusalem's municipal council, and a lawyer. He spoke Greek, Turkish, and Arabic: Greek because of his membership in the Orthodox church, Turkish because that was the second language of upwardly mobile elites and aspiring elites throughout the Ottoman Empire who sought advancement in late Ottoman society. Neither Wasif nor his father lived in a monoglot society.

Wasif's father took up silk farming later in his life. Silk farming took off in Palestine during the 1850s, again as a result of expanded trade with Europe. The marriage between urban and rural life was typical in Ottoman/Arab society of the time. As discussed earlier, the Ottoman Land Code of 1858 enabled notable families and ambitious individuals with money to invest to gain access to rural property. The land code was one reason for the appearance of large landed estates in the Arab provinces of the empire. Such landed estates would remain part of the Arab Middle Eastern scene until the mid-twentieth century.

The consolidation of large landed estates had important social implications as well. During the second half of the nineteenth century, a new class of absentee urban landowners began to dominate local politics in Greater Syria. These urban landowners not only took advantage of the 1858 land code, they also took advantage of new forms of governance introduced into the empire to make themselves indispensable both to the renovated Ottoman imperial system and local society. For example, by the close of the nineteenth century the imperial government had ordered the establishment of municipal councils in cities throughout the empire. The Jerusalem municipal council, of which Wasif's father was a member, was established in 1863. Before then, cities had no independent existence: They could not tax, nor could they commission the construction of municipal infrastructure. The establishment of municipal councils opened the way for the absentee landowners to gain access to positions of power and opportunities to enrich themselves further. Members of municipal councils were able to skim off taxes, register lands in their own names, and direct municipal resources to themselves and their friends. Like their contemporaries in the Tammany Hall political machine of New York, they "seen their opportunities and they took'em." And like their contemporaries they attracted a devoted following of people who sought to take advantage of their social betters' access to power and their ability to bestow bounty on their followers. Wasif Jawhariyyeh's father thus attached himself to the Husseini family, the most prominent family in Jerusalem. He began his career looking after the extensive Husseini family estates in the villages to the west of Jerusalem.

Jawhariyyeh describes his youth with a great deal of nostalgia for the "good old days." While a bit idealistic, this description gives us a view of day-to-day life among people of his class in Jerusalem. Take, for example, the following entry into his diaries:

> During the summer months of 1904 [when Jawhariyyeh was nine years old] we would sit around the lowered table for the main meal. Food was served in enameled zinc plates. That year we stopped eating with wooden spoons imported from Anatolia and Greece and replaced them with brass ones. We replaced the common drinking bowl tied to the pottery jar with individualized crystal glasses. In 1906 my father acquired single iron beds for each of my siblings, thus ending the habit of sleeping on the floor. What a delight it was to get rid of the burden of having to place our mattresses into the wall enclaves every night.

As a youth, Jawhariyyeh received a rather eclectic education. Although Orthodox, his father had him memorize the Qur'an. At the age of nine, he entered a Lutheran school. There, he learned basic Arabic grammar, dictation, reading, arithmetic, German, and Bible recitation. After being beaten by an instructor whom he allegedly mocked, Wasif went to the "progressive" Dusturiyyeh (constitutional) National School, where corporal punishment was forbidden. At the Dusturiyyeh, he learned grammar, literature, mathematics, English, French, Turkish, physical education, and Qur'anic studies for Christians.

Two of these subjects are particularly noteworthy. First, physical education was associated with the cult of the body popular in Europe at the time and spreading into the Middle East. Physical education had become an important part of "Christian renewal"—what is known as muscular Christianity—and was, of course, of vital concern to nationalist movements throughout Europe. Educators, clerics, and politicians promoted physical

The cult of the body: student athletes at the American University of Cairo, 1924. (From: Fondation Arabe pour l'image, Beirut.)

education to prevent physical and moral weakness that were seen as detrimental to the "body politic." This tendency was later taken up in Egypt with the establishment of the Young Men's Muslim Association, modeled on the Young Men's Christian Association that had been founded in England in 1844. Its spread to the Middle East demonstrates in a different form the impulse toward "renewal" that will be discussed in the next chapter.

The second item on the curriculum that bears scrutiny is Qur'anic studies for Christians. Christians studied the Qur'an because it was believed that the text was an important part of the literary and cultural tradition of the Middle East—their literary and cultural tradition. In other words, by the beginning of the twentieth century the Qur'an did not only have a religious function, it took on another function as well. For many in the region, the Qur'an became part of a shared cultural heritage that distinguished the culture of the region from the culture of the West. One prominent scholar writing from Istanbul at the time explicitly linked the creation of a shared culture and efforts to revitalize the Middle East as follows:

> The Germans differed in religion in a manner similar to the way Persians and Afghans differ in religion. When this difference was manifested in politics, the Germans were weak. But when they returned to their authentic culture, when they heeded the call of national unity and the general interest, God returned their power and they became the rulers of Europe and dominated its politics.

Like this particular scholar, many Ottoman cultural elites of the time thought that the creation of a common culture that superseded sectarian, regional, or linguistic divisions was necessary for imperial revitalization.

Jawhariyyeh describes his education in the Qur'an in the following manner:

> I received my copy of the Qur'an from al-Hajjah Um Musa Kadhem Pasha al-Husseini . . . who taught me how to treat it with respect and maintain its cleanliness. [Um Musa was, of course, a woman.] My Qur'anic teacher was Sheikh Amin al-Ansari, a well-known *faqih* [legal scholar qualified to rule on matters pertaining to shari'a] in Jerusalem. The headmaster's idea was that the essence of learning Arabic lies in mastering the Qur'an, both reading and incantation. My Muslim classmates and I would start with Surat al-Baqara and continue. . . . I can say in all frankness that my mastery of Arabic music and singing is attributable to these lessons—especially my ability to render classical poetry and *muwashahat* to musical form.

Jawhariyyeh was compelled to leave the school and enroll in another "in order to gain knowledge of the English language and build a solid base for my future." He remained in this school for another two years until it was closed at the beginning of World War I.

The story of Jawhariyyeh's education demonstrates the fluidity of boundaries in Ottoman Jerusalem during Jawhariyyeh's youth. In the contemporary world, peoples' identities and social and political roles are relatively fixed. In the world of Jawhariyyeh's youth, boundaries separating the lives of Christians or Jews from Muslims were more fluid, as were urban social boundaries and the boundaries separating so-called traditional and modern ways of life. The ceremonies and rituals of each religious group borrowed elements from the others, and the festivals celebrated by one group often marked the occasion for citywide revelry. Looking back from contemporary Jerusalem, it is hard to imagine a time when Muslim children would dress up in costumes alongside Jewish children to celebrate the Jewish feast of Purim (Jewish children joined their Muslim contemporaries as well in celebrating the festival of the prophet Muhammad), or when an Orthodox Christian musician like Jawhariyyeh would play at Jewish weddings, or when a native Palestinian would accompany an Ashkenazi (European Jewish) choral group on his oud (a popular Middle Eastern stringed instrument). Even gender roles and gender relations were less rigid during Jawhariyyeh's youth than they are today: The role of women in society varied from place to place, from city to countryside, and from social class to social class. Although women, like men, faced social pressures to conform, no state or political movement forced women to dress in a manner that would make them walking billboards for either the "new nationalist woman" or the "devout Islamic woman." It seems that for every set of boundaries the modern world has broken down, it has created others.

One should not, of course, paint a picture of Jawhariyyeh's youthful world that is too rosy. Nevertheless, if one looks closely enough, over the course of the diaries one can detect a dramatic shift away from a world that appears remote to one that appears all too familiar. Take, for example, the spatial and cultural boundaries separating rich from poor. Although Jerusalem's rich and poor certainly enjoyed different levels of creature comforts, before the mid-nineteenth century they lived side by side in urban quarters. During the late nineteenth and early twentieth centuries, notable families began to move out of densely packed urban areas and into suburban areas outside the city walls where life was cleaner and more spacious. The spatial separation of rich and poor was reflected in an emerging cultural separation as well. During Jawhariyyeh's youth what might be termed a genteel, bourgeois culture began to emerge among the wealthier families of Jerusalem. This genteel, cosmopolitan, bourgeois culture in many ways mimicked the dominant culture of Europe, not just in terms of the physical trappings of refinement—overstuffed couches and gaudy chandeliers—but in cultural terms as well.

In turn-of-the-century Jerusalem, both gentility and cosmopolitanism, on the one hand, and its bohemian opposition, on the other, were maintained and reproduced through a thriving salon culture. Wealthier Jerusalemites as well as their more fancy-free neighbors gathered nightly in homes and apartments to enjoy each other's company. Throughout his diaries, Wasif Jawhariyyeh describes nightly episodes of drinking, dancing, card playing, music, and hashish smoking in bachelor apartments kept by single men from notable families. Muslims, Christians, and Jews all participated in these entertainments, and Jawhariyyeh earned his living as a musician playing at such gatherings.

The music played by Jawhariyyeh reflected a mixture of conventional and Western styles and themes and typifies the culture of the educated urban elites of his time. Like many other children of relative privilege, Jawhariyyeh received a rigorous training in both classical Arabic poetry and contemporary writers associated with the *nahda*—the Arabic literary renaissance of the nineteenth century. The writers, playwrights, and poets of the *nahda* attempted to fuse Arabic and European forms of expression. Jawhariyyeh even tried his hand at creating a system of musical notation that would convert Ottoman/Arab music to a Western system of notation, much as *nahda* writers attempted to simplify the Arabic language and script so that it might be accessible to a wider audience.

The influence of *nahda* culture on Jawhariyyeh can also be seen from the themes he selected for his compositions. For his first public performance, Jawhariyyeh chose to play a work based on Salamah Hijazi's translation of *Romeo and Juliet*. Like Farah Antun (who rendered the Oedipus cycle into Arabic), Khalil Matran (who translated and produced the works of Sophocles, Molière, and Shakespeare), and 'Uthman Jalal (an actor who specialized in playing characters created by Molière), Hijazi cultivated a devoted following among educated audiences. The pinnacle of Hijazi's influence took place in June 1920, when he staged two outdoor performances of his *Romeo and Juliet* in Damascus as part of the ceremonies marking Syria's post–World War I declaration of independence. The performances were reportedly received with enthusiasm, and Hijazi's influence lasted longer than Syria's initial flirtation with independence, which was terminated by the French within a month.

Musical ensemble, Aleppo, Syria, ca. 1900. (From: The Collection of Wolf-Dieter Lemke.)

Many in the Middle East saw the aping of Western ways among society's elites as just another aspect of Western corruption and imperialism. Some chose to fight this by espousing what might be termed a new Islamic orthodoxy. The new orthodoxy attempted to standardize and enforce rules for proper Islamic conduct. In Damascus, ulama led the campaign to shut down the city's only dance hall. In Basra, a city in the south of contemporary Iraq, other ulama protested the raising of a statue of a famous reforming governor. They argued that the statue would violate Islamic proscriptions against representational art. Throughout the Middle East, the issues of the veiling of women and the mixing of men and women in public took on a new urgency. For adherents to the new orthodoxy, the concern of Westerners and Westernizers about the status of Middle Eastern women in Middle Eastern society was part of an imperialist conspiracy against Islam. What made this conspiracy so insidious was that it was launched at a segment of society that those adherents claimed was particularly vulnerable to foreign intrigue. One orthodox periodical republished an article allegedly written in a French journal in which a French missionary stated, "The education of girls in convent schools leads to our gaining our true purpose and the arrival at our goal. In fact, I believe that the education of girls in this manner is the one means for finishing off Islam." It would not be a stretch to say that the roots of contemporary Islamic movements, with their obsession over issues of gender and personal conduct, lie in the attempts made by these early twentieth-century ulama and their followers to defend Islam against foreign influences.

The disputes between the adherents to the new, cosmopolitan culture and the adherents to the equally new orthodoxy actually boiled down to a single question: Who would control the new public sphere and determine how that public sphere was to be used? The public sphere is an imaginary space where citizens contest issues of common (that is, public) concern. These issues included everything from imperial politics to the role of women in society. While it would be a mistake to associate the emergence of a modern public sphere with democratization, it would not be a mistake to say that the emergence of a modern public sphere was essential for the emergence of mass political movements. In future chapters we shall see how the emergence of a modern public sphere allowed for the spread of constitutionalism and nationalism in the region.

One factor that set the stage for the emergence of a modern public sphere was the reconstruction of cities. There were a number of reasons why cities took on new attributes at this time. New technologies such as tramways were introduced into the region. These technologies broadened the territorial reach of urban environments and literally broke down the walls separating semiautonomous urban quarters from each other. Newly empowered municipal councils directed centralized planning and policing. Sultans, shahs, and khedives imported conceptions of municipal order from abroad. The new cities of Port Said and Isma'iliyya on the Suez Canal, for example, were laid out according to a checkerboard pattern, and the Egyptian khedive, Isma'il, and the shah of Persia, Nasr ed-Din Shah, were so impressed by late nineteenth-century Paris that they rebuilt parts of their capitals in imitation, with wide boulevards, public parks, and landscaped roads. The reconstruction of cities introduced new conceptions of space into urban areas and created spaces where public ceremonies could be held and individuals could meet and talk.

Then there were coffeehouses. Coffeehouses were not new to the Middle Eastern urban landscape. Indeed, the first coffeehouses in the region date from the fifteenth and sixteenth centuries. But in the nineteenth century coffeehouses were ubiquitous in Middle Eastern cities. Located both on main thoroughfares in the heart of cities and in market areas adjacent to semiprivate lanes, they were one of the main sites in which an expanding public sphere could be found. During Jawhariyyeh's lifetime, it was common for the more popular and centrally located coffeehouses to cater to several hundred clients a day. Coffeehouse patrons passed their time sipping coffee, playing backgammon (*tawula*), smoking water pipes (*narghiles*), trading gossip, reading aloud one or more of the seven newspapers published in Jerusalem at the time, and watching shadow plays, which were frequently remade as political and social satire. Coffeehouses also served as centers for new entertainment technologies that catered to mass audiences. For example, phonographs were initially too expensive for private ownership, and Jawhariyyeh heard his first Edison recordings in a coffeehouse:

> I would take a matleek [small Ottoman coin] from my father and go to Ali Izhiman's café near the Damascus gate. A blind man by the name of Ibrahim

al-Beiruti operated the phonograph. The machine was raised on a wooden cabinet full of 78 r.p.m. records and covered by red velvet to protect it from the evil eye. I used to throw my matleek in a brass plate and cry to the blind man: "Uncle, let us hear (such-and-such)." The blind man would immediately pull the requested record from the cabinet—only God knows how—and would play it on the phonograph. Later my music teacher would say, "Listening to this music is like eating with false teeth."

Wasif Jawhariyyeh's brother opened up one such coffeehouse in Jerusalem in 1918 called the Café Jawhariyyeh. Wasif's brother had learned how to tend bar in Beirut while stationed there as a member of Turkish army, putting the time he spent in the military to good use. It was at his brother's cafe that Jawhariyyeh honed the craft that would make him famous.

Phonographs were not the only imported marvel that Jawhariyyeh describes in his diaries. He saw his first movie at the Russian compound in Jerusalem soon after he experienced his first phonograph record. He saw his first car (a Ford) in 1912 when it passed through the streets driven by an American driver. He saw his first airplane in the summer of 1914 when it was flown to Jerusalem by two Ottoman pilots, and when the plane crashed he composed a eulogy on their behalf. To get a sense of the speed with which these technologies entered the lives of people like Jawhariyyeh, one need only compare Wasif's experiences with those of his father, which Jawhariyyeh also records in his diaries:

> When I was thirteen, in 1850 [the father states], I recall that we did all our travel on individual beasts: mules, donkeys, horses, and even camels. I did not see any animal driven carriages until a few years later when the French brought the "tambour"—a two wheel carriage driven by mules—to transport bricks for the roof of the French church in Abu Ghush. Boys of my generation used to run after this amazing new invention until we reached the approaches of Lifta.

Although Jawhariyyeh's diaries continue for a half century after the close of World War I in 1918, it is appropriate to end our discussion here. In the immediate decades following World War I, a new set of issues emerged that commanded Jawhariyyeh's attention. For example, the year 1936 lies at the exact midpoint of Jawhariyyeh's diaries. The year is significant because it was then that the first great uprising in modern Palestinian history broke out: the Great Revolt of 1936–1939, which will be discussed in a later chapter. The revolt had two underlying causes: distress caused by the Great Depression of the 1930s and the dramatic rise of European Jewish immigration into Palestine. The Great Depression and the accompanying collapse of international trade and the international market for agricultural products caused extreme economic hardship in an economy that was still, fundamentally, rural. Jewish immigration into Palestine sparked a resistance among non-Jewish Palestinians. The motivations that drove Palestinians to revolt ran the gamut from the desire to settle old scores to blind anger at what many considered an alien presence in their midst. But many of the rebels and their leaders were motivated by nationalist aspirations as well.

Overall, the Great Revolt of 1936–1939 was emblematic of a Palestine firmly entrenched in the modern world economic system and, as signified by the spread of nationalism in Palestine, a world political order defined by nationalism and nation-states. The Palestinian world of the 1930s was a world in which rapid demographic change and political instability had ravaged much of the genteel, bourgeois culture that had shaped Jawhariyyeh. It was a world in which hard-and-fast ideologies and exclusive loyalties would shortly become the norm. Palestine in the 1930s represented a very different world from the Palestine of Jawhariyyeh's youth.

THE GREAT
TRANSFORMATION

Darwish Street, during the late Ottoman period. (From: The Collection of the author.)

Darwish Street, during the French Mandate. (From: The Collection of the author.)

Port Said, on the Suez Canal, laid out as a checkerboard. (From: The Collection of Wolf-Dieter Lemke.)

Place de l'Opera, Cairo. (From: The Collection of Wolf-Dieter Lemke.)

Al-Kamel Street, ca. 1900. (From: The Collection of Wolf-Dieter Lemke.)

Ezbekiya Gardens, ca. 1900. (From: Fondation Arabe pour l'image, Beirut.)

114

Museum in Gulestan Palace, Tehran. (From: Philip Mansel, Sultans in Splendor: Monarchs of the Middle East, 1869–1945. [London: Parkway Publishing, 1988], pp. 70–71.)

Covered market (Suq al-Hamidiyya), Damascus, after it was elongated and refurbished in the French arcade style in 1885. (From: The Collection of Wolf-Dieter Lemke.)

Ottoman infantry, drilling: Iraq, 1911. (From: Gertrude Bell Collection, University of Newcastle.)

Istanbul fire company, drilling, date unknown. (From: The Collection of Wolf-Dieter Lemke.)

Ottoman customs house on Kurdish frontier, 1911. (From: The Gertrude Bell Collection, University of Newcastle.)

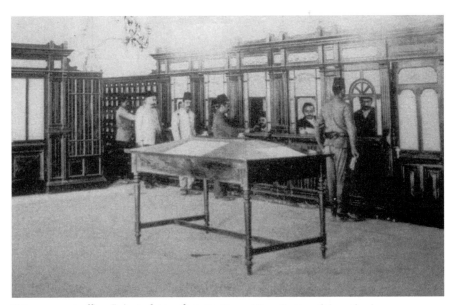

Ottoman post office, Beirut, date unknown. (From: The collection of the author.)

An "Arab gentleman," 1905. (From: The Gertrude Bell Collection, University of Newcastle.)

Sunbathing, Istanbul, ca. 1900. (From: The Collection of Wolf-Dieter Lemke.)

Steamships on the Tigris River. (From: The Collection of Wolf-Dieter Lemke.)

Marking the opening of the Istanbul Tramway with a sacrifice of a lamb. (From: Jacques Benoist-Méchin, La Turquie se dévoile, 1908–1938 [Paris: PML Editions, n.d.], p. 157.)

Coffeehouse, Cairo, late nineteenth century. (From: The Collection of Wolf-Dieter Lemke.)

Studio photograph, Alexandria, 1927. (From: Fondation Arabe pour l'image, Beirut.)

Carpet workshop, Aleppo, date unknown. (From: The Collection of Wolf-Dieter Lemke.)

Silk thread factory, Brusa (Anatolia), date unknown. (From: The Collection of Wolf-Dieter Lemke.)

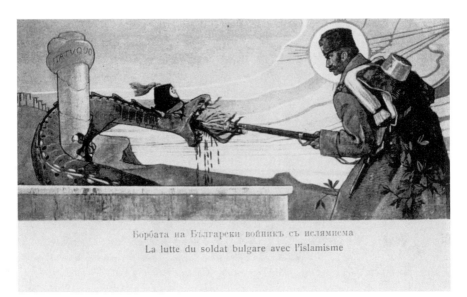

Bulgarian propaganda card with inscription: "A Bulgarian Soldier Struggles against Islam." (From: The Collection of Wolf-Dieter Lemke.)

Ottoman propaganda card showing Italian soldiers in Libya about to massacre women and children. Inscription reads: "Italian Civilization in Tripolitania." (From: The Collection of Wolf-Dieter Lemke.)

Eight

The Life of the Mind

As should now be obvious, the period stretching from the eighteenth century to the beginning of the twentieth was a time in which social and economic life in the Middle East underwent an extraordinary transformation. There was yet another aspect to this transformation that cannot go unexamined: the life of the mind. The eighteenth and nineteenth centuries mark a period of striking intellectual ferment in which new ideological and religious movements emerged and contended. Some of these movements faded into obscurity, others are with us to this very day. These movements affected cultural and sometimes political life throughout the region.

The previous chapter described one such nineteenth-century movement and its effects on a Jerusalem musician. Poets, novelists, and playwrights of the *nahda* sought to rejuvenate Arabic literature to recover it from what they described as *inhitat* (decline). They experimented with techniques to simplify forms of expression, expand the reach of their works among Arabic speakers, and shatter literary conventions by infusing their works with new, sometimes borrowed, forms. Similar literary ventures were undertaken by belletrists writing in Turkish and Persian.

More often than not, intellectuals who identified with the *nahda* were Syrian and Lebanese Christians from Beirut and Damascus and Syrian and Lebanese emigrants living throughout the region and in such far-flung places as Europe and the Americas. While it was certainly the case that these intellectuals often consciously borrowed ideas and forms of expression from the West, they represented only a segment of cultural producers in the region and only a tiny part of the population. Thus, to focus on the cohort of Westernizing cultural producers to the exclusion of others would cause us to lose track of the bigger picture.

The intellectual currents that emerged during the eighteenth and nineteenth centuries sprang from a variety of sources and took a number of forms. In contrast to the endeavors of Westernizers, for example, some intellectual movements arose in direct opposition to Western imperialism or the influx of Western ideas. We have seen one example of this in the previous chapter: the attempt made by some late nineteenth-century ulama to formulate a new Islamic orthodoxy. As we shall see later, this attempt was hardly as untainted by ideas originally produced in the West as its adherents claimed.

Other intellectual and religious movements emerged in indirect response to the effects of integration and peripheralization, defensive developmentalism, and imperialism. A good example of this sort of movement is the Baha'i movement in Persia. The roots of Baha'ism can be traced back to 1844, the one-thousandth anniversary of the occultation of the twelfth imam, when a merchant from Shiraz proclaimed himself first to be the "gate" (bab) through which the hidden imam communicated, then the hidden imam himself. For his efforts, he was executed by the Persian government. While the message the bab proclaimed was cloaked in what might be described as traditional religious garb, the movement he and his followers initiated was hardly traditional. Like other social/religious movements of the mid- to late nineteenth century—the Taipings in China (1851–1864), who launched a civil war that claimed more than thirty million lives, or the Native American Ghost Dance movement (1889–1895)—the Babi movement, as it was called, grew in response to the adverse conditions in which its members increasingly found themselves. The bab's followers advocated the abolition of taxes and private property and equal rights for men and women—an understandable response in a society affected by widespread economic and social dislocation associated with nineteenth-century developments. And, like other movements of the time, the Babi movement was supported by diverse layers of the population—in this case peasants, minor ulama, artisans, and guild members who had been adversely affected by nineteenth-century events. After being suppressed by the Persian government, many in the Babi movement, apparently believing discretion to be the better part of valor, became pacifists and disavowed politics. These are the Baha'is who have been persecuted off and on (now it is on) in Persia/Iran ever since.

While the Babi/Baha'i movement situated a modern social movement within the framework of conventional religious images and language, there were numerous intellectual currents that cannot be traced, either directly or indirectly, to integration and peripheralization, defensive developmentalism, and imperialism. It was often the case that scholars contributed to fields of knowledge such as Islamic law and theology in seeming isolation from the outside world, much as academics claim to do today. These scholars were, in effect, holding a dialogue with their predecessors. They expressed their end of the dialogue in much the same way that Muslim scholars had fashioned their arguments for centuries. This is not to say that their arguments did not have implications for the world outside the walls of their schools and seminaries. Nor is it to say that there was no relationship between the most "convincing" arguments and the political, social, or economic circumstances of the time. We shall look at one such dispute between two schools of Shi'i theology and its effects on subsequent developments later in this chapter.

This brings us to another important aspect of the intellectual and cultural movements of the eighteenth and nineteenth centuries: their implications for politics and political culture. Some of the movements discussed in this chapter had direct political ramifications, others did not. All the former movements had at least one thing in common: To be successful, their vision of political community had to be compatible with a world system of nation-states and the modern world economy. Those movements that were not initially compatible with both (such as the Sanusiyya movement of Libya or Wahhabism in Arabia, both of which will be discussed shortly) had to become compatible once their advocates achieved power. If not, these movements would simply not survive as a touchstone for political life. Thus, the state established by the Wahhabis in the early nineteenth century failed, but the state established by their descendants in the early twentieth century (Saudi Arabia), so far has not.

Although the intellectual and cultural movements with political implications needed to be compatible with the world system of nation-states and the modern world economy, they often used widely divergent arguments to justify their actions. For example, from 1878 until 1908 Sultan Abdulhamid II of the Ottoman Empire couched his policies of centralization and "modernization" within a rhetoric that drew from Islam. While the Young Turks who took over the Ottoman Empire in 1908 initially couched their policies in a rhetoric that drew from the latest scientific theories and secular philosophies, they followed pretty much the same centralization and modernization policies as the sultan they would depose. There is nothing mysterious about this. As discussed many times earlier, the modern state is far more capable of harnessing the social power of its citizens than any of its precursors, and so any political movement that wanted to survive had to adapt to the ways of the modern world, no matter what language it used to justify its policies.

The intellectual and cultural movements that arose in the Middle East during the eighteenth and nineteenth centuries thus ran the gamut from those that directly borrowed from Western Enlightenment traditions to those that developed in isolation from those traditions. It would be impossible to do justice to all these currents within the space of one chapter. Accordingly, this chapter will focus on just one type of movement: the sort that sought to reform society by reforming Islam.

During the eighteenth and nineteenth centuries, many in the Middle East looked around and concluded that Islam and the Islamic world had, indeed, fallen on hard times. Many attributed the predicament in which Islamic societies had found themselves to that fact that those societies had abandoned the original teachings and doctrines of Islam. These were, after all, the teachings and doctrines that allowed Muslims to establish a vast empire that had stretched from Spain to Afghanistan at a time when Europe was in its Dark Ages. In order to restore the glory of Islam—or at least stand up to the threat from the West—they felt that they had to eliminate from Islam everything that had contributed to its decline.

Many intellectual currents in the eighteenth and nineteenth centuries identified two sources of decline. On the one hand, many in the region questioned the tendency for Muslims to follow blindly the teachings of earlier generations of religious scholars who, they claimed, had contributed to Islam's decay. The harshest among them condemned their predecessors for misinterpreting or falsifying the original precepts of Islam. Others accused Islamic societies themselves of corrupting those precepts by mixing Islam with folk customs, such as saint worship, mysticism, and divination (prophesying the future by supernatural means). Movements that started from either of these two premises often encouraged Muslims to look to the first community established by Muhammad at Medina as a model for the moral and political regeneration of Islam. Because the first generation of Muslims was called *al-salif al-salih* (the "pious ancestors"), those who advocated using their community as a model were called salafis.

Salafis disregarded all Islamic sources but two: the Qur'an and the hadith (reports of the sayings and activities of the prophet). But there was an interesting flip side to the return to authoritative sources. Relying on these two sets of texts exclusively was easier in theory than in practice. After all, Islamic societies in the modern world confronted situations that the first Islamic community never had to face. Was it legal to use the telegraph to transmit the sighting of the new moon marking religious holidays? Did the digging of artesian wells violate the injunction forbidding Muslims from drinking from standing pools of water? How should Muslims respond to the dictates of their colonial rulers? To deal with new situations, many advocated that Muslims exercise independent judgment based upon reason—an established legal procedure called *ijtihad*. In the hands of some, *ijtihad* became a tool for preserving Islam in the face of modern conditions. In the hands of others, *ijtihad* became a tool for subordinating Islam to European ideas and the "spirit of the age."

Nineteenth-century salafism had its precursor in what some historians call the "moral reconstruction" movement of the eighteenth century. As discussed earlier, the eighteenth century was not a particularly auspicious period for Middle Eastern governments and the people they ruled. Local notables and warlords were effectively challenging the authority of imperial governments. Ottoman and Persian armies met with failure after failure in their confrontation with the armies of Europe. Peasants were unable to count on weak central governments to provide rural security and often sought shelter in inhospitable cities. Artisans were displaced by Europeans who dumped finished products on the Middle Eastern market. There was no lack of awareness of these problems among bureaucrats, scholars, and common people in the region. In response, many searched for the reasons behind the malaise and ways to overcome it. One solution they came up with was to rebuild society from the ground up, that is, to rebuild society by reconstructing the social and moral fabric that bound its members to one another. There was no more accessible or appropriate model for this project than that provided by the life and the activities of the prophet and the pious ancestors.

The moral reconstruction movement was powerful in part because it was transmitted through networks of like-minded people. Sometimes the networks were confined to a single quarter of a city or to all the local practitioners of a trade. Sometimes the networks stretched for thousands of miles, joining like-minded Muslims from as far away as India and Indonesia with Muslims living in Persia, Egypt, Syria, and North Africa. Networks might take the shape of informal clubs or study groups, or they might be much more formal. And they were very popular. One historian has estimated that by the beginning of the nineteenth century, almost every male of every class in Cairo belonged to at least one such network.

These networks were called *turuq* (sing: *tariqa*). *Turuq* were not new to the Middle East. Sufis—those who adhered to popular, sometimes mystical forms of Islam—had used this structure for centuries to link initiates with their spiritual guides and with each other. But in the eighteenth century many mainstream Muslims, such as artisans and merchants, joined *turuq* to find solutions to common problems. To find those solutions, members of these *turuq* went back to the Qur'an and hadith to see how the prophet and first community might have handled similar problems. While hadith had always been a pillar of Islamic law, the idea that sufis would turn to hadith to resolve day-to-day problems was hardly conventional. In other words, these *turuq* adopted the form of earlier *turuq* but used them for the very practical ends of reestablishing a sense of community and determining the rules for ethical/legal conduct.

Turuq thus became the vehicles for purification and revival. Since certain *turuq* and sufi masters were important in some cities, merchants, ulama, and the like would travel from city to city, cross-fertilizing ideas from one part of the Ottoman Empire or Persia with ideas from another—from Istanbul to Damascus to Mecca and Medina to Cairo, with its great Islamic university, al-Azhar.

At the same time, on the fringes of the Ottoman Empire where central control was particularly weak or the presence of imperialists was particularly strong, moral reconstruction based on the Medinan model took on a more overtly political form. The Sanusiyya *tariqa* that flourished in the territory that now constitutes Libya was typical. Founded by Muhammad ibn 'Ali al-Sanusi (1787–1859), who had studied in Egypt and Mecca and who preached a rigid puritanism, the *tariqa* spread throughout North and West Africa, uniting diverse tribes on the basis of a back-to-basics theology. Within a few years, there were approximately 140 Sanusiyya lodges across North Africa. These lodges participated in religious study, agricultural settlement, and trade. Later, they would play a central role in the fight against the Italians who invaded North Africa in the beginning of the twentieth century.

Another famous puritanical movement was founded by Muhammad ibn 'Abd al-Wahhab in central Arabia. Ibn 'Abd al-Wahhab rejected many of the folk practices of Arabia (worship of saints, pilgrimages to local cult centers, and so on) and what he regarded as the quibbling of medieval scholars. In fact, he rejected any authority but the Qur'an and hadith. He joined forces with a local chieftain, Muhammad ibn Sa'ud, and, as the official version of events puts it, the combination of sword and message proved unbeatable in Arabia. By 1803, ibn Sa'ud's tribesmen had conquered Mecca, establishing a puritanical Islamic state based on the Medinan model there. This state was, however, soon suppressed by an Egyptian army under Mehmet Ali's son, Ibrahim, working at the behest of the Ottoman government.

In 1902, 'Abd al-'Aziz ibn Sa'ud, a descendant of Muhammad ibn Sa'ud, began his conquest of the peninsula from the central and eastern Arabian province of the Najd. Key to his conquests were a group called the *ikhwan*— nontribal levies attracted by the message of ibn 'Abd al-Wahhab—whom he settled, like Muhammad ibn 'Ali al-Sanusi, in agricultural settlements. By 1925, ibn Sa'ud had conquered western Arabia and its two holy cities. Several years later he combined eastern and western Arabia to form the country of Saudi Arabia. To this day, the doctrines of ibn 'Abd al-Wahhab are the official state ideology of Saudi Arabia. Ulama—many of whom are descendants of ibn 'Abd al-Wahhab and are related by marriage to the royal family—have a great deal of influence, the legal system of Saudi Arabia is based on the most conservative school of Islamic law, and the government claims, a bit disingenuously, that there is no need for a constitution because the state already has one: the Qur'an.

Some intellectuals took salafism in a very different direction. Embracing the institutions and ideas brought to the region by integration and peripheralization, defensive developmentalism, and imperialism, many sought to reconstruct Middle Eastern society along Western lines. They argued that the true Islam that had preserved Greek philosophy during Europe's Dark Ages was not incompatible with science and reason. If Islam would shed its recent superstitious additions and root itself in the very reason that had given it its power, they argued, it could act as the foundation for a Middle Eastern scientific and industrial revolution. Those who argued that true Islam is compatible with Western notions of progress and other modern ideas are called "Islamic modernists."

Some Islamic modernists had been exposed to Western ideas and frequently were acquainted with either English or French. Others developed their ideas as a result of the transformation of society, economics, and politics of the Middle East. Unlike the pure Westernizers, who frequently blamed Islam for the so-called backwardness of the Middle East and promoted the adoption of such Western ideas as secularism, Islamic modernists were more selective in what they chose to borrow. Some believed that most Western institutions and ideas were not appropriate for the Ottoman Empire or Persia or that Western ideas could somehow be reconciled with the Islamic beliefs of a majority of the population. Others were more cynical or realistic (depending on your point of view). They wanted drastic change, but felt that the Middle Eastern population was too backward or the power of the government or religious establishment was too entrenched to allow a frontal assault to succeed. Realizing that their opinions were not held by the majority of the population, they sought to manipulate forces greater than themselves to effect change. They did this by masking their ideas in a conservative, even religious rhetoric. Many of those who did this belonged to secret societies or were members of minority groups or despised religious sects (such as the Babis).

Islamic modernism took on various forms in the Ottoman Empire. In the heartland of the empire, a diffuse group of intellectuals known as the Young Ottomans argued that the *tanzimat* had failed. The *tanzimat* had, to be sure, strengthened the power of the sultan, but it did not stop European imperial expansion at the expense of the empire. The Young Ottomans claimed that the empire needed an ideology that could guarantee and inspire the loyalty of all citizens of the empire. This ideology had to be based on indigenous Islamic principles. Among those principles that informed this ideology was the principle of *shura*, that is, government by consultation. Although the concept of *shura* originally referred to such convocations as that held by elders of the early Islamic community to choose the successor to Muhammad, the Young Ottomans used it to argue for an Ottoman constitution and parliament. While the influence of the Young Ottomans was initially limited to a thin stratum of intellectuals, many of their ideas became widespread throughout the Middle East. Their influence can be found in the Ottoman constitutional movement of 1876, the 'Urabi rebellion in Egypt, and even in the Persian Constitutional Revolution of 1905.

Islamic modernists thrived on the same cross-fertilization of ideas that had contributed to the moral reconstruction movement discussed earlier. But rather than limiting themselves to the cross-fertilization of ideas from other Muslims alone, they brought in European ideas as well. Take, for example, the case of Islamic modernism in Persia. Beginning in the mid-nineteenth century, there arose a new class of intellectuals in Persia, many of whom had been educated in the Dar al-Funun in Tehran. Others received their education abroad, often in Europe. Because of their position in society, and because of their aspirations, both groups had a natural affinity with European political and social ideas of the time—particularly the thought of two European thinkers.

Auguste Comte (1798–1857) was a French intellectual who formulated a philosophy called Positivism. Positivism had many adherents in Europe, as it had in the Ottoman Empire and Persia. As a matter of fact, the Committee of Union and Progress that took over the Ottoman government in 1913 derived its name from two watchwords of Comte's philosophy: unity and progress. Positivism contained two ideas that were particularly appealing to intellectuals in the Middle East. Comte believed that societies evolve through stages like biological species: from religious-based societies through philosophically based societies to scientifically based societies. Thus, even though a society like Persia might be stuck at the first level, there was no reason why it might not rise to a higher level, as had European societies. Comte also believed that society should be guided by a class of technocrats known as *savants*. These were people who understood the scientific principles upon which society should be based. Of course, a Persian intellectual who thought of himself as a *monavvar al-fekr* (enlightened thinker), or, for that matter, an Arab intellectual who thought of himself as *mutanawwir* (enlightened), identified with this role.

The second major influence on Persian (and Ottoman) intellectuals was the philosophy of Henri Comte de Saint-Simon (1760–1825). Saint-Simon's philosophy was similar to Comte's in many ways, but he envisioned the establishment of a planned, socialist-style economy run by benevolent industrialists—the sort of people many of the graduates of the Dar al-Funun wanted to become.

In all, many Persian intellectuals thought of themselves as a privileged enlightened class that was united by its opposition to royal despotism, religious fanaticism, and foreign imperialism. It was difficult for graduates of the Dar al-Funun and their allies to organize against these problems openly. After all, royalty and clerics do not appreciate being told they are despotic and fanatic. Thus, many joined together in secret societies called *anjumanha* (sing.: *anjuman*), where they could engage in political conspiracy. Others simply masked their ideas.

While there were numerous participants in *anjumanha*, historians have highlighted the careers and influence of two in particular. Mirza Malkom Khan was an Armenian Christian who may or may not have converted to Islam. He grew up in Paris, then returned to Persia, where he taught at the Dar al-Funun. Malkom Khan's relationship with religion was ambivalent. Like Comte, Malkom Khan thought that religion would be superseded by "humanity" and "reason." But Malkom Khan also thought that religion in general and the ulama in particular could be harnessed to build a new Persia. He was particularly enamored by the idea of *ijtihad*, through which he believed reason could be applied to religion. Malkom Khan organized several secret societies that included intellectuals, guild leaders, ulama, and, on occasion, members of the Qajar family. Many of those who participated in the Constitutional Revolution of 1905 were affiliated with Malkom Khan's secret societies and may have been introduced to the idea of a constitution through Malkom Khan's *Book of Reform*, which, in turn, picked up constitutionalist ideas from the Young Ottomans.

Jamal al-Din al-Afghani was a second political conspirator of importance. In spite of his name (which means Jamal al-Din, the Afghan), Jamal al-Din was probably born in Persia and sought to obscure his Shi'i origins so that he might be more influential in the Sunni world. During his lifetime, he traveled widely, living in Paris, Cairo, and Istanbul, among other places. Like Malkom Khan, al-Afghani borrowed from European and Ottoman ideas about social evolution and the special role for an intellectual elite in society. Like Malkom Khan, al-Afghani sought to harness religion to the cause of social change. And, like Malkom Khan, he organized secret societies that were to be politically influential. One of al-Afghani's followers assassinated Nasir al-Din Shah in 1896, and many of his followers were active participants in the Constitutional Revolution of 1905.

The sources of Malkom Khan's and al-Afghani's ideas cannot be laid at the doorstep of European philosophy alone. To the contrary, both they and their followers grew up in an environment enriched by the Persian legal tradition as well, particularly the debates between two schools of legal thought.

Up until the early nineteenth century, there had been no consensus among the ulama of Persia regarding their role in society. On the one hand, followers of the Akhbari school claimed that the ulama were limited in their legal and doctrinal decisions to the traditions of the prophet and the teachings of the twelve imams. In contrast, members of the Usuli school asserted that select religious scholars—called *mujtahids*—could act as representatives of the hidden imam. *Mujtahids* were chosen informally from among the ulama because of their piety and learning. They had the right to give fresh interpretations to the law—to practice *ijtihad*—in order to make the law compatible with real-life conditions.

During the nineteenth century, the Usulis emerged victorious, in part because of the nature of the Qajar rule. Remember, the power of the Qajars was limited and their legitimacy was always suspect. The growth of the Usuli tendency was thus directly related to its belief that ulama should perform educational, judicial, and even legitimation functions for the Qajars. Usuli ulama held a monopoly over the educational apparatus and over civil law (laws not related to state administration and crimes against the state). Thus, unlike ulama in the Ottoman Empire and Egypt whose power was usurped by the state, the victory of the Usulis over the Akhbaris guaranteed that the ulama of Persia would have a direct and necessary role in society. This ensured that the participation or aloofness of the ulama could make or break such political movements as the Tobacco Protest, the Constitutional Revolution, and the revolution of 1978–1979.

Like the Usulis, Malkom Khan and al-Afghani believed that ulama had a key role to play in society, that Islam constantly had to be revised to be applicable to contemporary conditions, and that *ijtihad* could be harnessed for that revision. Both believed that Islam was ingrained in Eastern society and that any reform of society had to take that into account. At the same time, both preached that Muslims had much to learn from the West, particularly in the realm of science and technology.

But how could religion and science be made compatible? Could Islam—or, indeed, any religion—be used to promote modernity? From the Enlightenment through Comte and beyond, Western social philosophers have pronounced secularism to be a prime attribute of modernity and religion to be either the primitive ancestor of modernity or its mortal enemy. Whether or not this is the case is the subject of the next chapter.

Nine

Secularism and Modernity

In the contemporary Middle East, there is only one state—Turkey—that performs civil marriages. If, for example, Middle Easterners in other states want to get married they must go to their local clergyman and not to a nondenominational marriage license bureau. This, in effect, both discourages and obstructs interfaith marriages in the region. Thus, at a recent conference on marriage held in Beirut, one topic of discussion was whether interfaith marriages have the same chance of success as "normal" marriages.

Issues of personal status such as marriage are not the only ones in which religion matters. Article three of the current Syrian constitution specifies that the president of Syria must be a Muslim. Before the removal of Saddam Hussein in 2003, article four of the Iraqi constitution defined Islam as the religion of the state. What makes this all the more surprising is the fact that both constitutions were written by a political party whose official publication had once stated that "God, religions, feudalism, capitalism, imperialism, and all other 'isms' that had dominated society in the past are like mummies in a museum."

Many in the West look at the Middle East and decry the role religion plays in the public sphere. They claim that secularism is an essential part of modernity and that states that are not secular cannot be considered modern. Those who do this, however, assume that the attributes of *Western* modernity can be generalized for the entire world. Another interpretation of the relationship between secularism and modernity is possible, however. It might be argued that secularism developed in the West as a result of idiosyncrasies associated with that region's historical experience. Europe suffered from bloody religious wars in the sixteenth and seventeenth centuries. Over the course of the centuries that followed, many in the West came to believe that the way to prevent a recurrence of that bloodshed was by severing the connection between politics and religion. In the process, they made the state, not religion, the ultimate source of authority. And since European modernity became the gold standard for "civilization" throughout the world, secularism tagged along for the ride.

The historical experience of Middle Eastern states was quite different from that of European states. As a result, their evolution was also quite different. The prominent role religion plays in politics and political discourse of Middle Eastern states does not mean these states are not modern; rather, it means these states follow an alternative form of modernity.

The role religion plays in contemporary Middle Eastern life emerged during the second half of the nineteenth century. The transformation of the Middle Eastern state in the nineteenth century fostered a corresponding transformation of religious institutions and doctrines. As the region was integrated into the modern state system, the meaning and function of religion in society changed. Those Islamic institutions and beliefs that political and religious elites and nonelites found appropriate for changing circumstances grew stronger. Others diminished in value.

The influence of nineteenth-century events on religion was not restricted to Islam or to the Middle East. A similar institutional and doctrinal transformation occurred in the Roman Catholic Church as a result of its competition with the nineteenth-century European state, the emergence of mass politics, and the spread of market relations. After the Vatican Council of 1869, popes became infallible on issues of faith and morals (but not, significantly, on other issues that were consigned to the state). The church sanctioned the formation of mass-based Catholic political parties, and church institutions were redesigned to parallel or complement those of the modern state. In other words, both church structures and church doctrines came to reflect the social and political world in which the church functioned.

In the Ottoman Empire, where the "church" was not as centralized as in Catholic Europe, the transformation of religious institutions and doctrines occurred in two ways. Sometimes it occurred as a result of state initiative. At other times it emerged from below, as citizens of the empire reacted to new state structures or to European models.

As discussed in Chapter 5, historians have commonly divided the responses of the nineteenth-century Ottoman state to European economic, political, and military expansion into two periods. During the first, the so-called *tanzimat* period, the Ottoman state attempted to foster a notion of a political community made up of equal citizens bound together by their commitment to a common set of legal norms. This form of *osmanlilik* failed for a number of reasons, also described earlier. Under Sultan Abdulhamid II, the state introduced a new form of *osmanlilik*. In place of the idea that all Ottoman citizens were to be equal regardless of their religion, the Ottoman state under Abdulhamid II promoted an ideology that gave pride of place to an Ottoman/*Islamic* identity.

There were two reasons why the new interpretation of *osmanlilik* became feasible. First, the new interpretation would have been impossible had it not been for the intellectuals and political activists who had lain the foundation for it over the course of the nineteenth century. Islamic modernists and others discussed in the previous chapter picked up on European social theories and applied them to understand their own history and current circumstances. One of the first Middle Easterners to do this was Rifaʿa Rafiʿ al-Tahtawi, an Egyptian *ʿalim*. In 1826, Mehmet Ali sent al-Tahtawi to Paris at the head of an educational mission. When al-Tahtawi returned to Egypt five years later, Mehmet Ali appointed him director of the School of Languages, an institution where European books were translated into Arabic. Under al-

Tahtawi's directorship, the school not only translated European military manuals, but works on geography and history as well. As a result, the concepts and vocabulary of European philosophy and social theory entered the lexicon of the region.

Take, for example, the concept of "civilization." Before al-Tahtawi, Arabic books used the term "civilization" to indicate the high culture, refined manners, and luxurious trappings of urban life. Borrowing from the writings of the fourteenth-century scholar and traveler Ibn Khaldun, they contrasted civilization with the harshness and rusticity of desert and rural life. In the nineteenth century, the concept of "civilization" began to take on a new meaning in the region. Upon his return from Paris, al-Tahtawi introduced the notion of separate "Western" and "Eastern" civilizations then in vogue in Europe (as it now is in North America). Like his European contemporaries, al-Tahtawi believed that each civilization possessed a distinguishing characteristic that differentiated it from the other: While science defined Western civilization, Islam and Islamic law defined its counterpart. Later writers developed this notion of "civilization" further, and even introduced the notion of a "clash of civilizations." Thus, according to al-Afghani,

> The problem facing the "East" is its struggle with the "West." Both cloak themselves in the armor of religion. The Westerner is an adherent of Christianity and the Easterner of Islam, and the people of the two religions are like a hard projectile in the hands of their throwers.

For both al-Tahtawi and al-Afghani, then, Islam was not only a divine message but an expression of a culturally and geographically distinct civilization. Since the Ottoman Empire was the preeminent Muslim power of its time, it was logical that Sultan Abdulhamid II and his associates would link Islam and imperial identity. As the semiofficial newspaper *La Turquie* put it, "Islam is not only a religion, it is a nationality."

The second factor that made an Islamic *osmanlilik* feasible was the changing religious composition of the empire. The steady retreat of the Ottoman Empire from Europe during the nineteenth century naturally decreased the number of Christians under imperial rule. In addition, as Balkan nationalisms spread in southeastern Europe and Russian expansionism continued to the north and east, Muslim immigrants from Europe and the Caucasus flooded into the empire. As a result, the proportion of Muslims to Christians within the empire increased decidedly. In the 1860s and 1870s, more than two million Circassian, Chechen, Bosnian, Bulgarian, Romanian, and Greek Muslims immigrated into the empire. The Ottoman government dispersed these immigrants throughout its domains. It encouraged Circassian and Chechen immigrants to settle and pacify the unruly frontier that is now Jordan, and so many Muslims from outside the empire took up residence in Damascus that one of the districts of the city is still known as Muhajirin (literally, "emigrants"). Identified by their persecutors outside the Ottoman Empire as members of an inassimilable minority group, many of these immigrants themselves had come to associate religious affiliation with national identity. After all, why would displaced Chechens and Bosnians be consigned to the same fate except that members of both groups were Muslims? And why should the Ottoman Empire take them in, except for the fact that it was the foremost Muslim power?

Taking all this into account, it should be obvious that it was not a stretch for Abdulhamid II to assert an Islamic *osmanlilik*. Abdulhamid II asserted his role as caliph in a manner that was rare among Ottoman sultans. His government attempted to standardize Islamic belief, intermix state and religious institutions, and associate loyalty to the state with loyalty to Islam. Among the activities the Ottoman government undertook to achieve these goals during the Hamidian period were the following:

1. *Missionary Activity within the Empire*: During the late nineteenth century, the Ottoman government worried about the threat posed by Christian missionaries operating in the empire and about Wahhabism, which had established a foothold in the Arabian peninsula. It also worried about the rapid spread of Shi'ism among the tribes of southern Iraq. Shi'ism was, after all, the state religion of Persia, the Ottoman's rival to the east, and its spread in Iraq endangered Ottoman control there. The Ottoman government thus sought to reduce the threat posed by potentially subversive sects housed in the empire by sending out missionaries to convert members of those sects— Alawites in Syria and eastern Anatolia, Yazidis in Iraq, select sufi groups throughout the empire—to a form of Islam it regarded as orthodox.

2. *Dissemination of Propaganda and Official Islamic Texts*: In an attempt to make Islamic doctrine uniform and foster the idea of a unified Islamic "culture," the Ottoman state made the printing of the Qur'an a state monopoly and established a Commission for the Inspection of Qur'ans. The state also supported the publication of over four thousand books and pamphlets in the first fifteen years of Abdulhamid II's reign alone. These books not only included "classic" Islamic legal and religious texts, but books and pamphlets depicting the exploits of Muslim heroes such as Saladin, who had fought the enemies of Islam.

3. *Imperial Patronage and Employment of Religious Scholars*: In addition to expanded imperial patronage, ulama of all ranks from throughout the empire were integrated into imperial institutions, from municipal and provincial councils to the network of imperial schools. Ulama thus participated in the Military Council, the Council of Public Works, the Council of Finance, the Council of Agriculture, the Council of the Navy, the Council of Police, the Council of the Arsenal, and the Council of State, the central legislative body of the empire.

4. *Support for Religious Endowments and Infrastructure*: To bolster the Islamic credentials of the Ottoman government and the caliphal pretensions of the Ottoman sultan, the imperial government undertook the construction and restoration of Islamic monuments and expanded its contributions to religious endowments. For example, the imperial government supervised the reconstruction of the famous Umayyad Mosque in Damascus, partly de-

stroyed by fire in 1893. These activities received extensive coverage in the official gazettes published in provincial capitals.

The most famous building project during the Hamidian period was the Hijaz Railroad. The government intended the railroad to connect Istanbul with the holy cities of Mecca and Medina (it eventually reached the latter but not the former). Since the railroad was built to assist Muslims in making the annual pilgrimage to the two holy cities, the government presented the Hijaz Railroad as an *Islamic* railroad and financed it by encouraging Muslims throughout the world to underwrite its costs.

The Islamic *osmanlilik* promoted by Abdulhamid II survived beyond his reign. The Young Turks deposed Abdulhamid II in 1909. Once in power they attempted to restore the secular *osmanlilik* of the *tanzimat* to bind together what remained of the empire. They did this not only to differentiate themselves from Abdulhamid II, but because they believed that the "constraints imposed by the modern age had made religiosity a weaker influence in building social and political nations over time," as a Syrian newspaper put it a few years later. Eventually, they returned to the Islamic *osmanlilik* of the deposed sultan. Policies and institutions created over the course of the previous three decades were not easily abandoned, particularly since the goals of the Young Turks—development and centralization—so closely matched those of Abdulhamid II.

In addition, Abdulhamid II's policies had struck a chord with many in the empire. Soon after the Young Turk Revolution, soldiers, religious students, and others in such cities as Istanbul and Damascus went out into the streets in support of a countercoup on behalf of the sultan launched by an association called the Muhammadan Union. Inhabitants of the Maydan district of Damascus, for example, decorated and illuminated their streets in honor of the occasion, and marched through the streets of their quarter chanting, a bit prematurely, "God has granted victory to the sultan." Echoing the sentiments of *La Turquie*, a spokesman for the Muhammadan Union defended the failed countercoup by reaffirming his association's commitment to Abdulhamid II's Islamic *osmanlilik*: "The strongest bond of Arab, Turk, Kurd, Albanian, Circassian, and Laz [a people originally from the Caucasus inhabiting the Black Sea area]—and their nationhood—is nothing other than Islam." In the end, the countercoup failed.

Members of the short-lived Muhammadan Union were not the only ones who attempted to take the Hamidian blend of Islam and politics to the street. Two years after the Young Turks deposed Abdulhamid II, a group of orthodox ulama in Damascus began publishing a periodical, *al-Haqa'iq*, that urged both the Young Turks and the citizens of the empire not to abandon the policies of the former sultan. The members of this group were neither Westernizers nor Islamic modernists. They did not seek to reform Islam, nor did they seek to throw out the work of Islamic scholars who had interpreted the law for centuries. In fact, they claimed to be upholding religious tradition. Nevertheless, the Islam for which these ulama agitated was in fact an Islam that had been retooled for the modern age. Like the

Istanbul, 1909: Soldiers loyal to the Young Turks march "mutineers"—participants in the Muhammadan Union uprising—off to prison. (From: The Collection of Wolf-Dieter Lemke.)

Young Turks and their Westernizing and Islamic modernist supporters, the ulama who wrote for *al-Haqa'iq* embraced such European notions as the progress of nations, universal standards of civilization, and the division of the world into an "East" and a "West." They integrated these notions into their polemics. Unlike their opponents, however, they distinguished themselves by their defense of "traditional values" and by their incessant denunciations of "the corruption of morals," which, they maintained, their opponents encouraged by attempting to separate religion and politics.

Nations could only be strong and progress, these ulama claimed, if those nations remained true to the religion and customs that engendered and defined them and that bound together their citizens in a common struggle. "If one thinks that religion orders inactivity and laziness," one contributor to *al-Haqa'iq* wrote, "he is a base, bigoted, ignoramus, or a treacherous Westernizer. Does he not understand that religion is our path to civilization and progress?" The ulama associated with *al-Haqa'iq* thus called on their fellow citizens to safeguard the empire's Islamic character and to shun foreign influences that could only lead to its weakening. At the same time, they demanded that the Young Turk government continue Abdulhamid II's policies of defensive developmentalism to safeguard Islam from European imperialism. To accomplish both these goals, these self-proclaimed traditionalists called for the establishment of an Islamic political party to compete in the arena of the new mass politics.

That the ulama associated with *al-Haqa'iq* would even think of founding an Islamic political party to guarantee the "progress" of the "nation" demonstrates the extent to which the nineteenth-century cultural, social, and political transformation had influenced religious doctrines and institutions in the Ottoman Empire. And since this transformation was not limited to one city or region of the empire, associations such as the Muhammadan Union and the *al-Haqa'iq* group could be found throughout the empire. In the aftermath of World War I, when a collection of independent states came to replace the Ottoman Empire, associations and political parties committed to ideas similar to those recounted here forced their way into the political fray and extracted concessions from the new rulers. Thus, while many of the states that emerged from the Ottoman Empire did so under the supervision of European imperial powers, they did not produce a simple duplication of the public/private, religious/secular boundaries found in most states of Europe or North America.

Ten

Constitutionalism

On 11 December 1905, the governor of Tehran ordered the beating of two sugar merchants whom he accused of price gouging. The merchants claimed that they could not reduce the price they charged for sugar to levels demanded by the government. They argued that, unlike foreign merchants who paid only a 5 percent tariff on imported sugar, they had to pay 20 percent. They had to pass this additional cost on to their customers.

Word of the beating spread throughout Tehran. Two days later, about two thousand angry tradesmen, merchants, ulama, and theology students took refuge at the Shah ʿAbd al-ʿAzim Shrine in Tehran. Taking refuge, or *bast*, in a sanctuary—a shrine, a mosque, or even a government telegraph office— was a time-honored ritual of political protest in Persia, much as one-day strikes are in France.

During the month-long *bast*, the protesters drew up a list of demands, which they submitted to the prime minister. Their first two demands related directly to the incident that sparked the protest in the first place. The protesters demanded the dismissal of the governor of Tehran who had ordered the beatings of the merchants, as well as the dismissal of Joseph Naus, one of several Belgian administrators whom the shah had hired in 1899 to reorganize the collection of customs. As a foreigner, Naus had become a lightening rod for popular anger. For the protesters, he symbolized both the privileges the Persian government had accorded foreigners and imperialist designs on their country.

The third demand made by the protesters was more far-reaching. Moving beyond the immediate events that precipitated their *bast*, the protesters demanded the establishment of something they called a "House of Justice." Although the term "House of Justice" was ambiguous, it was widely interpreted to mean a parliament. That parliament, called a *majlis*, convened in October 1906, and representatives immediately began drafting a "Fundamental Law"—a constitution—to secure the gains the protests had brought. Thus began the Persian Constitutional Revolution of 1905.

Persia was not the only place in the Middle East where the desire for constitutional and parliamentary rule inspired political action. In the Ottoman Empire, bureaucrats and army officers, supported by popular protest, twice compelled the sultan to adopt a constitution and convene a parliament. The first instance occurred in 1876, when the empire was in the midst of crisis.

Drought and famine brought widespread suffering to peasants, the government found itself unable to pay its external debt or its army and navy, and, in the wake of revolts by Bosnian Serbs and Bulgarians, a conference of European powers convened in Istanbul to impose a Balkan settlement on the empire. Roused by the multiple failures of the Ottoman government, theological students rioted in Istanbul, demanding the dismissal of the grand vizier (the sultan's chief minister) and chief mufti (the highest ranking Muslim religious official in the empire). According to the British ambassador, who was a witness to the unfolding events:

> The word "Constitution" was in every mouth; that the softas [religious students], representing the intelligent public opinion of the capital, knowing themselves to be supported by the nation—Christian as well as Mahometan—would not, I believed, relax their efforts till they obtained it, and that, should the Sultan refuse to grant it, an attempt to depose him appeared almost inevitable; that texts from the Koran were circulated proving to the faithful that the form of government sanctioned by it was properly democratic, and that the absolute authority now wielded by the Sultan was an usurpation of the rights of the people and not sanctioned by the Holy Law; and both texts and precedents were appealed to, to show that obedience was not due to a Sovereign who neglected the interests of the state.

Soon after these events, constitution-minded bureaucrats deposed Sultan Abdulaziz I, replaced him with his alcoholic son, and then replaced the replacement with Abdulhamid II, another son of Abdulaziz I. Before they threw their support to Abdulhamid II, however, they extracted from him a promise to rule in accordance with a constitution.

The first constitutional period lasted a mere two years. In 1878, Sultan Abdulhamid II, using the outbreak of war with Russia as a pretext to break his promise, suspended the Ottoman constitution, dismissed the elected parliament, and concentrated power in his own hands. Not until thirty years later, when a mutiny of Young Turk military officers stationed in Macedonia sparked a wider rebellion, was the constitution restored. That constitution remained in effect until World War I.

As we have seen in previous chapters, the transformation of society during the late nineteenth century laid the foundations for the emergence of a modern public sphere in the Middle East. In cities throughout the Ottoman Empire and Persia, all sorts of new ideas germane to new social, political, and economic realities emerged and competed with each other. The new Islamic orthodoxy that inspired the Muhammadan Union and the *al-Haqa'iq* group represented one intellectual current that attracted a following. Constitutionalism represented another. Accordingly, during this period a significant group of Westernizing intellectuals and Islamic modernists, working in alliance with urban crowds and political reformers, devoted their political energies to the realization of constitutional rule. Ottoman civil servants and soldiers, socialists in the northern Persian city of Tabriz, and even the partisans of Ahmad 'Urabi who demanded a charter from the Egyptian

PROCLAMATION DE LA CONSTITUTION OTTOMANE
le 11/24 Juillet 1908
La foule arrivant devant le Konak pour entendre la proclamation
de la Constitution par l'Inspecteur général Hilmi Pacha

Crowd in Istanbul listening to the announcement of the restoration of the Ottoman constitution, July 1908. (From: The Collection of Wolf-Dieter Lemke).

khedive in 1881–1882 all viewed constitutionalism as a panacea for the ills that beset their states.

Both local and international factors inspired the rise of constitutionalist movements in the region. As we have seen, local factors—the beating of sugar merchants in Persia, a crisis of legitimacy in the Ottoman Empire, an army mutiny in Egypt—provided the spark that touched off constitutionalist movements in the Middle East. But this spark was, in turn, touched off in a context defined by growing pains in the world economy, the consolidation of territorial states, intensified imperialist pressure and interimperialist rivalry, and the emergence of new social classes whose role in politics and society had yet to be determined. These conditions were not exclusive to the Middle East. They influenced events throughout the globe. Thus, any explanation for constitutionalism in the Middle East must take into account the fact that constitutionalist movements also emerged in such places as Japan (1874), Russia (1905), Mexico (1910), and China (1911). In each of these places, constitutionalists thought that the key to solving the predicament their states found themselves in was political reform, and political reform meant constitutional and parliamentary rule.

The first Ottoman constitutional revolution, the 'Urabi Revolt, and the Persian Constitutional Revolution took place during periods of global economic crisis. Of course, in none of these cases did the economic crisis define the direction political protest would take. Nevertheless, economic crisis did prompt widespread dissatisfaction and this dissatisfaction often found expression in constitutional movements.

In 1873, the collapse of the Viennese stock market precipitated a period of world depression that, according to some economists, lasted until 1896. The Depression of 1873 may not have been the first truly worldwide depression. Some economists give that honor to the "panic" of 1856–1857. And, of course, attributing such a cataclysmic event to the collapse of a stock market in Vienna would be as glib as attributing the Great Depression of the 1930s to the collapse of the New York Stock Exchange. But whatever the actual cause of the depression—rampant stock speculation; the emergence of the United States and Germany as new industrial powers; the spread of cash-cropping to the far reaches of the globe and the introduction of new technologies, from refrigeration to railroads, which glutted markets with agricultural products and mineral wealth—its magnitude and breadth was unprecedented. The 1873–1896 depression affected countries from Argentina to the Dutch East Indies. In Europe, the price of wheat declined 30 percent. In the United States, two-thirds of all railroads went under. In the Middle East, the collapse of international trade and commodity prices bred discontent among merchants and farmers. It also resulted in Ottoman and Egyptian bankruptcy and foreign supervision of the finances of each. Money that had gone into public works, military salaries, and the expansion of services vital to the functioning of modern states now went to repaying European creditors. Many in the region were resentful.

In every country hit by depression, popular movements emerged. The ideologies expressed by these movements reflected local conditions and conventions: thus, communism, trade unionism, and anarchism in the cities and factories of Western Europe and North America; populism on the Great Plains of North America; and anti-Semitism in any place in Europe where Jews could be found. In the Middle East, discontent was often channeled into constitutionalism. And why not? Governments that seemed to have brought such disaster to the region, that were unresponsive and did not allow those best fit for governance any role in decision making, needed to be expanded and made responsible to their citizens. Constitutions and parliaments, many believed, would guarantee that expansion and assumption of responsibility.

The economic background for the Persian Constitutional Revolution was a bit different from that which stimulated constitutionalism in the Ottoman Empire. During the late nineteenth and early twentieth centuries, the Persian economy was hit by a double whammy. First, there was the depression of 1873–1896, which affected Persia just as it did every other economy locked into the world system. Then, just as much of the world was climbing out of depression, another shock hit the economies of China, Japan, India, and Persia. Unlike the economies of the West, which used a gold standard, the economies of these states were silver-based. During the late nineteenth century, two events occurred that caused the silver-backed currencies of these countries to lose value. Both events bear a striking resemblance to those

Persian parliamentarians in session. (From: The Collection of Wolf-Dieter Lemke).

which many historians argue took place in the sixteenth century. First, as more and more countries bound themselves to the gold standard, silver flooded east, where it had a higher value. Second, the discovery of new deposits of silver, such as the Comstock Lode in Nevada, flooded the international market with the precious metal. This, too, affected economies and politics around the world. Cash-strapped, indebted farmers in the United States demanded that the United States Mint coin silver so that they not be "crucified on a cross of gold," as the 1896 Democratic presidential candidate William Jennings Bryan put it. In Persia, where coining silver was already the practice, prices skyrocketed 600 percent between 1850 and 1890. The Persian government borrowed heavily as a result of this inflation, and soon had to take out additional loans to pay back previous ones.

At the same time as the collapse of the international economy, both the Ottoman Empire and Persia experienced increasing political pressures that threatened their sovereignty and stimulated an anti-imperialist response. Many historians trace the increase in interimperialist rivalries directly to the Depression of 1873. After the onset of the depression, protectionist sentiments challenged free market liberalism, and Europeans and North Americans sought to establish overseas empires from which they could exclude foreign competition. Both Middle Eastern empires felt the sting of the "new imperialism" in forms that ranged from debt commissions to increased competition for concessions. In both empires, constitutionalists blamed autocratic government for the weak response to the threats to national sovereignty and demanded constitutional reform to strengthen their states. Constitutionalists also hoped that constitutions and parliaments would demonstrate to European powers that their empires were civilized members of the world community rather than carcasses to be picked clean by various imperialist powers or nationalist movements.

However much they might have protested European imperialism, those who led constitutional movements were the products of the world created by imperialism and defensive measures taken by non-European states in response to imperialism. For example, Midhat Pasha, the chief engineer of Ottoman constitutionalist intrigue in 1876, had studied briefly at a palace school established by an early *tanzimat* sultan, Mahmud II. Designed to prepare students to participate in a renovated bureaucracy, the school encouraged students to stay abreast of the latest intellectual trends in Europe. Midhat Pasha also participated in an Istanbul salon dedicated to discussing such topics as Western literature and philosophy. Taking advantage of Ottoman provincial reorganization, Midhat Pasha went on to organize "model" provinces in Bulgaria, Baghdad, and Syria. These provinces might be considered laboratories in which *tanzimat* ideas were applied and tested.

Like Midhat Pasha, the military officers, bureaucrats, and intellectuals who formed the nucleus of constitutional movements throughout the region—and, indeed, throughout the world—had often received advanced educations that included a good dose of Western social science and technical know-how. The core group of army officers that founded the Committee of Union and Progress and restored the Ottoman constitution in 1908 were graduates of the military medical school in Istanbul, and many of the intellectuals who organized the *anjumanha*—the building blocks of the Persian Constitutional Revolution—had either been educated in the West or at the Dar al-Funun in Tehran. Their ideas drew from both Western and indigenous sources. Thus, the Ottoman constitution was modeled on the constitution of Belgium and justified by ideas advanced by the Young Ottomans. Because of their advanced education, leaders of constitutionalist movements demanded a greater role in determining the future of their states. They thought that that role would be guaranteed through constitutions and parliaments.

Constitutionalists also felt perfectly at ease in a world where ideas could be spread by newspapers and popular support mobilized through the railroads and telegraph lines that connected the countryside with their capital cities. The introduction of modern techniques of communications, the formation of émigré communities outside the view of imperial surveillance, and labor migration played a key role in making constitutionalism an international movement. Constitutionalist movements were mutually reinforcing. Many Egyptians who joined the 'Urabi movement in 1881 were influenced by the doctrines of the Young Ottomans and by the example of the Ottoman constitution, which had been announced only five years earlier. Emigré Persians in Istanbul followed closely the Ottoman constitutional movement as well as the 'Urabi rebellion. Ottoman military officers knew what was going on in Persia in 1905 before they launched their own constitutional rebellion in 1908. And constitutionalists throughout the region took solace in the Russo–Japanese War of 1904–1905. Here, for the first time, was an Asiatic power that had defeated a European one—and the Asiatic power had a constitution while the European one did not. The Russo–Japanese War precipitated Russia's own constitutional revolution, which observers to the south also followed closely before embarking on theirs.

The close proximity of Russia affected constitutionalism in Persia in another way as well. Just as news spread from one state to another, so did techniques for mass political organizing. In the Persian case, laborers from northern Persia who had gone to Russia to work in the oil fields of Baku brought these techniques back with them when they returned home. By 1905, there were approximately three hundred thousand Persians in Russia, making up about a quarter of the oil field workers. About 80 percent of these workers eventually returned to Persia, bringing back with them ideas about trade unionism and socialism. Some organized an affiliate to the Russian Social Democratic Workers Party called Hemmat, which promoted a combination of Islamic modernist and socialist ideas. This is one of the reasons why the northern city of Tabriz became a hotbed of pro-constitutionalist and social democratic ideas. Constitutionalists in Tabriz built a mass movement by infusing their political program with a social and economic program that advocated, among other things, an eight-hour workday, free public education, an expansion of women's legal rights, and the ownership of land by those who tilled it. After the shah launched a counterattack against the constitutionalists and closed the Persian *majlis*, Tabrizis established a pro-constitutionalist commune while an army composed of social democrats and Armenian and Muslim radicals marched from the northern city of Rasht to Tehran to restore the parliament.

In the end, constitutionalism failed in both the Ottoman Empire and Persia. In the former case, constitutional rule was replaced by the rule of a triumvirate of military leaders who took over the reins of government in 1913. They ruled the Ottoman Empire until the end of World War I. Although the constitution theoretically remained in effect in Persia, the Russians invaded from the north, destroyed the Tabrizi experiment, and dismissed the *majlis* in Tehran. The fact that elections for another majlis took place in 1914 is as much a testament to the inconsequence of government structures in Persia as it is evidence for the survival of constitutionalism there. Thus, the era of constitutionalism ended not so much with a bang as with a whimper. Why, then, bother with it at all?

There are two reasons constitutionalism in the Middle East is important for subsequent developments. First, constitutional movements, to a greater or lesser extent, brought about a change in the political culture of the Middle East. They made the state the site of political contestation. In other words, in the wake of the constitutional movements, control of the state apparatus became the focus of political activity. They spread the representative principle—the idea that individuals had the right to participate in governance and in selecting those who stood for their interests. They reinforced among the inhabitants of the Ottoman Empire and Persia the notion that they were citizens, not subjects. And they made ideology—not dynasty—the foundation for political legitimacy.

Furthermore, constitutionalist movements both embodied and spread mass politics. Even in the Ottoman Empire, where constitutionalism was twice put in place by means other than mass movements, there were widespread demonstrations in support of—as well as against—the constitutionalists. Here is how one (obviously unsympathetic) observer described demonstrations held in Damascus in support of the restoration of the Ottoman constitution:

> Imagine some five hundred illiterate young men, some with swords in their hands, others with revolvers and many with prohibited rifles stolen from the government, this whole crowd followed by a great multitude pass through the streets and the bazaars shooting and shouting. On the 8th instant, the orations in general were exceptionally liberal. A "Young Turk" having the grade of "Usbashy" stood on the platform, took out his sword and asked the people to stand up and repeat after him an oath to the meaning that if tyranny shall reign again, they would overthrow it no matter how dear it might cost them. They solemnly declared that they were ready to sacrifice for liberty their wives, their children and their blood! After this solemn oath three times three cheers were given for liberty, the Army and the sultan.

Damascus, it should be remembered, was also one of the centers for the anti-constitutionalist, anti–Young Turk Muhammadan Union demonstrations described in the previous chapter. While the success of constitutional movements in spreading the gospel of constitutions and parliaments may thus have been less than sweeping, constitutional movements were instrumental in fostering a new style of politics in the Middle East.

DOCUMENTS

Commercial Convention (Balta Liman): Britain and the Ottoman Empire

As a price for assisting the Ottomans in expelling Mehmet Ali from Syria, the British insisted that the sultan sign the 1838 Treaty of Balta Liman. By lowering duties and abolishing monopolies in Ottoman territories, the treaty opened up the Ottoman Empire to British free trade policy.

Art. I. All rights, privileges, and immunities which have been conferred on the subjects or ships of Great Britain by the existing Capitulations and Treaties, are confirmed now and for ever, except in as far as they may be specifically altered by the present Convention: and it is moreover expressly stipulated, that all rights, privileges, or immunities which the Sublime Porte now grants, or may hereafter grant, to the ships and subjects of any other foreign Power, or which may suffer the ships and subjects of any other foreign Power to enjoy, shall be equally granted to, and exercised and enjoyed by, the subjects and ships of Great Britain.

Art. II. The subjects of Her Britannic Majesty, or their agents, shall be permitted to purchase at all places in the Ottoman Dominions (whether for the purposes of internal trade or exportation) all articles, without any exception whatsoever, the produce, growth, or manufacture of the said Dominions; and the Sublime Porte formally engages to abolish all monopolies of agricultural produce, or of any other articles whatsoever, as well as all *Permits* from the local Governors, either for the purchase of any article, or for its removal from one place to another when purchased; and any attempt to compel the subjects of Her Britannic Majesty to receive such *Permits* from the local Governors, shall be considered as an infraction of Treaties, and the Sublime Porte shall immediately punish with severity any Vizirs and other officers who shall have been guilty of such misconduct, and render full justice to British subjects for all injuries or losses which they may duly prove themselves to have suffered.

Art. III. If any article of Turkish produce, growth, or manufacture, be purchased by the British merchant or his agent, for the purpose of selling the same for internal consumption in Turkey, the British merchant or his agent shall pay, at the purchase and sale of such articles, and in any manner of trade therein, the same duties that are paid, in similar circumstances, by the most favoured class of Turkish subjects engaged in the internal trade of Turkey, whether Mussulmans or Rayahs.

Art. IV. If any article of Turkish produce, growth, or manufacture, be purchased for exportation, the same shall be conveyed by the British merchant or his agent, free of any kind of charge or duty whatsoever, to a convenient place of shipment, on its entry into which it shall be liable to one fixed duty of nine per cent. *ad valorem*, in lieu of all other interior duties.

Subsequently, on exportation, the duty of three per cent., as established and existing at present, shall be paid. But all articles bought in the shipping ports for exportation, and which have already paid the interior duty at entering into the same, will only pay the three per cent. export duty.

ART. V. The regulations under which Firmans are issued to British merchant vessels for passing the Dardanelles and the Bosphorus, shall be so framed as to occasion to such vessels the least possible delay.

ART. VI. It is agreed by the Turkish Government, that the regulations established in the present Convention, shall be general throughout the Turkish Empire, whether in Turkey in Europe or Turkey in Asia, in Egypt, or other African possessions belonging to the Sublime Porte, and shall be applicable to all the subjects, whatever their description, of the Ottoman Dominions: and the Turkish Government also agrees not to object to other foreign Powers settling their trade upon the basis of this present Convention.

ART. VII. It having been the custom of Great Britain and the Sublime Porte, with a view to prevent all difficulties and delay in estimating the value of articles imported into the Turkish Dominions, or exported therefrom, by British subjects, to appoint, at intervals of fourteen years, a Commission of men well acquainted with the traffic of both countries, who have fixed by a tariff the sum of money in the coin of the Grand Signior, which should be paid as duty on each article; and the term of fourteen years, during which the last adjustment of the said tariff was to remain in force, having expired, the High Contracting Parties have agreed to name conjointly fresh Commissioners to fix and determine the amount in money which is to be paid by British subjects, as the duty of three per cent upon the value of all commodities imported and exported by them; and the said Commissioners shall establish an equitable arrangement for estimating the interior duties which, by the present Treaty, are established on Turkish goods to be exported, and shall also determine on the places of shipment where it may be most convenient that such duties should be levied.

The new tariff thus established, to be in force for seven years after it has been fixed, at the end of which time it shall be in the power of either of the parties to demand a revision of that tariff; but if no such demand be made on either side, within the six months after the end of the first seven years, then the tariff shall remain in force for seven years more, reckoned from the end of the preceding seven years; and so it shall be at the end of each successive period of seven years.

J. C. Hurewitz, *The Middle East and North Africa in World Politics: A Documentary Record, vol. 1: European Expansion, 1535–1914* (New Haven, Conn.: Yale University Press, 1975), pp. 265–66.

The Hatt-i Sharif of Gulhane

The two cornerstones of the *tanzimat* were the *Hatt-i Sharif* of Gulhane (1839) and the *Islahat Fermani* (1856), imperial edicts that set out an agenda for Ottoman administrative reform and defined the rights of Ottoman citizens. The latter document reaffirmed and expanded on the promises and program of the former.

All the world knows that since the first days of the Ottoman State, the lofty principles of the Kuran and the rules of the Şeriat were always perfectly observed. Our mighty Sultanate reached the highest degree of strength and power, and all its subjects [the highest degree] of ease and prosperity. But in the last one hundred and fifty years, because of a succession of difficulties and diverse causes, the sacred Şeriat was not obeyed nor were the beneficent regulations followed; consequently, the former strength and prosperity have changed into weakness and poverty. It is evident that countries not governed by the laws of the Şeriat cannot survive.

From the very first day of our accession to the throne, our thoughts have been devoted exclusively to the development of the empire and the promotion of the prosperity of the people. Therefore, if the geographical position of the Ottoman provinces, the fertility of the soil, and the aptitude and intelligence of the inhabitants are considered, it is manifest that, by striving to find appropriate means, the desired results will, with the aid of God, be realized within five or ten years. Thus, full of confidence in the help of the Most High and certain of the support of our Prophet, we deem it necessary and important from now on to introduce new legislation to achieve effective administration of the Ottoman Government and Provinces. Thus the principles of the requisite legislation are three:

1. The guarantees promising to our subjects perfect security for life, honor, and property.

2. A regular system of assessing taxes.

3. An equally regular system for the conscription of requisite troops and the duration of their service.

Indeed there is nothing more precious in this world than life and honor. What man, however much his character may be against violence, can prevent himself from having recourse to it, and thereby injure the government and the country, if his life and honor are endangered? If, on the contrary, he enjoys perfect security, it is clear that he will not depart from the ways of loyalty and all his actions will contribute to the welfare of the government and of the people.

If there is an absence of security for property, everyone remains indifferent to his state and his community; no one interests himself in the prosperity of the country, absorbed as he is in his own troubles and worries. If, on the contrary, the individual feels complete security about his possessions, then he will become preoccupied with his own affairs, which he will seek to expand, and his devotion and love for his state and his community will steadily grow and will undoubtedly spur him into becoming a useful member of society.

Tax assessment is also one of the most important matters to regulate. A state, for the defense of its territory, manifestly needs to maintain an army and provide other services, the costs of which can be defrayed only by taxes levied on its subjects. Although, thank God, our Empire has already been relieved of the affliction of monopolies, the harmful practice of tax-farming [*iltizam*], which never yielded any fruitful results, still prevails. This amounts to handing over the financial and political affairs of a country to the whims of an ordinary man and perhaps to the grasp of force and oppression, for if the tax-farmer is not of good character he will be interested only in his own profit and will behave oppressively. It is therefore necessary that from now on every subject of the Empire should be taxed according to his fortune and his means, and that he should be saved from and further exaction. It is also necessary that special laws should fix and limit the expenses of our land and sea forces.

Military matters, as already pointed out, are among the most important affairs of state, and it is the inescapable duty of all the people to provide soldiers for the defense of the fatherland [*vatan*]. It is therefore necessary to frame regulations on, the contingents that each locality should furnish according to the requirements of the time, and to reduce the term of military service to four or five years. Such legislation will put an end to the old practice, still in force, of recruiting soldiers without consideration of the size of the population in any locality, more conscripts being taken from some places and fewer from others. This practice has been throwing agriculture and trade into harmful disarray. Moreover, those who are recruited to lifetime military service suffer despair and contribute to the depopulation of the country.

In brief, unless such regulations are promulgated, power, prosperity, security, and peace may not be expected, and the basic principles [of the projected reforms] must be those enumerated above.

Thus, from now on, every defendant shall be entitled to a public hearing, according to the rules of the Şeriat, after inquiry and examination; and without the pronouncement of a regular sentence no one may secretly or publicly put another to death by poison or by any other means. No one shall be allowed to attack the honor of any other person whatsoever. Every one shall possess his property of every kind and may dispose of it freely, without let or hindrance from any person whatsoever; and the innocent heirs of a criminal shall not be deprived of their hereditary rights as a result of the confiscation of the property of such a criminal. The Muslim and non-Muslim subjects of our lofty Sultanate shall, without exception, enjoy our imperial concessions. Therefore we grant perfect security to all the populations of our Empire in their lives, their honor, and their properties, according to the sacred law.

As for the other points, decisions must be taken by majority vote. To this end, the members of the Council of Judicial Ordinances [Meclis-i Ahkam-ı Adliyye], enlarged by new members as may be found necessary, to whom will be joined on certain days that we shall determine our Ministers and the high officials of the Empire, will assemble for the purpose of framing laws to regulate the security of life and property and the assessment of taxes. Every one participating in the Council will express his ideas and give his advice freely.

J. C. Hurewitz, *The Middle East and North Africa in World Politics: A Documentary Record, vol. 1: European Expansion, 1535–1914* (New Haven, Conn.: Yale University Press, 1975), pp. 269–70, 315–18.

The Islahat Fermani

Let it be done as herein set forth.

To you, my Grand Vizier Mehemed Emin Aali Pasha, decorated with my imperial order of the medjidiye of the first class, and with the order of personal merit; may God grant to you greatness and increase your power.

It has always been my most earnest desire to insure the happiness of all classes of the subjects whom Divine Providence has placed under my imperial sceptre, and since my accession to the throne I have not ceased to direct all my efforts to the attainment of that end.

Thanks to the Almighty, these unceasing efforts have already been productive of numerous useful results. From day to day the happiness of the nation and the wealth of my dominions go on augmenting.

It being now my desire to renew and enlarge still more the new institutions ordained with a view of establishing a state of things conformable with the dignity of my empire and the position which it occupies among civilized nations, and the rights of my empire having, by the fidelity and praiseworthy efforts of all my subjects, and by the kind and friendly assistance of the great powers, my noble allies, received from abroad a confirmation which will be the commencement of a new era, it is my desire to augment its well being and prosperity, to effect the happiness of all my subjects, who in my sight are all equal, and equally dear to me, and who are united to each other by the cordial ties of patriotism, and to insure the means of daily increasing the prosperity of my empire.

I have therefore resolved upon, and I order the execution of the following measures:

The guarantees promised on our part by the Hatti-Humayoun of Gulhané, and in conformity with the Tanzimat, to all the subjects of my empire, without distinction of classes or of religion, for the security of their persons and property, and the preservation of their honor, are to-day confirmed and consolidated, and efficacious measures shall be taken in order that they may have their full entire effect.

All the privileges and spiritual immunities granted by my ancestors *ab antiquo*, and at subsequent dates, to all Christian communities or other non-Mussulman persuasions established in my empire, under my protection, shall be confirmed and maintained.

Every Christian or other non-Mussulman community shall be bound within a fixed period, and with the concurrence of a commission composed *ad hoc* of members of its own body, to proceed, with my high approbation and under the inspection of my Sublime Porte, to examine into its actual immunities and privileges, and to discuss and submit to my Sublime Porte the reforms required by the progress of civilization and of the age. The powers conceded to the Christian patriarchs and bishops by the Sultan Mahomet II and to his successors shall be made to harmonize with the new position which my generous and beneficent intentions insure to these communities. . . . My Sublime Porte will take energetic measures to insure to each sect, whatever be the number of its adherents, entire freedom in the exercise of its religion. Every distinction or designation pending to make any class whatever of the subjects of my empire inferior to another class, on account of their religion, language, or race, shall be forever effaced from administrative protocol. The laws shall be put in force against the use of any injurious or offensive term, either among private individuals or on the part of the authorities.

As all forms of religion are and shall be freely professed in my dominions, no subject of my empire shall be hindered in the exercise of the religion that he professes, nor shall he be in any way annoyed on this account. No one shall be compelled to change their religion.

The nomination and choice of all functionaries and other employes of my empire being wholly dependent upon my sovereign will, all the subjects of my empire, without distinction of nationality, shall be admissible to public employments, and qualified to fill them according to their capacity and merit, and conformably with rules to be generally applied.

All the subjects of my empire, without distinction, shall be received into the civil and military schools of the government, if they otherwise satisfy the conditions as to age and examination which are specified in the organic regulations of the said schools. Moreover, every community is authorized to establish public schools of science, art, and industry. Only the method of instructions and the choice of professors in schools of this class shall be under the control of a mixed council of public instruction, the members of which shall be named by my sovereign command.

All commercial, correctional, and criminal suits between Mussulmans and Christians, or other non-Mussulman subjects, or between Christian or other non-Mussulmans of different sects, shall be referred to mixed tribunals.

The proceedings of these tribunals shall be public; the parties shall be confronted and shall produce their witnesses, whose testimony shall be received without distinction, upon an oath taken according to the religious law of each sect.

Suits relating to civil affairs shall continue to be publicly tried, according to the laws and regulations, before the mixed provincial councils, in the presence of the governor and judge of the place.

Special civil proceedings, such as those relating to successions or others of that kind, between subjects of the same Christian or other non-Mussulman faith, may, at the request of the parties, be sent before the councils of the patriarchs or of the communities.

Penal, correctional, and commercial laws, and rules of procedure for the mixed tribunals, shall be drawn up as soon as possible and formed into a code. Translations of them shall be published in all the languages current in the empire.

Proceedings shall be taken, with as little delay as possible, for the reform of the penitentiary system as applied to houses of detention, punishment, or correction, and other establishments of like nature, so as to reconcile the rights of humanity with those of justice. Corporal punishment shall not be administered, even in the prisons, except in conformity with the disciplinary regulations established by my Sublime Porte, and everything that resembles torture shall be entirely abolished.

Infractions of the law in this particular shall be severely repressed, and shall besides entail, as of right, the punishment, in conformity with the civil code, of the authorities who may order and of the agents who may commit them.

The organization of the police in the capital, in the provincial towns and in the rural districts, shall be revised in such a manner as to give to all the peaceable subjects of my empire the strongest guarantees for the safety both of their persons and property.

The equality of taxes entailing equality of burdens, as equality of duties entails that of rights, Christian subjects, and those of other non-Mussulman sects, as it has been already decided, shall, as well as Mussulmans, be subject to the obligations of the law of recruitment.

The principle of obtaining substitutes, or of purchasing exemption, shall be admitted. A complete law shall be published, with as little delay as possible, respecting the admission into and service in the army of Christian and other non-Mussulman subjects.

Proceedings shall be taken for a reform in the constitution of the provincial and communal councils in order to insure fairness in the choice of the deputies of the Mussulman, Christian, and other communities and freedom of voting in the councils. My Sublime Porte will take into consideration the adoption of the most effectual means for ascertaining exactly and for controlling the result of the deliberations and of the decisions arrived at.

As the laws regulating the purchase, sale, and disposal of real property are common to all the subjects of my empire, it shall be lawful for foreigners to possess landed property in my dominions, conforming themselves to the laws and police regulations, and bearing the same charges as the native inhabitants, and after arrangements have been come to with foreign powers.

The taxes are to be levied under the same denomination from all the subjects of my empire, without distinction of class or of religion. The most prompt and energetic means for remedying the abuses in collecting the taxes, and especially the tithes, shall be considered.

The system of direct collections shall gradually, and as soon as possible, be substituted for the plan of farming, in all the branches of the revenues of the state. As long as the present system remains in force all agents of the government and all members of the medjlis shall be forbidden under the severest penalties, to become lessees of any farming contracts which are announced for public competition, or to have any beneficial interest in carrying them out. The local taxes shall, as far as possible, be so imposed as not to affect the sources of production or to hinder the progress of internal commerce.

Works of public utility shall receive a suitable endowment, part of which shall be raised from private and special taxes levied in the provinces, which shall have the benefit of the advantages arising from the establishment of ways of communication by land and sea.

A special law having been already passed, which declares that the budget of the revenue and the expenditure of the state shall be drawn up and made known every year, the said law shall be most scrupulously observed. Proceedings shall be taken for revising the emoluments attached to each office.

The heads of each community and a delegate, designated by my Sublime Porte, shall be summoned to take part in the deliberations of the supreme council of justice on all occasions which might interest the generality of the subjects of my empire. They shall be summoned specially for this purpose by my grand vizier. The delegates shall hold office for one year; they shall be sworn on entering upon their duties. All the members of the council, at the ordinary and extraordinary meetings, shall freely give their opinions and their votes, and no one shall ever annoy them on this account.

The laws against corruption, extortion, or malversation shall apply, according to the legal forms, to all the subjects of my empire, whatever may be their class and the nature of their duties.

Steps shall be taken for the formation of banks and other similar institutions, so as to effect a reform in the monetary and financial system, as well as to create funds to be employed in augmenting the sources of the material wealth of my empire. Steps shall also be taken for the formation of roads and canals to increase the facilities of communication and increase the sources of the wealth of the country.

Everything that can impede commerce or agriculture shall be abolished. To accomplish these objects means shall be sought to profit by the science, the art, and the funds of Europe, and thus gradually to execute them.

Such being my wishes and my commands, you, who are my grand vizier, will, according to custom, cause this imperial firman to be published in my capital and in all parts of my empire; and you will watch attentively and take all the necessary measures that all the orders which it contains be henceforth carried out with the most rigorous punctuality.

The d'Arcy Oil Concession

The first Middle Eastern oil concession was granted by the Qajar government of Persia to William Knox d'Arcy in 1901. It became the prototype for subsequent oil concessions in the region.

Between the Government of His Imperial Majesty the Shah of Persia, of the one part, and William Knox d'Arcy, of independent means, residing in London at No. 42, Grosvenor Square (hereinafter called "the Concessionnaire"), of the other part;

The following has by these presents been agreed on and arranged—viz.:

ART. 1. The Government of His Imperial Majesty the Shah grants to the concessionnaire by these presents a special and exclusive privilege to search for, obtain, exploit, develop, render suitable for trade, carry away and sell natural gas petroleum, asphalt and ozokerite throughout the whole extent of the Persian Empire for a term of sixty years as from the date of these presents.

ART. 2. This privilege shall comprise the exclusive right of laying the pipelines necessary from the deposits where there may be found one or several of the said products up to the Persian Gulf, as also the necessary distributing branches. It shall also comprise the right of constructing and maintaining all and any wells, reservoirs, stations and pump services, accumulation services and distribution services, factories and other works and arrangements that may be deemed necessary.

ART. 3. The Imperial Persian Government grants gratuitously to the concessionnaire all uncultivated lands belonging to the State which the concessionnaire's engineers may deem necessary for the construction of the whole or any part of the above-mentioned works. As for cultivated lands belonging to the State, the concessionnaire must purchase them at the fair and current price of the province.

The Government also grants to the concessionnaire the right of acquiring all and any other lands or buildings necessary for the said purpose, with the consent of the proprietors, on such conditions as may be arranged between him and them without their being allowed to make demands of a nature to surcharge the prices ordinarily current for lands situate in their respective localities.

Holy places with all their dependencies within a radius of 200 Persian archines are formally excluded.

ART. 4. As three petroleum mines situate at Schouster, Kassre-Chirine, in the Province of Kermanschah, and Daleki, near Bouchir, are at present let to private persons and produce an annual revenue of two thousand tomans for the benefit of the Government, it has been agreed that the three aforesaid mines shall be comprised in the Deed of Concession in conformity with Article 1, on condition that, over and above the 16 per cent mentioned in Article 10, the concessionnaire shall pay every year the fixed sum of 2,000 (two thousand) tomans to the Imperial Government.

ART. 5. The course of the pipe-lines shall be fixed by the concessionnaire and his engineers.

ART. 6. Notwithstanding what is above set forth, the privilege granted by these presents shall not extend to the provinces of Azerbadjan, Ghilan, Mazendaran, Asdrabad and Khorassan, but on the express condition that the Persian Imperial Government shall not grant to any other person the right of constructing a pipe-line to the southern rivers or to the South Coast of Persia.

ART. 7. All lands granted by these presents to the concessionnaire or that may be acquired by him in the manner provided for in Articles 3 and 4 of these presents, as also all products exported, shall be free of all imposts and taxes during the term of the present concession. All material and apparatuses necessary for the exploration, working and development of the deposits, and for the construction and development of the pipe-lines, shall enter Persia free of all taxes and Custom-House duties.

ART. 8. The concessionnaire shall immediately send out to Persia and at his own cost one or several experts with a view to their exploring the region in which there exist, as he believes, the said products, and in the event of the report of the expert being in the opinion of the concessionnaire of a satisfactory nature, the latter shall immediately send to Persia and at his own cost all the technical staff necessary, with the working plant and machinery required for boring and sinking wells and ascertaining the value of the property.

ART. 9. The Imperial Persian Government authorises the concessionnaire to found one or several companies for the working of the concession.

The names, "statutes" and capital of the said companies shall be fixed by the concessionnaire, and the directors shall be chosen by him on the express condition that, on the formation of each company, the concessionnaire shall give official notice of such formation to the Imperial Government, through the medium of the Imperial Commissioner, and shall forward the "statutes", with information as to the places at which such company is to operate. Such company or companies shall enjoy all the rights and privileges granted to the concessionnaire, but they must assume all his engagements and responsibilities.

ART. 10. It shall be stipulated in the contract between the concessionnaire, of the one part, and the company, of the other part, that the latter is, within the term of one month as from the date of the formation of the first exploitation company, to pay the Imperial Persian Government the sum of £20,000 sterling in cash, and an additional sum of £20,000 sterling in paid-up shares of the first company founded by virtue of the foregoing article. It shall also pay the said Government annually a sum equal to 16 per cent of the annual net profits of any company or companies that may be formed in accordance with the said article.

ART. 11. The said Government shall be free to appoint an Imperial Commissioner, who shall be consulted by the concessionnaire and the directors of the companies to be formed. He shall supply all and any useful information at his disposal, and he shall inform them of the best course to be adopted in the interest of the undertaking. He shall establish, by agreement with the concessionnaire, such supervision as he may deem expedient to safeguard the interests of the Imperial government.

The aforesaid powers of the Imperial Commissioner shall be set forth in the "statutes" of the companies to be created.

The concessionnaire shall pay the Commissioner thus appointed an annual sum of £1,000 sterling for his services as from the date of the formation of the first company.

ART. 12. The workmen employed in the service of the company shall be subject to His Imperial Majesty the Shah, except the technical staff, such as the managers, engineers, borers and foremen.

ART. 13. At any place in which it may be proved that the inhabitants of the country now obtain petroleum for their own use, the company must supply them gratuitously with the quantity of petroleum that they themselves got previously. Such quantity shall be fixed according to their own declarations, subject to the supervision of the local authority.

ART. 14. The Imperial Government binds itself to take all and any necessary measures to secure the safety and the carrying out of the object of this concession of the plant and of the apparatuses, of which mention is made, for the purposes of the undertaking of the company, and to protect the representatives, agents and servants of the company. The Imperial Government having thus fulfilled its engagements, the concessionnaire and the companies created by him shall not have power, under any pretext whatever, to claim damages from the Persian Government.

ART. 15. On the expiration of the term of the present concession, all materials, buildings and apparatuses then used by the company for the exploitation of its industry shall become the property of the said Government, and the company shall have no right to any indemnity in this connection.

ART. 16. If within the term of two years as from the present date the concessionnaire shall not have established the first of the said companies authorised by Article 9 of the present agreement, the present concession shall become null and void.

ART. 17. In the event of there arising between the parties to the present concession any dispute or difference in respect of its interpretation or the rights or responsibilities of one or the other of the parties therefrom resulting, such dispute or difference shall be submitted to two arbitrators at Teheran, one of whom shall be named by each of the parties, and to an umpire who shall be appointed by the arbitrators before they proceed to arbitrate. The decision of the arbitrators or, in the event of the latter disagreeing, that of the umpire shall be final.

ART. 18. This Act of Concession, made in duplicate, is written in the French language and translated into Persian with the same meaning.

But, in the event of there being any dispute in relation to such meaning, the French text shall alone prevail.

J. C. Hurewitz, *The Middle East and North Africa in World Politics: A Documentary Record,* *vol. 1: European Expansion, 1535–1914* (New Haven, Conn.: Yale University Press, 1975), pp. 483–84.

Algeria: The Poetry of Loss

The following poems, transmitted orally and later written down by a French anthropologist, were composed by a young Algerian Qur'an-school student who bore witness to the French invasion of Algeria in 1830.

The days, my brothers, place diversity into the hours,
The century turns around and brusquely swerves
(Algiers), The Splendid, has had its flag, its wujak*
Nations have trembled before her on the continent and on two seas
But when God wanted it to be, the appointed time came upon her.
She was delivered by Allah's men, by the Saints.
The Frenchman marched against her and took her.
It was not one hundred ships that he had, nor two hundred;
He proudly had his flotilla defile before her,
Surging forth from the high seas, with powerful armies,
We were unaware of how many they were, their numbers becoming
embroiled, lost to our eyes.
Fiercely the Rumis† *came against the Splendid city.*
    Regarding al-Jazair,‡ *Gentlemen, my heart is mourning! . . .*

    Conquering her without fighting, he took her, the dog.
They carried away her treasures, those brothers of demons.
After having gone to Stawali and having seized it,
With their drums, their soldiers and their flags,
They secured the cafe of al-Biar and its villas
And they climbed toward Buzareah in a moment.
They brought down their forces in front of the "Pines"
And they took the Fort of My Lord Maulay Hussain.
In the night, the Rumis *advanced: they made their drums resound:*
And the Believers shed tears, O Muslims!
Some left the city; others waited resolutely.
They held the enemy in the gardens for about two days.
They left for adventures abandoning their homeland,
And they dispersed into diverse countries, poor exiles.
Be patient, people of Muhammad, endure the days the foreigners bring you!
It is the test the Master of the Universe has decreed for you.
    Who would have said of al-Jazair, of its fortifications,
Of its wujak, *that even the evil eye would have come to it?*
Alas! Where is the place of its sultan and of its people?
They have gone and other faces have taken their places.
Alas! Where are their beys *and their* qaids?
Who knows what has become of those famous qasbajis§
And the Bailiff's guards of the station house?
And those militia men?

---

*wujak: corps of janissaries, Turkish military unit.
†*Rumis*: Algerian term to refer to Frenchmen and other Europeans.
‡*al-Jazair*: Transliteration of the Algerians' own name for Algiers.
§*qasbaji*: officer of the qasabah or fort.

Alas! Where is the palace of the council and its dignitaries?
And the places of justice full of majesty?
Alas! Where are those shawush-es *and their arrogance?*
Alas! Where are those haughty Turks? . . .

May your servants regain peace, may all their grief be ended
And may this oppression which crushes the Muslims cease!
Let us cry over the muftis, *over the* qadis,
Over the ulama *of the city, those guides of the religion.*
Let us cry over the mosques and their sermons
And over their pulpits of elevated marble.
Let us weep over their minarets* *and the calls of the* muezzins[†];
and over the classes of their teachers and over their cantors of the Qur'an.
Let us lament the private chapels whose doors have been locked
And which have sunk today, yes Sir, into oblivion.
Alas where are the precious trinkets of the city, where are its houses?
Where are their low apartments and the elevated rooms for the enunchs?
They are no longer but a parade ground and their traces have disappeared.
So much does that cursed one breathe to plague us!
The Christians have installed themselves in the city;
Its appearance has changed;
It no longer has seen anything but impure people.
The janissaries' *houses! They have razed their walls;*
They have torn down its marble and its sculptured balustrades,
The iron grills which protected the windows
Have been put to pieces by those impious ones, enemies of the Religion.
Likewise, they have named that Qaisariya "the Square",
Where the Books and their binders were formerly found.
The Magnificent Mosque which was next to it
Has been destroyed by them simply in order to spite the Muslims. . . .

Alf Andrew Heggoy, *The French Conquest of Algiers, 1830: An Algerian Oral Tradition*
(Athens, Ohio: Ohio University Center for International Studies/Africa Studies
Program, 1986), pp. 32–36.

Huda Shaarawi: A New Mentor and Her Salon for Women

Men such as Wasif Jawhariyyeh were not the only ones to participate in the salon culture of the late nineteenth- and early twentieth-century Middle East.
Women did as well. In this selection, Egyptian feminist Huda Shaarawi describes
her experiences at one such salon in Cairo:

Eugénie Le Brun, a Frenchwoman, was the first wife of Husain Rushdi Pasha.
I met her for the first time at a wedding reception and was immediately taken
by her dignity, sensitivity and intelligence. In spite of my extreme youth I at-

---

*minaret: slender tower attached to mosques. Balconies on the minaret are the
place from where people are called to prayer.
[†]muezzin: Muslim official who calls the faithful to prayer (from the minaret).

tracted her attention as well. We were introduced by Rushdi Pasha's sister and spent most of the evening in delightful conversation. Some time later, my brother arranged for me to take a day's excursion on the Nile to the Delta Barrage with Mme Rushdi and a number of other European women. The hours I spent in her company on that occasion were the beginning of a close relationship. She soon became a dear friend and valued mentor. She guided my first steps in 'society' and looked out for my reputation. . . .

Mme Rushdi not only guarded my reputation, but also nourished my mind and spirit. She took it upon herself to direct my reading in French. She would assist me over difficult passages in a book and when I had finished it she would discuss it with me. In that way, she helped me perfect my French and expand my learning.

Soon, at her request, I began to attend her Saturday salon during the hours set aside for women. She would tell me, 'You are the flower of my salon.' On the days when I was unable to attend I used to send flowers. Once she responded with a sweet note saying that the flowers I had sent could not make up for the absence of her 'beloved flower'. She begged me to lessen the number of bouquets so I would not diminish her joy. Her growing affection toward me made some of her friends jealous but others applauded her devotion to me.

As mistress of the salon, Mme Rushdi adroitly guided the discourse from issue to issue. There were debates about social practices, especially veiling. She confessed that although she admired the dress of Egyptian women, she thought the veil stood in the way of their advancement. It also gave rise to false impressions in the minds of foreigners. They regarded the veil as a convenient mask for immorality. Plenty of lurid tales were circulated by ignorant outsiders about Egyptian morals. Foreigners not infrequently departed from Egypt under the mistaken impression they had visited the houses of respectable families when, in truth, they had fallen into the lands of profiteers who, under the guise of introducing them into the harems of great families, had in fact led them merely to gaudy brothels.

The conversation would move to another topic such as offspring and immorality. Mme Rushdi believed that people who had children never died, as their children were extensions of themselves who kept their memories alive. 'I have no children to perpetuate my memory,' she would say, 'but I shall remain alive through my books.' She once revealed that she had provided for a burial plot in the cemetery of Imam al-Shafai. In answer to our surprised looks she said, 'You didn't know that I embraced Islam after my marriage? I wish to be buried in the Muslim cemetery next to my husband so we shall never be separated in this world or the next.'

Speaking of her books, she said, 'I have signed them, as I have written them— Niya Salima ('In Good Faith'). My purpose in *Harem et les musulmanes* (*The Harem and Muslim women*) was to describe the life of the Egyptian woman, as it really is, to enlighten Europeans. After it appeared in Europe, I received many letters saying my book had cleared up false impressions of life in Islamic countries. They said it had corrected outsiders' images of Egyptians. In fact, they said Egyptians seemed not unlike themselves.' That restored her peace of mind, she said. She had been very upset when she heard that many Egyptians had thought she had criticized the condition of women in Egypt.

'However,' she continued, 'my second book is different. I decided to attack the problem of the backwardness of Egyptian women, demonstrating it arose from the persistence of certain social customs, but not from Islam, as many Europeans believe. Islam, on the contrary, has granted women greater justice than previous religions. While working on the book I attended sessions of the *Shariah* Courts (religious courts where person status or family law cases are heard) to find out for myself how women fared. I was aghast to see the blatant tyranny of men over women. My new book will be called, *Les Repudiées (The Divorcees).'* Mme Rushdi read me portions of the book as she completed them, asking for my reactions.

Huda Shaarawi, *Harem Years: The Memoirs of an Egyptian Feminist (1879–1924)*, trans. and ed. Margot Badran (New York: The Feminist Press at the City University of New York, 1986), pp. 76–81.

Rifaʿa Rifiʿal-Tahtawi: The Extraction of Gold or an Overview of Paris

Mehmet Ali sent Rifaʿa Rafiʿ al-Tahtawi to Paris as the head of the first Egyptian educational mission. Upon his return, al-Tahtawi became head of the School of Languages, where he developed his ideas based upon his experiences in Europe and in Mehmet Ali's Egypt. Here is al-Tahtawi on patriotism and the responsibilities of citizenship.

Patriots who are faithful in their love of homeland redeem their country with all their means, and serve it by offering all they possess. They redeem it with their soul, and repel anyone who seeks to harm it the same way a father would keep evil away from his child. The intentions of the children of the country must always be directed toward the country's virtue and honor, and not toward anything that violates the rights of their countries and fellow countrymen. Their inclination should be toward that which brings benefit and goodness. Likewise, the country protects its children from all that harms them, because of its possession of those characteristics. The love of homeland and the promotion of the public welfare are among the beautiful characteristics that get inculcated into each person, constantly, throughout one's life, and make every one of them loved by the others. No one could be happier than the human beings who are naturally inclined to keep evil away from their homeland, even if they must harm themselves to do so.

The quality of patriotism requires not just that humans demand the rights they are owed by their homeland. They must also carry out their obligations toward the country. If the children of the homeland fail to earn the rights of their country, then the civil rights to which they are entitled will be lost.

In olden times, the Romans used to force citizens who reached twenty years of age to give an oath that they would defend their country and their government. They required a pledge to this effect, the text of which is:

"May God be my witness that I shall carry the sword of honor to defend my country and its people whenever there is a chance I would be able to assist it. May God be my witness that I am willing to fight with the army or on my own for the protection of the country and religion. May God be my witness that I shall not disturb the serenity of my country, nor betray it or deceive it, and that I shall sail on the seas whenever necessary in all conquests that the government orders, and that I pledge to follow present and future laws and customs in my country. May God be my witness that I shall not tolerate anyone who dares violate them or undermine their order."

Based on this, it is understood that the Roman nation firmly adhered to the love of country, and that is the reason it reigned over all the countries of the world. When the quality of patriotism was removed, failure beset the members of this nation, its affairs were ruined, and the order of its system disintegrated by the numerous disagreements of its princes and the multiplicity of its rulers. After being ruled by one Caesar, it was divided between two Caesars in the east and the west, the Caesar of Rome and the Caesar of Constantinople. Power that had belonged to one mighty force was split into two minor forces. All its wars ended in defeat, and it retreated from a perfect existence to nonexistence. This is the fate of any nation whose government is in disarray, and whose state is disorganized.

Charles Kurzman, ed., *Modernist Islam, 1840–1940: A Sourcebook* (Oxford: Oxford University Press, 2002), p. 35.

Muhammad ʿAbduh: The Theology of Unity

The Islamic modernist Muhammad ʿAbduh (1849–1905), an Egyptian associate of Jamal al-Din al-Afghani, sought to make Islam compatible with the dogmas and doctrines of nineteenth-century rationalism. In this selection, he argues that Muslims cannot simply rely on the authoritative interpretation of texts done by medieval clerics (a procedure known as *taqlid*); rather, they must use reason to keep up with changing times.

Islam will have no truck with traditionalism, against which it campaigns relentlessly, to break its power over men's minds and eradicate its deep-seated influence. The underlying bases of *taqlīd* in the beliefs of the nations have been shattered by Islam.

In the same cause, it has alerted and aroused the powers of reason, out of long sleep. For whenever the rays of truth had penetrated, the temple custodians intervened with their jealous forebodings. 'Sleep on, the night is pitch dark, the way is rough and the goal distant, and rest is scant and there's poor provision for the road.'

Islam raised its voice against these unworthy whisperings and boldly declared that man was not created to be led by a bridle. He was endowed with intelligence to take his guidance with knowledge and to con the signs and tokens in the universe and in events. The proper role of teachers is to alert and to guide, directing men into the paths of study.

The friends of truth are those 'who listen to what is said and follow its better way.' (Surah 39.18.) as the Qur'ān has it. It characterizes them as those who weigh all that is said, irrespective of who the speakers are, in order to follow what they know to be good and reject what gives evidence of having neither validity nor use. Islam threw its weight against the religious authorities, bringing them down from the dominance whence they uttered their commands and prohibitions. It made them answerable to those they dominated, so that these could keep an eye on them and scrutinize their claims, according to their own judgement and lights, thus reaching conclusions based on conviction, not on conjecture and delusion.

Further, Islam encouraged men to move away from their clinging attachment to the world of their fathers and their legacies, indicting as stupid and foolish the attitude that always wants to know what the precedents say. Mere priority in time, it insisted, is not one of the signs of perceptive knowledge, nor yet of superior intelligence and capacity. Ancestor and descendant compare closely no doubt in discrimination and endowment of mind. But the latter has the advantage over his forebears in that he knows events gone by and is in a position to study and exploit their consequences as the former was not. It may be that such traceable results which men of the present generation can turn to profit will also illustrate the ill-effects of things done in earlier times and the dire evils perpetrated by the men of the past. 'Say: Go through the world and see what was the fate of those who disbelieved.' (Surah 6.11.) The doors of the Divine favour are not closed to the seeker: His mercy which embraces everything will never repel the suppliant.

Islam reproves the slavish imitation of the ancestors that characterizes the leaders of the religions, with their instinct to hold timidly to tradition-sanctioned ways, saying, as they do: 'Nay! We will follow what we found our fathers doing.' (Surah 31.21) and 'We found our fathers so as a people and we will stay the same as they'. (Surah 43.22.)

So the authority of reason was liberated from all that held it bound and from every kind of *taqlid* enslaving it, and thus restored to its proper dignity, to do its proper work in judgement and wisdom, always in humble submission to God alone and in conformity to His sacred law. Within its bounds there are no limits to its activity and no end to the researches it may pursue.

Hereby, and from all the foregoing, man entered fully into two great possessions relating to religion, which had for too long been denied him, namely independence of will and independence of thought and opinion. By these his humanity was perfected. By these he was put in the way of attaining that happiness which God had prepared for him in the gift of mind. A certain western philosopher of the recent past has said that the growth of civilisation in Europe rested on these two principles. People were not roused to action, nor minds to vigour and speculation until a large number of them came to know their right to exercise choice and to seek out facts with their own minds. Such assurance only came to them in the sixteenth century AD—a fact which the same writer traces to the influence of Islamic culture and the scholarship of Muslim peoples in that century.

Islam through its revealed scripture took away the impediment by which the leaders of the religions had precluded rational understanding of the heavenly books on the part of their possessors or adherents, in that they arrogated the exclusive right of interpretation to themselves, withholding from those who did not share their habit or go their way the opportunity of acquiring that sacred role.

Muhammad ʿAbduh, *The Theology of Unity*, trans. Ishaq Masaʿad and Kenneth Cragg (London: Allen and Unwin, 1966), pp. 126–28.

Namik Kemal: Extract from the Journal Hürriyet

Namik Kemal (1840–1888) was an Islamic modernist and, as a member of the
Young Ottomans, an avid supporter of constitutionalism in the Ottoman Empire. He wrote this article defending the idea of consultation between ruler and
ruled for *Hürriyet* (*Liberty*), a journal he and like-minded exiles published while
in London.

As for the imagined detrimental effects that would stem from the adoption of
the method of consultation, in reality these have no basis. First, it is said that
the establishment of a council of the people would violate the rights of the sultan. As was made clear in our introduction, the right of the sultan in our country is to govern on the basis of the will of the people and the principles of freedom. His title is "one charged with kingship" [*sahib al-mulk*], not "owner of
kingship" (*malik al-mulk*, a title reserved for God in the Qur'an, Sura 3, Verse
26]. His Imperial Majesty the sultan is heir to the esteemed Ottoman dynasty,
which established its state by protecting religion. It was thanks to this fact that
the [Ottoman sultan] became the cynosure of the people and the caliph of Islam. The religion of Muhammad rejects the absolutist claim to outright ownership [of the state] in the incontrovertible verse: "Whose is the kingdom today? God's, the One, the Omnipotent." [Qur'an, Sura 40, Verse 16]

Second, it is argued that the religious and cultural heterogeneity of the Ottoman lands and the ignorance of the people are reasons against this [the adoption of consultation]. In the gatherings of highly important personages, it is
asked how a people speaking seventy-two different tongues could be convened
in one assembly, and what kind of response would be given if [some of] the
deputies to be convened opposed dispatching troops to Crete because they
wished to protect the Greeks, or raised an objection to appropriations for holy
sites and pious foundations.

O my God! In all provinces there are provincial councils. Members from all
denominations serve in these councils, and all of them debate issues in the official language [Turkish]. How can anybody speak of linguistic heterogeneity
in light of this obvious fact? Is it supposed that a council of the people is a
seditious assembly whose members are absolutely independent, and whose
administration is not based on any rules? Once the fundamental principles and
the internal regulations of the assembly are issued, who would dare to protect
those, like the rebels of Crete, who desire to separate themselves from the integral nation? Who would dare to say a word about [Islamic] religious expenditures [purchasing non-Muslim land], in return for which [non-Muslim
communities] have acquired real estate valued several times more?

Let us come to the matter of ignorance. Montenegro, Serbia, and Egypt each
have councils of the people. Why should [our people's] ignorance prevent us
[from having a council], if it did not prevent these lands? Are we at a lower
level of culture than even the savages of Montenegro? Can it be that we could
not find people to become deputies, whose only necessary qualification will
be attaining the age of majority, when we can find people in the provinces to
become members of the State Council, membership in which is dependent upon
possessing perfected political skills?

O Ottoman liberals! Do not give any credit to such deceptive superstitions.
Give serious thought to the dangerous situation in which the nation finds it-

self today. While doing do, take into consideration the accomplishments that the opposition has already achieved. It will be obvious that the salvation of the state today is dependent upon the adoption of the method of consultation, and upon continuing the opposition aimed at achieving this method of administration. If we have any love for the nation, let us be fervent in advancing this meritorious policy. Let us be fervent so that we can move forward without delay.

Charles Kurzman, ed., *Modernist Islam, 1840–1940: A Sourcebook* (Oxford: Oxford University Press, 2002), pp. 147–48.

The Supplementary Fundamental Law of 7 October 1907

The Fundamental Law of 1906 and the Supplementary Fundamental Law of 1907 provided the foundation for the Persian constitution. The following excerpts come from the latter document.

In the Name of God the Merciful, the Forgiving

The Articles added to complete the Fundamental Laws of the Persian Constitution ratified by the late Shahinshah of blessed memory, Muzaffaru'd-Din Shah Qajar (may God illuminate his resting-place!) are as follows:

General Dispositions

Article 1. The official religion of Persia is Islam, according to the orthodox Jafari doctrine of the *Ithna Ashariyya* (Church of the Twelve Imams) which faith the Shah of Persia must profess and promote.

Article 2. At no time must any legal enactment of the Sacred National Consultative Assembly, established by the favor and assistance of His Holiness the Imam of the Age (may God hasten his glad Advent!), the favor of His Majesty the Shahinshah of Islam (may God immortalize his reign!), the care of the Proofs of Islam [the *mujtahids*] (may God multiply the like of them!), and the whole people of the Persian nation, be at variance with the sacred principles of Islam or the laws established by His Holiness the Best of Mankind [the Prophet Muhammad] (on whom and on whose household be the Blessings of God and His Peace).

It is hereby declared that it is for the learned doctors of theology (the *ulama*)—may God prolong the blessing of their existence!—to determine whether such laws as may be proposed are or are not conformable to the principles of Islam; and it is therefore officially enacted that there shall at all times exist a Committee composed of not less than five *mujtahids* or other devout theologians, cognizant also of the requirements of the age, [which committee shall be elected] in this manner. The ulama and Proofs of Islam shall present to the National Consultative Assembly the names of twenty of the ulama possessing the attributes mentioned above; and the members of the National Consultative Assembly shall, either by unanimous acclamation, or by vote, designate five or more of these, according to the exigencies of the time, and recognize these as

Members, so that they may carefully discuss and consider all matters proposed in the Assembly, and reject and repudiate, wholly or in part, any such proposal which is at variance with the Sacred Laws of Islam, so that it shall not obtain the title of legality. In such matters the decision of this Ecclesiastical Committee shall be followed and obeyed, and this article shall continue unchanged until the appearance of His Holiness the Proof of the Age (may God hasten his glad Advent!).

Article 3. The frontiers, provinces, departments and districts of the Persian Empire cannot be altered save in accordance with the Law.

Article 4. The capital of Persia is Teheran.

Article 5. The official colors of the Persian flag are green, white, and red, with the emblem of the Lion and the Sun.

Article 6. The lives and property of foreign subjects residing on Persian soil are guaranteed and protected, save in such contingencies as the laws of the land shall except.

Article 7. The principles of the Constitution cannot be suspended either wholly or in part.

Rights of the Persian Nation

Article 8. The people of the Persian Empire are to enjoy equal rights before the Law.

Article 9. All individuals are protected and safeguarded in respect to their lives, property, homes, and honor, from every kind of interference, and none shall molest them save in such case and in such way as the laws of the land shall determine.

Article 10. No one can be summarily arrested, save *flagrante delicto* in the commission of some crime or misdemeanor, except on the written authority of the President of the Tribunal of Justice, given in conformity with the Law. Even in such case the accused must immediately, or at latest in the course of the next twenty-four hours, be informed and notified of the nature of his offense.

Article 11. No one can be forcibly removed from the tribunal which is entitled to give judgment on his case to another tribunal.

Article 12. No punishment can be decreed or executed save in conformity with the Law.

Article 13. Every person's house and dwelling is protected and safeguarded, and no dwelling-place may be entered, save in such case and in such way as the Law has decreed.

Article 14. No Persian can be exiled from the country, or prevented from residing in any part thereof, or compelled to reside in any specified part thereof, save in such cases as the Law may explicitly determine.

Article 15. No property shall be removed from the control of its owner save by legal sanction, and then only after its fair value has been determined and paid.

Article 16. The confiscation of the property or possessions of any person under the title of punishment or retribution is forbidden, save in conformity with the Law.

Article 17. To deprive owners or possessors of the properties or possessions controlled by them on any pretext whatever is forbidden, save in conformity with the Law.

Article 18. The acquisition and study of all sciences, arts and crafts is free, save in the case of such as may be forbidden by the ecclesiastical law.

Article 19. The foundation of schools at the expense of the Government and the Nation, and compulsory instruction, must be regulated by the Ministry of Sciences and Arts, and all schools and colleges must be under the supreme control and supervision of that Ministry.

Article 20. All publications, except heretical books and matters hurtful to the perspicuous religion [of Islam] are free, and are exempt from the censorship. If, however, anything should be discovered in them contrary to the Press law, the publisher or writer is liable to punishment according to that law. If the writer be known, and be resident in Persia, then the publisher, printer and distributor shall not be liable to prosecution.

Article 21. Societies (*anjumans*) and associations (*ijtimaat*) which are not productive of mischief to Religion or the State, and are not injurious to good order, are free throughout the whole Empire, but members of such associations must not carry arms, and must obey the regulations laid down by the Law on this matter. Assemblies in the public thoroughfares and open spaces must likewise obey the police regulations.

Article 22. Correspondence passing through the post is safeguarded and exempt from seizure or examination, save in such exceptional cases as the Law lays down.

Article 23. It is forbidden to disclose or detain telegraphic correspondence without the express permission of the owner, save in such cases as the Law lays down.

Article 24. Foreign subjects may become naturalized as Persian subjects, but their acceptance or continuance as such, or their deprivation of this status, is in accordance with a separate law.

Article 25. No special authorization is required to proceed against government officials in respect of shortcomings connected with the discharge of their public functions, save in the case of Ministers, in whose case the special laws on this subject must be observed.

Powers of the Realm

Article 26. The powers of the realm are all derived from the people; and the Fundamental Law regulates the employment of those powers.

Article 27. The powers of the Realm are divided into three categories:
First, the legislative power, which is specially concerned with the making or amelioration of laws. This power is derived from His Imperial Majesty, the National Consultative Assembly, and the Senate, of which three sources each has the right to introduce laws, provided that the continuance thereof be dependent on their not being at variance with the standards of the ecclesiastical law, and on their approval by the Members of the two Assemblies, and the Royal ratification. The enacting and approval of laws with the revenue and expenditure of the kingdom are, however specially assigned to the National Consultative Assembly. The explanation and interpretation of the laws are, moreover, amongst the special functions of the above-mentioned Assembly.

Second, the judicial power, by which is meant the determining of rights. This power belongs exclusively to the ecclesiastical tribunals in matters connected with the ecclesiastical law, and to the civil tribunals in matter connected with ordinary law.

Third, the executive power, which appertains to the King—that is to say, the laws and ordinances—is carried out by the Ministers and State officials in the august name of His Imperial Majesty in such manner as the Law defines.

Article 28. The three powers above mentioned shall ever remain distinct and separate from one another.

Article 29. The special interests of each province, department and district shall be arranged and regulated, in accordance with special laws on this subject, by provincial and departmental councils (*anjumans*).

Rights of the Persian Throne

Article 39. No King can ascend the Throne unless, before his coronation, he appears before the National Consultative Assembly, in the presence of the Members of this Assembly and of the Senate, and of the Cabinet of Ministers, and repeat the following oath:

> "I take to witness the Almighty and Most High God, on the glorious Word of God, and by all that is most honored in God's sight, and do hereby swear that I will exert all my efforts to preserve the independence of Persia, safeguard and protect the frontiers of my Kingdom and the rights of my People, observe the Fundamental Laws of the Persian Constitution, rule in accordance with the established laws of Sovereignty, endeavor to promote the Jafari doctrine of the Church of the Twelve Imams, and will in all my deeds and actions consider God Most Glorious as present and watching me. I further ask aid from God, from Whom alone aid is derived, and seek help from the holy spirits of the Saints of Islam to render service to the advancement of Persia."

W. Morgan Shuster, *The Strangling of Persia: A Personal Narrative. Story of the European Diplomacy and Oriental Intrigue That Resulted in the Denationalization of Twelve Million Mohammedans* (New York: The Century Co., 1920), Appendix.

SUGGESTED READINGS

'Abduh, Muhammad. *The Theology of Unity.* Translated by Ishaq Musa and Kenneth Cragg. New York: Books for Libraries, 1980. Seminal work by one of the luminaries of the modernist movement in Islam.

Afary, Janet. *The Iranian Constitutional Revolution, 1906–1911: Grassroots Democracy, Social Democracy, and the Origins of Feminism.* New York: Columbia University Press, 1996. Revisionist account of the Persian Constitutional Revolution, with an emphasis on the processes and effects of popular mobilization.

Alavi, B. "Critical Writings on the Renewal of Iran." In *Qajar Iran: Political, Social, and Cultural Change,* edited by Edmond Bosworth and Carole Hillenbrand, 243–53. Edinburgh: University of Edinburgh Press, 1983. Explores the intellectual origins of defensive developmentalism in Persia.

Cole, Juan. *Colonialism and Revolution in the Middle East: Social and Cultural Origins of Egypt's 'Urabi Movement.* Princeton, N.J.: Princeton University Press, 1993. Comprehensive study of the social and cultural origins of the 'Urabi Revolt, along with a comparative analysis of revolution in the region.

Commins, David Dean. *Islamic Reform: Politics and Social Change in Late Ottoman Syria.* New York: Oxford University Press, 1990. Wonderfully written account of the development of Islamic modernist currents in Syria.

Davison, Roderic H. *Reform in the Ottoman Empire, 1856–1876.* New York: Gordian Press, 1973. Classic analysis of the final two decades of the Tanzimat Period.

Deringil, Selim. *The Well-Protected Domains: Ideology and the Legitimation of Power in the Ottoman Empire, 1876–1909.* London: I. B. Tauris, 1998. Path-breaking study looks at the changing sources for Ottoman legitimacy during the nineteenth century, including new sources of religious legitimation.

Dumont, Paul. "Said Bey—the Everyday Life of an Istanbul Townsman at the Beginning of the Twentieth Century." In *The Modern Middle East*, edited by Albert Hourani et al., 271–88. Berkeley: University of California Press, 1993. Said Bey's life shows an interesting parallel to that of Wasif Jawhariyyeh.

Fahmy, Khaled. *All the Pasha's Men: Mehmed Ali, His Army and the Making of Modern Egypt.* Cambridge, England: Cambridge University Press, 1997. Revisionist work on Mehmet Ali and state formation in Egypt, focusing on the central institution for that effort: the military.

Findley, Carter V. "The Advent of Ideology in the Islamic Middle East." *Studia Islamica* 15–16 (1982): 143–69, 147–80. While the theoretical underpinnings of this article are a bit old-fashioned, the argument is still convincing today.

Hanioglu, M. Sukru. *The Young Turks in Opposition.* New York: Oxford University Press, 1995. Detailed examination of the conspirators who took power in the Ottoman Empire in 1908 and the evolution of their ideas.

Hourani, Albert. *Arabic Thought in the Liberal Age: 1798–1939.* Cambridge, England: Cambridge University Press, 1983. Classic account of *nahda, salafi,* and Westernizing Arab intellectuals and intellectual trends of the long nineteenth century.

Karpat, Kemal H. *The Politicization of Islam: Reconstructing Identity, State, Faith, and Community in the Late Ottoman State.* Oxford: Oxford University Press, 2001. Dense but authoritative account of the transformation of the state and its impact on Islamic beliefs and institutions during last half-century of Ottoman rule.

Keddie, Nikki. *An Islamic Response to Imperialism: Political and Religious Writings of Sayyid Jamal al-Din "al-Afghani."* Berkeley: University of California Press, 1983. Analysis of the thought of Jamal al-Din, along with excerpts from his writings.

Kurzman, Charles. *Modernist Islam, 1840–1940: A Sourcebook.* Oxford: Oxford University Press, 2002. Good collection of documents from thinkers and activists who sought to make Islam compatible with the ideas of the modern age.

Makdisi, Ussama. *The Culture of Sectarianism: Community, History, and Violence in Nineteenth-Century Ottoman Lebanon.* Berkeley: University of California Press, 2000. Marvelous examination of the role played by European imperialism, Ottoman state policies, and local actors in creating religious boundaries and sparking violence in mid-century Lebanon.

Mitchell, Timothy. *Colonising Egypt.* Berkeley: University of California Press, 1991. Complex but rewarding analysis of the transformation of worldview in Egypt brought about by the combination of imperialism and the "self-colonization" of defensive developmentalism.

Owen, Roger. *The Middle East in the World Economy, 1800–1914.* London: Methuen, 1993. The gold standard of Middle East political/economic history in the nineteenth century.

Quataert, Donald. *The Ottoman Empire, 1700–1922.* Cambridge, England: Cambridge University Press, 2000. Concise yet excellent history of the empire after its initial expansion; particularly strong on economic and social history.

Robinson, Ronald. "Non-European Foundations of European Imperialism: Sketch for a Theory of Collaboration." In *Studies in the Theory of Imperialism*, edited by Roger Owen and Bob Sutcliffe, 117–42. London: Longman, 1972. Essay not only presents persuasive definition of imperialism, it also analyzes the reasons why imperialism took the various forms it did.

Rogan, Eugene. *Frontiers of State in the Late Ottoman Empire: Transjordan, 1850–1921.* Cambridge, England: Cambridge University Press, 1999. Excellent study of the application of defensive developmentalist policies in one of the frontier provinces of the Ottoman Empire.

Sohrabi, Nader. "Historicizing Revolutions: Constitutional Revolutions in the Ottoman Empire, Iran, and Russia, 1905–1908." *American Journal of Sociology* 100 (May 1995): 1383–1447. Thoughtful, theoretical comparison of three turn-of-the-century constitutional revolutions.

Tamari, Salim. "Jerusalem's Ottoman Modernity: The Times and Lives of Wasif Jawhariyyeh." *Jerusalem Quarterly File* 9 (2000): 5–34. Wonderful account of a musician and composer whose diary gives contemporary historians of the Middle East access to daily life in Jerusalem over the course of six decades.

Voll, John Obert. *Islam: Continuity and Change in the Modern World.* Boulder, Colo.: Westview Press, 1982. Probably the best overview of Islam throughout the world from the eighteenth century through the present day.

Part 3

WORLD WAR I AND THE MIDDLE EAST STATE SYSTEM

O n 28 June 1914, the heir to the Austrian throne, Archduke Franz Ferdinand, was shot by a Serbian nationalist while visiting the city of Sarajevo. With the backing of its ally, Germany, Austria presented an ultimatum to Serbia. The Austrians demanded that the Serbs rein in nationalist and anti-Austrian movements in their territory. Then, even after the Serbian government agreed to the ultimatum, the Austrians declared war.

While Germany was allied with Austria, Russia was allied with Serbia. The Russians feared that they would be at a disadvantage if war broke out and Germany had completed its military preparations before them. The Russian tsar thus ordered a general mobilization. Germany also mobilized and, to avoid fighting both Russia and France at the same time, decided to launch a knockout blow against France by striking at France through Belgium. Because Britain was committed by treaty to Belgian independence, it declared war on Germany. World War I had started.

When we think of World War I, we generally think of trench warfare on the Western Front in France. It is important to understand, however, that World War I was truly a world war. As a matter of fact, although the British and French referred to the war as the "Great War" until World War II, the Germans coined the phrase "world war" early on to describe the conflict. German strategists understood that the war was being waged among rival empires with worldwide interests. These empires depended on their colonial possessions to maintain their strategic position and economic well-being. Colonies were also indispensable for the French and British military effort, because both powers depended on them for manpower to replenish the depleted ranks of their armies. As a result, much of the globe was dragged into a war that had begun in Europe.

It has been estimated that the per capita losses in the Ottoman Empire and Persia were among the highest of all nations affected by the war. While Germany and France lost, respectively, about 9 and 11 percent of their populations as a result of the war, estimates for Ottoman losses run as high as almost 25 percent—approximately five million out of a population of twenty-one million. These casualties occurred both on and off the battlefield. As a matter of fact, four out of every five Ottoman citizens who died were noncombatants. Included among these were one to 1.5 million Armenians in the Ottoman Empire who died as a result of starvation and ethnic cleansing. While many Armenians believe the Ottoman government planned genocide at the highest levels, Turkish governments still claim that the tremendous losses suffered by the Ottoman Armenian community were an unfortunate accident of war. Although Persia was officially neutral in World War I, estimates put its per capita wartime losses in the same range as those incurred by the Ottoman Empire.

Many of the casualties suffered by the Ottoman Empire and Persia succumbed to famine. In Mount Lebanon, for example, famine killed upward of half the population. This tragedy still plays a central role in the Lebanese national narrative, which claims that the (Muslim) Ottoman government intentionally created the famine by requisitioning agricultural products and tools from the largely Christian population. While requisitioning certainly aggravated the problem, it was in fact the French and British blockade of eastern Mediterranean ports that had created it. In Persia, tribal insurrections, the collapse of the political order, and the destruction of infrastructure so devastated agricultural production that it did not reach pre-war levels again until 1925.

World War I thus had immediate, tragic consequences for the populations of the region. But the war had other consequences as well. World War I was the single most important *political* event in the history of the modern Middle East. This is not to say that the war changed everything. The great nineteenth-century transformation did more to revolutionize the social and economic relations of the inhabitants of the Middle East than did World War I. So did events during another period of immense change—the period stretching from the 1930s to the 1970s. Nevertheless, World War I did bring about a new political order in the region, one that has lasted to this very day. Four aspects of this new political order are particularly significant.

First, World War I brought about the creation of the current state system in the region. At the beginning of the war, the Ottoman Empire ruled, in law if not in deed, Anatolia, the Levant, Mesopotamia, Egypt, parts of the Arabian peninsula, and a small sliver of North Africa. By the early 1920s, Turkey was an independent republic, the Asiatic Arab provinces of the empire had been divided into what would become separate states, Egypt had evolved from an Ottoman territory to a quasi-independent state, and much of the Arabian peninsula had been united under the control of the dynasty of ibn Saud.

The ideological glue that bound together these states—and in some cases challenged them—was nationalism. After the war a variety of nationalist movements emerged in the territories previously controlled by the Ottoman Empire. Some of these movements were successful, others not. Nationalism itself was not new to the region. As the nineteenth-century Ottoman state extended its reach into the lives of its citizenry, many in the empire came to view themselves as part of expanded political communities, bound together by shared experiences and distinguishing traits. This is, after all, what nationalism is all about. But at the end of the war Ottoman nationalism—*osmanlilik*—was no longer an option. With the end of the Ottoman Empire, there no longer remained a political framework that could unite Arabs and Turks, the two largest ethno-linguistic groups housed within its boundaries. Nor was there a commonly accepted political framework to unite Arabs with one another. As a result, varieties of nationalism—Turkish nationalism, Arab nationalism, Syrian nationalism, Egyptian nationalism, and so on—spread throughout the region. Each nationalism claimed the exclusive right to command the loyalty and obedience of the citizens it sought to govern.

One other nationalist movement achieved success as a result of the war: Zionism. Zionism might be broadly defined as Jewish nationalism. Zionists believe that Jews have the same right to self-determination as other peoples. More often than not, they have placed the site of that self-determination in Palestine. Although Zionism was a product of the nineteenth century, World War I brought the international Zionist movement its first real diplomatic success. In November 1917, the Zionist movement achieved recognition by a world power. This recognition accorded Zionism enough prestige and drawing power to ensure that it would not follow in the footsteps of hundreds of other nationalist movements that had appeared briefly, then faded into obscurity. During the period between the two world wars, Jewish immigration to Palestine soared. This led to the first large-scale intercommunal violence between Jewish settlers and the indigenous inhabitants of the region. Thus, World War I not only marks a milestone on the road to the establishment of the State of Israel, it marks the beginnings of the Arab-Israeli conflict.

Finally, World War I brought about a political transformation in Persia. In the aftermath of wartime famine and political chaos, a military leader, Reza Khan, took control of Persia and established a political dynasty (if two rulers can be said to constitute a dynasty) that ruled until 1979. Reza Khan, who later adopted the title Reza Shah, and his son, Muhammad Reza Shah, centralized and strengthened the power of the state to an extent never previously accomplished in Persia. Their authoritarian but developmentalist strategy continues to influence economic, social, and political life in Iran to the present day.

Eleven

State-Building by Decree

The states that emerged in the Middle East in the wake of World War I were created in two ways. In the Levant and Mesopotamia, the site of present-day Syria, Lebanon, Palestine/Israel, Jordan, and Iraq, France and Britain constructed states. Guided by their own interests and preconceptions, the great powers partitioned what had once been the Ottoman Empire and created states where states had never before existed. The wishes of the inhabitants of those territories counted for little when it came to deciding their political future.

In contrast, Turkey, Iran, Saudi Arabia, and Egypt emerged as independent states as a result of anti-imperialist struggle (Turkey), *coup d'etat* (Iran), revolution (Egypt), and conquest (Saudi Arabia). In each of these cases, the national myth recounting the deeds of a heroic leader or founding generation created a firmer foundation for nation-building than that enjoyed by the states created in the Levant and Mesopotamia.

To understand the origins of the states that emerged in the Levant and Mesopotamia, it is necessary to return to World War I. World War I drew the final curtain on the century of relative peace that had begun in Europe in the wake of the Napoleonic Wars. But, in addition to marking the end of the nineteenth-century European order, World War I marks a turning point in the relations between Europe and the Middle East.

During the second half of the nineteenth century, European powers acting in concert had taken responsibility for resolving the various crises brought on by the Eastern Question. True, European nations nibbled at the edges of the Ottoman Empire. The French picked away at North Africa, the British were ensconced in Egypt, and the Italians invaded the territory that is contemporary Libya in 1911. Nevertheless, the concert of Europe provided a protective umbrella sheltering the Ottoman Empire from total dismantlement.

There is no telling what the future of the Ottoman Empire might have been had the concert of Europe remained in place. However, the unification of Germany in 1871 disrupted the European balance of power and crippled the ability of European states to act together on issues of common interest. By the beginning of the twentieth century, the concert of Europe no longer existed. Instead, on the eve of World War I European states divided themselves into two alliances. Britain, France, and Russia (and, after 1917, the

Sweaters, Sleeves, and the Crimean War

During the period between the end of the Napoleonic Wars and the rise of Germany, the concert of European powers went to war only once to resolve a crisis originating in the Middle East: the Crimean War (1853–1856). The origins of the war were so murky that after its conclusion the government of one of the principal combatants, Great Britain, appointed a commission to determine what, in fact, it had been all about. In part the war began as a result of great power rivalry within the Ottoman Empire: The Orthodox Russians and the Catholic French quarreled over access to holy sites in Palestine. In part it began because of Russia's attempt to extend its patronage to all Orthodox Christians in the Balkans, even those who resided in the Ottoman Empire. When the Russians moved troops into Ottoman Moldavia and Wallachia (in present-day Romania), the Ottomans, British, French, and Piedmontese (!) launched a military campaign to drive them out. They chose the Crimean peninsula, of all places, as the site on which to challenge the Russians. After a truly abysmal showing by both sides, including the famous (and irresponsible) charge of the light brigade, the Russians backed down. In the wake of the war, the Ottomans were admitted into the concert of Europe. Henceforth, the European powers promised to act together to guarantee the independence and territorial integrity of the Ottoman Empire.

However important its diplomatic and military effects, the Crimean War also deserves notice because of its impact on men's fashions. If not for the war, there would be no raglan overcoats or sleeves, named for Fitzroy James Henry Lord Raglan, the British field marshall in charge of the Crimea campaign. Nor would there be cardigan sweaters, named for James Brudenell, the seventh earl of Cardigan, who led the infamous charge of the light brigade. And lest we forget, there is the balaklava, named for the site of the famous battle in which the light brigade charged and the "thin red line"— the 93rd Highlander Regiment—held its position against a Russian attack. Balaklavas are knit caps that drape over the wearer's face, leaving only the eyes and mouth exposed. They remain the headgear of choice for bank robbers and terrorists the world over.

United States) formed the core of the entente powers. Germany, Austria, and the Ottoman Empire formed the core of the Central Powers. Other states in Europe and elsewhere also signed on to one alliance or the other.

The Ottoman Empire joined the Central Powers for several reasons. Not only did Germany enjoy extensive political and economic influence in the empire, the empire was unlikely to join any alliance that included its archrival, Russia. In addition, the Austrians, anxious to control Ottoman ambitions in the Balkans, actively solicited the empire's participation in the war on their side. On the other hand, the entente powers did not try very hard to attract the Ottomans to their side. Because the entente powers assumed that the war would be short, they believed that including the Ottoman Empire in their alliance would not affect its outcome. They also believed that attracting Greece and Italy into their alliance was more important (both countries laid claims to Ottoman territory) and that the Ottomans would make up their minds about which alliance to join based on the progress of the war.

As soon as it became clear that the war would not be over quickly, each of the entente powers began to maneuver to be in a position to claim the spoils it desired in the Middle East in the event of victory. Russia had its eye on two prizes. The Russian government hoped to realize its long-standing dream of acquiring a warm water port by laying claim to the Turkish Straits. What made this dream all the more compelling was the fact that almost 40 percent of Russia's exports passed through the straits. Russia also had interests in the heartland of the Ottoman Empire, particularly Ottoman Palestine. Not only were sites holy to the Orthodox Church located there, Orthodox Christians looked to Russia to protect their interests against Catholics, whose interests were backed by France. France, on the other hand, claimed to have "historic rights" in the region of the Ottoman Empire that lies in present-day Syria and Lebanon. France based this claim both on its role as protector of Lebanon's Maronite Christian population and on its economic interests in the region, such as investments in railroads and in silk production.

In contrast with the single-mindedness of the Russians and the French, the British were a bit flustered about the spoils of war they sought from the Ottomans. After all, until the eve of war, Britain had been the staunchest defender of Ottoman integrity. The British government thus appointed a special committee to determine its war aims in the Middle East. The committee was made up of representatives from a variety of ministries, from the foreign office to the India and war offices. Each of these ministries had different preoccupations. As a result, the committee returned with a laundry list of demands. For the most part, this list focused on Britain's long-standing obsession with the protection of the sea routes to India and on ensuring postwar security for British investment and trade in the region.

Starting in 1915, the entente powers began negotiating secret treaties that pledged mutual support for the territorial claims made by themselves or their would-be allies. By negotiating these treaties, entente powers hoped to confirm those claims, attract to their alliance outlying states such as Italy and Greece, and, as the war went on, keep the alliance intact by promising active combatants a payoff at the close of hostilities. For example, the British assumed that continued Russian pressure on Germany was the key to entente victory in Europe. To prevent Russia from signing a separate peace with the Central Powers and withdrawing from the war, the British and French negotiated a deal with the Russians. According to what became known as the Constantinople Agreement, Britain and France recognized Russia's claims to the Turkish Straits and the city that overlooked them, Istanbul. In return for their generosity, France got recognition for its claims to Syria (a vague geographical unit never defined in the agreement), and Britain got recognition for its claims to territory in Persia.

What makes the Constantinople Agreement important is not what it promised. Russia never got the straits nor did it remain in the war until the bitter end. France and Britain enjoyed only temporary control of the territories promised them. What makes the agreement important is that it established the principle that entente powers had a right to compensation for fighting their enemies and that at least part of this compensation should come in the form of territory carved out of the Middle East. Other secret treaties soon followed: the Treaty of London, the Sykes-Picot Agreement, the Treaty of Saint-Jean de Maurienne. All these treaties applied the principle of compensation. Sometimes the treaties stipulated that compensation should take the form of direct European control over territories belonging to the Ottoman Empire. At other times, the entente powers masked their ambitions by promising each other rights to establish or maintain protectorates or to organize zones of indirect control. In those zones, one European state would enjoy economic and political rights not granted to other states, but would not rule the zone per se. That would be the function of local power brokers who would receive the support of the European state in charge. In yet another attempt to arrive at a formula that would satisfy all entente powers, the alliance at one point committed itself to establishing an "international zone" in Jerusalem. This was done mainly to relieve Russian anxieties by making sure that no Christian group would be in a position to deny another access to the holy sites.

Britain not only initiated or signed on to secret agreements, it also made pledges to local or nationalist groupings to assure their support or, at least, quiescence. For example, the British offered to shelter ibn Saʿud within a "veiled (secret) protectorate" if he would only remain out of trouble. Far more important for the story of state-building in the Levant and Mesopotamia were two other pledges that most historians regard as contradictory, despite the efforts of diplomats to square the circle after the war. In 1915, the British made contact with an Arabian warlord based in Mecca, Sharif Husayn. Husayn promised to delegate his son, Amir Faysal, to launch a revolt against the Ottoman Empire. In exchange, the British promised Husayn gold and guns and, once the war ended, the right to establish an ambiguously defined Arab "state or states" in the predominantly Arab territories of the Ottoman Empire. The negotiations between Sharif Husayn and the British led to the famous Arab Revolt, guided by the even more famous British colonel T. E. Lawrence (Lawrence of Arabia). British military strategists championed the revolt because they thought it a useful way to harass the Ottomans and compel them to overextend their forces. They also believed the revolt would shore up the right flank of a British army invading Ottoman territories from Egypt. The leaders of the revolt, taking the British at their word, viewed it as a means to achieve Arab unity and independence from the Ottoman Empire. As we shall see later, the revolt was more successful in creating the legend of heroic Arab struggle and imperialist betrayal, in spreading the fame of T. E. Lawrence, and in advancing the careers of Peter O'Toole and Alec Guiness than it was in fostering Arab unity and independence.

While the negotiations that led to the Arab Revolt were held in private, the British government pledged support to another group openly on the pages of the *Times* of London. According to the Balfour Declaration of November 1917, the British endorsed the Zionist goal of establishing a "national home" in Palestine for Jews around the world. Historians disagree as to exactly why the British would make such a promise. Some assert that the British did so for strategic reasons. Because the Jewish settlers in Palestine would be far outnumbered by Muslim Arabs, they would remain dependent on the British and be more than willing to help the British preserve the security of the nearby Suez Canal. Others attribute the Balfour Declaration to a British overestimation of Jewish power in the United States and Russia. Britain wanted to maintain support in the United States for the entente side. It also wanted to keep Russia, which had just experienced a revolution, in the war. Thinking that Jews had a great deal of influence over the American president, Woodrow Wilson, and within the Bolshevik movement, the British figured that they had nothing to lose. As we know, the British underestimated the effects of the Balfour Declaration. Their wartime promise had consequences far beyond those they anticipated at the time.

While the secret agreements and pledges set a number of diplomatic and political precedents, they were relatively ineffective in determining the postwar settlement. There were a number of reasons why this was the case. First, the agreements were both ambiguous and mutually contradictory. Take the issue of Palestine, for example. According to the French reading of one of the secret treaties, the Sykes-Picot Agreement, Syria was promised to France and Palestine was part of Syria. According to the Russian reading of the same agreement, Palestine was simply the territory surrounding Jerusalem and Jerusalem was to be placed under international control. According to the Arab reading of the letters Sharif Husayn exchanged with the British government before the Arab Revolt, Palestine was to be part of the Arab "state or states." And then, of course, there was the Balfour Declaration.

Changed circumstances also muddied the waters of the postwar settlement. For example, during the war Britain had launched attacks on the Ottoman Empire from India and Egypt. At the close of the war British troops occupied Iraq and parts of the Levant. This gave them leverage in postwar negotiations with other victorious powers. At the same time, the Russian Revolution brought to power a government that, in theory at least, opposed the imperialist designs of the tsarist government. The new Bolshevik government of Russia not only renounced the claims made by its predecessor, it embarrassed the other entente powers by publishing the texts of the secret agreements signed by Russia. Furthermore, the Bolsheviks were ideologically committed to atheism and thus had no desire make an issue about Orthodox access to Christian holy sites. In other words, now there was no need to "internationalize" Jerusalem. Finally, a nationalist revolt broke out in Turkey. This prevented the Greeks, Italians, and French from dividing Anatolia as they had arranged in the secret treaties.

One last obstacle to implementing the secret agreements came from the United States. When the United States entered the war on the side of the entente powers, President Woodrow Wilson announced his intention to make his Fourteen Points the basis of a post-war peace. These points included such benign items as freedom of navigation on seas and free trade ("as far as possible"), but they also included two items that made European diplomats wince: the right of peoples to self-determination and an end to secret agreements. Indigenous nationalist leaders in particular seized on Wilson's call for an end to secret agreements and the right of the colonized to determine their own future. Increasingly frustrated British and French diplomats humored Wilson as best they could while they seethed in private. French president and foreign minister Georges Clemenceau reportedly scoffed at the Fourteen Points, remarking, "Even the good Lord contented himself with only ten commandments, and we should not try to improve on them." Nevertheless, Wilson had let the genie out of the bottle, and delegates to the peace conference ending the war were beset by Kurds, Arabs, Zionists, Armenians, and others, all demanding their right to self-determination.

Meeting in Paris, entente peace negotiators attempted to unravel the conflicting claims of their governments and lay the foundations for the postwar world. The negotiators agreed to establish a League of Nations to provide a permanent structure in which international disputes might be resolved peacefully. Although the original call for a league can be found in Woodrow Wilson's Fourteen Points, the United States did not join it once it had been created. Nor, initially, were Germany or the newly established Union of Soviet Socialist Republics members. This weakened the league from its inception. But while the league failed miserably in its main mission—its peacemaking activities were unfortunately interrupted by the onset of World War II—its charter did sanction French and British designs for the Levant and Mesopotamia. Article 22 of the charter dealt directly with the region, establishing the so-called mandates system there:

> To those colonies and territories which as a consequence of the last war have ceased to be under the sovereignty of the states which formerly governed them and which are inhabited by peoples not yet able to stand by themselves under the strenuous conditions of the modern world, there should be applied the principle that the well-being and development of such peoples form a sacred trust of civilization and that securities for the performance of that trust should be embodied in the covenant. The best method of giving practical effect to this principle should be entrusted to advanced nations who by reason of their resources, their experience, or their geographical position can best undertake this responsibility. . . . Certain communities formerly belonging to the Turkish empire have reached a stage of development where their existence as independent states can be provisionally recognized subject to the rendering of assistance by a mandatory [power] until such time as they are able to stand alone,

the wishes of the communities must be a principle consideration in the selection of the mandatory.

Accordingly, after World War I, France got the mandate for the territory that now includes Syria and Lebanon while Britain got the mandate for the territory that now includes Israel, the occupied territories, Jordan, and Iraq. The phrase "territory that is now Syria, Lebanon, Israel, the occupied territories, Jordan, and Iraq" is used here deliberately. The states known as Syria, Lebanon, Israel, Jordan, and Iraq had never before existed, but were created under the auspices of France and Britain.

Contrary to the Charter of the League of Nations, the inhabitants of the region were never seriously consulted about their future. For example, the elected parliament of Syria that met after the war, the Syrian General Congress, declared that it wanted Syria to be independent and unified. By unity, they meant that Syria should include territories of present-day Syria, Lebanon, Israel/Palestine, and Jordan. If Syria had to have a mandatory power overseeing it, a majority of the representatives declared, it should be the United States. Their second choice was Great Britain. For the representatives to the congress, France was unacceptable as a mandatory power. Nevertheless, a geographically diminished Syria went to France as a mandate.

Overall, the mandates system was little more than thinly disguised imperialism. Although they had to report their activities to a special committee of the League of Nations, the European mandatory powers had absolute rights over the internal affairs of their mandates, both economically and politically. They severed and joined the territories under their control as they wished. The British divided the Palestine mandate into two separate regions, one that would become Israel and the occupied territories and another that would become Jordan. They also created Iraq by joining together three former Ottoman provinces. For their part the French created what they thought would be a permanent Christian enclave on the coast by severing Lebanon from Syria. They included in Lebanon just enough territory to make it economically viable and strategically useful, but not enough to threaten Christian dominance—at least for the time being. They then divided and redivided the territory of present-day Syria into up to six ethnically and religiously distinct territorial ministates. While the French soon abandoned their ministate experiment, the local leaders they supported in each of them would remain a thorn in the side of Syrian governments for almost half a century.

Unfortunately for the British and French, implementing the mandates system was not as easy as planning it. Although Britain and France played the major role in the creation of states in the Middle East, a third actor was involved as well—the Hashemite family of Sharif Husayn of Mecca. In the wake of the Arab Revolt, troops under the command of Amir Faysal had occupied Damascus. Immediately after the war, Faysal tried to assume administrative control over the surrounding region as well. The French, supported by the League of Nations, opposed Faysal's pretensions and sent an army to Damascus to depose him. The British reacted somewhat passively to the French dismissal of their client. Fearing that only France stood between them and a resurgent Germany, the British had no desire to jeopardize their relations with France over some trivial problem in the Middle East. As British prime minister Lloyd George put it, "The friendship of France is worth ten Syrias." But by now the British had another problem on their hands.

After the French deposed Faysal, another son of Sharif Husayn, Amir 'Abdallah, began marching north from his home in Mecca to avenge his brother's humiliation. The British now faced two problems: what to do with their wartime ally, Faysal, and what to do about 'Abdallah, who was threatening to make war on their more important wartime ally, France. The British persuaded 'Abdallah to remain in the town of Amman, which was then a small caravan stop on the route to Syria, while they called a conference to determine what to do about the worsening situation in the Middle East. At the Cairo Conference of 1921, the British came up with a solution. To divert 'Abdallah, the British divided their Palestine mandate into two parts and offered their new protégé the territory east of the Jordan River as a principality. The territory lying across the Jordan River was first called, appropriately enough, Trans-Jordan. 'Abdallah made Amman his capital. No longer part of Palestine, the British closed this territory to Zionist immigration. After independence in 1946, Trans-Jordan became the Hashemite Kingdom of Jordan. Jordan has been ruled by the descendants of 'Abdallah ever since, and the present king of Jordan is his great-grandson. The territory west of the Jordan River (Cis-Jordan, or "this side of the Jordan") retained the name Palestine. Although also a mandate, the British ruled Palestine like a crown colony until they withdrew in 1948. This territory comprises present-day Israel and the occupied Palestinian territories.

While the British thus solved the problem of 'Abdallah, they still had the problem of Faysal to contend with. Once again, the British came up with an inventive solution. They granted Faysal the throne of Iraq, a realm they created by joining together the Ottoman provinces of Basra, Baghdad, and Mosul. The descendants of Faysal ruled Iraq until they were overthrown in 1958.

On paper, Iraq appeared to be a good idea. The northern territory of Mosul had oil, which would ensure the economic viability of the state and a ready supply of the valuable commodity for the mandatory power. Basra in the south provided the territory with an outlet to the Persian Gulf. The territory in between, irrigated by the Tigris and Euphrates rivers, includes rich farmland that the British planned to use as a granary for its colony in India. Ironically, however, the very mandates system that had created Iraq also conspired against its full political and economic development. In this, Iraq was not exceptional. The mandates system also frustrated the full political and economic development of Lebanon, Syria, and Jordan.

The League of Nations had entrusted the territories of the Ottoman Empire to Britain and France so that the European states could prepare their charges for self-rule. Whatever the charter had said about "the sacred trust of civilization," however, Britain and France accepted the mandates so that

Drawing Boundaries

In the aftermath of World War I, French and British diplomats created states and the boundaries separating them where none had previously existed. Sometimes, their decisions seem to lack any rationale. If you look at a map of Jordan, for example, you will see a strange indentation in its eastern border with Saudi Arabia. There is no reasonable explanation for that indentation. No river runs through the area, no mountain range forms a natural division between the two states.

Jordan (or Trans-Jordan, as it was then called) was created at the Cairo Conference of 1921. Winston Churchill, who presided over the conference as the British colonial secretary, later bragged that at the conference he had "created Jordan with a stroke of the pen one Sunday afternoon." But why did it take the shape it did?

Churchill was a man who enjoyed a good meal, which, more often than not, meant heavy food topped off with brandy or whiskey. According to legend, Churchill began to draw the boundary dividing Jordan from Saudi Arabia after a particularly bounteous repast. Midway through drawing the boundary line, Churchill hiccuped and his pen deviated from the straightedge. Hence, according to the legend, the strange indentation in Jordan's border—and hence the reason why some Jordanians call the indentation "Churchill's hiccup" to this very day. An apocryphal story, to be sure, but one that speaks to the artificial nature of the states created through the mandates system.

they could retain control over those areas in which they felt they had vital interests. The mandatory powers thus divided and combined territory into states to suit their own interests, rarely giving much thought to ensuring their mandates were both economically *and* politically viable. For example, the invention of Jordan solved a political problem for the British but created an economic nightmare: a country with virtually no economic resources. Since its earliest days, Jordan's economic survival has depended on the kindness of strangers. Foreign subsidies have maintained Jordan since 1921, when the British began paying ʿAbdallah a yearly stipend of five thousand pounds. Foreign subsidies increased steadily for the next half century, and by 1979 they provided over 50 percent of government revenue (the figure now is a little over 20 percent).

Iraq presents us with a different story. From its inception, the territory of Iraq has included populations with significant ethnic and religious differences. As we have seen, these differences took on new significance during the nineteenth century. It was then that the boundaries separating religious and ethnic communities became more rigid and religious and ethnic affiliation became the basis for claiming shares in the political system. Religious and ethnic affiliation has been associated with political claims ever since. A majority of those living in mandated Iraq were Shi'i Arab, although the ruling elites—Faysal and his cronies—were Sunni Arab. The northern area, Mosul, was inhabited in large measure by Sunni Kurds, many of whom would have preferred self-rule. As a result, Iraq was notorious for its political instability. Beginning in 1933, when Iraqi troops massacred a Christian group in the north called Assyrians, it also became notorious for dealing with political instability through violence. British policy makers well understood the problem they had created. Realizing that Iraqi leaders would have to continue to depend on British assistance and the Royal Air Force to remain in power, the British granted Iraq independence in 1932, ahead of the other mandated territories that were better prepared to withstand "the strenuous conditions of the modern world."

The mandates system also stacked the deck against economic development in the mandated territories. European investors were reluctant to invest in territories their governments were contractually bound to surrender. In addition, according to the terms under which the League of Nations granted mandates, mandatory powers could neither apply tariffs nor take any measures that could be construed as restricting trade. As a result, Europe maintained a colonial-style system of trade with the region, buying raw materials and agricultural products while dumping finished goods on unprotected markets. Industrial development languished in most of the region until World War II, when submarine warfare in the Mediterranean prevented European manufactures from reaching the region and the Allies promoted local industries to meet their wartime needs.

The thinly disguised colonialism that underlay the mandates system and led to the creation of modern Lebanon, Syria, Jordan, and Iraq affected the legitimacy of those states as well. State-building in the Levant and Mesopotamia was initiated by victorious European powers rather than by the inhabitants of the region. No Washington or Garibaldi forged nations through wars of national liberation. No Valley Forge became a mythic symbol of nation-building. No indigenous Bismarck or Napoleon stirred patriotism through conquest. States in the Levant and Mesopotamia were plotted on maps by diplomats and received their independence in stages, usually after painstaking treaty negotiations. The correspondence between patriotic sentiments and the national boundaries of newly independent states was, at best, sporadic, and many among the Arab population of the region saw the division of the Levant and Mesopotamia into separate nations as debilitating and unnatural. Many still do. This is one of the reasons for the emergence and persistence of pan-Arabism in the region, the sentiment that stresses the unity of all Arabs and, in its political form, calls for the obliteration of national boundaries separating them. This is also one of the reasons why many in the region—even those who should and do know better—could cast Saddam Hussein in the role of an Arab Bismarck after his invasion of Kuwait in 1990.

However much pan-Arabism might resonate with the populations of the Levant and Mesopotamia region, however, it must be stressed that years of state-building have strengthened national allegiances and have transformed pan-Arabism from a blueprint for political action to a nebulous sentiment. This can be seen by tracking the fate of Arab unity schemes, particularly those involving Syria, the "beating heart of the Arab nation." From 1946 through the 1960s, Syrian politicians seeking to exploit a popular issue proposed no less than nine schemes to unite Syria with various other countries of the region. Since the 1960s, there have been only three such proposals, and none of them recently. Throughout the region, crowds that had once demonstrated in support of Arab unification now march in support of the right of Palestinians to establish their own state, or in support of the Iraqi state's battle against what has been widely perceived to be foreign aggression. However rickety the foundations upon which it was built, the state system established in the Levant and Mesopotamia in the wake of World War I has held for over three-quarters of a century.

Twelve

State-Building by
Revolution and Conquest

When the League of Nations established the mandates system in the Middle East, its member states had no intention of applying the system beyond the Levant and Mesopotamia. Nor did they have the capacity to do so. Outside this region, in Anatolia, Egypt, Persia (officially called Iran since the 1930s), and Saudi Arabia, indigenous nationalist movements and nation-builders established states through revolution, conquest, and anti-imperialist struggle.

The establishment of Saudi Arabia was discussed in Chapter 8. Suffice it to say that in 1924, seven months after Husayn (the father of Faysal and ʿAbdallah) had himself proclaimed the caliph of all Muslims, ibn Saʿud kicked the unfortunate monarch out of western Arabia, thus continuing the run of bad Hashemite luck. Ibn Saʿud then united eastern and western Arabia into a single kingdom and, in 1932, officially proclaimed the formation of Saudi Arabia. The period between the two world wars was a particularly fortuitous one for the kingdom, for on the eve of World War II oil was discovered there, making this relative backwater of the Arab world into a player in international affairs. Until then, however, the attention of the great European powers was focused elsewhere in the region.

Egypt

World War I had both political and economic consequences for Egypt. Although Britain had occupied Egypt since 1882, Egypt had been legally part of the Ottoman Empire until World War I. In December 1914, after the outbreak of war, Britain declared Egypt a protectorate, ending Ottoman sovereignty once and for all.

British rule in Egypt had become increasingly unpopular over the course of its history, and by the end of World War I the British had managed to alienate virtually all segments of the Egyptian population. The peculiar circumstances created by the war did little to soothe Egyptian public opinion. During the war, the British established controls over the marketing of cotton, thereby alienating the influential stratum of large landowners. Wartime inflation devastated the living standards of civil servants, the urban poor, and even the peasantry. Peasants also suffered from famine during the war. The complaints of Egyptians found voice among an educated stratum of intellectuals and activists who, at the close of the war, found release from the constraints of wartime repression.

All that was needed to ignite the tensions between much of the Egyptian population and the British occupiers was a spark. That spark was touched off in November 1918, when a delegation of Egyptian politicians, testing the limits of Woodrow Wilson's promise of "self-determination of peoples," petitioned the British high commissioner in Cairo for permission to go to Paris to represent the Egyptian population at the peace conference. The leader of this group was Sa'd Zaghlul. Although born into a family of mid-level peasants, Zaghlul had married well (his wife was a daughter of an Egyptian prime minister). He procured a number of important positions in the Egyptian government, including those of minister of education, minister of justice, and vice president of the legislative assembly. During the war, Zaghlul used the last position to organize nationalist committees throughout Egypt.

When the British arrested and deported Zaghlul and his colleagues for their presumption, the committees founded during the war sprang into action. Demonstrations and strikes broke out throughout Egypt in the spring of 1919. They spread from students and labor activists to artisans and civil servants and even the urban poor of Cairo. Peasants, fearing imminent starvation, attacked the rail lines by which scarce food supplies might be taken to distant cities. Alongside the peasants were many rural landowners, who not only had complaints of their own but who feared social upheaval if they stood on the sidelines. The revolt—called by Egyptian nationalist historians the 1919 Revolution—lasted two months before the British were able to put it down by force.

In response to the uprising, the British government appointed a commission under Lord Milner to investigate its causes and to propose a solution. The Milner Commission concluded that Britain could not hope to keep direct control of Egypt and that British interests could best be maintained in Egypt if Britain gave Egypt conditional independence. Only then could the British hope to rein in the most vehement Egyptian nationalists. Thus, in 1922, the British granted Egypt conditional independence. The treaty they imposed on the Egyptians was a disappointment to Egyptian nationalists. The British asserted their right to control Egyptian defense and foreign policy, protect minorities and the Suez Canal, maintain their role (alongside the Egyptians) in the governance of the Sudan to the south, and safeguard the capitulations. Independence indeed. Making conditional independence into unconditional independence would be the focus of nationalist efforts for the next three decades, even after the British sought to placate Egyptian public opinion by negotiating a new treaty on the eve of World War II.

Independence was also hampered by the strange system of governance in Egypt that pit three powerbrokers against each other. On the one hand was the Wafd, the main nationalist party. The Wafd had been founded by Sa'd Zaghlul not as a party but as the platform representing the aspirations of the Egyptian nation. This can be seen in the name itself, which means "delegation" in Arabic and refers to the delegation Zaghlul had put together to represent Egypt at the Paris negotiations. In the contentious environment of interwar Egypt, however, the Wafd was soon joined by a number of other parties also seeking to become the platform for Egyptian aspirations. Arrayed against the Wafd were the king (still a descendant of Mehmet Ali) and the British ambassador. Although the Wafd was extremely popular, both the king and the British conspired against unfettered parliamentary rule. Ultimate power rested, of course, in the hands of the British. The British only allowed the Wafd to take power when it needed to exploit the party's popularity in times of crisis. The first time was in 1936, when the British, fearing the rise of the original "axis of evil," needed to negotiate a new, less provocative treaty with the Egyptians. The second time was in 1942 when, in the midst of World War II, German field marshall Erwin Rommel's troops threatened Egypt.

In the decades following World War I, the mainstream nationalist movement in Egypt did not advocate radical social change. Indeed, the mainstream nationalist movement in Egypt represented the interests of two groups in particular that feared unbridled democratic rule and social revolution: large landowners and members of the upwardly mobile intelligentsia. Neither group rejected Europe or European ideas, and their brand of nationalism demonstrated the role European conceptions of nation and state had in shaping their worldview. In 1914, one of Zaghlul's more articulate colleagues put the mission of the nationalist movement as follows:

> The wave of civilization has come to us with all its virtues and vices, and we must accept it without resisting it. All that we can do is to Egyptianize the good that it carries and narrow down the channels through which the evil can run. We must possess that civilization as it is, but not try to control it.

By narrowing their concerns to independence and by representing the interests of layers of the population that were anything but plentiful, the nationalist movement failed to encompass or even control the totality of the Egyptian public sphere. This left the door open to a host of other political movements that posed alternatives to the mainstream nationalist movement. A communist party, capitalizing on the success of the revolution in Russia and resurgent labor activism, opened its doors in the early 1920s. Toward the end of the decade, that apotheosis of modern Islamist organizations, the Egyptian Muslim Brotherhood, began recruiting its first members in the Suez Canal city of Isma'iliyya. Like the mainstream nationalists, the Muslim Brotherhood had also made its peace with the modern nation-state system and even nationalism. Like the nationalists, the Muslim Brotherhood claimed to be the true voice of Egypt. According to its founder, Hassan al-Banna,

> The love for one's country and place of residence is a feeling hallowed both by the commands of nature and the injunctions of Islam. . . . The desire to work for the restoration of the honour and independence of one's country is a feeling approved by the Qur'an and by the Muslim Brotherhood. . . . However, the love for party-strife and the bitter hatred of one's political opponents with all of its destructive consequences, is a false kind of nationalism. It does not benefit anybody, not even those who practise it.

On the other hand, the brotherhood articulated its message in a language that differed dramatically from that used by the mainstream nationalist movement. It was able to speak to layers of the population left unmoved by or alienated from the mainstream nationalist movement.

Turkey

In both Turkey and Iran, leaders seeking to centralize their authority and "modernize" their states took power in the wake of World War I. At the end of the war, the entente powers occupied Istanbul and held the Ottoman sultan virtual prisoner. In 1920, the government of the sultan signed the Treaty of Sèvres, which formally severed the connection between Turkish and non-Turkish regions of the Ottoman Empire. It also divided western Anatolia among Greece, Italy, and France. While all three states sent armies of occupation to affirm their claims, Greek ambitions in Anatolia were particularly expansive. Greek nationalists were inspired by what they called the *megali idea* (grand idea). They sought to unite all Greeks from the Mediterranean islands to the Black Sea coast into one state, thereby restoring the glory of the Byzantine Empire. They thus sought to snatch as much territory in Anatolia as possible. But Greek ambitions were also particularly obnoxious to many Turks who chafed at the idea that a former vassal state would now attempt to turn the tables on its former overlord. Throughout unoccupied Anatolia, popular "Committees for the Defense of Rights" sprang up to resist the occupiers. To restore order, the government in Istanbul sent General Mustafa Kemal east to suppress the committees.

Mustafa Kemal hailed from Salonika, formerly part of the Ottoman Empire but now the second largest city in Greece. Trained in various military academies, he fought for the Ottomans in Libya (against the Italians) and in the Balkan Wars (against the Serbs, Bulgarians, and Greeks). He achieved his greatest fame as a military commander at the Battle of Gallipoli in 1915. The entente powers conceived the Gallipoli campaign as a quick stroke to knock the Ottoman Empire out of World War I by seizing the peninsula south of Istanbul, then marching on the Ottoman capital. Rather than a quick stroke, the battle degenerated into trench warfare that was catastrophic even by World War I standards. Between one-third and one-half of the British, Australian, New Zealand, French, and Ottoman combatants were killed, wounded, or succumbed to disease. Nevertheless, the Ottomans repulsed the invaders and Mustafa Kemal emerged from the battle a national hero.

Instead of suppressing the Committees for the Defense of Rights, Mustafa Kemal took charge of the rebellion. In a costly war that lasted two years, he forced foreign troops from Anatolia. In the wake of his victory, Mustafa Kemal adopted the name "Ataturk" (father of the Turks) and guided the establishment of a Turkish Republic that has ruled over an undivided Anatolia ever since.

Mustafa Kemal has been at the center of a Turkish cult of personality whose vehemence seems bizarre to outsiders. When *Time* magazine asked readers worldwide to choose the most influential "Men of the [Twentieth]

Century," it received over two hundred thousand votes for Mustafa Kemal, not only in the category of "Warriors and Statesmen," but in the categories of "Scientists and Healers," and "Entertainers and Artists." While, presumably, most of these votes came from Turkey, something of a cult has developed around Mustafa Kemal outside Turkey as well. Mustafa Kemal has served as the model for those who claim that the only future for the Middle East is Westernization. Unlike, for example, the Islamic modernists who sought to find a compromise between Islam and Western ideas, Mustafa Kemal and his acolytes sought to impose a model for modernity borrowed directly from the Western experience.

In the early days of the new Turkish Republic, Mustafa Kemal abolished the caliphate, nationalized religious endowments, and abolished Islamic courts and sufi orders. In other words, he established Turkey as a secular state in which private beliefs were tolerated but religion was not allowed to enter into the public sphere. He changed the calendar to a Western calendar and he "Latinized" the Turkish alphabet, making it easier to read than the Ottoman script, which had used Arabic letters. Mustafa Kemal granted women the right to vote in municipal elections in 1930 and in national elections in 1934, eleven years before women were allowed to vote in France. He even passed legislation forbidding women from wearing the veil in public and men from wearing the conical hat, the fez, that had been associated with high Ottoman modernity. Although breaking down the fashion barrier between east and west was not far from his mind, state-builders such as Mustafa Kemal regularly legislated on matters of clothing during this period. They wanted to eliminate all clothing styles that alluded to regional, religious, or ethnic identities that might compete with the state for the loyalty of its citizens. They also wanted to advertise government policies (in this case, Westernization) by making citizens into walking billboards for them. Furthermore, they regulated clothing because they could. By attacking something as personal as clothing, governments demonstrated their ability to cow their citizens. The reason why so many Turkish peasants to this very day dress like characters out of the comic strip "Andy Capp" can be attributed to Mustafa Kemal's policies.

In addition to introducing unabashed Westernization into Turkey, Mustafa Kemal might also be viewed as an heir to the great defensive developmentalists of the nineteenth-century Ottoman Empire. Like his predecessors, he attempted to expand the role of the state, centralize power, and spread a single, official ideology to bind citizens to each other and to the state. Following in their footsteps, Mustafa Kemal introduced policies to standardize Turkish legal institutions and educational curricula. Unlike his predecessors, however, he was able to harness twentieth-century technologies and assumptions about governance in support of this project. For example, while free market doctrines and political liberalism hamstrung the efforts of the *tanzimat* statesmen, Mustafa Kemal ruled during a period in which centralized economic planning had become second nature to policy makers. He thus had a list of blueprints from which to draw, from the "New

Mustafa Kemal shown demonstrating the new Turkish alphabet. (From: Jacques Benoist-Mechin, La Turquie se devoile, 1908–1938 (Paris: PML Editions, n.d.), p. 231.)

Deal" model adopted in the United States to the Fascist model of Italy to the Soviet model. Ultimately, the economic policies adopted by the Turkish government came to resemble the latter two models more closely than the former one. The era of state-directed economic planning and supervision lasted until 1950.

Overall, the fact that Turkey is today a republic and that many Turks consider their country to be part of Europe might be attributed to Ataturk's policies. In contemporary Turkey there are elections that are relatively free, particularly by Middle Eastern standards. Parliamentary representatives include members of minority groups, such as Kurds, although the formation of political parties based on ethnicity is forbidden. Nevertheless, the transformation of Turkey into a secular republic was not as easy, humane, or thorough as many of the devotees of Mustafa Kemal have made it out to be. When Mustafa Kemal took charge of the Committees for the Defense of Rights, no one fighting by his side could have realized the breadth or depth of the changes he would attempt to implement. In fact, many fought in the name of Islam. Others fought merely to eliminate a foreign presence from Anatolia. Thus, from its inception "Kemalism" met with opposition, and that opposition continues to color Turkish politics to this day.

Sometimes, the opposition to Kemalism has broken down along ethnic lines. For example, the Kurds have resisted the "Turkification" policies of the government. Although one former Turkish prime minister claimed that Kurds were merely "mountain Turks," Kurds continue to assert an ethnic and linguistic identity separate from Turks. To this day, some Kurds demand cultural autonomy while others go so far as to demand separation from Turkey. At other times, the opposition to Kemalism comes from those put off by the uncompromising secularism of the Turkish constitution. As early as 1950, the Democratic Party, which had distanced itself from the official secularist line and wrapped itself in Islamic imagery, emerged the victor in Turkish national elections. In November 2002, the Justice and Development Party—a party with Islamist roots—won close to two-thirds of the seats in the Turkish parliament. Just what that victory means is disputed. Those who claim that the party's votes were mere protest votes point to widespread disillusionment caused by the collapse of the Turkish economy and corruption in politics. They also point to the fact the more "hardcore" Islamist party, the Felicity Party, failed to gain even one seat in parliament. Others view the electoral victory as a reflection of the trend toward Islamism taking place outside Turkey's borders and as the harbinger of the collapse of the firewall separating religion and politics in Turkey.

Because Kemalism met with opposition, it has been enforced through repression. This is, of course, not unique to Kemalism. It is in the nature of all nationalisms to enforce uniformity to some degree or another. Soon after the Turks expelled the Greek army from Anatolia, the governments of the two states arranged a population transfer. The Turks forced up to 1,300,000 Christian Turks out of the country. Many had lived for centuries in Anatolia, spoke Turkish as their native language, and only differed from their neighbors in terms of the religion (Orthodox Christianity) that they practiced. In return, about 380,000 Greek Muslims went to Turkey. Like the ethnic cleansing of Armenians that took place during World War I and the ongoing war to suppress Kurdish separatism, the transfer of "Greeks" to their "ancestral homeland" displays the dark side of nationalism in all its grisly detail.

Finally, Turkish democracy works until it doesn't. When the Turkish military has felt that stability or the principles of Kemalism is threatened, it has stepped into the political process to "restore order" and "uphold the constitution." Mustafa Kemal may have set the precedent for this himself. In the wake of an internal rebellion in 1925, he assumed sweeping emergency powers for four years. In the course of its recent history, the Turkish military assumed emergency powers three times, in 1960, 1971, and 1980, and forced the replacement of the prime minister in 1997. Like Mustafa Kemal, it relinquished control a short time later, after "cleansing" the political system by disbanding political parties, jailing, and, in some cases, torturing those it deemed enemies of the state. In sum, any assessment of Turkish democracy has to balance a lively electoral and parliamentary tradition with a pattern of military intervention into politics.

Iran

At the beginning of World War I, the Russians occupied northern Persia while the British occupied the south. When the Bolsheviks toppled the tsarist

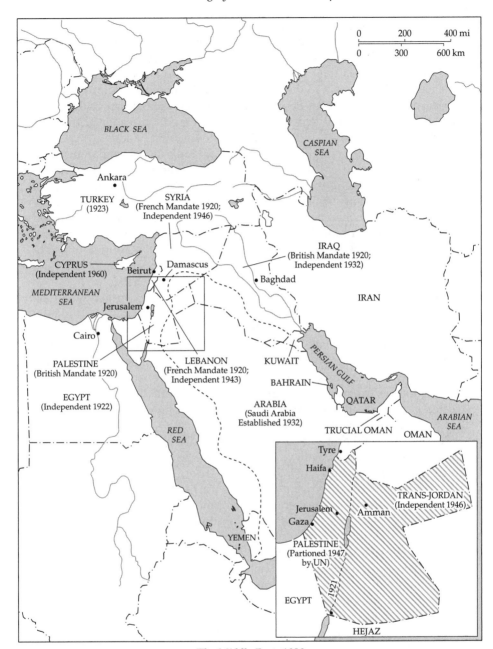

The Middle East, 1923

government, they withdrew Russian troops from Persia and the British occupied the entire country. After the war, the British attempted to impose a
treaty on their hosts that would have made Persia into a virtual British protectorate. At the same time, the communist government in Russia backed
separatist movements in the north.

The Anglo-Persian Treaty of 1919 was so unpopular that no Persian government could afford to ratify it. This created a dilemma for the British. British policy makers wanted to maintain their position in Persia to protect their oil interests and their Indian colony. They also wanted to prevent the expansion of Bolshevism to the south. But Britain could not afford to maintain an occupation force in Persia. Fearing a total breakdown of their Persian "buffer state," local British envoys encouraged the leader of the Cossack Brigade, Reza Khan, to take matters into his own hands.

Reza Khan came from a Turkish-speaking family in Mazandaran by the Caspian Sea. He had enlisted in the Cossack Brigade at the age of fifteen and rose through the ranks. Soon after the British forced the replacement of Russian officers with British officers in 1920, he became the force's commander. Reza Shah marched on Tehran with three thousand men and forced the shah to appoint him defense minister. Within a few years he had outmaneuvered his political opponents. After toying with the idea of establishing a republic in Persia with himself as the first president, he had himself proclaimed shah in 1926. Reza Khan became Reza Shah.

Like Mustafa Kemal, Reza Shah was one of several strongmen who took power in the wake of World War I and changed the paradigm for statebuilding. As a matter of fact, Reza Shah deliberately modeled his policies on those of Mustafa Kemal, as well as those of another strongman who rose to power at the same time: Benito Mussolini of Italy. Like his exemplars, Reza Shah was a self-proclaimed modernizer, a centralizer, and a nationalist. Also like his exemplars, Reza Shah disdained liberal democracy and mistrusted parliamentary rule. All three state-builders believed that the masses had to be led by a powerful leader.

Reza Shah was barely literate and reportedly had little patience with abstract discussions of policy. Nevertheless, he promoted an economic and political blueprint called the "New Order," a name that Mussolini also used to describe his own policies. At the heart of the New Order was national consolidation, economic development, and Westernization. To accomplish the first, he expanded the military and bureaucracy, waged war against the tribes and secessionist movements that threatened the territorial integrity of Persia, and promoted a single nationalist ideology. The nationalism promoted by Reza Shah traced an uninterrupted history of the Persian nation from pre-Islamic times to the present. Islam did not play a role in this nationalist ideology, and the Arab/Islamic conquest was presented as the beginning of a period of darkness. Changing the official name of the country from Persia to Iran, described earlier, was one of the actions Reza Shah took to highlight the pre-Islamic, "Aryan" roots of his domains.

Reza Shah undertook a number of actions to spread a notion of loyalty to the nation and to the approved national ideology. On the one hand, he outlawed ethnic and regional clothes, commissioned the Iranian Academy to eliminate Turkish and Arabic words from the Persian language (a project that proved unsuccessful because about 40 percent of Persian words come from Turkish and Arabic), and replaced Arabic or Turkish place names with

Persian ones. The province of Arabistan thus became the province of Khuzistan. On the other hand, he commissioned new primary and secondary school curricula to disseminate the official ideology and set up the Society of Public Guidance, modeled on the propaganda machines of Italy and Nazi Germany, to publish journals, pamphlets, newspapers, and textbooks, and to script radio broadcasts.

Like Mustafa Kemal and Mussolini, Reza Shah adopted a state-directed economic policy to eliminate foreign control over the economy and to ensure rapid development. To end foreign interference, the shah cancelled foreign concessions, established the National Bank of Iran to take the place of the British-run "Imperial Bank," and took control of posts, telegraph, and customs from foreigners. He also set high tariffs to protect the infant industries he was setting up. To accumulate capital for investment, the state confiscated landholdings of many of the wealthiest landlords and ulama and set up government monopolies. In addition, the state acquired revenues from oil sales. By accumulating capital from these three sources, the state began what later was called "import substitution industrialization." In other words, rather than importing goods from Europe and elsewhere, Iran attempted to produce everything from soft drinks to steel itself. Thus, the policies of Reza Shah (and Mustafa Kemal) differed from those of nineteenth-century state-builders in a significant way. While the most of their predecessors tried to modernize by integrating their states further into the modern world economy, Reza Shah and Mustafa Kemal sought to modernize by freeing their nations of the constraints of the world system.

Reza Shah, like Mustafa Kemal, associated modernization with Westernization. Westernization took a variety of forms for Reza Shah. First, it included secularization. Reza Shah legislated against religious display and the participation of ulama in positions of authority. He replaced the ulama in the judicial system and introduced the French Civil Law Code and the Italian Penal Code, thus eliminating the role played by the shariʿa in all matters save for those concerning personal status. He also refused to give exit visas to pilgrims wishing to go to Mecca and Medina or the Shiʿi holy cities of Karbala and Najaf in Iraq, and restricted Shiʿi rituals he deemed "barbaric" or potentially subversive. To rub the ulama's nose in it, Reza Shah erected statues of himself in town squares throughout Iran, violating the religious injunction against the representation of the human form.

In addition to secularization, Reza Shah, like Mustafa Kemal, also adopted other attributes of Western modernity wholesale. For example, like Mustafa Kemal, Reza Shah prescribed the appropriate clothing for the "modern Iranian." After a trip to Turkey in 1934, he prohibited women from wearing the veil and required all adult men to wear Western clothes and a brimmed hat that obstructed one of the positions for prayer. His visit to Turkey also resulted in legislation promoting women's legal rights. He had legislation passed that ensured female education and outlawed discrimination against women in public facilities. Women, in other words, were placed in roles similar to the roles they had in the West: Iranian women, like their Western sisters, were to be the mothers of the nation. To train their sons to be good citizens, they had to have an education. Iranian women did not have the right to vote (as they do now in the Islamic Republic), but then again, voting under Reza Shah did not mean much anyway. While the promotion of women's rights is often associated with an expansion of individual freedoms, Reza Shah, like Mussolini (another advocate of women's legal rights) had a different goal in mind. Both state-builders sought to expand the reach of the state into the home and to replace the "private patriarchy" of the family unit with a "public patriarchy" defined by the state.

Reza Shah's New Order certainly changed Iran in a number of ways. It resulted in a massive expansion of the state and the spread of a nationalist myth so powerful that it still provides the foundation for Iranian identity. It also brought about social changes, from the end of Persia's "tribal problem" to the creation of an industrial working class. But since the Iranian Revolution of 1978–1979, these changes are more often than not disparaged, particularly when the effectiveness of Reza Shah's policies is compared to that of Mustafa Kemal's.

Many historians cite three reasons for the "success" of the Turkish experiment and the "failure" of the Iranian. First, they assert that defensive developmentalism in the Ottoman Empire during the nineteenth century had had a greater impact on society than defensive developmentalism in Persia. In Turkey, the successor state to the Ottoman Empire, the state had already expanded its role before World War I and had taken over functions that were still in the hands of nongovernment institutions in Iran. Therefore, the changes in Iran were more novel than those in Turkey and fostered a greater resistance. Second, historians commonly cite the fact that Mustafa Kemal created a state and government simultaneously, so that the one became fused with the other. Reza Shah, on the other hand, created a government in a state that had been self-governing, in one form or another, since the sixteenth century. Rather than starting totally anew, he had to contend with institutions and traditions that far predated his government. He also had to contend with popular memories about the way things had been and therefore were supposed to be. Finally, historians argue that Mustafa Kemal established his state and government through a popular war of national liberation, whereas Reza Shah took power in a *coup d'etat* and ruled by decree.

The argument about Mustafa Kemal's "success" and Reza Shah's "failure" is not so clear cut, however. First of all, the jury is still out in the case of Turkey's tilt toward Europe, particularly in light of the recent upsurge in support for Islamic political movements. In addition, the argument underestimates the ability of the world system of nation states and the world economy to integrate and transform the nature of political movements and the states in which they arise. As we shall see in later chapters, contemporary Islamist movements, such as the one that took power in Iran in 1979, are just as "modern" as the secularizing movements represented by Mustafa Kemal and Reza Shah.

Thirteen

The Introduction and Spread of Nationalism

In the spring of 1919, about six months after the end of World War I, political posters festooned the streets of Damascus. A pedestrian taking an evening stroll would thus not have been surprised to see a poster ending in the following phrase: "The Arab nation is indivisible. The Arabs make up a single nation that demands independence." Turning the corner, that same pedestrian might have encountered another poster, this time ending with the following slogan: "We demand complete independence for Syria within its natural boundaries." That pedestrian might be forgiven for wondering just who he was supposed to be. Was he a member of the Arab nation, the Syrian nation, both, or was there yet a fourth option? One year earlier it is doubtful that he would have had to ponder the question. The year before he had been, after all, an Ottoman.

In the aftermath of World War I, a variety of nationalist movements emerged and spread in the Middle East. Representatives of the Armenian, Arab, and Kurdish "nations" descended on Paris to lobby the peace conference, while Turkish, Egyptian, Syrian, and Lebanese ("Phoenician") nationalists made their voices heard in other ways. Each of these movements claimed to represent the political aspirations of populations that had previously been ruled by the Ottoman Empire. Each claimed that the Ottoman Empire had been little better than an imperial prison that had kept their nations in captivity. But as the nineteenth-century French philosopher Ernest Renan once put it, "Getting history wrong is part of being a nation." Despite the claims of nationalist movements, those movements did not represent age-old nations yearning to reestablish their freedom after four hundred years of bondage. They created those nations. Furthermore, it was the very Ottoman Empire the movements vilified that had laid the basis for the explosion of nationalisms in the post–World War I Middle East.

To understand why this was the case, it is necessary to understand something of the nature of nationalism. Although every nationalist movement and creed asserts its uniqueness, all are, in fact, comparable. All share a common set of assumptions about the proper ordering of human society. All nationalists believe that humanity is naturally divided into smaller units, or nations. All nationalists believe that nations can be identified by certain characteristics that all its citizens hold in common. These characteristics include the linguistic, ethnic, religious, or historical traditions that make a nation distinctive. All nationalists believe that times might change but nations retain their essential characteristics. According to Persian nationalists, for example, Persians who listened to the "national poet," Firdawsi, in the eleventh century are members of the selfsame nation as those who memorized Firdawsi in schools built by Reza Shah. They are linked across time by language, literary tradition, and history. All nationalists believe that peoples have a special relationship to some particular piece of real estate in which their ancestors first emerged as a distinct group and flourished. Zionists "belong" in Palestine, Egyptians in Egypt, Persians in Persia. All nationalists believe that nations possess something called a "common interest," and it is the role of the state to promote it. Indeed, all believe that the only form of government that can assure the common interest of the nation is self-government.

In the modern world, these assumptions need no explanation or justification. They just *are*. And the very fact that they appear obvious and commonsensical means that nationalism, when used in its most general sense, might be called an "ideology."

All nationalist movements draw their assumptions from this ideology. All nationalist movements take one or more linguistic, religious, or ethnic attributes of a given group of people and claim that the attributes they have highlighted makes that group a nation and entitles it to political independence in its ancestral homeland. Yet it is important to keep in mind that the ideology of nationalism and the nationalist movements that draw from that ideology are different. The ideology of nationalism has proven to be extraordinarily resilient wherever it has taken hold. In the modern world, everyone must belong to a nation. Nationalist movements, on the other hand, come and go all the time. Thus, the Ottoman nationalism that Ottoman state-builders had floated during the nineteenth century (*osmanlilik*) could join Confederate nationalism in the dustbin of history in the twentieth. Because all nationalist movements and creeds are rooted in a common set of assumptions, it is relatively easy for people to switch from one to another as circumstances demand. Over the course of the twentieth century, for example, loyal Ottoman citizens could become Arabs or Syrians or, over time, both, and some of these could later become Lebanese or Palestinians. Nationalists? Always. Ottoman or Arab or Palestinian nationalists? Maybe, sometimes.

True believers, of course, swear that their particular brand of nationalism deserves to succeed because it represents the authentic identity and aspirations of a given people. Most historians, on the other hand, wince at the idea of authentic identities and aspirations. For them, nationalist movements succeed or fail not because they represent true or false identities and aspirations, but because of the often unpredictable circumstances in which nationalist movements find themselves. After all, who is to say what the subsequent history of the Middle East might have been had the entente powers supported the establishment of a unified Arab state, or had the Arab nationalist movement been anchored in a state that had the power to coerce and persuade its citizens?

The ideology of nationalism differs from the various nationalist movements that draw on its assumptions in another way as well. Because the ideology of nationalism deals with assumptions about the organization of state and society, its advent in any given territory represents a truly revolutionary departure for the inhabitants of that territory. The ideology of nationalism transforms subjects into citizens and citizens into cogs of a machine grinding away for something called "the common good" (or common wealth). Such transformations began to take place in the Ottoman Empire during the mid-nineteenth century. The rise and fall of various nationalist movements, on the other hand, is more superficial than revolutionary in nature. When compared to the extraordinary social and political changes induced by Ottoman attempts to create an ideology that could unite all inhabitants of the empire as citizens, the fact that some of those citizens would later apply that ideology to assert some local identity is of negligible importance.

Nationalism in both senses of the word is a relatively new phenomenon in world history. We can trace it back only as far as the eighteenth century. Historians disagree about where nationalism first emerged. Theories range from the usual suspects, Britain and France, to the Netherlands, Germany, and even the Americas. Wherever it emerged, however, it took a little over one hundred years for nationalism to traverse the globe. Nationalism struck roots in various territories when both international and local circumstances were ripe. In the case of the Ottoman Empire, we can identify two such circumstances.

On the most fundamental level, nationalism came to the Ottoman Empire with the spread of the modern world economic and state systems to the Middle East. As we saw in Chapter 3, the modern state first appeared in Europe in the wake of the commercial revolution. Modern states proved to be far more efficient than previously existing political units. They were small enough to enable governments to regulate production and trade, while at the same time they were large enough to foster a single integrated market and labor pool within their boundaries. The ideology of nationalism emerged with the modern state. By defining a group of people as a nation deserving a state of their own, by endowing that group of people with a common identity and common interest, and by making the state responsible for advancing that common interest, nationalism gave the modern state legitimacy and purpose. Conversely, nationalism also proved useful to state-builders, who used it to mobilize and harness the energies of their populations. As the modern world economy spread throughout the globe, so did the modern state system. Because the ideology of nationalism was inextricably connected to the modern state, it hitched a ride when the modern state system broadened its reach.

This brings us to the second condition for the emergence of nationalism in the Ottoman Empire. The spread of the modern economic and state systems throughout the world encouraged the spread of modern institutions of governance and market relations within every territory, principality, or empire with which those twinned systems had contact. The Ottoman Empire, like the Habsburg, Russian, and Chinese empires, may have continued to call itself an empire. Nevertheless, over the course of the nineteenth and twentieth centuries it increasingly came to resemble a modern state. For example, the *tanzimat* decrees established the notion of citizenship as a legal principle. The announcement of this principle quickly struck roots among many in the empire. As early as the 1840s, peasants began asserting their newly acquired rights in local disputes. So did others, who also sought to use these rights to their advantage. Along with new rights, the Ottoman state demanded new obligations from its citizenry. It therefore increased its control and coercive capabilities over that citizenry. By taking responsibility for functions it had previously disregarded, by standardizing institutions, by attempting to set norms for public and even private behavior, the state created the conditions in which new ties among its citizens might emerge.

Those ties also emerged as a result of the spread of market relations within the empire. Over the course of the nineteenth century, for example, peasants who had furnished most of their own needs and artisans who had produced for local markets found themselves bound up in larger economic networks. Sometimes these networks were regional. At other times, they were imperial or even international. The introduction of new transportation technologies such as railroads and steamships not only opened up new markets, it expanded the traffic in labor and goods between cities and countryside. On the one hand, peasants might migrate seasonally to urban centers to supplement their incomes by engaging in wage labor. On the other hand, increased urban economic control over the countryside broadened and deepened the spread of market relations in rural areas. The expanded interchange between city and countryside brought urban values and norms to outlying areas. It also enlarged the social, economic, and cultural space in which people lived their lives.

Just how the spread of modern technologies and market relations affected notions of social, economic, and cultural space—and paved the way for regional loyalties that would later provide the basis for nationalist movements—can be seen in the case of Greater Syria. Over the course of the nineteenth century, trade and infrastructural development established Greater Syria as a distinct economic unit. By 1861, a British-built telegraph connected Aleppo, Beirut, and Damascus. By the 1880s a system of carriage roads connected the inland cities of Damascus and Homs with the coastal cities of Tripoli, Sidon, and Beirut. By the 1890s, rail service connected Beirut with Damascus and Damascus with the grain-producing region of the Hawran to the south. Commerce increasingly flowed along the lines of the new railroads and carriage roads. Urban-based merchants enriched by that commerce increasingly loaned money to and frequently repossessed the lands of peasants inhabiting the hinterlands of Syrian cities. Peasants increasingly swelled the population of nearby urban centers in search of jobs in industries fueled by that commerce. Elite families in Damascus, Jerusalem, and Aleppo increasingly sought marriage alliances with their peers in Sidon, Nablus, and Beirut in an effort to supplement commercial ties with family ties. All this contributed to the emergence of a Greater Syrian social and economic space.

At the same time that a regional social and economic space emerged in Greater Syria, the connections between Greater Syria and areas with which it was not so well integrated loosened. For example, over the course of the nineteenth century, Greater Syria and the territory that is now Iraq emerged as distinct economic units. By the beginning of the twentieth century, little remained of the overland trade that had connected the two regions in earlier centuries. After the opening of the Suez Canal in 1869, farmers of the upper Tigris valley began to ship grain via the Persian Gulf to Europe. This allowed them to abandon less profitable markets in geographic Syria. Not that it mattered all that much to the Syrian economy. With the opening of rail connections and ports, Syrian merchants could increase their profit margins as well by orienting to the Greater Syrian market or to the west.

The evolution of Greater Syria as a distinct unit capable of inspiring loyalty would rouse later generations of nationalists to champion the establishment of a Greater Syrian state. As we have seen, their plan ran afoul of the mandates system. Nevertheless, the legacy of the regional economic, social, and cultural ties that emerged in the empire in the nineteenth century affected even Arab nationalists. Most of the plans Arab nationalists floated to unite the eastern Arab world called for regional autonomy within a federated Arab state. And if economic integration affected Greater Syria in this manner, imagine how it affected the Ottoman province of Egypt, where the process of economic integration was much further advanced.

The economic, social, and cultural integration of a region does not necessarily mean that a nationalist movement will emerge there, of course. If that were the case, a California nationalism would have emerged years ago. For a nationalist movement to emerge, there must be nationalists to articulate its principles and mobilize a population to realize its goals. Sometimes these nationalists work through states to produce what are called "official nationalisms." We have seen this in the case of the Ottoman Empire, and it would take place again among the various states that emerged in the aftermath of World War I. At other times, freelance nationalists work either in the absence of a state (as Palestinian nationalists have done) or in opposition to one (as, for example, Balkan nationalists did). The Ottoman state had created the environment in which such nationalists might work. By instituting new mechanisms to discipline and oversee its populations, by encouraging the spread of market relations, and by promoting a particular brand of nationalism as a prototype, the Ottoman state had created what might be called a "culture of nationalism." This culture of nationalism affected elites and nonelites alike. As a result, the nationalist movements that emerged within the empire found an audience that was not mystified by what those movements were trying to accomplish.

Groups of nationalists began to emerge in the Ottoman Empire during the nineteenth century for several reasons. Some bureaucrats and imperial functionaries consciously copied European techniques for state-building. The result was *osmanlilik*. Other groups of nationalists soon emerged both as a result of imperial state-building and in opposition to specific policies undertaken by the state-builders. On the one hand, defensive developmentalism had created new social strata, such as a Christian bourgeoisie in the port cities of the Ottoman Empire; urban notables who counted on Istanbul for positions of influence; and the professionals, intellectuals, and military officers who played such a key role in constitutional movements. These strata had been raised in an environment defined by the culture of nationalism introduced by an expanding international state-system and imperial state-builders. They were accustomed to the modern public sphere and an urban environment in which new techniques of mass politics could be deployed.

On the other hand, many from these strata had reasons to be dissatisfied. For urban notables, there was just so much imperial patronage to go around. Some were sure to feel slighted. Many among the Christian bourgeoisie felt excluded from a state that professed an Islamic *osmanlilik*. The same went for many professionals, intellectuals, and military officers who, as we have seen, failed to achieve the power and influence they felt they deserved. These were the layers that were at the forefront of oppositional nationalist movements.

The more the Ottoman state intruded into the lives of its citizens, and the more it attempted to establish norms of acceptable behavior and belief, the more the disgruntled members of these strata resisted. For example, some historians trace the origins of Arab nationalism to attempts made by the Young Turks to "turkify" the Ottoman Empire in the early twentieth century. Because the Young Turks sought to make Turkish the official language of the empire and eliminate non-Turks from positions of authority, these historians claim, some in the empire became conscious of themselves as members of a distinct Arab nation and demanded the right to rule themselves.

It is interesting to note that here as elsewhere a nationalist movement invented a nation. Before the nineteenth century, the word "*ʿarab*" did not have the same meaning among Arabic speakers it has today. Instead, the word was commonly used as a term of contempt by town-dwellers when referring to "savage" bedouin. Only in the nineteenth century did intellectuals begin using the term to refer to their linguistic and cultural community. Their nationalist descendents then appropriated the term and used it for their own purposes.

(Lest any Turkish or Persian nationalist feel smug, both the idea of a "Turkish nation" and "Persian nation" have similarly shallow roots. During the nineteenth century, Ottoman and Persian intellectuals, trained in Europe or in elite institutions that borrowed their methods and curricula from those of Europe, began to apply assumptions about historical evolution and social cohesion to trace the genealogies of their respective societies. Using the tools of the newly established disciplines of archaeology and philology, they traced the lineages of their respective cultures and languages from pre-Islamic times forward. These intellectuals were not necessarily nationalists. Nevertheless, they provided a cultural, linguistic, and/or ethnic argument for the continuous existence of the Turkish and Persian nations that later nationalists, such as Ziya Golkalp and Sayyid Hasan Taqizadeh, could apply. When Mustafa Kemal and Reza Shah took power, they found the ideas of these nationalist ideologues useful for their nation-building projects and used the institutions of state to disseminate them.)

Arab nationalism was, of course, just one of the nationalist movements that emerged in the Arab Middle East. It was not the first. That distinction belongs to the Egyptian nationalist movement. A nationalist movement emerged in Egypt before the other Arab provinces because of the peculiarities of Egyptian history. Under the mamluks and then Mehmet Ali and his descendents, Egypt had been virtually autonomous. This made it easier for the more politically motivated of its inhabitants to think of Egypt as a single unit that should be independent. At the same time, the effectiveness of Mehmet Ali's policies of defensive developmentalism, combined with the integration of Egypt into the world economy and British administrative practices, caused the breakdown of social structures that reinforced local identities: the autonomous village, the guild, the town quarter. This enabled the inhabitants of the province to see themselves as part of a wider, yet clearly bounded, political community. Egypt also was home to a large and concentrated stratum of intellectuals and political activists. Some of these intellectuals were exiles from other Arab provinces who found shelter from Hamidian repression in British-controlled Egypt. Others were homegrown, the products of Western or Western-style institutions that defensive developmentalism had fostered. These intellectuals played the same role in fostering Egyptian nationalism as their counterparts would later play in fostering Arab nationalism. Finally, the British occupation had created an obvious target against which a nationalist movement could mobilize. All these factors contributed to the rise of a nationalist movement in Egypt that was distinctly Egyptian.

Beginning in 1907, a number of nationalist parties and associations began to materialize on the Egyptian scene. The first such party, the Nationalist Party, was organized by Mustafa Kamil (not to be mistaken for Mustafa Kemal of Turkey), a French-educated lawyer and newspaper publisher. Another party, the Umma Party, followed soon afterward. Although both parties wanted to bring the British occupation to an end, they divided along tactical lines. The Nationalist Party took a more combative stance than its rival, whose approach was anything but combative. Leaders of the Umma Party felt that Egyptians should cooperate with the British and hoped that the British would learn from this that Egyptians were ready to enter the "civilized" world as an independent nation. The British consul general called the Umma Party the "Girondists of Egypt," a reference to the "moderates" of the French Revolution who clashed with (and were decimated by) the more radical Jacobins of Robespierre fame.

Nationalist demonstration in Aleppo, Syria, 1920. (From: 'Abd al-'Aziz al-'Azma, Mir'at al-Sham: Tarikh Dimashq wa ahliha (London: Riad El-Rayyes Books, 1987) p. 218.)

Nationalist parties in the proper sense of the word did not emerge in the Levant and Mesopotamia until after World War I. That is not to say that no nationalists existed. There were a number of associations with branches in various cities of the Levant and Mesopotamia that advocated Arab or Syrian or Mesopotamian autonomy and, eventually, even independence from the Ottoman Empire. But these associations were small and had limited influence. Because their members feared repression, and because they were more inclined to engage in conspiracies than mass organizing, these associations did not attract a large following. The largest of them, the Damascus-based al-Fatat, included only about seventy members before the war.

Arab, Syrian, and, to a lesser extent, Iraqi nationalist movements attracted a larger following in the aftermath of World War I. The Ottoman Empire had been destroyed and there was a political vacuum at the top that had to be filled. We have already seen how larger and more popular nationalist movements in Turkey and Egypt were able to take advantage of post-war realities. Nationalist movements in the Levant and Mesopotamia were less successful in realizing their goals. Arab nationalism had to compete with regional nationalisms, and both fell victim to the mandates system and its heir, the regional state system. As we shall see in a later chapter, the nationalisms associated with established states appear to have taken hold—at least for the time being—but only as a result of state-building and the support the international state system offers to the regional state system. The states in the region jealously guard their borders, rewrite their histories, and, indeed, have produced enough of their own history to coax the loyalty of their citizens. All the while, international guarantees assure the durability of the state system created in the aftermath of World War I. The key words here are, of course, "for the time being," particularly in a period as volatile as the current one. Regardless of the fate of particular nationalist movements, however, the ideology of nationalism remains the only game in town for those who need a blueprint for defining political communities. And, in spite of the protests of globalization enthusiasts, it is likely to remain so for a long time to come.

Fourteen

The Origins of the
Israeli-Palestinian Dispute

The British short story writer Saki (H. H. Munro) once described the island of Crete as a place that has produced more history than could be consumed locally. The same might be said of Palestine, the territory that includes the contemporary state of Israel and the occupied territories. The territory itself is quite small. It stretches from the Mediterranean Sea in the west to the Jordan River in the east, and from Lebanon in the north to the Gulf of Aqaba and the Sinai Peninsula on the south. The state of Israel is roughly the size of New Jersey. And Israel comprises almost 80 percent of historic Palestine.

The population of Palestine is also small. Israel's population is about 6.5 million, less than 10 percent of the population of Turkey, Iran, or Egypt. There are approximately three to 3.5 million Palestinians in the occupied territories—roughly the population of Chicago. (Estimates for total number of Palestinians in the world run as high as nine million.) Since 1948, wars between Israel and its neighbors have claimed upward of 150,000 casualties. These wars were certainly tragic, but they just as certainly pale in horror when compared with the most grievous squandering of lives in the region during its recent history. During the Iran–Iraq War, which lasted from 1980 to 1988, there were 500,000 to one million deaths and one to two million wounded.

In spite of the fact that the size of Palestine and the number of people directly affected by its political problems are minuscule in comparative terms, the dispute between Israel, on the one hand, and the Palestinians and various Arab states, on the other, has been at the forefront of international attention for over fifty years. The so-called Arab-Israeli dispute has gone on for such a long time and has been the subject of so much heated debate that it is easy to lose sight of the fundamental issue involved. The dispute is, simply put, a real estate dispute. Jewish immigrants and their descendents, united by their adherence to the nationalist ideology of Zionism, and the Palestinian Arab inhabitants among whom the Zionists settled both claim an exclusive right to inhabit and control some or all of Palestine.

Zionism is a nationalist movement that redefined a religious community—Jews—as a national community. Like other nationalist movements, Zionism asserts the right of this nation to an independent existence in its historic

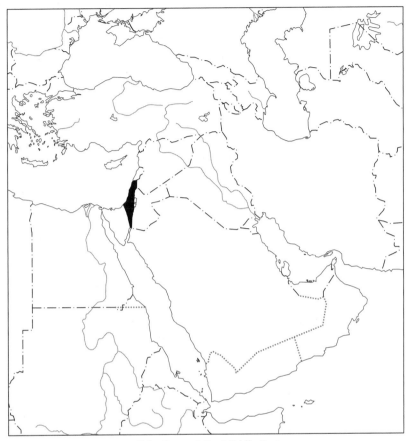

Palestine and the Middle East

homeland. The Zionist movement was typical of nationalist movements that arose in Europe during the nineteenth century. And, like other nationalist movements, the Zionist movement has its own pantheon of heroes who were instrumental in articulating its doctrines and organizing for its goals.

Perhaps the most important figure in the early history of Zionism was a Viennese journalist, Theodor Herzl (1860–1904). Herzl was the son of a Hungarian merchant whose family had moved to Vienna at a time when that city seemed to promise so much to upwardly mobile Jews who wished to assimilate into mainstream European society and culture. Herzl received a secular education and acquired a doctorate in law. He went on to become the French correspondent for a prestigious Viennese newspaper. It was while he was in Paris that Herzl became a Zionist.

According to many accounts, Herzl converted to Zionism as a result of the Dreyfus Affair. In 1894, Alfred Dreyfus, a French army captain, was accused of spying for Germany. Dreyfus was, like Herzl, an assimilated Jew. The trial of Alfred Dreyfus became a *cause célèbre* in France and the rest of Europe. For many, it was clear that Dreyfus had been guilty of little more than being a successful Jew in Catholic France. Among these was the French novelist Emile Zola, who condemned those who accused Dreyfus in the following words:

> It is a crime to poison the minds of the small and simple and to excite the passions of reaction and intolerance while seeking refuge behind that hateful anti-Semitism of which great liberal France—France of the rights of man—will die, unless she is cured of her disease.

The Dreyfus Affair demonstrated to Herzl that if France could play host to virulent anti-Semitism, Jews could not be secure anywhere. What the Jews needed was a homeland of their own in which they would form a majority of citizens.

At first, Herzl was ambivalent about just where that homeland should be. In various writings, he advocated establishing a Jewish home in Argentina or in the western United States. Others were not so ambivalent. Since the first century, when Jews were exiled from Palestine by the Romans, Palestine was remembered in texts and rituals of Jews who lived, sometimes uncomfortably, sometimes in peril, as a scattered community throughout the world. Thus, Zionism combined Herzl's call for the establishment of a Jewish national home with the historical memory of Palestine.

Theodor Herzl was not the first Zionist. Nor was he the movement's most brilliant advocate. Indeed, there were a number of Zionist thinkers who contributed more ideas to Zionism than Herzl. But few offered more passion. Herzl's organizational talents proved essential for the success of the Zionist cause. In 1897, Herzl organized the First Zionist Congress in Basel, Switzerland. The Zionist Congress created the World Zionist Organization, which continues to speak for the international Zionist movement. It also issued the Basel Program, which not only called for the establishment of a "Jewish home" in Palestine, but specified the tactic to achieve that goal. The Basel Program stipulated that Zionists should commit themselves to obtaining that home through diplomacy.

While Herzl and others attempted to gain support from a variety of powers (including the Ottoman Empire), the Zionist movement achieved its first real success in 1917 when the British issued the Balfour Declaration. The Balfour Declaration stated, in part, "His Majesty's Government view with favor the establishment in Palestine of a national home for the Jewish people, and will use their best endeavors to facilitate the achievement of this object . . . " This declaration marked a milestone in the efforts that culminated in the creation of the State of Israel. The British, who received the mandate for Palestine from the League of Nations, allowed Zionist immigration to Palestine (which, after the creation of Trans-Jordan, they defined as the territory between the Mediterranean Sea and the Jordan River).

Jewish immigration to Palestine began even before the Balfour Declaration was issued and continued long after the end of the war, however. Immigration took place in waves, called in Hebrew "*aliyot*" (sing.: *aliya*). The first *aliya* was significant because its members attempted to install a settler-plantation colony in Palestine similar to the French settler-plantation colony in Algeria. For the most part, their efforts failed. The second and third *aliyot*, which took

The Jewish settlement Nes Zionah, near Jaffa, was established in 1883. (From: The Collection of Wolf-Dieter Lemke.)

place during 1904–1914 and 1918–1923, had more lasting results. During these *aliyot*, sixty-five thousand Jews emigrated to Palestine from Europe. These immigrants shaped many of the institutions and ideals that still exist in Israel. Influenced by both socialism and romantic, back-to-the-land ideas that were then popular in Germany, the new immigrants established agricultural settlements, including collective farms (*moshavim*, sing.: *moshav*) and communal farms (*kibbutzim*, sing.: *kibbutz*). They organized a labor federation (the Histadrut), which established schools and hospitals and which provided a variety of social and welfare services for the immigrant community. And they resurrected the biblical language of Hebrew for use as the national tongue.

Perhaps most important for the future of the Middle East was the labor policy adopted by the new immigrants. The Zionists of the second and third *aliyot* expressed their aspirations in two slogans: "conquest of land" and "conquest of labor." The first slogan refers to the need these Zionists felt to make their imprint on the land of Palestine by "taming the wilderness" through settlement activity. The second refers to the need these Zionists felt to remake the Jewish people by having Jews fill all jobs in the economy. Whereas the peculiar circumstances of Jews in Europe had restricted them to certain urban occupations, these Zionists wanted Jews to expand beyond commerce and the professions. Only by doing this, they believed, could Jews overcome their crippling experience as an exile community and become a true nation. The belief that the Jewish nation had to purge itself of the ill effects of centuries of exile is called "the negation of exile." It, too, played a central role in Zionist polemics.

Although the "conquest of labor" idea had its ideological roots in utopian socialism and romanticism, there were practical reasons for European Jewish settlers to shun Arab labor. Although one of early Zionist slogans was "a land without a people for a people without a land," Arab labor was, in fact, plentiful and Arabs were willing to work for lower wages than would European emigrants. The expansion of the labor force to include low-wage workers would drive wages down and discourage the immigration of new settlers. As a result, influential Zionists felt that the success of their project depended on severing the economic links connecting the two communities. Thus, after the Zionists bought land, often from absentee landlords, they frequently displaced Palestinian farmers whose services were no longer required.

The indigenous inhabitants of Palestine did resist Zionist settlement policies. This resistance took a variety of forms, from land occupations to violence against settlers and destruction of property. But, while the indigenous inhabitants of Palestine resisted Zionist settlement from the start, this resistance was mainly defensive, devoid of political goals, and rather haphazard. No Palestinian national movement existed until after World War I. Even then it had to compete with other nationalist movements for support. Before World War I, most educated Palestinians viewed themselves as Ottoman subjects and later as Ottoman citizens. As we saw in Chapter 13, the fact that educated Palestinians would express their political aspirations in the form of nationalism was inevitable. That they would advocate Palestinian nationalism was not. After World War I, when an Ottoman identity was no longer a viable option, some Palestinians were attracted to Arab nationalism. Others viewed themselves as Syrians.

In addition to the competition a Palestinian national movement faced from rival national movements, there were other factors that hindered its consolidation. The Palestinian community was hardly as well organized or as unified as the Zionist community. As citizens of the Ottoman Empire, there had been no need. Although the Zionist community was notorious for the fractiousness of its politics, most of its members did, after all, play by the same rule book. The Zionist community embraced the mandates system and organized itself accordingly. Political elites in the Arab community in Palestine accepted neither the Balfour Declaration nor the British mandate. They thus did not organize themselves in a way that could take advantage of the mandate. Further hindering the organization of a unified Palestinian national movement was the problem of internal fissures in the Arab community—fissures that were exacerbated by British policies. While political elites had competed with each other for positions and prestige under the Ottomans, the British were not reluctant to use that competition for their own ends. The British also continued the Ottoman policy of allowing each religious community to organize its own affairs. Because the Arab community of Palestine included both Muslims and Christians, each community maintained parallel but separate institutions for such functions as social welfare and law.

Over the course of the mandate period, both the Arab nationalist and the Syrian nationalist options became less and less viable. The mandates system not only divided the Arab world into a variety of states, but severed Palestine from Syria. Because the Palestinian Arab community could not reasonably expect to unite with Syrians, the lure of Syrian nationalism eventually lost its hold on it. Over time, the history and institutional development of Palestine and Syria also diverged. Syrian elites, for example, would further their education by studying in France and felt at ease in French culture. Since Britain held the mandate for Palestine, educated elites in Palestine would often learn English, complete their studies in Britain, and come to regard British institutions and traditions, not French, as a model to be emulated.

But there was a second reason why a separate Palestinian identity began to emerge during the mandate period. The inhabitants of Palestine faced a problem that no other inhabitants of the region faced: Zionist settlement. Zionist settlement was very different from the imperialism practiced in Syria or Iraq under the mandates system. The British and French ruled their mandated territories indirectly, through local collaborators. They did not appropriate land, establish a rival and competing economy, or establish rival and competing political structures. Because they faced a different type of adversary, the response of Palestinians was different from the response of their neighbors.

The fact that Palestinian nationalism developed later than Zionism and, in fact, developed in response to Zionist immigration does not mean that Palestinian nationalism is any less legitimate than Zionism. All nationalisms arise in opposition to some internal or external nemesis. All are defined by what they oppose. Zionism itself originally arose in reaction to anti-Semitic and nationalist movements in Europe. It would be perverse to judge Zionism as somehow less valid than European anti-Semitism or those nationalisms. Furthermore, Zionism itself was also defined by its opposition to the indigenous Palestinian inhabitants of the region. Both the "conquest of land" and the "conquest of the labor" slogans that became central to Zionist thinking originated as a result of the confrontation of Zionism with its Palestinian "other."

During the late 1920s and 1930s tensions between the two communities escalated. Both local and international events contributed to these tensions. As a result of the spread of anti-Semitism in Europe during the 1930s, Jewish immigration to Palestine expanded dramatically. From 1931 to 1935, the Jewish population of Palestine rose from 175,000 to four hundred thousand. To put it another way, the Jewish population expanded from 17 to 31 percent of the total population in Palestine. Zionist land purchases struck a Palestinian population already reeling from an agricultural crisis. Palestinian society was predominantly rural, and the collapse of agricultural prices and international trade caused by the Great Depression had put it under tremendous strain. By 1931, Zionist land purchases had led to the ejection of approximately twenty thousand peasant families from their lands. Close to 30 percent of Palestinian farmers were landless and another 75 to 80 percent did not have enough land for subsistence.

Thus, in 1936 Palestine exploded in violence. What Palestinians call the Great Revolt was, after the 1948 War, the most traumatic event in modern history for Palestinians. The British quickly suppressed the revolt in urban areas, but met with more difficulty in rural areas. There, the revolt lasted three years. By the autumn of 1937, up to ten thousand rebels roamed the countryside. To put down the revolt, the British launched a brutal counterinsurgency campaign, employing tactics all too familiar to Palestinians today: collective punishment of villages, "targeted killings" (assassinations), mass arrests, deportations, and the dynamiting of homes of suspected guerrillas and their sympathizers. The revolt, and the British reaction to it, ravaged the natural leadership of the Palestinian community and opened up new cleavages in that community. Many wealthy Palestinians fled rather than face what they considered to be the extortionate demands of rival Palestinian gangs, while the British imprisoned many of the community's leaders or forced them into exile. Palestinian society never recovered. The roots of what Palestinians called the *nakba* (calamity) of 1948 can be found in the Great Revolt.

In the wake of the Great Revolt, the British attempted to find some diplomatic solution to the Palestine imbroglio. In 1937, they proposed dividing Palestine into two separate territories, one Zionist, one Palestinian. In 1939, they backed away from partition and issued a White Paper that had just the right ingredients to offend leaders of both communities. The White Paper of 1939 advocated putting restrictions on (but not ending) Jewish immigration, closer supervision of (but not ending) land sales, and independence within ten years. Both communities felt betrayed by the White Paper. Both communities rejected it.

Although the White Paper remained official British policy during World War II, Palestine was relatively quiet. Much of the Zionist community balked at the idea of sabotaging the British war effort against the Nazis, and the Arab community of Palestine was still recovering from the trauma of the Great Revolt. Furthermore, the war was an economic boon to Palestine, as it was to much of the rest of the region. But the lull was not to last. As the ten-year deadline stipulated by the White Paper loomed on the horizon, the struggle between the two communities—and between the two communities and the British—resumed. By 1947, at a time when India was about to achieve independence and the cold war was in its initial stages, the British had to station one hundred thousand soldiers in Palestine to keep the peace. Their soldiers and diplomats targeted by Zionist splinter groups, their economy in shambles, the British decided that enough was enough and dumped the Palestine issue in the lap of the newly established United Nations. The United Nations was, after all, the successor organization to the League of Nations, which had granted Britain the mandate to begin with. Following the recommendations of the United Nations Special Committee on Palestine (UNSCOP), the General Assembly of the United Nations voted to terminate the mandate and partition Palestine between Zionist and Palestinian communities.

In the wake of the United Nations' vote to partition Palestine, a civil war broke out between the two communities. The civil war was followed by the intervention of surrounding Arab nations on behalf of the Palestinians. The war for Palestine—called by Israelis the War of Independence and by Palestinians the *nakba*—affected all combatants in dramatic ways. For Zionists, the war led to the creation of the State of Israel whose de facto borders corresponded to the ceasefire lines. Although the state quickly received international recognition, no peace treaties were signed between Israel and its

Palestinian houses demolished by the British during the Great Revolt. (From: Fondation Arabe pour l'image, Beirut.)

neighbors—only armistice agreements. For the next forty-five years, the attention of the world would focus on getting Israel and its neighbors to sign such treaties. In other words, for the next forty-five years most of the international community chose to view the conflict between two peoples—Zionists and Palestinians—as an "Arab-Israeli" conflict among sovereign states. After more than half a century, only two peace treaties between Israel and any of its neighbors have been signed: one between Israel and Egypt (1979), the other between Israel and Jordan (1994).

On the other hand, the war devastated Palestinian society. About 720,000 Palestinians fled their homes and were trapped behind enemy lines, unable to return. Although the reasons for their flight have been a subject of debate for over fifty years, a consensus has begun to emerge in the scholarly community, mainly as a result of research undertaken by a group of Israeli scholars called the New Historians. Most scholars now agree that a combination of factors led to the birth of the Palestine refugee problem. On the one hand, Palestinians, like most refugees, naturally fled from a war zone. On the other hand, there were expulsions, particularly in the north, while other Palestinians were deliberately frightened into leaving by acts of terror committed by Zionist forces. In the village of Dayr Yassin alone, between 110 and 240 men, women, and children were butchered, and the bodies of many were stuffed in the village well. Acts such as that one were hardly kept secret. After all, as Lenin once put it, the purpose of terrorism is to terrorize.

Most Palestinian refugees ended up in the West Bank (which was occupied by Jordan until 1967), the Gaza Strip (which was occupied by the Egyp-

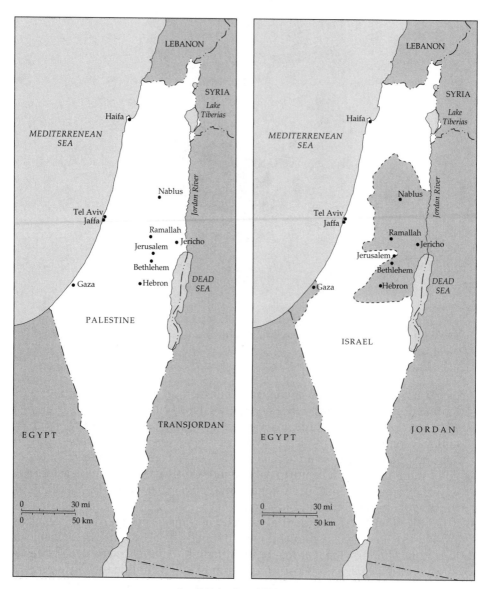

Israel/Palestine, 1921, 1948

tians until the same year), and neighboring Arab countries. Those who had
an education or money tried to rebuild their lives as best they could on their
own. Others who were not so lucky ended up in camps supported by the
United Nations Relief and Works Agency (UNRWA), where they and their
descendents have lived to this very day. Those Arabs who remained in Israel were subject to martial law until 1966.

The 1948 war also affected Arab states—not just those that fought in the
war, but states throughout the region. Groups of military officers in Egypt,

Syria, and Iraq felt they had been betrayed by their governments. While the Palestine war was not the only reason these officers were dissatisfied, the Arab defeat came to symbolize a host of grievances these officers held against their governments. They accused those governments of entering the war half-heartedly (which they did) and blamed their defeat on the incompetence and corruption of those governments. They also equated the defeat of the Arab forces with the inability or unwillingness of Arab governments to promote the sort of economic and social development that would have assured success on the field of battle. Taking matters into their own hands, these officers launched *coups d'etat* in Syria (1949), Egypt (1952), and Iraq (1958) against their governments. As we shall see in the next chapter, these coups would change the course of Arab politics and transform the bond connecting the states of the Middle East with their citizens.

DOCUMENTS

Resolution of the Syrian General Congress at Damascus, 2 July 1919

In the aftermath of World War I, the Syrian General Congress met and agreed upon a program for the future of a Syrian nation. In violation of Article 22 of the Covenant of the League of Nations, the following resolution of the congress was ignored by the entente governments.

We the undersigned members of the Syrian General Congress, meeting in Damascus on Wednesday, July 2nd, 1919, made up of representatives from the three Zones, viz., the Southern, Eastern, and Western, provided with credentials and authorizations by the inhabitants of our various districts, Moslems, Christians, and Jews, have agreed upon the following statement of the desires of the people of the country who have elected us to present them to the American Section of the International Commission; the fifth article was passed by a very large majority; all the other articles were accepted unanimously.

1. We ask absolutely complete political independence for Syria within these boundaries. The Taurus System on the North; Rafah and a line running from Al Jauf to the south of the Syrian and the Hejazian line to Akaba on the south; the Euphrates and Khabur Rivers and a line extending east of Abu Kamal to the east of Al Jauf on the east; and the Mediterranean on the west.
2. We ask that the Government of this Syrian country should be a democratic civil constitutional Monarchy on broad decentralization principles, safeguarding the rights of minorities, and that the King be the Emir Feisal, who carried on a glorious struggle in the cause of our liberation and merited our full confidence and entire reliance.
3. Considering the fact that the Arabs inhabiting the Syrian area are not naturally less gifted than other more advanced races and that they are by no means less developed than the Bulgarians, Serbians, Greeks, and Roumanians at the beginning of their independence, we protest against

Article 22 of the Covenant of the League of Nations, placing us among the nations in their middle stage of development which stand in need of a mandatory power.

4. In the event of the rejection by the Peace Conference of this just protest for certain considerations that we may not understand, we, relying on the declarations of President Wilson that his object in waging war was to put an end to the ambition of conquest and colonization, can only regard the mandate mentioned in the Covenant of the League of Nations as equivalent to the rendering of economical and technical assistance that does not prejudice our complete independence. And desiring that our country should not fall a prey to colonization and believing that the American Nation is farthest from any thought of colonization and has no political ambition in our country, we will seek the technical and economical assistance from the United States of America, provided that such assistance does not exceed 20 years.

5. In the event of America not finding herself in a position to accept our desire for assistance, we will seek this assistance from Great Britain, also provided that such assistance does not infringe the complete independence and unity of our country and that the duration of such assistance does not exceed that mentioned in the previous article.

6. We do not acknowledge any right claimed by the French Government in any part whatever of our Syrian country and refuse that she should assist us or have a hand in our country under any circumstances and in any place.

7. We oppose the pretentions of the Zionists to create a Jewish commonwealth in the southern part of Syria, known as Palestine, and oppose Zionist migration to any part of our country; for we do not acknowledge their title but consider them a grave peril to our people from the national, economical, and political points of view. Our Jewish compatriots shall enjoy our common rights and assume the common responsibilities.

8. We ask that there should be no separation of the southern part of Syria known as Palestine, nor of the littoral western zone, which includes Lebanon, from the Syrian country. We desire that the unity of the country should be guaranteed against partition under whatever circumstances.

9. We ask complete independence for emancipated Mesopotamia and that there should be no economical barriers between the two countries.

10. The fundamental principles laid down by President Wilson in condemnation of secret treaties impel us to protest most emphatically against any treaty that stipulates the partition of our Syria country and against any private engagement aiming at the establishment of Zionism in the southern part of Syria; therefore we ask the complete annulment of these conventions and agreements.

The noble principles enunciated by President Wilson strengthen our confidence that our desires emanating from the depths of our hearts, shall be the decisive factor in determining our future; and that President Wilson and the free American people will be our supporters for the realization of our hopes, thereby proving their sincerity and noble sympathy with the aspiration of the weaker nations in general and our Arab people in particular.

We also have the fullest confidence that the Peace Conference will realize that we would not have risen against the Turks, with whom we had participated in all civil, political, and representative privileges, but for their violation of our national rights, and so will grant us our desires in full in order that our political rights may not be less after the war than they were before, since we have shed so much blood in the cause of our liberty and independence.

We request to be allowed to send a delegation to represent us at the Peace Conference to defend our rights and secure the realization of our aspirations.

J. C. Hurewitz, *The Middle East and North Africa in World Politics: A Documentary Record, vol. 2: British–French Supremacy, 1914–1945* (New Haven, Conn.: Yale University Press, 1979), pp. 180–82.

Theodor Herzl: A Solution of the Jewish Question

Theodor Herzl (1860–1904) was one of the founders of the Zionist movement. In an 1896 article written for the London weekly *The Jewish Chronicle*, he outlines his argument for the establishment of a Jewish homeland and discusses alternative sites for the location of such a homeland.

The Jewish Question still exists. It would be foolish to deny it. It exists wherever Jews live in perceptible numbers. Where it does not yet exist, it will be brought by Jews in the course of their migrations. We naturally move to those places where we are not persecuted, and there our presence soon produces persecution. This is true in every country, and will remain true even in those most highly civilised—France itself is no exception—till the Jewish Question finds a solution on a political basis. I believe that I understand antisemitism, which is in reality a highly complex movement. I consider it from a Jewish standpoint, yet without fear or hatred. I believe that I can see what elements there are in it of vulgar sport, of common trade, of jealousy, of inherited prejudice, of religious intolerance, and also of legitimate self-defence. . . .

We are one people—One People. We have honestly striven everywhere to merge ourselves in the social life of surrounding communities, and to preserve only the faith of our fathers. It has not been permitted to us. In vain are we loyal patriots, in some places our loyalty running to extremes; in vain do we make the same sacrifices of life and property as our fellow-citizens; in vain do we strive to increase the fame of our native land in science and art, or her wealth by trade and commerce. In countries where we have lived for centuries we are still cried down as strangers; and often by those whose ancestors were not yet domiciled in the land where Jews had already made experience of suffering. Yet, in spite of all, we are loyal subjects, loyal as the Huguenots, who were forced to emigrate. If we could only be left in peace. . . .

We are one people—our enemies have made us one in our despite, as repeatedly happens in history. Distress binds us together, and thus united, we suddenly discover our strength. Yes, we are strong enough to form a state, and a model state. We possess all human and material resources necessary for the purpose. . . . The whole matter is in its essence perfectly simple, as it must necessarily be, if it is to come within the comprehension of all.

Let the sovereignty be granted us over a portion of the globe large enough to satisfy the requirements of the nation—the rest we shall manage for ourselves. Of course, I fully expect that each word of this sentence, and each letter of each word, will be torn to tatters by scoffers and doubters. I advise them to do the thing cautiously, if they are themselves sensitive to ridicule. The creation of a new state has in it nothing ridiculous or impossible. We have, in our day, witnessed the process in connection with nations which were not in the bulk of the middle class, but poor, less educated, and therefore weaker than ourselves. The governments of all countries, scourged by antisemitism, will serve their own interests, in assisting us to obtain the sovereignty we want. These governments will be all the more willing to meet us half-way, seeing that the movement I suggest is not likely to bring about any economic crisis. Such crisis, as must follow everywhere as a natural consequence of Jew-baiting, will rather be prevented by the carrying out of my plan. For I propose an inner migration of Christians into the parts slowly and systematically evacuated by Jews. If we are not merely suffered to do what I ask, but are actually helped, we shall be able to effect a transfer of property from Jews to Christians in a manner so peaceable and on so extensive a scale as has never been known in the annals of history. . . .

Shall we choose [the] Argentine [Republic] or Palestine? We will take what is given us and what is selected by Jewish public opinion. Argentina is one of the most fertile countries in the world, extends over a vast area, and has a sparse population. The Argentine Republic would derive considerable profit from the cession of a portion of its territory to us. The present infiltration of Jews has certainly produced some friction, and it would be necessary to enlighten the Republic on the intrinsic difference of our new movement.

Palestine is our ever-memorable historic home. The very name of Palestine would attract our people with a force of extraordinary potency. Supposing His Majesty the Sultan were to give us Palestine, we could in return pledge ourselves to regulate the whole finances of Turkey. There we should also form a portion of the rampart of Europe against Asia, an outpost of civilisation as opposed to barbarism. We should remain a neutral state in intimate connection with the whole of Europe, which would guarantee our continued existence. The sanctuaries of Christendom would be safeguarded by assigning to them an extra-territorial status, such as is well known to the law of nations. We should form a guard of honour about these sanctuaries, answering for the fulfillment of this duty with our existence. This guard of honour would be the great symbol of the solution of the Jewish Question after nearly nineteen centuries of Jewish suffering. . . .

Paul Mendex-Flohr and Jehuda Reinharz, *The Jew in the Modern World: A Documentary History* (New York: Oxford University Press, 1995), pp. 534–36.

The Balfour Declaration, 2 November 1917

The following is the text of the Balfour Declaration in its entirety.

I have much pleasure in conveying to you, on behalf of his Majesty's Government, the following declaration of sympathy with Jewish Zionist aspirations which has been submitted to and approved by the Cabinet:—

His Majesty's Government view with favour the establishment in Palestine of a national home for the Jewish people, and will use their best endeavours to facilitate the achievement of this object, it being clearly understood that nothing shall be done which may prejudice the civil and religious rights of existing non-Jewish communities in Palestine, or the rights and political status enjoyed by Jews in any other country.

I should be grateful if you would bring this declaration to the knowledge of the Zionist Federation.

J. C. Hurewitz, *The Middle East and North Africa in World Politics: A Documentary Record, vol. 2: British–French Supremacy, 1914–1945* (New Haven, Conn.: Yale University Press, 1979), pp. 180–82.

Mahmud Darwish: Eleven Planets in the Last Andalusian Sky

Mahmud Darwish is considered by many Palestinians to be their national poet. Born in a village destroyed during the 1948 war, Darwish has spent most of his life in exile. The experience of exile provides a touchstone for many of his poems—as it does for the poems of other Palestinian poets. The poem that follows is entitled "Eleven Planets in the Last Andalusian Sky." According to the Qur'an, the patriarch Joseph saw "eleven planets" in a prophetic vision. "The last Andalusian sky" is an allusion to the expulsion of the Moors from Spain.

On the last evening
we tear our days down from the trelisses
tally the ribs we carry away with us
and the ribs we leave behind.

On the last evening
we bid farewell to nothing,
we've no time to finish,
everything's left as it is,
places change dreams the way they
change *casts of characters.*

Suddenly we can no longer be lighthearted,
this place is about to play host to nothing.

On the last evening
we contemplate mountains surrounding the clouds,
invasion and counter-invasion,
the ancient era handing our door keys over to a new age.
Enter, O invaders, come, enter our houses,
drink the sweet wine of our Andalusian songs!
We are night at midnight,
no horseman galloping toward us
from the safety of that last call to prayer
to deliver the dawn.

Our tea is hot and green—so drink!
Our pistachios are ripe and fresh—so eat!
The beds are green with new cedarwood
    —give in to your drowsiness!
After such a long siege, sleep on the
    soft down of our dreams!
Fresh sheets, scents at the door, and many mirrors.
Enter our mirrors so we can vacate the premises completely!

Later we'll look up what was recorded in our history
    about yours in faraway lands.

Then we'll ask ourselves,
"Was Andalusia
here or there? On earth
or only in poems?"

Mahmud Darwish, *Adam of the Two Edens: Selected Poems*, ed. Munir Akash and Daniel Moore (Syracuse, N.Y.: Syracuse University Press, 2001), pp. 147–70.

SUGGESTED READINGS

Batatu, Hanna. "Of the Diversity of Iraqis, the Incohesiveness of Their Society, and Their Progress in the Monarchic Period toward a Consolidated Political Structure." In *The Modern Middle East*, edited by Albert Hourani et al., 503–28. Berkeley: University of California Press, 1993. The absurdity of the mandates policy presented in graphic detail.

Chehabi, Houchang E. "Staging the Emperor's New Clothes: Dress Codes and Nation-Building Under Reza Shah." *Iranian Studies* 26 (Summer/Fall 1993): 209–21. Explains the origins and experiences of Reza Shah's policies with respect to clothing.

Doumani, Beshara. *Rediscovering Palestine: Merchants and Peasants in Jabal Nablus, 1700–1900*. Berkeley: University of California Press, 1995. Pathbreaking social, economic, and cultural history of central Palestine over two centuries.

Fromkin, David. *A Peace to End All Peace: Creating the Modern Middle East*. New York: Henry Holt, 1989. Very readable account of great power bargaining and conflict over the Middle East in the wake of World War I.

Gelvin, James L. *Divided Loyalties: Nationalism and Mass Politics in Syria at the Close of Empire*. Berkeley: University of California Press, 1998. Close examination of the development of both popular and elite nationalism in the Levant in the aftermath of World War I.

Gelvin, James L. *The Israel-Palestine Conflict: One Hundred Years of War*. Cambridge, England: Cambridge University Press, 2005. Readable interpretation of the conflict from the nineteenth century through the present.

Gelvin, James L. "The League of Nations and the Question of National Identity in the Fertile Crescent." *World Affairs* (Summer 1995): 35–43. Concise overview of nationalism and state-building in the region in the aftermath of World War I.

Gelvin, James L. "Modernity *and* Its Discontents: On the Durability of Nationalism in the Arab Middle East." *Nations and Nationalism* 5, no. 1 (January 1999): 71–89. Investigation of the origins and persistence of nationalism in the Middle East.

Halliday, Fred. "The Nationalism Debate and the Middle East." In *Middle Eastern Lectures*, edited by Martin Kramer, 3. Syracuse, N.Y.: Syracuse University Press, 1999. Presents a cogent theoretical model for understanding nationalism in the region, then applies it.

Hertzberg, Arthur, ed. *The Zionist Idea: A Historical Analysis and Reader*. New York: Atheneum, 1981. Excerpts from a broad range of Zionist authors, with an excellent introduction on the intellectual history of Zionism.

Hurewitz, J. C. "The Entente's Secret Agreements in World War I: Loyalty to an Obsolescing Ethos." In *Palestine in the Late Ottoman Period*, edited by David Kushner, 341–48. Jerusalem: Yad Izhak Ben-Zvi, 1986. Situates the agreements made by the entente powers during World War I within the context of the breakdown of the European concert of powers.

Jankowski, James, and Gershoni, Israel, eds. *Rethinking Nationalism in the Arab Middle East*. New York: Columbia University Press, 1997. Excellent collection of essays on all aspects of nationalism in the Arab Middle East, including the historiography of nationalism.

Karpat, Kemal H. *An Inquiry into the Social Foundations of Nationalism in the Ottoman State: From Social Estates to Classes, From Millets to Nations*. Princeton, N.J.: Princeton University Research Monograph 39 (July 1973). An extremely valuable study that looks at the rise of nationalisms within the Ottoman Empire from the standpoint of comparative social history.

Khoury, Philip S. *Syria and the French Mandate: The Politics of Arab Nationalism, 1920–1945* Princeton, N.J.: Princeton University Press, 1987. The definitive study of the effects of French mandatory policies on the rise of nationalism in Syria.

Mardin, Serif. "Religion and Secularism in Turkey." In *The Modern Middle East*, edited by Albert Hourani et al., 347–74. Berkeley: University of California Press, 1993. Puts the policy of Ataturk in historical perspective.

Shafir, Gershon. "Zionism and Colonialism: A Comparative Approach." In *Israel in Comparative Perspective: Challenging the Conventional Wisdom*, edited by Michael N. Barnett, 227–44. Albany: State University of New York Press, 1996. A comparison between Zionist settlement in Palestine and contemporaneous movements in other parts of the world.

Smith, Charles D. *Palestine and the Arab-Israeli Conflict: A History with Documents*. Boston: Bedford/St. Martin's, 2001. Probably the best comprehensive history of the conflict over Palestine.

Swedenburg, Ted. "The Role of the Palestinian Peasantry in the Great Revolt (1936–1939)." In *The Modern Middle East*, edited by Albert Hourani et al., 467–501. Berkeley: University of California Press, 1993. Overview of the Great Palestine Revolt with a good dose of social history.

Part 4

THE CONTEMPORARY ERA

If a Middle Eastern Rip van Winkle had fallen asleep in the decade following World War I and then awoke seventy or eighty years later, there would be much that he would recognize. The state system that had been in embryo at the beginning of his nap was, by the time of his awakening, fully realized. While various nationalisms had emerged or withered during his sleep, the populations of the region still looked to the principles of nationalism to organize their political communities—much as they had done when van Winkle's eyes were just getting heavy. The confrontation between Zionist settlers and the indigenous inhabitants of the region had changed to a confrontation involving Israel, its neighbors, and a seasoned Palestinian national movement. Yet the conflict remained a lasting and seemingly intractable problem. The influence of Britain and France had waned, but great power meddling in the region continued under the aegis of the United States. And, although an Islamic republic had replaced the Iranian monarchy, Iran's boundaries remained much as they had been in the aftermath of World War I. Certainly, the postrevolutionary Iranian state did not surrender any of the powers the state had accumulated under Reza Shah and his heir.

In many ways, World War I and its aftermath had a profound influence on the subsequent history of the Middle East. That influence should not be overestimated, of course. History is cumulative, and so-called revolutionary events are as much the product of change as they are the source of it. No nationalist movements or state system could have arisen in the Middle East had not the great nineteenth-century transformation prepared the ground for them. Furthermore, the war hardly affected the nature of economic and social relations in the region at all. That would come later. Nevertheless, World War I remains a useful benchmark, so long as we remember its usefulness has limitations.

One should also be wary of glossing over the equally profound changes that took place in the region subsequent to World War I. But how should the historian approach those changes? Historians writing today are so close to the events of the past three-quarters of a century that they are unable to gain the perspective distance provides. To put it another way, few historians would deny the significance of the French Revolution, although there are many disagreements about exactly what its significance was. On the other hand, how can historians be expected to judge the significance of the Iranian Revolution of 1978–1979? As in the case of journalists, the best that historians writing about the past three-quarters of the century can offer is a first draft of history.

This should not discourage historians from attempting to make sense of the most recent period, however. Thus far, this book has argued that the establishment of a modern world economy and the modern state system distinguish the modern period from previous epochs. If we continue to use the world economic and state systems as our guideposts, it might be argued that the history of the contemporary period can be subdivided into two parts. The first began during the 1929–1945 interval and ended in the early 1970s. This period started with the onset of the Great Depression and World War II. Both events changed the nature of social, economic, and political relationships in the region. In the aftermath of the economic crisis spawned by the Great Depression and industrial growth spawned by World War II, more and more people in the region moved to cities, sold their labor, and became integrated into the political process. While governments in the region were hardly democratic, they did have to respond to the aspirations and needs of newly urbanized and politicized populations to survive. Middle Eastern states responded by adopting an increasingly popular-nationalist rhetoric that appealed to those populations. More important, those states responded to popular demands and expectations by taking on many of the trappings of post–World War II welfare states in Europe and North America. Over time, they introduced new labor laws, workman's compensation policies, food subsidies, and welfare for their most impoverished citizens.

Three factors encouraged this process. The first was ideology. In the aftermath of World War II, Western governments (particularly the United States), the United Nations, and international banking institutions adopted an approach to the "underdeveloped world" called "modernization theory." Modernization theorists believed that the only way the underdeveloped world could progress and avoid crippling social revolution—communist revolution—was through economic development. They assumed that if a country had an entrepreneurial middle class; a strong government committed to economic growth or middle-class values; small, independent farmers no longer bound to rich landowners; political participation; or some other "magic bullet," it could achieve growth, stability, and, eventually, Western-style democracy. The institutions and governments modernization theorists ran or advised thus sought to bring about modernization by financing or encouraging the emergence of that elusive "magic bullet" in each underdeveloped country. To accomplish this end, the United States encouraged "modernizing" military officers to take over the reins of government in a number of Middle Eastern countries. Once they did, it encouraged them to adopt one or another development program. The United States also encouraged the shahs and monarchs it supported in the region to adopt similar programs.

Modernization theorists found kindred spirits in much of the periphery of the modern world economic system. There, a remarkable generation of leaders—Marshal Tito of Yugoslavia, Achmed Sukarno of Indonesia, Jawaharlal Nehru of India, Ahmed Sékou Touré of Guinea, Patrice Lumumba of the Congo, Kwame Nkrumah of Ghana, among others—formulated a doctrine known as "Third Worldism." Like the modernization theorists, Third Worldists believed in modernization and economic development for their countries. Like the modernization theorists, Third Worldists felt that modernization and economic development could only be brought about by strong, guiding hands. Unlike the modernization theorists, however, Third Worldists advocated social revolution to overcome economic inequities in their societies, quasi-socialist policies to bring social justice to their nations, and nonalignment in international affairs to avoid being caught up in the dispute between the United States and the Soviet Union. For them, the cold war was an irrelevant but dangerous dispute between two rival imperialist blocs. Third Worldists celebrated the masses they claimed to represent and inveighed against the injustices perpetrated by colonialism. Many adherents to Third Worldism found a local hero in Egyptian president Gamal 'Abd al-Nasser, who came to personify the doctrine in the Middle East.

The decades of the 1950s and 1960s were the highwater mark of modernization theory and Third Worldism. In the Middle East, the doctrines became more than abstract ideologies as a result of two phenomena. First, as a result of decolonization and military *coups d'etat*, new ruling elites emerged in much of the region, from Algeria to Iraq. These new ruling elites had reached political maturity in a political environment in which it was assumed that states had to foster economic growth and social solidarity. Modernization theory and Third Worldism provided them with a roadmap. But the revolutionary Middle East was not alone in adopting development strategies associated with modernization theory. Even those countries that did not directly experience military takeovers—Saudi Arabia, Lebanon, Jordan, Iran—saw which way the wind was blowing and adopted development strategies modeled on those introduced by the "revolutionary states." As in the case of revolutionary states, ruling elites in those countries proclaimed their commitment to full national independence, social equality, and economic development. They, too, grasped at theoretical straws as they made the state the motor propelling social and economic transformation. In Turkey and Iran, where state-directed economies and social engineering were nothing new, modernization theory provided a new foundation for policies that post–World War I governments had adopted to achieve "modernization."

Full national independence, social equality, and economic development were quite a burden for a state to take on. But in their efforts to assume new powers, states in the region had an ace in the hole. They were able to accumulate the money necessary for development through the nationalization of foreign properties and those belonging to "enemies of the state," foreign aid, and, perhaps most decisively in the Middle East, oil revenues. Every state in the region used one or more of these sources of revenue to concentrate an inordinate amount of power in its hands, build institutions, and take on new functions. In the process, populations in the Middle East came to expect more from their states. The criteria for political legitimacy changed, and as states became the arbiters of political, economic, and social life, they also became the focus of popular anger when things went wrong.

By the mid-1970s, many states in the Middle East were in crisis. In large measure, the roots of this crisis were international. In 1971, the international financial arrangement that had ushered in a twenty-five year period of growth and economic stability in the West was coming apart at the seams. From 1945 through the late 1960s, the United States had been the unrivalled economic power in the world. The American dollar was strong and the U.S. government guaranteed that dollars could be exchanged for gold at an official, fixed rate. The dollar provided the foundation for international exchange. All other Western countries pegged their currencies to the dollar. By the early 1970s, however, the United States was no longer the unrivalled economic power it had been in 1945. Germany and Japan challenged America's position of preeminence and began to accumulate dollars at a rate that alarmed financial experts. By 1971, the value of American imports outran the value of its exports for the first time in the post–World War II period, and the dollars held outside the United States began to exceed the gold reserves in Fort Knox that backed those dollars.

In August 1971, the United States government severed the relationship of the dollar to gold and allowed the dollar to "float." In point of fact, it sank. The dollar ceased to be the "go to" currency. Instead, a new arrangement emerged. International currencies would no longer be linked to the dollar directly, but to a mixture of currencies. The value of those currencies, which had been fixed to the dollar, now rose and fell according to circumstances. To prevent financial chaos, the governments of the seven major Western economies—the United States, Japan, Germany, Britain, France, Canada, and Italy—agreed to coordinate their economic policies. A new multipolar world economy arose from the ashes of a unipolar (American-centered) world economy.

The protectionist and state-guided economic development policies adopted by states in the aftermath of the Great Depression had found expression in modernization theory and Third Worldism. Likewise, the new realities also found expression in ideology. Competition over scarce and more expensive commodities, stalled economies in the West, and the failure of modernization in the underdeveloped world gave rise to the notion that there were limits to growth. States would just have to learn to curb their ambitions. At the same time, the new financial arrangements that dispersed financial decision making among a "Group of Seven" led to the first predictions that the world economy would be truly "globalized" in the future. Globalization would become a full-fledged mantra in the wake of the Soviet collapse and the end of the cold war. Globalization depended upon open markets that operated with a minimum of government interference. "Neo-liberalism" replaced "modernization theory" as the dogma of bankers.

All this had momentous effects on the Middle East. Arab states were already under severe pressure as a result of the disastrous 1967 War against Israel. The war not only discredited the revolutionary regimes but improved the position of the United States in the region. Anwar al-Sadat, the president of Egypt from 1970 to 1981, once remarked that after the war the United States held "99 percent of the cards" in the Arab Middle East. The conservative oil monarchies came to play an expanded role in the interregional balance of power in the wake of the war as well. These states were enriched by the elevated price of oil and were major donors of financial aid to oilless states in the region. Because they had a stake in the success of the new international financial arrangements, they used their leverage to convince the revolutionary regimes to moderate their internal and external goals. In addition, states from Egypt to Iran were weakened as a result of the inefficiencies of centralized economic planning and social dislocations caused by the sudden rise and equally sudden collapse of oil prices. All these factors contributed to creating an environment in the Middle East in which states would pin their hopes on the new economic dogmas.

Under pressure from the United States and international institutions, states began to renege on the commitments they had made to their populations in the 1950s and 1960s. Because no state could risk doing this openly, each adopted piecemeal solutions. States continued to distribute many of the high-profile goodies they had promised in the 1950s and 1960s, such as subsidies on basic commodities and employment guarantees. At the same time, they began to "liberalize" some sectors of their economies to encourage private enterprise and foreign investment. Limited liberalization proved ineffectual. Productivity did not increase. On the other hand, the gap separating rich from poor did. States ended up with the worst of both possible worlds: popular frustration and stalled economies. As often as not, when governments showed themselves unable or unwilling to meet the needs and aspirations of their populations, Islamist movements stepped into the breach.

Islamist movements trumpeted the same commitment to social justice and social welfare as had governments before the 1970s. That commitment still resonated with the inhabitants of the region. Their own populist credentials in tatters, states throughout the region answered those who challenged them with repression. In the case of Iran, this did not work. In 1978–1979, a broad-based revolutionary movement overthrew the shah. In other cases, repression has provided what may prove to be only temporary relief. It is a bit ironic that in the post–cold war "Age of Democratization" and "Age of Globalization," so much of the Middle Eastern population has thus found itself enmeshed in the twin snares of authoritarianism and economic stagnation.

Fifteen

State and Society in the Contemporary Middle East: An Old/New Relationship

When the cold war ended in the early 1990s, many statesmen and political scientists predicted that the world was entering a new period in which democratic governments would be the rule, not the exception. And at the beginning of the post–cold war era, there seemed to be plenty of evidence to support their optimism. After all, the last great totalitarian system—communism—seemed to be in eclipse throughout the world. That "prison-house of nations," the Soviet Union, had come and gone and its "subject peoples" were now free to determine their own futures. From China to Latin America to Eastern Europe, pro-democracy movements inspired fear in authoritarian governments and, at least in the latter two cases, achieved some notable successes. Yes, it appeared that a new democratic order was about to emerge throughout the world.

Or parts of the world. When statesmen and political scientists talked of democratization they rarely, if ever, cited trends in the Middle East. Even after American policy makers announced that "regime change" in Iraq would unleash a "democratic tsunami" in the region, their vision met with a chorus of doubt. "The idea of instant democratic transformation in the Middle East," a report issued by the Carnegie Endowment for International Peace pronounced, "is a mirage." How has it come to pass that the Middle East has become a bastion for authoritarian governments resisted by equally authoritarian opposition movements? Why do the governments in the region appear so tenacious and powerful?

A number of factors contributed the emergence of strong states ruled by authoritarian governments in the Middle East. The great powers certainly played a part. Over the course of the twentieth century, the great powers not only established states, they intervened directly into their internal affairs. The great powers have also used their leverage in both the political and economic spheres to dictate policy to governments and have granted them financial assistance. Underwriting democracy was not a high priority for the great powers. Governments in the region could also count on other financial resources to bolster their power. For example, almost all Middle Eastern states are directly or indirectly enriched by oil. Those states not fortunate enough to have oil lying under their territory have received financial assistance from those that are. Because governments, not individuals or private corporations, control revenues derived directly or indirectly from oil, governments—not individuals or private corporations—have achieved unrivaled economic power throughout the region. With unrivaled economic power came unrivaled political power.

A third factor contributed to the emergence and endurance of strong, authoritarian governments in the region as well. Over the course of the past two centuries, both elites and nonelites in the Middle East increasingly came to equate economic development with social justice and nation-building. They have also come to view government as the primary engine for economic development. The widely held belief that a leading function of government is to guide economic development and ensure social justice enabled governments in the region to concentrate an inordinate amount of power in their hands.

What might be termed a "developmentalist ethos" emerged in the Middle East during the nineteenth century. It spread among the populations of the region in much the same way as did the ideology of nationalism. Both found an avid following in an environment in which state capabilities had begun to expand dramatically. In those regions where states were most effective in imposing new institutions and structures and in mobilizing and harnessing the energies of their populations in the name of the "common interest," a change occurred. The populations affected by state initiatives began to internalize the principles by which the state justified its actions and adopt them as their own. In effect, it was the defensive developmentalist activities of rulers and bureaucrats that generated a shared developmentalist ethos amongst the inhabitants of the territories they governed.

Nationalists interested in the practical details of state-building were, of course, among the most vocal advocates of developmentalism. Zia Gokalp, the so-called father of Turkish nationalism, thus wrote in the early twentieth century,

> In the future Turks must possess the same economic well-being that they once enjoyed in the past, and the wealth which is earned must belong to everyone. . . . The large sums that will result from collecting surplus values in the name of society will serve as capital for the factories and farms to be established for the benefit of society. Earnings of these public enterprises will be used to establish special refuges and schools for paupers, orphans, widows, invalids, cripples, the blind and the deaf, as well as public gardens, museums, theatres and libraries; to build housing for workers and peasants; and to construct a nation-wide electric power network.

But overt nationalists like Gokalp were not the only ones to believe in these ideals. For example, in 1899 the Islamic modernist and grand mufti (chief religious figure) of Egypt, Muhammad 'Abduh, issued a religious ruling that included the following sentences:

Establishing industries is a delegated duty. The nation must have a group within it to establish industries necessary for survival. . . . If the industries are not available, whoever is in charge of the affairs of the nation must establish them so that they might provide for the needs of the people.

Shortly after 'Abduh's ruling, orthodox ulama in Damascus joined the chorus, warning the Young Turk government, "Whoever does not work to advance the economy strays from Islam."

Thus, by the early twentieth century, the developmentalist ethos had become widespread in those areas of the Middle East that had been most affected by defensive developmentalism during the previous century. When, in the wake of World War I, new governments began expanding their power over territories that had once been beyond the reach of imperial authority, the territorial stretch of the developmentalist ethos expanded along with it. The developmentalist ethos achieved its greatest influence in the region during the 1950s and 1960s, when modernization theory and Third Worldism were at their peak and when a series of military *coups d'etat* established new regimes in Egypt, Syria, and Iraq. These new regimes based their legitimacy on their ability to bring about economic development and social justice. They also established new norms for state behavior that continue to influence both governments and populations throughout the region.

Few observers looking at Egypt, Syria, and Iraq in the immediate aftermath of World War I would have imagined that within a few decades those states would be regional trendsetters. Egypt won its sovereignty under conditions largely defined by an outside power. The latter two states were directly created by outside powers. The structure of the governments of all three reflected the imperialist legacy.

During the period between the two world wars, both the British and the French relied on local notables and sympathetic rulers to maintain their influence in the region. They found notables and rulers reliable proxies for a number of reasons. The economic interests of most notables matched those of Britain and France. After all, most notables derived their wealth from landownership. The lands they owned produced agricultural commodities such as cotton and silk, which sustained British and French mills. Furthermore, the populations of the mandated territories and Egypt would have chafed at direct control from Paris or London. On the other hand, the British and French banked on the fact that those populations would tolerate indirect control by their compatriots. Besides, indirect control was also cheaper. This was a primary concern for powers that had endured such large losses of men and matériel during World War I. Finally, relying on notables and sovereigns made British and French control easier. Competition among notables and between notables and sovereigns for power and influence impeded the emergence of unified nationalist movements that might have dislodged the imperialist powers. We have already seen how this worked in Egypt, where the palace, often with the connivance of the British ambassador, prevented the Wafd from dictating the course of Egyptian politics. For all these reasons, the states left by the British and the French in the Levant, Mesopotamia, and Egypt were initially weak, unrepresentative, and divided.

There had been, of course, no tradition of kingship in Egypt or Iraq before World War I. Egypt did not become a monarchy until 1922. In Iraq, the establishment of a royal house coincided with the invention of the state itself. But just as kings were a new phenomenon in Egypt and Iraq, so was the class of landowning notables upon whom the British and French also relied. Some of these notables could trace the roots of their wealth only as far back as the nineteenth century, when high prices for cash crops and the Ottoman Land Code of 1858 made real estate an attractive arena for investment. The roots of others were even more shallow. In Syria and Iraq, the French and British granted tracts of land to rural and tribal leaders during the mandates period. They did this in order to buy their loyalty and counterbalance the power of urban notables. The holdings of both urban and rural notables were not negligible. By the mid-twentieth century, 1 percent of the population of Syria owned about 50 percent of the land. In Egypt, about 1 percent of the population held about 72 percent of the land. The newness of many of these holdings and the disparities in wealth in societies that were still predominantly rural would make land reform a hot-button issue in the period following World War II.

All this has not prevented historians and others from looking back on the period stretching from the 1920s through the mid-1930s—and in some cases even later—with a great deal of nostalgia. This period, they point out, was one of cosmopolitanism in culture and the "liberal experiment" or the "liberal age" in politics. There is much to commend this view. As late as the 1940s, 40 percent of the population of Alexandria, Egypt, was "foreign." It consisted mainly of Greeks, Italians, Syrians, and Jews. Until the early 1950s, the largest single group in the multiethnic, multireligious capital of Iraq, Baghdad, was Jews. Today, the population of Alexandria is overwhelmingly made up of descendants of native-born Egyptians, and less than a handful of Jews remain in Baghdad. In the realm of politics, those who call some slice of the interwar period the "liberal age" describe it as such because during this period parliaments were convened, political parties formed, constitutions promulgated, secular rights institutionalized, and newspapers published. Egyptian feminism even celebrated a founding moment during this period. In 1923, Egyptian feminists returning from a women's conference in Italy removed their veils in public.

But celebrating the moment of unveiling also points to a fundamental weakness in the "liberal age" argument. Veiling was practiced among upper-class women only. Whether they donned or doffed veils was of little concern to most Egyptians. Looking at the period as a golden age draws attention away from the social cleavages that permeated Arab Middle Eastern societies and made the "liberal age" liberal for only a few. In cosmopolitan Alexandria, for example, the foreign community enjoyed privileges unavailable to most Egyptians. As a matter of fact, it was common practice for native Egyptians to be segregated in or excluded from tramways, clubs, and cafés and to fill the least rewarding niches of the economy. While it is

Upper class Egyptian woman, 1920s. (From: The Collection of the author.)

also true that during this period states in the Arab East often took on the formal trappings of democratic life, more often than not these trappings masked underlying practices and social divisions that were undemocratic. Although there were parliaments, the franchise was limited and assemblies were unrepresentative. Although political organizations and trade unions were founded, associational life was restricted and often curtailed by imperialist powers or local autocrats. Although newspapers were published, they were subject to censorship.

The overriding fact of political life from the 1920s through the 1940s was that there was little that governments or nationalist parties in Egypt, Syria, and Iraq could or would do to change this state of affairs. Governments were weak and unstable and governed at the sufferance of the imperialist powers that maintained a presence throughout the region. Nationalist movements reflected the interests of the elites who dominated them. They concentrated their efforts on gaining or confirming national independence and paid only limited attention to social and economic concerns.

Nevertheless, during the period between 1918 and the end of World War II, the developmentalist ethos not only continued to find adherents, it became a key element in the politics of the three states. Merchants, home-grown industrialists, and even landowners played an important role in this. Working through the governments they dominated, these groups planned rudimentary programs for economic development, if for no other reason than it would be beneficial to all involved. For example, all supported the construction of basic infrastructure like roads, which would enable governments to maintain control over the countryside, industrialists to obtain labor and raw materials for their factories, and landowners to ship goods to market. Likewise, all supported a rudimentary expansion of educational facilities, centralized planning, and incentives for private enterprise.

Groups of industrialists and bankers that emerged first in Egypt in the early 1920s, then in Syria and Iraq, played a particularly important role in energizing the doctrine of developmentalism. They made developmentalism a key component of nationalism by spreading a doctrine known as "economic nationalism." Not only did they encourage Egyptians, for example, to "buy Egyptian," they attempted to infuse nationalist movements with enthusiasm for economic and social reform. True independence, they claimed, was not limited to political independence. True independence meant economic independence as well. Economic independence could only be achieved through economic development and establishing a social system that would allow all to participate in nation-building.

The message of the economic nationalists was spread by new types of mass political parties and associations. As poverty in the countryside increased during the Great Depression, and as cities began to lure peasants with the promise of employment or educational opportunities, the population of urban centers exploded. In 1917, for example, the population of Cairo and Alexandria together was one and a quarter million; by 1947, it was over three million. As urban populations increased, so did the number of those available for political mobilization. A host of political parties and associations emerged, splintered, and re-formed during this period, from assorted communist parties and Muslim brotherhoods to the Syrian Social Nationalist Party, the League of National Action (in Syria), the National Democratic Party (in Iraq), and the Wafdist Vanguard and Young Egypt. These parties and associations differed from earlier nationalist parties in three ways: They were tightly structured, they possessed a middle-class leadership and middle-class and lower middle-class following, and they championed doctrines that went beyond mere calls for political independence. They sought to address the bread-and-butter concerns of their new constituents. The founder of the Syrian Social Nationalist Party put it this way:

> The aim of the Syrian Social Nationalist Party is the achievement of unity which
> will enable the Syrian nation to excel in the struggle for existence. This national
> unity cannot be obtained within an unsound economic system just as it can-
> not be realized within an unwholesome social order. That is why the achieve-

ment of social and economic justice is of extreme importance to the success and triumph of the Syrian Social Nationalist Party.

Ironically, the activities of the Great Powers encouraged the spread of new political movements and their developmentalist doctrines as well. Britain, France, and, during World War II, the United States introduced into the region new administrative practices that they had devised to meet the challenges of the Great Depression or World War II. These practices expanded the capabilities of governments, made populations accustomed to close governmental supervision of economic affairs, raised popular expectations, and opened up fresh possibilities for developmentalist currents. For example, during the Depression, French mandatory authorities in Syria introduced measures designed to stabilize the economy and maintain order. These measures were based on the welfare-state policies introduced by the Popular Front government that governed France from 1936 to 1938. But once price supports, wage guidelines, labor codes, poor relief, commodity subsidies, and the like were put in place, urban Syrians increasingly viewed them as an obligation of government, not a gift from government.

The activities of the Middle East Supply Center (MESC) reinforced the developmentalist ethos even further. The MESC was designed by the Allies in World War II to collect data on consumer needs in the region so that they might allocate cargo space on freighters more efficiently. Over the course of the war, the MESC expanded its role. By the time the program was terminated, the MESC was regulating imports, guiding and supporting industrial investment, distributing essential commodities, and supervising production in Egypt and the Levant. The MESC fostered a 40 percent increase in manufacturing output in Egypt. Investment in Syrian industry quadrupled during the war years. The activities of the MESC not only set a standard for state-led economic development but provided the developmental blueprint for post-war governments to follow.

The developmentalist policies promoted by elites and popular political associations, along with the intrusive activities of foreign powers, redefined the criteria for political legitimation in Egypt, Syria, and Iraq. More often than not, the "old guard" politicians who dominated parliamentary politics had to respond to new demands. But more often than not they responded in word rather than in deed. All this was to change over the course of the next two decades. Beginning in 1949, cliques of military officers launched *coups d'etat* against civilian politicians in all three countries and then against already empowered military regimes in Syria and Iraq.

While the first military coup in the post–World War II period took place in Syria, it was the Free Officers coup in Egypt in 1952 that would set the standard and provide a model for other states in the region. The Free Officers movement was established in the late 1940s by a group of mostly younger officers. Soon after the coup, Gamal ʿAbd al-Nasser emerged as the group's leader. Nasser had been born in 1918 in a village near Alexandria. He was the son of a postal clerk and had risen in the Egyptian military to the rank of colonel. He had fought in the 1948 Palestine war, during which he was seriously wounded. For him, like many in his cohort, the war was a turning point. It represented the corruption, ineptitude, and treason of the old regime. The Free Officers claimed to have launched their coup to put an end to that corruption, ineptitude, and treason. They did not, at first, offer a grand ideological vision. Instead, they promised to work with the private sector and the least objectionable political parties, and to restore democracy once they had ironed things out. For this reason, the Free Officers referred to themselves and their coup merely as a "movement." Only later did they retrospectively overstate their sense of purpose by replacing the word "movement" with "revolution."

This is not to say, however, that the Free Officers or other military cliques who seized power between 1949 and 1958 were ideologically barren. As urban dwellers, graduates of military academies, and the products of lower middle- or middle-class upbringing at a time when those classes formed the nucleus of new political currents, military officers were steeped in the political controversies of the day. They also had been raised in an environment that provided them with a set of assumptions about modernity and progress. Once in power, even the unimaginative Husni al-Za'im, who seized power in Syria in 1949, was instinctively drawn to the sort of policies that came to be associated with all military-led revolts in the region. Colonel al-Za'im, who ruled for only three months, reportedly proclaimed "Give me five years and I will make Syria as prosperous and enlightened as Switzerland" shortly before he was deposed.

Nevertheless, military conspirators throughout the region only began promoting comprehensive programs to restructure their economies and societies after the Suez War of 1956. The war was a debacle, an ill-conceived invasion of Egypt by British, French, and Israeli forces that is still called the Tripartite Aggression by Egyptians. The three states launched their invasion to topple Nasser's government because the Egyptian leader had proved himself to be a thorn in the side of all three. He had nationalized the Suez Canal, was supporting Algerian insurgents against French rule, and had just concluded an arms deal with Czechoslovakia that threatened to upset the regional balance of power. The British, French, and Israelis felt he clearly had to go.

The invasion did not topple Nasser's government. To the contrary. International pressure forced the invading states to withdraw their forces before they could achieve their aim. As a result of the failure of Britain, France, and Israel to realize their goal, the war actually raised Nasser's political stock both at home and throughout the region. Overall, the invasion had three results for the eastern Arab world and Egypt. First, it convinced Nasser that the Free Officers had not yet eliminated the twin threats of domestic reaction and foreign imperialism. From that moment on, the regime would no longer seek accommodation with the forces of reaction and imperialism, but would take control of its own destiny. It would do that by seizing the property of reactionaries and imperialists and using it to finance rapid economic and social development.

Gamal ʿAbd al-Nasser greeted by supporters in Port Said after the Suez War. (From: Fondation Arabe pour l'image, Beirut.)

The Suez War also created a political atmosphere in Iraq that made the overthrow of the monarchy by a military coup almost a foregone conclusion. That coup took place in 1958. It was soon followed by others, which introduced to Iraq policies first sampled in Egypt. Finally, Nasser's anti-imperialist stance incited political groupings in Syria to demand unification with Egypt. Foremost of these groupings was the Baʿth (Resurrection) Party. Founded in 1949, the party found support among romantic intellectuals who waxed eloquent about Arab unity as well as among hardcore organizers. This latter group had received its political education during the Depression of the 1930s. It thus brought to the party populist demands for economic and social reform. Baʿthist regimes, a bit less ideological but no less fervent about holding onto power, still control the government of Syria and retained control of Iraq until 2003. The unification of Egypt and Syria took place in 1958 with the establishment of the United Arab Republic. It lasted for three years. During that time, the Egyptians exported their model for development directly to Syria.

Wherever military officers and their "civilianized" successors took control (first in Egypt, Syria, and Iraq, then in Yemen, Libya, and the Sudan), their first goal was to weaken or break the power of previously existing elites. They did this in several ways. In some cases—Egypt, Iraq, and Libya—they deposed a monarch, confiscated his properties, and dissolved the venue for distributing royal patronage, the court. Coup leaders also dismissed parliaments that had provided landowning notables with a base for their political operations and disbanded political parties they felt were more part of the problem than part of the solution.

Alongside these political measures, the coup leaders destroyed the power of the old elites by striking at their economic power. One of the ways they did this was through land reform.

Land reform was hardly a revolutionary idea. Even the American and British governments and the World Bank had advocated land reform in the region to alleviate rural poverty and build a class of rural consumers who might buy goods produced in cities. There also appeared to be a crying need for land reform. On the eve of the 1963 revolution in Syria, for example, 60 percent of peasants were landless. In Iraq, the figure was 80 percent. But whatever the need, the military rulers found land reform to be a convenient way to weaken their rivals. At the same time, the new regimes viewed land reform as a means to gain the support of the rural masses and extend their control over those masses.

The Egyptian program of land reform was typical of the sort of program other states would come to adopt. The Egyptian government placed ceilings on the amount of land that individuals or families could own. Those ceilings were initially set at two hundred feddans, then reduced to one hundred, and finally to fifty. By 1971, nearly one million feddans had been distributed to about 350,000 peasant families. Peasants who received land had to join cooperatives set up by the state to organize and improve production, control the sale and pricing of agricultural goods, and provide credit. In effect, the cooperatives were created to enable the government to take over activities like money lending and marketing that had previously been in the hands of landholding elites. At their height, there were five thousand cooperatives with three million members. Similar cooperatives and even communes were established in Syria and Iraq.

The weakening or elimination of entrenched political elites paved the way for new political elites to rise to power. Military coups empowered what modernization theorists called the "new middle classes," as well as representatives of provincial and rural society. Many modernization theorists saw the military officers as the vanguard for these groups. This vanguard, they believed, would usher in a new era in which governments would be responsive to the aspirations of those classes that had the greatest stake in ensuring economic development and social justice. Being composed of military men, this vanguard would not hesitate to impose their programs by force. In Egypt, eight of the twelve members of the governing Revolutionary Command Council established after the Free Officers coup had rural roots. Nasser himself came from a provincial, middle-class background. In a like manner, thirteen of the fifteen members of the Revolutionary Command Council that ruled Iraq from 1968 to 1977 came from small peasant or petit-bourgeois backgrounds. Throughout the region, employees of the expanded bureaucracy came from similar provincial and lower middle-class backgrounds. As a result of this expansion of political and bureaucratic power to those who had previously been excluded, governments responded to the needs and ideals of strata that had never before been the object of government concern. These strata became the main beneficiaries of expanding services, such as healthcare, education, rent stabilization, and food subsidies provided by governments.

To pay for these services, military governments promoted programs for state-sponsored economic development. Governments sought to promote industry to end their nations' dependence on international markets and the industrialized West, break the back of industrialists and others who had, more often than not, proven themselves hostile to the new rulers, and to expand their control over their populations. The state mobilized resources and directed them through expanded state planning and investment.

Often, states mobilized resources by taking over (nationalizing) foreign or private holdings. Through nationalizations, the regimes not only gained control over the properties and businesses they seized, but acquired revenue to invest as they chose. Furthermore, nationalizations enabled the regimes to diminish the influence of foreigners, political enemies, and "resident-aliens" over the economies of their countries. In the case of Egypt, this last category included many of the Greeks, Italians, Syrians, and Jews whose families had lived in Egypt for decades, if not centuries. The Egyptian government not only took control of the Suez Canal and most British and French investments in the country, but took charge of the hundred million Egyptian pounds locked in the vaults of the largest bank in Egypt. By the mid-1960s, the Egyptian government found itself in control of banks, insurance companies, textile mills, sugar-refining and food-processing facilities, air and sea transport, public utilities, urban mass transit, cinemas, theaters, department stores, agricultural credit institutions, fertilizer production, and construction companies. According to recent statistics, government expenditures still account for about 60 percent of the Egyptian gross domestic product.

If measured by profit, state control over so much of the economy was highly inefficient. But the success of nationalizations and the ensuing program of "state socialism" or "state capitalism" (depending on your point of view) cannot be measured in terms of efficiency alone. By administering so many productive and commercial establishments, the state was able to allocate resources for its own ends and to gain control over strategic industries. Furthermore, the state was able to cut unemployment and even guarantee employment to many of its citizens. The 1962 Egyptian constitution, for example, promised employment to all graduates of the national university. Unfortunately, college graduates who work for the government are, more often than not, underemployed and paid ridiculously low salaries. Many have been forced to supplement their incomes by spending their off hours working in the private sector.

Controlling economic resources enabled states to expand their role in society and to rearrange society so that they might control it better. Through centrally planned economies and unopposed state power, governments have used economic incentives to gain the compliance of their citizens and reward those sectors of society the governments claimed to represent. The benefits states delivered have been extensive. States undertook road and school construction, rural electrification, and healthcare and literacy campaigns. States expanded educational opportunities by reducing or eliminating school fees. Enrollment at Damascus University, for example, doubled between 1963–1968, with half the students coming from a rural background. States have also kept food and commodities affordable by providing subsidies for many essentials: wheat, flour, cooking oil, rice, sugar, tea, petroleum, and gas. At the present time, subsidies on food, education, and healthcare account for over 50 percent of the Egyptian government's expenditures.

In addition to rewarding their supporters and punishing their opponents economically, the governments of Egypt, Syria, and Iraq have attempted to manipulate society by recognizing certain groups as legitimate and withholding recognition from others. The former groups are given the right to participate in the councils of government (if that phrase can be applied to party congresses and rubber stamp parliaments) and to bicker with other recognized groups over the division of spoils from the state. For example, during the 1960s the Egyptian government recognized five groupings as the building blocks of the new society: peasants, workers, intellectuals and professionals, national ("good") capitalists, and the army. Hand-picked representatives of these groups were called upon to ratify the 1961 Charter for National Action, and to keep their constituents informed of government decisions.

Interestingly, while this system diminished the rights enjoyed by some groups in Nasserist Egypt and Ba'thist Syria and Iraq, it had the opposite effect on the rights enjoyed by others. For example, the system substantially curtailed the rights of workers. In all three countries the state destroyed the organizational independence of trade unions. First, the state purged liberals, leftists, and Islamists from union leadership. Then, the state integrated unions into broader labor confederations. These confederations held the exclusive right to represent their members to the government. Other groups that had organized themselves before the onset of the revolutionary period, such as the press and professional and trade associations, likewise lost their independence.

But while the revolutionary states curtailed the rights of workers, they expanded the rights of women. The Egyptian government, for example, recognized women as a distinct category of society whose needs were deemed worthy of special consideration. The Egyptian constitutions of 1956 and 1962 guaranteed equal opportunities to all Egyptians regardless of gender. The Egyptian state granted women the right to vote (as had the Syrian state after its first military coup), and guaranteed women paid maternity leave and the right to child care if employed at a large facility. The Ba'thist regimes of Syria and Iraq legislated similar measures in the 1970s. Like the Egyptian government during the same period, they also expanded women's rights in marriage and protected women's rights of inheritance. Notwithstanding their stated commitment to social justice, the regimes stepped into this social minefield and promoted "state feminism" for two other reasons. First, they aspired to appease middle-class sentiment and to displace feminist organizations that had been active in the region since the 1920s. These organizations might have participated in liberal challenges to their rule. In addition, the regimes sought to further their control over the private lives of their citizens in much the same way as had Mustafa Kemal Ataturk and Reza Shah before them.

The military regimes thus pioneered approaches to politics and economics that were novel in the region. By doing so, they provided a model from which other Middle Eastern states drew. Even states in the region that had not experienced military takeovers adopted many of the administrative, economic, and social measures Nasser had imposed in Egypt or the Ba'thists had imposed in Syria and Iraq. In some cases, they did this to win the hearts and minds of their populations who were literally listening to the siren song of Gamal 'Abd al-Nasser on Radio Cairo. Imagine being King Hussein of Jordan and hearing Radio Cairo call on Jordanians to "take the dwarf [King Hussein, whom the British and the Americans called "our PLK"—plucky little king] and hang him from the gates of the British embassy." In other cases, states adopted Nasser's strategy because he had established a highly centralized government that brooked no challenge. They wished to follow suit.

Although almost all states in the region adopted institutions and programs similar to those adopted in Egypt, Syria, and Iraq, it is important to note that not all of them took their developmentalist cues directly from their turbulent neighbors. Influenced by modernization theory and Third Worldism, the governments of these states followed a path that paralleled the separate path followed by Nasserist Egypt and Ba'thist Syria and Iraq.

For example, in 1963–1964 the Ba'th Party took control over governments in both Syria and Iraq. The party presided over the most radical attempt to restructure the economics and politics of their countries yet. Governments of both states nationalized banks, insurance companies, and commercial and industrial establishments. A key element of their program was the expansion of land reform. At the same time, the shah of Iran announced his own plan for development known as the White Revolution. Like the Ba'thists, the shah committed his government to wideranging social and economic reforms, including a land reform program. The shah felt that land reform would placate American policy makers who continued to believe that land reform imposed from the top would prevent a social upheaval from below. The shah also sought to take the wind out of the sails of his liberal and leftist opponents who were influenced by Third Worldist doctrines. Besides, land reform would break the power of rural landlords and strengthen the power of the central government. The program restricted the number of villages that landowners could own and redistributed land to those peasants who could prove they had sharecropping rights. Landowners were compensated with shares in state-owned industries that the White Revolution also expanded. Unfortunately for the shah, many were left unsatisfied. Historians often cite the unpopularity or failure of the White Revolution when cataloguing the reasons behind the Iranian Revolution of 1978–1979.

Because most states in the region have copied or reproduced on their own the economic and political strategies pioneered by the self-described "revolutionary republics," their political systems hold a lot in common. From republican Egypt to monarchic Saudi Arabia to Islamist Iran, governments still play a major role in the economic sphere. In most states a small, close-knit ruling group stands above the fray, dispensing goodies to favored clients. This has bound populations to their governments and made those populations complicit in a political system that otherwise excludes them. In most states, what passes for political debate entails little more than disputes over the allocation of resources. In most states, the government has effectively pitted social groups against each other for shares in the economic bounty. This policy has all too often encouraged the fragmentation of society along kinship, ethnic, regional, and/or religious lines.

Then there is the problem of repression. Because the revolutionary regimes claimed to represent the "will of the nation," they have repressed their opponents and classified whole layers of society as "enemies of the people." The governments of Egypt, Syria, and Iraq have not been reluctant to use force when they have felt threatened or when it has suited their purposes. Within a month of taking power, the Free Officers of Egypt brutally suppressed a strike that had broken out at a textile factory. They arrested 545 workers and staged a show trial, after which two workers were hanged to demonstrate the commitment of the Free Officers to maintaining order. Far worse was yet to come. Nasser filled his jails with political dissidents, from leftists to Islamists. When the Syrian government faced an Islamist rebellion in the city of Hama, it shelled the city and killed from ten to twenty thousand of its residents. During the notorious Anfal campaign waged by the Iraqi government against its own Kurdish citizens in 1988, government troops killed between fifty thousand to 150,000 Kurdish fighters and noncombatants.

The heyday of the so-called revolutionary model in the Arab East was short-lived. The economies of Egypt, Syria, and Iraq had been buoyed from their inception through the 1970s by a combination of nationalizations, foreign assistance, and oil revenues. By the early 1980s, all three were compelled to change course. Centralized economic planning had proved to be just as inefficient in the Arab Middle East as it had in other parts of the world. States had run out of properties to nationalize and, after a rapid climb, oil prices once again bottomed out. Governments had proved themselves as incapable of defeating Israel as their predecessors had been, and with the end of the cold war, both Syria and Iraq had lost their Soviet patron. To make matters even worse for all three states, the world economy had entered into a crisis period. As a result of new international economic conditions, international lending institutions and the governments that stood behind them began to distance themselves from states that maintained closed and tightly regulated economies. The revolutionary model was no longer as enticing as it had once been.

A Joke

According to the father of psychoanalysis, Sigmund Freud, jokes provide the means by which one part of the brain outwits the "psychic censors" of another part of the brain, thereby transforming pain into pleasure. Because psychic censors are not the only censors present in the Arab Middle East, jokes there perform another function as well: They allow Middle Easterners to vent their grievances in a medium that flies under the radar of the state.

Here is a story I first heard in Syria, then soon after in Jordan and Egypt. For the latter versions, just substitute the words "Jordanian" or "Egyptian" for the word "Syrian":

> One day, the world's best intelligence agencies decided to stage a contest to see which was, indeed, the best. Invited to the contest were America's C.I.A., Russia's K.G.B., Israel's Mossad, and Syria's *mukhabarat* (secret intelligence agency). To determine which was the best agency, a rabbit was to be released into a forest. The first intelligence agency to bring the rabbit out of the forest would be deemed the finest in the world.
>
> And so a rabbit was released and given a brief head start. Shortly thereafter, teams from the various intelligence agencies went in after it. After about an hour, the American team emerged with the rabbit. The contest was over. Two hours later the K.G.B. team emerged (rabbitless, of course), followed by the Israeli team.
>
> One day passed, then two, yet the Syrian team still did not emerge from the forest. After a week, the other teams decided to send in a search party. The search party scoured the forest, searching for the missing Syrians. Finally, the search party came to a clearing. In the middle of the clearing was a tree on which a donkey had been strapped. The Syrian team was surrounding the tree, while one of the Syrian agents was beating the donkey with a stick shouting, "Admit it—you're a rabbit."

While none of the revolutionary republics was so foolish as to attempt to abandon the goal of economic development as a basis for political legitimacy, all adopted policies of limited economic liberalization. Egypt, always the pioneer, was the first to experiment with such policies. Three years after the death of Gamal 'Abd al-Nasser in 1970, the newly installed president of Egypt, Anwar al-Sadat, launched a program of economic liberalization known as the *infitah* ("opening up"). The *infitah* was an idiosyncratic mixture of "Arab socialist" and free-market economics. It combined a strong state sector with incentives for foreign investment and private enterprise. State welfare programs were maintained as well. Anwar al-Sadat learned through bitter experience that any attempt to revitalize the Egyptian economy could not be undertaken at the expense of those programs. The attempt to curtail them ended disastrously with widespread strikes by industrial workers in 1975–1976, regime-threatening breadriots throughout the country in 1977, and a surge in support for the Islamist opposition. Syria and Iraq also experimented with limited economic liberalization during the 1980s. As in Egypt, however, economic liberalization in Syria and Iraq did not entail a weakening of the public sector or a politically dangerous withdrawal of subsidies, employment guarantees, or social security benefits from the population. Instead, both states attempted to reinvigorate the economy by applying private initiative to support a languid public sector.

Political scientists debate whether or not economic liberalization leads to political liberalization. Those who think there is a connection between the two argue that governments cannot open up an economic space for private initiative without opening up a political space at the same time. Others are more skeptical. They argue that the states in the region are so powerful that they do not have to "bargain" with their populations about expanding democratic rights. They also argue that states themselves have already successfully "decoupled" economic and political liberalization. In the 1974 *October Paper* that laid out the blueprint for the *infitah*, for example, al-Sadat warned that the social progress realized since the Free Officers revolution could only be protected if the government maintained a firm control over the political process. Since the announcement of the *October Paper*, Egyptian governments have parried half-hearted foreign pressure and domestic (mostly Islamist) threats by adopting the formal trappings of pluralist democracy. All the while, they have attempted to ensure regime survival by repressing potential opponents, manipulating the electoral system, continuing the welfare policies initiated under Nasser, and playing off the divisions created in society by the regimes themselves against one another. As in the past, the Egyptians may very well have provided a model from which other states in the region will continue to draw.

Sixteen

Oil

During the 1950s and 1960s, promises of economic and social development became the linchpins of government policy throughout the Middle East, just as they did in other areas on the periphery of the modern world system at the same time. Middle Eastern states supported the expansion of their activities with revenues they acquired from a variety of sources. Governments acquired revenues from the nationalization of properties of foreigners and "enemies of the state." They acquired revenues from foreign aid. And they acquired revenues, directly or indirectly, from the exploitation of oil.

Economists call the type of revenue generated from these sources "rent." They define rent as income acquired by states from sources other than taxation. Some economists call states that are dependent on rent for a certain proportion of their income "rentier states." Other economists call them "allocation states" because the states distribute the rent they receive to favored clients and projects. In no other area of the world have so many states been so reliant on income derived from rent as in the Middle East. Every state in the region depends on income from rent to a greater or lesser extent. Kuwait and Saudi Arabia might be placed in the "greater extent" category. In the early 1990s, about 98 percent of government expenditures in Kuwait came from rent (mainly oil sales) while the figure for Saudi Arabia was about 80 percent. Before the disastrous war with Iran (1980–1988), revenues from oil accounted for more than half the Iraqi income. At around the same time nontax revenue accounted for one-third and one-quarter of government revenues in Egypt and Syria, respectively. In the case of the former, assistance from the United States—about two billion dollars a year—has played a major role in sustaining the state. Syria has had to be more creative, combining lackluster revenues from oil sales with protection money paid by other states in the region seeking peace and quiet from their often troublesome neighbor. For the sake of comparison, it is worth noting that even moderately successful core states such as France derive well under 10 percent of their revenues from rent.

At the present time, oil constitutes the largest source of rent in the region. Nevertheless, oil was not an important commodity for the Middle East until the twentieth century. In fact, oil was not a particularly important commodity anywhere until the last decades of the nineteenth century. What economic historians call the "first industrial revolution" began during the last

"And up through the ground came a bubblin' crude": oil seeping to the surface in Iraq, 1909. (From: The Gertrude Bell Collection, University of Newcastle.)

decades of the eighteenth century. The "dark satanic mills" most of us identify with the first industrial revolution were fueled first by water power, then by coal. During most of the nineteenth century, coal generated heat for homes and fueled the great navies of the world. People even derived the kerosene used in lamps from coal. The importance of coal to modern life began to decrease during the second half of the nineteenth century with the onset of the "second industrial revolution." If textile mills and the primitive factory system have come to symbolize the first industrial revolution, the internal combustion engine, oil-burning naval ships, and the petro-chemical industry might be used to symbolize the second. The second industrial revolution thus established petroleum-based economies.

Even after the uses for oil expanded in the late nineteenth century, however, there were other sources closer to Europe and North America than the Middle East. In 1900, Russia was the world's largest producer of oil—just as it is today. About 50 percent of the world's supply of oil came from Russia. Among the other sources for oil at that time were the United States, Mexico, and Romania. Oil was not even discovered in Saudi Arabia until 1931. Production there did not begin for another seven years.

Most historians trace the history of the exploitation of oil in the Middle East from the d'Arcy concession of 1901, discussed in Chapter 5. The d'Arcy concession underscored the importance of sharing risk when it came to the oil business. Because the business requires a huge outlay of capital to begin operations, d'Arcy ran out of money before he was able to draw a profit. He was thus forced to sell the rights he had been granted to the British government, which established the Anglo-Persian Oil Company. This lesson was not lost on investors when the Ottoman government granted a similar concession several years later. The Turkish Petroleum Company (later the Iraq Petroleum Company), which received the right to exploit all the oil in the imperial domains, was a joint effort bringing together the Anglo-Persian Oil Company, Royal Dutch Shell (which, as its name suggests, traces its history to a trading company that dealt in abalone shells for cameo jewelry), and various German interests. The Anglo-Persian Oil Company owned 50 percent of the shares of the venture, while the others held 25 percent each. This sort of arrangement is known as a consortium (pl.: consortia). A consortium is a group of companies that band together to undertake a project that would be beyond the means of any single company. After the d'Arcy concession, all concessions were granted to consortia.

The concessions granted in the first thirty years of the twentieth century resembled one another in other ways as well. Like the d'Arcy concession, all subsequent concessions were of long duration, usually from sixty to seventy-five years (the d'Arcy concession was granted for sixty years). They covered huge areas, such as most of Persia or all of Kuwait. The consortia had the right to pursue all operations connected with the industry, including exploration, production, refining, transport, and marketing. In return for the concession, the consortia paid the state that granted it royalties and fees. Only later, in the 1950s, did the consortia begin to pay the governments of oil-producing states a share of their profits. Finally, the consortia, not the governments of the oil-producing countries, had a free hand in determining the quantity and price of the output. Thus, beginning in the twentieth century and continuing for more than half a century, the West was able to exploit the oil resources of the Middle East with little interference from, and few benefits for, the states from which that oil was extracted.

The so-called oil revolution that culminated in the 1970s was nothing more than a step-by-step whittling down of the these privileges by the countries under whose territory oil lay. For example, in 1961 the Iraqi government asserted its right to drill for oil in areas of Iraq not being exploited by the Iraq Petroleum Company. The oil-producing countries won the right to set oil prices, along with the terms of concessions, themselves only in 1971. Only in 1975 did the first Persian Gulf oil-producing nations, Kuwait and Dubai, take full control over the consortia operating in their countries. Rather than using the term "nationalization," which would have set off red flags in the minds of Western diplomats, most oil-producing states called their takeovers "100 percent participation" in the consortia working in their territories. Most did not attempt to acquire 100 percent participation overnight. For example, in 1973 the government of Saudi Arabia acquired 25 percent of the shares of ARAMCO (Arabian-American Oil Company), the consortium that controlled the oil business in the kingdom. A year later, it acquired 60 percent. It was not until 1980 that it acquired 100 percent participation. One hundred percent participation is, in effect, nationalization.

Oil-producing states were able to assume greater control over their most important resource in part because they acted in concert. The idea for an association to represent the common needs of producers, the Organization of Petroleum Exporting Countries (OPEC), originated in South America, not the Middle East. At the close of World War II, Venezuela was the world's third largest oil producer. The government of Venezuela proposed the formation of a producers' association in 1947 to prevent the United States from importing lower-priced Middle Eastern oil to undercut the prices set by the Latin American nation. The Venezuelan government argued that a producers' association would prevent the United States from setting oil exporters against one another. The idea finally bore fruit in 1960. In the wake of a recession in the West, oil companies slashed prices to stimulate demand. By this time, the consortia were paying most oil-producing nations 50 percent of their profits. A drop in prices thus meant a drop in revenues for producing nations. Outraged, representatives from five nations—Venezuela, Kuwait, Saudi Arabia, Iran, and Iraq—agreed on "the unification of the petroleum policies of member countries and the determination of the best means for safeguarding their interests."

OPEC came into its own during the international financial crisis of the 1970s. The famous price hike of 1973, which stimulated the influx of enormous wealth into the Middle East, can be traced to the American devaluation of the dollar in 1971. Confronted by an economic crisis that would change the nature of the international financial system, the American government was forced to sever the official relationship between the dollar and gold and lower the value of the dollar in comparison to other currencies. Oil was priced in dollars. Although oil producers continued to receive the same number of dollars for a barrel of oil, the devaluation meant that those dollars would be worth less. Using the 1973 Arab–Israeli war as a pretext, Arab members of OPEC temporarily decreased production, thereby limiting supply and raising prices. The price of oil jumped 380 percent and wealth flowed back into the region from the industrialized, petroleum-importing world.

The final transformation of OPEC took place in 1982 when the organization became a cartel. Economists define cartels as groups of businesses, or in this case states, that coordinate policies to limit competition. This enables them to ensure a high price for their product. By 1982, the price of oil had leveled off, despite the spectacular price rise of 1973 and another price spurt in the wake of the Iranian Revolution of 1978–1979. To keep prices high, the OPEC countries decided to assign themselves shares of the international market.

OPEC ministers meet regularly to decide how much oil each producer should pump. The meetings are usually contentious. Saudi Arabia, with an estimated population one-quarter that of Iran, will never become an industrial powerhouse and will never overcome its dependence on revenues from oil. Saudi Arabian ministers have traditionally fought to keep prices down to prevent new sources of oil from becoming economical. After the price hike of 1973, for example, the exploitation of North Sea and Alaskan oil fields became profitable. In a way, Saudi fears have already been realized. Whereas OPEC nations once accounted for about three-quarters of the world's supply of oil, they currently produce only about 40 percent. The Saudis also fear that high oil prices would encourage the West to turn to alternative sources of energy, such as nuclear or solar power. Iran, on the other hand, has a large population and an industrial infrastructure that Saudi Arabia can only envy. Since the 1950s, it has sought to end its dependence on oil revenues by becoming an industrial power. Iranian ministers therefore argue for higher prices so that they may reap immediate profits to invest to build their industrial economy of the future. Then there is Iraq. Before the Gulf War of 1991, Iraq demanded an equivalent market share with its neighbor to the east. Although Iraq has a population one-third the size of Iran's, it has had a history of contentious relations with that neighbor. After a great deal of haggling, OPEC ministers return home with production quotas in hand for their governments. Then their governments cheat on those quotas anyway.

In spite of attempts at price-fixing, complaints by Western politicians and consumers that they are being held hostage by a greedy cartel is a little like Claude Rains in "Casablanca" discovering there is gambling going on in Humphrey Bogart's nightclub. Before 1973, a cartel of Western oil companies known as the "seven sisters"—Exxon (Standard Oil of New Jersey), Mobil (Standard Oil of New York), Chevron (Standard Oil of California), Gulf, Texaco, and British Petroleum (Anglo-Persian Oil Company)—controlled all aspects of the oil industry. Because of the importance of oil for national economies, the cartel could count on the support of Western governments in their negotiations or confrontations with their hosts. Thus, in 1951, when the Iranian government had the temerity to nationalize the holdings of the Anglo-Iranian Oil Company (previously the Anglo-Persian Oil Company), the British and American governments imposed sanctions on Iran, arranged for an international boycott of Iranian oil, and organized a *coup d'etat* that brought the Iranian government down. The oil revolution merely replaced one cartel with another—and a not particularly effective one at that.

The decade of the 1970s thus seemed to mark the beginning of a new era for both the Middle East and the rest of the world. Fernand Braudel, the great French historian, speculated at that time that the oil revolution might be epoch-making because it would reverse the flow of wealth from the East to the West that had been ongoing for two centuries. From the Middle Ages through the eighteenth century, he wrote, wealth flowed from west to east as the value of goods Europeans bought from the East—spices, silks, etc.—exceeded the value of goods bought by the peoples of the East from Europeans. Beginning in the eighteenth century and continuing through the first three quarters of the twentieth, the value of goods the peoples of the East bought from the West—mostly finished products—exceeded the value of goods the peoples of the West bought from the East. It was entirely feasible, Braudel surmised, that the oil revolution would herald the beginning of an epoch in which the flow of riches would be reversed once again.

Three decades later, it is clear that the effects of the oil revolution have not been as epoch-making as, for example, the European discovery of the Americas or the onset of the industrial revolution. Middle Eastern oil producers and Western oil consumers are not two adversaries locked in combat. They are more akin to codependents locked in an uneasy embrace. The Middle Eastern oil producers must sell their oil. The West must buy it. Hence, in spite of the continued animosity between the United States and Iraq in the aftermath of the first Gulf War, and in spite of the fact that the United States continued to enforce sanctions on the regime in Baghdad, the United States was the biggest consumer of the oil that the Iraqi government was permitted to sell. Large sums of money from the West did go to the Middle East, but much of it returned to the West as investments or was deposited in Western banks, where it was "recycled." In other words, no dramatic change took place in the relative positions of the West and the Middle East as a result of the oil revolution. In fact, oil has had much the same effect on the twentieth-century Middle East as had cotton on nineteenth-century Egypt. Both reinforced a pattern of trade that has been favorable to the West.

This is not to say that the oil revolution brought no changes to the region. Rather, it is to say that the changes brought about by the oil revolution have mainly affected economic, political, and social life within the Middle East itself. For example, as discussed in Chapter 15, access to rent has sustained governments in the region and has given them an unprecedented ability to control and direct their states. What this means for the future of the region is, however, controversial. Some political scientists argue that an overdependence upon rent is actually the Achilles heel of Middle Eastern governments. They assert that governments in the region have been dangerously dependent on the international market or on the good will of foreign governments. If those sources of revenues dry up—if, for example, the price of oil plummets or foreign governments cut off aid—states have no safety net to make up the shortfall. Because citizens of rent-dependent states are bound to their governments in the same way that clients are bound to patrons, once the subsidies or jobs or welfare benefits dry up, the bond connecting them may very well break. And because governments have gone out of their way to let the citizenry know just who is responsible for their good fortune when times are flush, when the pickings are slim that same citizenry knows just whom to blame.

Some political scientists have thus ascribed the Iranian Revolution to the collapse of oil prices in 1975–1977. No longer able to meet the expectations of its citizenry and no longer able to balance repression with bribery, the government of the shah was doomed to collapse. Other political scientists note that this explanation, like any other "monocausal" explanation for the Iranian Revolution, is simplistic. They argue that this explanation fails to account for the fact that other states overly dependent on revenues from the sale of oil, such as Saudi Arabia, did not experience revolutions. Nor does this explanation account for the fact that states with little or no oil, from

Wealth from oil revenues once financed this public housing project in Baghdad. (From: Fondation Arabe pour l'image, Beirut.)

Nicaragua to Poland to the Philippines, experienced revolutionary upsurges at around the same time.

In addition to affecting individual states in the Middle East, there is a regional dimension to the oil revolution as well. In the wake of the revolution, the lines dividing rich from poor states in the region became more tightly drawn. The former states export oil. The latter export labor to the oil-producing nations. This division between rich and poor has had a number of repercussions. The Gulf region, considered a social and cultural backwater by many in the more populous and cosmopolitan regions of the Middle East, assumed a new and important role in the inter-Arab balance of power. For example, after the 1967 Arab-Israeli War, Saudi Arabia, Kuwait, and Libya (at that time a conservative monarchy) began paying subsidies to the so-called frontline states bordering on Israel to enable them to restock their arsenals. Because the payments were made in quarterly installments, the oil states maintained constant leverage over the foreign policies of Egypt, Jordan, and Syria.

At the same time, the labor-exporting states have become increasingly dependent on remittances—money sent home by expatriate laborers employed abroad—to ease their financial burdens. Remittances are a peculiar form of rent. They go to individuals and families, not to governments. For this reason, some political scientists argue that remittances actually weaken the governments of labor-exporting states by lessening the dependence of the citizenry on them for economic favors. Again, this view is not undisputed. Skeptics maintain that the export of labor may act as a safety valve in states where population growth and the spread of education have far outpaced economic opportunities. Whatever the case, the oil revolution sparked a migration of labor that has affected all states within the region. In 1968, for example, no more than ten thousand Egyptians worked abroad. Within ten years that number increased to over half a million. Between 1973 and 1985, one-third of all rural Egyptian men worked at some time during their lives in the Gulf. During the same time, 40 percent of the Jordanian workforce was abroad.

Like the uneven distribution of oil, the export of labor has had political effects on the region. Remittances have become an important source of supplementary income for the states that export labor. As a result, the threat that labor importers will expel guest workers can be a potent tool in their hands to exact concessions from their labor-exporting neighbors. During recent years, labor-importing nations have moved beyond merely making threats. On the eve of the Gulf War, Iraq expelled one million Egyptian workers. Egypt was a member of the Gulf War coalition. After the war, Kuwait expelled upward of seventy thousand Palestinians whom they accused of acting as a fifth-column for the Iraqis. Not to be outdone by their smaller neighbor, Saudi Arabia expelled one million Yemeni guestworkers the same year to protest Yemen's support for Iraq. Labor migration has thus further strengthened the hand of labor importers in the regional balance of power.

Labor migration has also affected social life throughout the region. For example, the employment of male workers in the Persian Gulf has led to what one Egyptian sociologist has called the "feminization of the Egyptian family" and a shift in women's roles there. In the absence of men, lower- and middle-class Egyptian women have become temporary heads of households, play a greater role in domestic decision making, and have built broad, community-based networks outside the home and family upon which they have come to depend. But if labor migration has created new forms of community bonds in Egypt, it has had an opposite effect in many states that import labor. There, labor migration has created cleavages between citizens who are entitled to government benefits and noncitizens who are not. Currently, noncitizens (from within and without the region) make up one-third of the inhabitants of Saudi Arabia and Libya, two-thirds of the inhabitants of Kuwait, and four-fifths of the inhabitants of Qatar. While the Pakistanis and Bangladeshis who live in the impoverished Kuwaiti towns of Fuhayhil, Jahrah, Hawalli, or Kaifan, for example, provide unskilled labor for the oil-rich principality, they are shunned by the privileged minority of native-born citizens.

The divide separating guest workers from citizens is not the only cleavage opened up by the oil revolution. Another has emerged as the oil-producing countries of the Gulf have had to balance the aspirations of their more Westernized citizens with the social norms of societies that had been little more than frontier territories before the contemporary period. The split between "traditionalists" and "Westernizers" often takes place within a context of a struggle pitting former elites against royal households. Tribal leaders, merchants, landowners, and ulama, claiming to represent the "traditional" values of society, often resist the policies and practices of the Westernizers. Those policies and practices, not coincidentally, would further reduce their already diminished power. On the other hand, many of the so-called Westernizing policies and practices in the smaller Gulf states are imposed from the top by kings and shaykhs. Not coincidentally, those policies and practices would increase the popularity of the central government among the more cosmopolitan elements of the population and strengthen its power.

What makes the squabble between old and new elites so intriguing is the fact that on closer inspection the "tradition" of kingdoms and shaykhdoms in the Gulf turns out not to be so traditional after all. Although royal households appear to be sanctioned by timeless custom, they are, in fact, novel to the region. It was the British who transformed influential families in Kuwait, Oman, Bahrain, Qatar, and the United Arab Emirates into royal dynasties by signing agreements with them during the nineteenth and early twentieth centuries. The British supported their dynastic ambitions. The newly anointed "rulers" recognized special British rights in their territories. All this provides the context for the bizarre confrontation that pit Kuwaiti "traditionalists" against Kuwaiti "Westernizers" in 1999. After the "traditional-but-progressive" amir of Kuwait decreed that women would have the right to vote, his decree was overturned by a majority of the members of that most Western of all institutions—a parliament.

Oil has had one further effect on the Middle East that merits mention here. Oil has made the region strategically important to outside powers, particularly the United States. Think of it this way: The United States has a historic connection to the West African country of Liberia. Liberia was founded by freed American slaves in 1822 and over the course of the nineteenth and twentieth centuries Liberia resembled an American colony, in deed if not in word. Between 1989 and 1996, Liberia experienced a bloody civil war in which a quarter of a million of its citizens died (another civil war broke out in 1999). On the other hand, the United States has no historic connection to Kuwait, which was a British protectorate until its independence in 1962. According to Amnesty International, during the Iraqi occupation of Kuwait (1990–1991), far fewer Kuwaitis—several hundred—were killed than the numbers of Liberians who perished in that country's civil wars. Yet the United States put together an international coalition and sent five hundred thousand of its own troops to liberate Kuwait. The American response to events in Liberia was tepid at best. Even after the secretary general of the United Nations, Kofi Annan, personally appealed to the American administration to send peacekeeping troops to Liberia in 2003, the United States sent only a token force of two hundred marines. Kuwait is one of the world's largest producers of oil (currently number thirteen) and is located in the midst of one of the biggest pools of oil in the world. Even the Liberian government classifies Liberia's oil reserves as "moderate."

It would be just as simplistic to say the United States waged the Gulf War just for oil as it would to deny the importance of oil in the calculations of policy makers. The objectives of American foreign policy in the region, as well as the effects of that policy, are the subjects of the next chapter.

Seventeen

The United States and the Middle East

During the latter part of the cold war, an eminent historian described American–Soviet competition in the Middle East as "new wine in old bottles." What he meant by this was that the cold war struggle for influence in the region might be seen as an extension of the Eastern Question of the nineteenth century. Once again, great powers outside the Middle East intervened in the region to gain strategic advantage over their rivals. Only the cast of players and their immediate goals changed. Instead of the main actors being Great Britain, imperial Russia, and France, the main actors in the cold war drama were the United States and the Soviet Union. Instead of great powers defining their interests in terms of protecting their route to India or seeking warm water ports, the great powers defined them in terms of a struggle between rival ideological systems locked in a titanic contest for the future of the world. Each viewed their competition in the Middle East as just one more front in that contest.

Now that the cold war has ended and a new international diplomatic order is in the process of formation, it might be a good time to take another look at the role of the great powers in the region. The world in which we currently live is a world defined by the defeat of the Soviet Union in the cold war by the United States and its allies. It is also a world in which the United States holds, at least temporarily, an indisputedly dominant position in international affairs. For this reason, this chapter is written from the standpoint of the sole remaining superpower, the United States.

Before World War II, the Middle East held little interest for the U.S. government. This is not to say that private citizens and nongovernmental groups ignored the region. Ever since the first governor of the Massachusetts colony, John Winthrop, called on colonizers to make their new home a "city on the hill," this image has resonated with Americans. Accordingly, over the course of American history, many Americans have felt a special affinity for that original city on the hill, located in the "Holy Land." American missionaries and travelers went to the region to save souls and survey sites from the Bible. They also founded schools and hospitals. In 1866, American missionaries established the Syrian Protestant College, now known as the American University in Beirut. Its motto was, and continues to be, "That they might have life and have it in abundance." In other words, American missionaries assumed the burden of bringing civilization and progress to the site of Christianity's birth—a site that, after the rise of Islam and centuries of "Turkish" rule, they believed had fallen on hard times.

The American government did undertake the occasional and desultory diplomatic and even military foray into the region before the cold war. Thomas Jefferson sent a naval expedition to "the shores of Tripoli" (in present-day Libya) after a local warlord attacked American merchant vessels in an attempt to extort more protection money from the United States. President Abraham Lincoln sent a brace of pistols as a gift to ʿAbd al-Qadir al-Jazaʾiri, the former Algerian resistance leader who, while in exile in Damascus, had intervened to protect Christians during the 1860 sectarian riots there. Lincoln also signed a treaty of commerce and navigation with the Ottoman Empire at a time when much of the world was unsure that there would be a United States for much longer. When a Moroccan bandit, Ahmad al-Rasuli, kidnapped an American businessman, Ion Pericardis, President Theodore Roosevelt won public acclaim by storming, "Pericardis alive or Rasuli dead." While Roosevelt was strutting around with his "big stick," the Moroccan government quietly paid the ransom. During and immediately after World War I, U.S. presidents and Congress weighed in on the Armenian massacres and Zionism (they deplored the former, supported the latter). Overall, however, when it came to foreign policy, the interest of the U.S. government lay outside the region. The Middle East—that is, the Ottoman Empire—was, after all, part of the concert of Europe throughout much of the nineteenth century. The United States thus let Europeans deal with Middle Eastern problems.

Even when the U.S. government stepped in to protect American oil interests in the Gulf from the "rapacity" of British and French oilmen during the interwar period, it was with the idea that others—the French and particularly the British—had the primary imperial responsibility for the area. Only in the wake of World War II did American policy makers work to replace the old imperialist powers in the region. It was not until after 1956, in the wake of the Suez War, that the United States accomplished this, finally replacing France and Britain as the primary Western power in the region.

Surprisingly, American policy with regard to the Middle East remained fairly stable throughout the second half of the twentieth century. This can be seen by comparing a policy statement made at the beginning of the cold war with one made toward its end. In July 1954, the National Security Council sent to President Dwight D. Eisenhower a report entitled "United States Objectives and Policies with Respect to the Near East." Under the section entitled "Objectives," the report lists the following:

a. Availability to the United States and its allies of the resources, the strategic position, and the passage rights of the area and the denial of such resources and strategic positions to the Soviet bloc.

b. Stable, viable, friendly governments in the area, capable of with-standing communist-inspired subversion from within and willing to resist communist aggression.

c. Settlement of major issues between the Arab states and Israel as a foundation for establishing peace and order in the area.

d. Reversal of the anti-American trends of Arab opinion.

e. Prevention of the extension of Soviet influence in the area.

f. Wider recognition in the free world of the legitimate aspiration of the countries in the area to be recognized as, and have the status of, sovereign states; and wider recognition by such countries of their responsibility toward the area and toward the free world generally.

In April 1981, Peter Constable, deputy assistant secretary of state for Near East and South Asian affairs in the administration of Ronald Reagan, testified before Congress "to provide an integrated picture of our policies toward the Middle East and Persian Gulf region." He listed the fundamental American objectives in the region as promoting the security of friends, assuring the security and availability of resources, and protecting vital transportation and communications routes. Constable then identified three "threats and challenges." First and foremost was Soviet expansion, both direct and indirect. Constable's testimony took place two years after the Soviet invasion of Afghanistan. The second threat to American interests was regional disputes and conflicts that jeopardized regional stability and provided fertile opportunities for external (Soviet) exploitation. Although a number of conflicts—the Lebanese Civil War, Iran vs. Iraq, Ethiopia vs. Somalia, and so on—posed a danger in American eyes, Constable focused much of his remarks on the Arab-Israeli conflict. Constable stated that "deep divisions and unresolved issues. . . . will continue to affect United States interests, relationships, and objectives until they can be composed on broadly accepted terms." Finally, Constable pointed to the destabilizing effects of political change, social development, and economic growth. In the minds of policy makers in the post-1971 world, "change," "development," and "growth" did not bring stability. They brought false hope and instability.

Between 1954 and 1981, and continuing through the end of the cold war, policy planners issued other pronouncements delineating American goals in the region. Although there were a few changes in the margins, most repeated pretty much the same policy objectives as the National Security Council and Peter Constable. Overall, then, we can identify six such objectives that guided American policy toward the region for over forty years.

First and foremost among American goals in the region was the containment of the Soviet Union. That is to say, the primary objective of the United States in the Middle East, as in all other areas of the cold war world, was to prevent the expansion of Soviet influence into the region. The United States had every reason to worry. The Soviet Union was located in the geographic heartland of the Eurasian continent and there was no reason to believe that its geopolitical ambitions were different from those of its predecessor, imperial Russia. As a matter of fact, the first cold war confrontation between the United States and the Soviet Union took place in the Middle East. In 1946, the Soviet Union refused to remove its troops from northern Iran, which it had occupied during World War II. It eventually withdrew them, but only under pressure. The heartland of the Middle East became a battle-ground between the two superpowers as Soviet strategy shifted in the late fifties. Under Nikita Khrushchev, who led the Soviet Union in one capacity or another from 1953 to 1964, Soviet strategists sought to spread Soviet influence by leapfrogging over surrounding states into the wider world. By doing so, Soviet strategists believed they could break containment, take advantage of anti-imperialist sentiments and the Third Worldist clamor for social revolution, and outflank the United States without directly confronting its nuclear-armed nemesis. Thus, from 1955 onward, the Soviet Union sought out allies in the heartland of the Middle East, including the three revolutionary republics: Egypt, Syria, and Iraq.

The second goal of the United States in the Middle East was to assure Western access to oil. There are two reasons for this: economic and strategic. Access to oil for domestic consumption has been, of course, a major concern for American policy planners for many years. At the beginning of the cold war, however, the United States did not depend on the Middle East for its oil. As a matter of fact, in the 1950s the international oil market was so glutted that President Eisenhower imposed import quotas to protect oil companies from falling prices. It was only in 1969 that the United States began importing crude oil from the region for domestic consumption. By the time of the oil crisis of 1973, the United States was importing more than a third of its oil from the Middle East. Currently, the United States imports approximately a fifth of its oil from the region.

But if oil for domestic consumption was not an immediate concern for the United States at the onset of the cold war, oil as a strategic commodity was. After World War II, the United States sustained European and Japanese economic recovery with cheap Middle Eastern oil. The United States viewed economic recovery in those regions as essential to prevent social revolutions—communist revolutions. American policy makers have viewed oil as a strategic commodity ever since. Europe still gets over a third of its oil from the Middle East; Japan gets close to 80 percent.

The third goal of American policy in the Middle East was to ensure the peaceful resolution of conflicts and the maintenance of a regional balance of power in the region. The U.S. government feared that regional conflicts—most of all the Arab-Israeli conflict—would polarize the region. This would encourage some states to turn to the Soviet Union (always the second-best option for Middle Eastern states during the cold war) and might destabilize the governments of America's friends. The best way to ensure stability in the region was to establish some sort of regional balance of power. During the Truman administration, the United States and its allies agreed to coordinate arms sales to Israel and surrounding Arab states to make sure neither side would have a clear advantage. After that policy broke down, most

American policy makers sought to assure peace by keeping Israel at least as strong as the sum total of its potential adversaries. American policy makers also sought to establish a balance of power in the Gulf. As a result, the United States "tilted" toward Iraq during the Iran-Iraq War and, three years after the war ended, led a coalition against Iraq in the Gulf War.

To ensure regional stability, the United States promoted stable, pro-Western states in the region. Furthermore, policy makers believed that if the states of the region were strong, and if they fulfilled the aspirations of their populations, they and their populations would resist Soviet blandishments. At first, American policy makers defined popular aspirations in terms of anti-imperialism, nationalism, and economic development. Thus, in the immediate aftermath of World War II, state department officials, policy planners, and Central Intelligence Agency spooks often supported the "modernizing" military officers who took power in military *coups d'etat*. As a result, the annals of contemporary Middle Eastern history are filled with stories—some probably fabricated—of ambassadors giving winks and nods to colonels and CIA agents distributing suitcases of money to local politicians and military officers.

The United States also supported the economic development of the states in the region, both as a contributor of foreign assistance and as an advocate in international economic institutions such as the World Bank. As was the trend during the 1950s, development experts often advocated the construction of colossal projects that they believed would provide the magic bullet for economic development. From 1953 to 1955, for example, the Eisenhower administration sent Eric Johnston, the former head of the Motion Picture Association, to the Middle East to negotiate a comprehensive plan for dividing the waters of the Jordan River among Israel, Lebanon, Jordan, and Syria. The plan, which included a blueprint for agricultural development, was modeled on the Tennessee Valley Authority, the showpiece of Depression-era public planning in America. Johnston's efforts failed, as did all American peace-through-economic-development schemes proposed during the 1950s and 1960s. (A Jordanian government official actually told the American ambassador there, "We've been impoverished for a thousand years. Rather than making peace with Israel, we'll be impoverished for another thousand.") The United States (and Great Britain) also backed Egypt's request for World Bank financing to build the Aswan High Dam. Like the Johnston Plan, the Aswan High Dam was a megaproject that, by regulating the flow of the Nile and harnessing its waters, was expected to provide the foundation for Egyptian development. When the United States, angered by Nasser's recognition of "Red" China, withdrew its support from the project, Nasser sought to make up the shortfall by nationalizing the Suez Canal. The nationalization set off the chain of events that led to the Suez War of 1956.

Although the United States replaced Britain and France as the dominant outside power in the Middle East in the wake of the Suez War, it soon found its ambitions in the region threatened by the very anti-imperialism and nationalism it had sought to channel. The United States had supported Nasser and the Free Officers in Egypt in 1952, but by 1958 Secretary of State John Foster Dulles was referring to Nasser as "nothing but a tin-horn Hitler." In the wake of the 1958 *coup d'etat* in Iraq, the United States placed itself in opposition to Nasser and the pan-Arab nationalism Nasser personified. About a decade and a half later, with the onset of the international financial crisis, it did the same with state-guided economic development. By the close of the cold war, the United States, once again in conjunction with international financial institutions, was preaching the message that economic development and political stability could only be achieved in the Middle East if states would liberalize their economies and give vent to private initiative.

The fifth goal of American policy during the cold war was the preservation of the independence and territorial integrity of the state of Israel. The American/Israeli alliance did not begin immediately. The decision made by President Truman to recognize Israel in 1948 was by no means a sure thing. Policy planners feared that the partition of Palestine would lead to a bloodbath that would divert American troops and attention away from Europe. They also feared that U.S. recognition of Israel would jeopardize American relations with the Arab world and thus jeopardize European and Japanese economic recovery. When President Truman announced at a closed-door meeting with policy makers that he planned to endorse partition, Secretary of State George Marshall stated, "Mr. President, if you proceed with that position, in the next election I will vote against you." Eight years later, Eisenhower was so outraged by Israel's participation in the Suez conspiracy that he threatened economic retaliation if Israel did not withdraw from Egyptian territory. It was not until John F. Kennedy that an American president used the word "ally" when referring to Israel.

Nevertheless, the United States has consistently reaffirmed its commitment to Israeli sovereignty and security. Numerous factors contributed to the American/Israeli alliance, from ideological to strategic to domestic. In terms of ideology, the Israelis have presented their case well in the United States, portraying Israel as the sole democracy and repository of American values in the region. In terms of strategy, U.S. policy makers oftentimes viewed Israel as a proxy in the fight against Soviet influence in the region. In terms of domestic politics, presidents and congressmen have attempted to garner Jewish—and, more recently, Christian evangelical—votes by portraying themselves as supporters of Israel. None of this means, however, that the American-Israel relationship has been trouble free, or that the United States has agreed with Israel across the board on such issues as borders, Israeli settlement policies in the occupied territories, approaches to ending the Arab-Israeli conflict, or the status of Jerusalem.

The final objective of American policy during the cold war was the protection of sea lanes, lines of communications, and the like, connecting the United States and Europe with Asia. The Middle East is, after all, the *middle* East. Its geographic position alone made it a prize worth fighting for by any power with global pretensions.

In the most abstract sense, then, American objectives in the Middle East—containing the Soviet Union, maintaining access to oil, achieving a peaceful resolution of conflicts and a balance of power among states of the region, safeguarding Israel, and capitalizing on the strategic location of the region—remained consistent over the course of the forty-year cold war. Why, then, does it appear to have been otherwise?

There are several reasons why U.S. policy appears to have been inconsistent. First of all, although American administrations faithfully advocated the same six policy objectives for forty years, the approaches the American government used to achieve them varied over time. For example, during the course of the cold war there were two main strategies of containment: peripheral containment and strong-point containment. The idea behind peripheral containment was to ring the Soviet Union with an unbroken string of pro-American states linked together through a system of alliances. This seemed the appropriate response to Soviet expansion across its borders during the early cold war period.

While the most famous and most successful of these alliances was the North Atlantic Treaty Organization (NATO), there were others. In 1955, for example, the British organized the "Baghdad Pact," made up of Britain, Turkey, Iraq, Pakistan, and Iran. The pact was a failure. Because Egypt and Iraq were locked in a rivalry for leadership of the Arab world throughout much of the cold war, Egypt opposed it. The Egyptians signed an arms deal with the Soviet bloc state of Czechoslovakia in 1955, thus rendering the alliance irrelevant. After military officers deposed the Iraqi monarchy in 1958, Iraq withdrew from the alliance anyway. All that was left was an empty shell called the Central Treaty Organization (CENTO), made up of the remaining states. In all, the Baghdad Pact and CENTO proved as effective in preventing the spread of Soviet influence in the Middle East as SEATO (Southeast Asia Treaty Organization) did in Southeast Asia.

With the failure of peripheral containment in regions outside Europe, American policy makers adopted the strategy of strong-point containment. Strong-point containment called for the judicious strengthening of a few "fortress" allies in various regions. It was hoped that this would prevent the Soviets from projecting their power abroad through proxy states bound to the Soviet Union by treaty. The United States chose its fortress states on the basis of the strength of their economy or military or government apparatus. Thus, during the 1970s the United States came to depend on Israel in the western Middle East to prevent the Soviets from using their Syrian ally to spread their influence. In the eastern Middle East, the United States supported the Iranian government (and, to a lesser extent, Saudi Arabia) to prevent the Soviets from using Iraq in the same way. While successful in the short term, strong-point containment in the Middle East ultimately contributed to disastrous consequences for the United States in the region: the Iranian Revolution of 1978–1979 and the Israeli invasion of Lebanon in 1982.

The containment of the Soviet Union was one policy goal that might be achieved in multiple ways. The preservation of the independence and territorial integrity of the state of Israel was another. During the cold war, some policy makers believed that this goal could be achieved by regarding Israel as a "strategic asset," a phrase coined during the Reagan administration. Another approach was expressed in the title of an article written in 1977 by that embodiment of the pipe-smoking American foreign policy establishment, George Ball. The article was entitled "How to Save Israel in Spite of Herself." According to Ball, Israel's long-term security depends on a settlement of the Arab-Israel dispute and good relations with its neighbors. Israeli intransigence not only prolongs the atmosphere of hostility, but undermines the governments of moderate neighbors, such as Jordan, which have nothing to show for their moderation. Therefore, if the United States truly has Israel's best interests at heart, it should adopt a more "evenhanded approach" and drag Israel, kicking and screaming if need be, to the bargaining table to negotiate a fair peace. Needless to say, successive Israel governments and their supporters in the United States have had problems with Ball's approach.

A second reason why U.S. cold war policy in the region seems inconsistent is that policy planners often attempted to achieve one objective at the expense of others. In 1970, President Richard Nixon alluded to what would become known as the Nixon Doctrine in his annual State of the Union Address. The United States was, at that time, embroiled in Vietnam and was looking for ways to avoid similar entanglements in the future. According to the Nixon Doctrine, the United States would give support to regional surrogates engaged in the fight against international communism without itself deploying forces. The idea was to put teeth in the words of Nixon's predecessor, Lyndon Baines Johnson, who announced (falsely as it turned out), "We are not about to send American boys nine or ten thousand miles away from home to do what Asian boys ought to be doing for themselves." Soon thereafter, OPEC decided for the first time to raise oil prices unilaterally. The U.S. government hardly let out a whimper. After all, price increases would allow America's regional surrogates (particularly Iran) to use their newly acquired wealth to buy the American weapons that, in turn, would enable them to block Soviet and Iraqi ambitions in the Gulf. In this case, containment trumped oil.

U.S. policy also seems to have been inconsistent because of what might be termed "the law of unexpected results." When formulating and implementing Middle East policy, the United States does not operate in a vacuum. For every move the United States made in the Middle East, the Soviets and local actors could be expected to make a countermove—very often an unexpected countermove—thereby forcing the United States to reevaluate its tactical or strategic approach.

Moves that the United States made not only affected individual states, they frequently had effects—often unexpected—on the regional balance of

power. Although Jimmy Carter was widely applauded for his role in medi-
ating the Camp David Accords between Israel and Egypt, the accords had
consequences none of the negotiators anticipated. After Egypt signed a peace
treaty with Israel, it was expelled from the Arab League. This left Iraq as the
dominant force in the inter-Arab balance of power. Many political scientists
argue that Iraq invaded Iran in 1980 to consolidate its hegemonic position
in the Gulf. Many also trace the Israeli invasion of Lebanon in 1982 to Camp
David. The clauses in the Camp David "Framework for Peace in the Middle East" dealing with a solution to the Palestinian question were stillborn.
According to some scholars, the Israeli government thus decided to impose
its own solution on the Palestinians. All that stood between Israel and that
solution was the Palestine Liberation Organization (PLO), safely ensconced
in Lebanon. The Israeli government therefore thought it could kill two birds
with one stone: destroy the PLO once and for all and impose a settlement
for the West Bank and Gaza Strip unilaterally. It is doubtful that the Israeli
government would have committed itself to this adventure had it not believed that Egypt would abide by the peace treaty it signed and not threaten
Israel from the south. Add to the mix the assassination of Anwar al-Sadat,
which came about as a direct or indirect result of Camp David (depending
on whom you ask), and the handshake on the White House lawn loses much
of its luster.

Finally, U.S. policy during the cold war appears to have been inconsistent
because even a superpower does not have a boundless ability to impose its
will on the world and failures prompted the reassessment of policies. As
successive American administrations learned from attempts to move Israelis
and Arabs to the bargaining table, impose unpopular economic policies in
Egypt, or to build a viable state in Lebanon, the American ability to direct
events or reconstruct states in its own image is, at best, limited.

Consistent or not, was American policy in the region successful during
the cold war? Before the events of 11 September, former National Security
Council member William Quandt wrote a number of articles arguing that it
was. Quandt compares the costs of U.S. policy in the region with the benefits the United States derived from that policy. According to his tally, U.S.
policy in the Middle East was far more successful than United States policy
in many other parts of the world. During the forty-year cold war, approximately five hundred Americans lost their lives in service to their country in
the Middle East. Almost half that number were American marines killed in
a single incident in Beirut in 1983. Compare that figure with the number of
Americans killed in ten years (1965–1975) in Southeast Asia—over fifty thousand. And America was far more successful in achieving its objectives in the
Middle East than in Southeast Asia. Of its six policy objectives, the United
States clearly accomplished five (containment, oil, stable states, Israel, sea
lanes and communications) and split on one (the United States was not able
to end regional conflicts, particularly the Arab-Israeli dispute, but for the
most part was able to maintain a regional balance of power). All this, for a

mere expenditure of an estimated 150 to two hundred billion dollars over forty years. (This figure apparently includes the one million dollar bribe allegedly paid by the U.S. government to Gamal ʿAbd al-Nasser soon after he took power.) In terms of current value, it is less than half the amount spent by the United States to wage the futile Vietnam War. Holding the expenditures in blood and treasure against the results the United States gained from those expenditures, it might be said that Americans got "more bang from the buck" (to borrow a phrase from the Eisenhower administration) from their involvement in the Middle East during the cold war than from probably any other region in the world.

Quandt does qualify his triumphalism a bit. He does not ignore the fact that American policy in the region had its share of disasters and near disasters during the cold war. In the first category we might include the inability of the United States to foresee or deal effectively with the Iranian Revolution. In the latter category, we might include the narrowly averted nuclear confrontation with the Soviet Union that occurred at the tail end of the 1973 Arab-Israeli War. Quandt is also conscious of the fact that his cost/benefit analysis weighs success in American terms and takes no account of the effects of American policy on the region itself. The United States has achieved its goals by supporting truly appalling regimes, for example, and U.S. policy has inflicted its own share of horrors on the population of the region as well. American weapons have been used against civilian populations in Lebanon in 1982 and in the occupied territories to this very day. The United States cynically abandoned Palestinians and Lebanese to their fate in 1983, the Kurds to theirs in 1975 and 1988, and the Shiʿis of southern Iraq to theirs in 1991. The United States pressured regimes in the region to adopt economic policies that have more often than not brought economic hardship rather than economic growth. These effects might be more easily brushed away as unfortunate side effects of an otherwise successful U.S. policy if it were not for 9/11. It is to the aftermath of that event that we must now turn.

The Road to Iraq

According to an old cliché, American foreign policy has historically swung between two poles: messianic idealism, on the one hand, and hard-headed realism, on the other. Idealists believe that America is more than just a country—it is also that shining "city on a hill" mentioned earlier. Thus, idealists hold that the United States has a special mission in the world, and that mission is to promote "American values" such as freedom, justice, or liberty internationally. Perhaps the most famous idealist in American history was Woodrow Wilson, who called Americans to arms in World War I to "make the world safe for democracy." And as we have seen, he also pressed Britain and France to adopt the "noble principles" embedded in his Fourteen Points as the price the two countries had to pay for American entry into the war— much to their chagrin. Realists, on the other hand, believe that the United States is a state like any other and that states are not driven by ideals, but rather by self-interest. They also believe that the international system can only attain stability when competing states achieve a balance of power among themselves, and that it is the duty of wise policy makers to pursue such a balance. Perhaps the most famous recent practitioner of realism was Henry Kissinger, whose doctoral dissertation, later published as *A World Restored*, lauded the role played by the conservative Austrian prince Metternich in establishing the post-Napoleonic European balance of power. As secretary of state, Kissinger supported the overthrow of a democratically elected leftist government in Chile and escalated the bombing of Vietnam and its neighbors while simultaneously pursuing détente with the Soviet Union and opening relations with "Red" China—all in the interest of maintaining America's strategic position within a durable world order.

Like all clichés, the idealism/realism divide is an oversimplification. Woodrow Wilson well understood the benefits to the United States of a world in which protected colonial markets were open to all. Similarly, those who would reduce America's 2003 invasion of Iraq to the idealist impulse to spread democracy tend to forget American policy makers' very unidealist concerns about oil supplies and America's strategic position in the Middle East. And many of those policy makers who have recently called for promoting democracy and free markets worldwide have not been shy about linking the spread of those values to American hegemony in international affairs. Nevertheless, like all clichés there is a germ of truth in this one as well.

Under the guidance of Henry Kissinger, American foreign policy during the first half of the 1970s was firmly in the hands of realists. But not all policy makers and pundits approved of Kissingerian *Realpolitik*. Some argued that Kissinger and like-minded realists underestimated both Soviet strength and intentions and that, as a result, détente endangered American security. Their hand was strengthened by a number of government officials who resented Kissinger's success as a bureaucratic infighter—success that diminished their own authority and their capacity to mold foreign policy. Others were appalled at the realist assumption that the United States and the Soviet Union were equivalent players on an international chessboard and that the United States might disavow its moral authority in the cold war. Among them were conservative Democrats alienated by the rise of the anti-Vietnam war faction in their party, by their party's support for any number of social experiments at home, or both.

The anti-realists of the 1970s were thus an eclectic group. There were old-fashioned Republican cold warriors who aligned themselves with disgruntled public officials working on the foreign policy fringes. There were Democrats affiliated with Senator Henry "Scoop" Jackson of Washington (also known as the "Senator from Boeing" because of his ties to the Seattle-based defense contractor), who pushed for a stronger defense and took up causes—freedom for Soviet dissidents and the right of Jews to emigrate from the Soviet Union—that highlighted the totalitarian nature of America's adversary. There were former Marxist-Jewish intellectuals in New York who felt the sting of the Left's abandonment of Israel as well as its infatuation with hot-button domestic programs like affirmative action. And there were intellectuals inspired by University of Chicago-based philosopher Leo Strauss, whose philosophy challenged moral relativism and championed a special role for intellectual elites in making public policy. The more ideologically motivated of these anti-realists came to be known as neoconservatives.

While neoconservatism is, at best, an imprecise category, most neoconservatives agree that American interests are linked to the spread of American values, that America's friends are those nations that adhere to those values and its enemies are those that oppose them, that it is legitimate to use force in the pursuit of policy goals, and that the United States cannot trust international institutions, international law, or international agreements to protect American interests. And at the end of the cold war, most neoconservatives came to believe that the United States was and had to remain the sole dominant power in the world. This meant that the United States was free to do what it wanted, where it wanted, when it wanted, regardless of whatever roadblocks other members of the international community might put in its way. Some even began to talk of a "benevolent American empire."

Beginning in the second half of the 1970s, neoconservatives and their allies undertook a number of activities to keep their realist adversaries off balance. They joined think tanks, wrote op-ed pieces, and edited magazines. They participated in special commissions that accused the CIA of underestimating Soviet strength and intentions. They took out full-page ads in major newspapers warning of the Soviet threat and the danger of American lethargy. And they found a hero in Ronald Reagan, who increased defense spending, supported anticommunist movements from Central America to Eastern Europe, and referred to the Soviet Union as an "evil empire."

The collapse of the Soviet Union confirmed for neoconservatives the effectiveness of Reagan's muscular defense policy. It also left a void at the center of American strategic planning for the first time in half a century. Reagan's immediate successor, George H.W. Bush, adopted a posture of cautious realism. Thus, although the United States drove Iraq out of Kuwait in 1991, it did so only after winning international sanction for its efforts and with the help of a multinational force. And once Iraqi troops were defeated, the United States made no attempt to "democratize" Iraq and left Iraqi president Saddam Hussein in power. Bill Clinton wavered between realism (no humanitarian intervention in Rwanda) and idealism (humanitarian intervention in Kosovo), but for the most part focused American foreign policy on the opportunities afforded by globalization. Even George W. Bush, who filled his administration with neoconservatives and their allies, began his presidency as a realist. Then came 9/11.

After the al-Qaeda attacks on the United States, the neoconservatives and their enablers in the Bush administration came to the fore. Although the administration won international support for its campaign against al-Qaeda and the Taliban government in Afghanistan that gave al-Qaeda sanctuary, big changes were in the offing. Almost immediately after the attacks, the Bush administration announced a "global war on terror," ignoring those who argued that fighting terrorism was a law enforcement problem as well as those who argued against a nation declaring war on a tactic and the open-endedness of this undertaking. Within a year of the attacks, the National Security Council issued a new set of foreign policy guidelines that reflected the neoconservative agenda. Henceforth, the National Security Council proclaimed, American policy would rest on three pillars: a right to take preemptive and unilateral action when necessary, unchallengeable American dominance of international affairs, and the active promotion of pro-American democracies throughout the world. The guidelines also underscored the danger posed by weapons of mass destruction falling into the hands of terrorists or "rogue states" such as Iraq, Iran, and North Korea— states dubbed by George W. Bush "the axis of evil."

No one could doubt that Iraq was a rogue state of special interest to the administration. Iraq had been in neoconservative sights since the abrupt end of the first Gulf War. For the neoconservatives, the fact that Saddam Hussein not only remained in power but thumbed his nose at the sanctions imposed by the international community after the war made a mockery of America's claim to dominance of global affairs. As early as the fall of 2001, military planners were busy making preparations and soon thereafter troops and equipment were redeployed from the Afghanistan front for the coming invasion of Iraq. At first, the administration tried to link Saddam Hussein to al-Qaeda and international terrorism. When met with skepticism, it focused on Iraq's pursuit of weapons of mass destruction. None were ever found. Finally, the administration unveiled its ultimate justification for making war on Iraq: By liberating Iraq and imposing democracy there, the United States would create a model for the democratic transformation of the entire region and dry up the authoritarian swamp that breeds terrorism.

As everyone knows, things did not go as planned. Some have placed the blame on "tactical" miscalculations made by American war planners and occupation authorities. These miscalculations range from deploying an inadequate force to secure the country to disbanding the Iraqi army and loosing on Iraqi civilians hordes of armed and unemployed young men. Others point to the mistaken assumptions and fundamental errors in judgment made by neoconservative advocates of the war. Rather than being greeted as liberators by all but a few regime loyalists (as Iraqi exiles in the United States had predicted), American forces found themselves fighting a stubborn insurgency. Rather than providing a model for democratization throughout the region and drying up the terrorist swamp, Iraq descended into sectarian violence and the invasion created an anti-American backlash in the region of unprecedented proportions. Rather than demonstrating American dominance on the world stage, the American campaign in Iraq stretched American capabilities to the breaking point and enhanced the regional power of another member of the access of evil—Iran. Iran, after all, had advocated the removal of Saddam Hussein since his attack on that country in 1980. With Hussein gone, there has been no power in the Persian Gulf to counterbalance Iran. Faced with a weakened Iraq or an Iraq dominated by its Shi'i (and pro-Iranian) majority, Iran seems to be facing a win-win situation. Finally, there are the costs in lives and treasure: As alluded to in the Introduction, as of this writing more than three thousand Americans and between fifty thousand and one hundred thousand Iraqis have been killed, and the United States has spent well over three hundred billion dollars on its Iraq adventure, not to mention the cost of rebuilding ruined or destroyed Iraqi infrastructure.

The criticisms voiced against neoconservatives have ranged far beyond Iraq. According to some, American unilateralism has dissipated the goodwill the United States had gained after the events of 11 September. It will be, they claim, a long time before the French newspaper *Le Monde* again runs a headline like the one that dominated the front page of its 12 September 2001 edition: "We are all Americans." Others argue that the neoconservative quest for American global superiority is bound to provoke a reaction among other powers (Europe, China, Russia), if it has not done so already. Furthermore, while neoconservatives believe that their Manichean division of the world into good and evil provides policy makers with a clear road map for action, many policy makers believe it actually limits America's options in the world. During the conflict between Hizbullah and Israel in the summer of 2006, for example, the United States refused to talk to the only powers that might have had any influence on Hizbullah, Iran and Syria, because their "terrorist connections" put them beyond the pale. Compare that reaction with the shuttle diplomacy of Henry Kissinger, who not only parleyed with Syrians, Israelis, and Egyptians after the 1973 Arab-Israeli War, but managed to keep the Russians in the loop as well. Finally, criticism of neoconservatives has come from the American Right: Since when are social engineering and nation building conservative values?

It is, of course, still too early to know if the recent ascendancy of the neoconservative movement marks a sea change in the history of American foreign policy or is merely a hiccup. In 1898, America was all abuzz about liberating Cuba and the Philippines from the clutches of Spain, shouldering the "white man's burden," and "civilizing" the inhabitants of those unfortunate isles. A century later, America's great imperialist adventure has been all but forgotten. Forgotten among Americans, that is. Cubans and Filipinos still remember.

Eighteen

Israel, the Arab States, and the Palestinians

The 1948 war between Zionists and Palestinians, then between Israel and Arab states, left two unresolved issues. First, although the State of Israel received the recognition of most other states in the world, the surrounding Arab states did not extend it recognition. Indeed, after the initial round of negotiations they refused to sit down with their Israeli counterparts at conferences held to resolve the dispute, and soon after the war the Arab League imposed an economic boycott on Israel. The second unresolved issue was what to do about the problem of the Palestinian refugees.

Israel was unlike most states that emerged in the wake of World War II. It entered into its independence period with a strong heritage of institutions built over the course of the previous half century. Because most of those who opposed the Zionist program—most Palestinians—were no longer there, the fractiousness that divided many emerging states was kept within limits. During its early years it also had access to rent that was unavailable to most other new states in the world. Israel received contributions and investment from Jews from around the globe, reparations from the German government for the Holocaust, then foreign aid from France and later the United States.

Rather than comparing Israel with other states that emerged during the period of decolonization, one Israeli scholar has suggested that it might be more accurate to compare Israel during its immediate post-independence period with the United States during its period of mass immigration, 1880–1920. Immigrants who flooded into Israel in the mid-twentieth century, like immigrants who flooded into the United States thirty to seventy years earlier, found political and economic institutions already intact. While their arrival in such large numbers certainly did modify the existing institutions, immigrants did not have to build those institutions from scratch. Furthermore, they found upon their arrival a political system with established "rules of the game." In the case of Israel, those rules had pretty much been set by the members of the second and third *aliyot*, who, along with their descendents, continued to form the aristocracy of Israeli society.

The first ten years of the Israel's existence might be thus considered a period of demographic change and institutional continuity. The demographic change was the result of two factors. Most obviously, there was the flight of the Palestinians. Israel only repatriated a tiny number of the Palestinians who fled after the war—a gesture it made to win the goodwill of the international community. The issue of repatriation and restitution is a complex one that has yet to be resolved. Israel is a Jewish state. In 1950, the Israeli parliament, the *knesset*, passed the Law of Return guaranteeing Jews from around the world citizenship. Israel could hardly retain its Jewish character if it allowed the right of citizenship to large numbers of non-Jews, such as Palestinians.

The problem of repatriation and restitution was made all the more complex by the fact that the Israeli government took over the property abandoned by the Palestinians who fled and then distributed it to Jewish Israelis. Some Palestinians attempted to reclaim their property by crossing the armistice lines to harvest crops or carry away moveable property to their new homes. Others crossed the lines to commit acts of sabotage. The Israeli government did not differentiate between the two groups. To deal with the problem of "infiltration," it launched reprisal raids against the states from which the infiltration occurred. In part, the Israeli government adopted this policy to encourage the emergence of the "new Zionist man." In the words of the first prime minister of Israel, David Ben Gurion, "We must strengthen their [the Israelis'] backs and demonstrate that those who attack them will not get away unpunished, that they are residents of a sovereign state which is responsible for their safety." The second reason why reprisal was adopted as a policy was that the Israeli government felt that this strategy would induce the Arab states to police their borders more diligently. Obviously, the policy of reprisals did little to endear Israel to its neighbors. In 1953, an Israeli raid into Jordan resulted in sixty-six civilian casualties. In 1955, an Israeli raid into Egypt, led by future Israeli prime minister Ariel Sharon, left thirty-eight Egyptian soldiers dead and about forty wounded.

The other factor that changed the demographic balance of Israel was immigration. During the first four years of Israel's existence, approximately seven hundred thousand new immigrants arrived. This doubled the state's population. Another seven hundred thousand arrived over the next fifteen years. A large number of the new immigrants came from Muslim countries. Some Arab Jews immigrated to Israel at the urging of Israeli Zionists. Others came because they were persecuted at home. For example, beginning in 1947 the Iraqi government passed discriminatory legislation against Iraqi Jews that restricted their freedom of movement and required them to put up a bond if they wanted to leave Iraq. In 1948, discrimination against Jews became systematic in Iraq. There were anti-Jewish riots in Baghdad, probably encouraged by the Iraqi government, Jews were arrested, and Jews who worked for public concerns (ports, railroads, and the like) were dismissed from their jobs. There was even a show trial and execution of a prominent Jewish Iraqi businessman. Most of the Jewish community of Iraq saw the writing on the wall. Over 120,000 Iraqi Jews emigrated to Israel. They joined or were joined by thirty-one thousand Jews from Libya, forty thousand from

Yemen, eighty thousand from Egypt, and ten thousand from Syria, among others.

While the Arab states that surrounded Israel never granted it recognition, and while the dismal showing of the Arab states in the 1948 war contributed to the rash of *coups d'etat* that began in the region in 1949, the focus of those states was initially elsewhere. When the Free Officers took power in Egypt, for example, they were too involved in consolidating power, devising land reform and other economic programs, and negotiating the withdrawal of British troops from the Suez Canal Zone to pay Israel much mind. Israel only became an important issue for Nasser after the bloody border incident of 1955 and the 1956 "Tripartite Aggression." After 1956, Nasser increasingly saw the West in conspiratorial terms—a vision that was not far from the truth. He sought the unity of Arab states against that conspiracy and viewed Israel as an integral part of it. He also viewed Israel as a hindrance to Arab unity. Israel was, as he put it (referring to Israel's shape), a "dagger aimed at the heart of the Arab nation." The Syrians, who by the early 1960s were involved in escalating battles with the Israelis over the allocation of Jordan River water, concurred.

In the spring of 1967, in solidarity with the Syrians, Nasser ordered the entrance of the Red Sea closed to Israeli shipping. Because this effectively quarantined the southern Israeli port city of Eilat, and because the Israelis (and the Americans) considered that part of the Red Sea an international waterway, the Israelis regarded the Egyptian action as an act of war. On 5 June 1967, Israel launched an attack against its neighbors.

The 1967 war lasted a mere six days and resulted in a resounding defeat for the Arab armies. The Israeli army captured all of Jerusalem (which had been divided between Israel and Jordan since 1948), the West Bank, the Sinai peninsula, the Gaza Strip, and part of Syria (the Golan Heights). The war fundamentally changed the equation of the Arab-Israel dispute. Before the war, the issue at stake for both Israelis and their Arab neighbors had been the existence of Israel. After the war, the issue at stake was no longer the existence of Israel. Instead, the return of the territories occupied during the hostilities became the overriding concern for the Arab states. For their part, the Israelis demanded recognition and peace settlements as the price for the return of land. The exchange of land for peace—embodied in United Nations Security Council Resolutions 242 and 338—became the basis for all subsequent peace negotiations between Israel and the Arab states. For example, as stipulated by the 1978 Camp David Accords, Israel withdrew from the Sinai Peninsula in exchange for recognition by, and peace with, Egypt.

The exchange of land for peace is a simple formula. Nevertheless, it has been hard to accomplish for four reasons. First, it is (purposely) ambiguous. U.N. Resolution 242 calls for the withdrawal of Israeli forces "from territories occupied during the recent conflict." The Israelis like to point out that the resolution nowhere states that the Israelis must withdraw from *all* the territories it occupied. The resolution also calls for the "termination of all claims or states of belligerency and respect for and acknowledgement of the

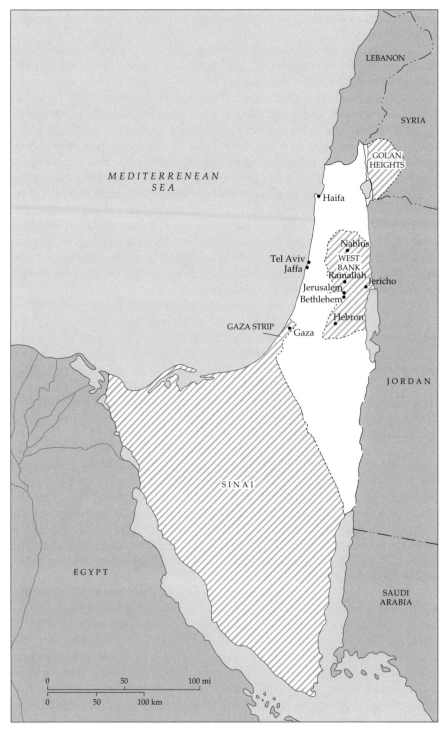

Israel and the Occupied Territories after 1967

sovereignty, territorial integrity, and political independence of every state in the area and their right to live in peace within secure and recognized boundaries free from threats or acts of force." The Arab states like to point out that the resolution does not call for formal peace treaties with Israel. They have claimed that they could fulfill the terms of the resolution simply by issuing statements of nonbelligerency.

Then there was the postwar strategy adopted by the Arab states. Soon after the war, the heads of the Arab states met in Khartoum, Sudan, to negotiate a unified position. At Khartoum, Arab leaders decided on the famous "three no's": no negotiations with Israel, no peace with Israel, no recognition of Israel. Although this seems the height of intransigence, it marked a subtle tactical shift. The Arab states agreed to unify efforts to "eliminate the effects of aggression"—not eliminate Israel. And although they pledged not to negotiate with Israel, they did not pledge not to negotiate. The Arab heads of state instead looked to the superpowers—the United States and the Soviet Union—to resolve the dispute. Since the Soviet Union had broken diplomatic relations with Israel, they counted on the United States to bring the Israelis around. This is how the United States came to hold "99 percent of the cards" in the region.

This tactic was dangerous for the Arab states because it assumed that the Americans so wanted a settlement that they would put pressure on Israel. This assumption was overly optimistic. American politicians are fond of saying that the issue of Social Security is the "third rail" of American politics. What they mean by this is that any politician who touches the issue is bound to get singed. The same might be said about Arab-Israeli politics. Appearances aside, since the 1970s most American presidents have initially avoided getting involved in the issue until circumstances forced them to.

After the 1967 war, the United States was all too willing to sit back and wait for the Arab states to come around. After all, the Arab states wanted their land back and all they had to do to get it back was to sign peace treaties with Israel. To re-engage the Americans, Egypt engaged Israel in the so-called War of Attrition—artillery duels and aerial dogfights across the Suez Canal. Then Egypt and Syria once again launched a war against Israel in October 1973. The October war resulted in eleven to sixteen thousand more Arab and Israeli casualties, was used by Arab members of OPEC as an excuse to hike oil prices, and brought the United States and the Soviet Union to the brink of nuclear war. It certainly caught American attention. At a time when the United States had bigger fish to fry—the United States was still involved in Vietnam, had just opened up relations with China, and had to figure out the intricacies of détente (cooperation) with the Soviet Union—the American secretary of state, Henry Kissinger, was spending his time shuttling between Damascus, Cairo, and Tel Aviv working out minutiae of Israeli and Arab troop redeployments.

The Israelis also contributed to complicating the "land for peace" equation. Immediately after the 1967 war, the Israeli government declared Jerusalem to be Israel's eternal, indivisible capital. Settlers began moving in and the municipal boundaries were extended far into the West Bank. Currently, there are approximately two hundred thousand Jewish settlers in Arab East Jerusalem, and the new municipal boundaries of Jerusalem comprise a little over 10 percent of West Bank territory. The Israelis also built settlements in the West Bank (called by the Israeli government "Judea and Samaria," after its biblical name), the Golan Heights, and the Gaza Strip. The first settlements were built along the Jordanian border, ostensibly for security reasons. Then came religious settlers and those interested in low-cost housing subsidized by the Israeli government. Currently, there are approximately two hundred thousand settlers in the West Bank, not including Greater Jerusalem.

Most of the international community considers the settlements to be a violation of international law, specifically the Fourth Geneva Convention of 1949, which stipulates that an "occupying power shall not deport or transfer parts of its own civilian population into the territory it occupies." By giving tax incentives and other forms of encouragement to settlers, it is argued, the Israeli government is encouraging the transfer of population. Before the Reagan administration, the U.S. government called Israeli settlements illegal; until Spring 2004 the official American position was that they were "an obstacle to peace."

In addition to building and populating settlements in the occupied territories, the Israeli government has transformed the economy and society of the West Bank and Gaza Strip. Over the course of the occupation, the Israelis linked the West Bank electrical grid and water table to their own. The Israelis also grew dependent on buying labor and agricultural goods from the West Bank and Gaza, while Palestinians in the territories grew dependent on selling both in Israel. Although unskilled Palestinian workers had to go back to their homes in the occupied territories every evening, they continued to travel back and forth to Israel daily because jobs were available there and wages and prices for produce were higher in Israel than in the territories. The overall effect of Israeli policies has thus been to make separation that much more difficult and to create a dependent economy in the territories. Whenever the Israelis close the border separating Israel from the occupied territories, it brings widespread suffering to the Palestinian population. Ever since the recent surge in violence between the two peoples, "closure" has become commonplace.

Ironically, while the Israeli policy of closure has caused severe economic stress among Palestinians, it has had a negative impact on Israeli society as well. Beginning in 1993, Israel began replacing Palestinian workers with workers imported from East and South Asia, Eastern Europe, and Africa. Within three years, there were two hundred thousand such workers in Israel, about half of whom were in the country illegally. Currently, about one-sixth of the population of Tel Aviv is guest workers. Because the guest workers are not Jewish, Israel faces a dilemma: If it grants them the rights of citizens, it may risk its identity as a Jewish state; if it refuses them the rights of citizens, it will face the same quandaries as its caste-ridden neighbors in the Gulf. By replacing the Palestinian labor upon which it had grown dependent, Israel simply replaced one problem with another.

The final problem with the "land for peace" solution is that it reduced the conflict to one between states. There is another actor involved, however: the Palestinians. Until the 1993 Oslo Accord, the Israelis did not recognize the existence of a Palestinian nation. Nevertheless, such a nation does exist simply because most Palestinians believe that it does and nothing has shaken that belief. Indeed, the idea of Palestinian nationhood has only strengthened over time, partly as a result of the efforts of its political incarnation, the Palestine Liberation Organization (PLO).

The PLO was founded in 1964 at the instigation of Gamal 'Abd al-Nasser, who wanted to maintain control of the Palestinian movement. It was initially led by a fairly worthless career diplomat, Ahmad Shuqairy, whose dubious contribution to the Palestinian cause was to proclaim on the eve of the 1967 war that the Arabs would "push the Jews into the sea." In the wake of the 1967 war, the leader of the largest Palestinian guerilla group, Yasir Arafat, was chosen leader of the PLO by its main representative body. He led it until his death in 2004.

Arafat was born in the Gaza Strip in 1929. He studied engineering at King Fuad University in Egypt during the early 1950s, the golden age of Arab anti-imperialism and secular Arab nationalism. Arafat's ideas have certainly been within the anti-imperialist and secular nationalist mold. But early on Arafat differed from many of his cohorts in a fundamental way. According to an associate who knew him then,

> Yasser Arafat and I knew what was damaging to the Palestinian cause. We were convinced, for example, that the Palestinians could expect nothing from the Arab regimes, (which were in 1951) for the most part corrupt or tied to imperialism, and that they were wrong to bank on any of the political parties in the region. We believed that *the Palestinians could rely only on themselves.*

Thus, as early as the 1950s, we see the two elements that made the politics of Yasir Arafat and his closest colleagues distinctive from the politics of many other politically savvy Palestinians: the idea that the Palestinians themselves, not established Arab states, would have to be responsible for the liberation of Palestine, and the idea that Palestinians would have to form their own organizations that cooperated with, but were independent of, established states and parties in the region. The 1967 war bore out Arafat's skepticism about the ability of the Arab states to liberate Palestine. Seven years later, the PLO achieved its greatest political coup. In 1974, the Arab states recognized the PLO as the "the sole legitimate representative of the Palestinian people."

Under Arafat, the PLO was dominated by a fairly durable group of leaders from the largest guerrilla groups. The fact that the PLO is a coalition of these and other groups has made change in strategy and objectives slow and difficult. Nevertheless, such changes have taken place. Initially, the PLO advocated the liberation of all of historic Palestine. For some in the PLO, historic Palestine included Jordan. Hence, the slogan of one of the guerilla groups that constitute the PLO, "The road to Jerusalem leads through Amman [Jordan]." Since 1977, the PLO has advocated the establishment of a Palestinian mini-state in the West Bank and Gaza Strip. At first, some PLO leaders asserted that this mini-state would be a temporary condition, until all Palestine could be liberated. In time, the PLO accepted the fact that this mini-state would be the best they could hope for. In terms of tactics, Arafat worked hard (but not entirely effectively) to demonstrate that the hijackings and terrorist operations that had marked PLO tactics in the 1970s had given way to a responsible government in the process of formation.

In spite of the efforts of the PLO to keep the Palestinian issue up front in international politics, the dispute between Israelis and Palestinians continued to be defined as a dispute among states during the period stretching from 1948 to 1993. All this changed with the Oslo Accord of 1993, which transformed the dispute back to one between two peoples.

The Oslo Accord and the subsequent Oslo II Agreement consisted of two components: an exchange of letters of mutual recognition and more concrete proposals to establish Palestinian rule in the territories. The exchange of letters was significant for both the Palestinians and Israelis. For the Palestinians, mutual recognition meant that the establishment of an independent Palestinian state in the West Bank and Gaza Strip was all but inevitable. Just how big that state would be, and just how independent it would be, would be determined by circumstances. For the Israelis, the fact that the Palestinians accorded them recognition meant that the close to 80 percent of Palestine that they had won in the 1948 war was forever removed from the bargaining table. While other aspects of the Oslo process have been suspended or failed—Palestinian self-rule in parts of the West Bank, the phased Israeli withdrawal from the occupied territories—this exchange of letters changed the nature of the dispute forever.

Oslo was born of desperation. Other than the mutual recognitions, Oslo died in an atmosphere of violence and distrust. Palestinians signed on to the accord because life under Israeli occupation had been difficult and the conditions in the occupied territories were deplorable. By 2000, unemployment in the Gaza Strip had reached over 40 percent and the territory had become the most densely populated area on earth. To make matters worse, the PLO had been chased out of Jordan (1970) and Lebanon (1983), only to end up in far-off Tunis. Beginning in the early 1990s, the PLO's dominance over the Palestinian movement was being challenged by Islamic groups—the most important of which was Hamas—based in the occupied territories. The PLO desperately needed a political breakthrough to maintain its leadership. (Significantly, in January 2006, after the breakdown of the "Oslo process" and widespread Palestinian disillusionment with PLO governance, Hamas defeated the PLO handily in parliamentary elections.) In addition, because of the end of the cold war and their support for the Iraqi invasion of Kuwait in 1990, the PLO could no longer count on East Bloc or Gulf Arab financial and diplomatic assistance. For their part, since 1987 the Israelis had confronted a seemingly interminable insurgency in the occupied territories known as the "intifada." Many Israelis longed for a "normal" existence and anticipated the economic benefits of peace in the post-cold war "age of globalization."

But Oslo was based on the premise that trust between the two peoples would slowly build so that by the end of the Oslo process they could tackle the most difficult issues, such as Jerusalem and the Palestinian right of return to Israel. Trust was never built. The Israelis blamed Palestinian terror and halted the entire process during a second intifada launched by the Palestinians in 2000. The Palestinians blamed Israeli intransigence and bad faith. During the Oslo process, they maintain, the number of settlers in the occupied territories doubled, new settlements and "bypass roads" connecting those settlements to each other and to Israel were built, and land confiscations continued, as did the destruction of Palestinian homes and orchards by the Israeli army.

With the concrete proposals of Oslo going the way of the Rhodes Talks, the Palestine Conciliation Commission, the Johnston Plan, the Rogers Plan, the Rogers Initiative, the First Geneva Conference, the Second Geneva Conference, the 1978 Framework for Peace in the Middle East, the Schultz Plan, the Reagan Plan, and the Madrid Conference, the government of Israel began preparations to break the deadlock. In 2002, Israel began construction of a separation barrier—a series of walls, fences, and trenches that in some places stretched far into the West Bank. While the Israelis argued that they were building the barrier to prevent Palestinian suicide bombers from infiltrating into Israel, Palestinians, along with much of the international community and many Israelis, feared that by building the barrier, Israel was taking the first step toward abandoning negotiations forever and drawing its final boundaries unilaterally. These fears seemed to be realized when Israel withdrew from its settlements in the Gaza Strip and drew up plans to consolidate its settlements in the West Bank. By the summer of 2006, a unilateral settlement imposed by Israel seemed a done deal—until renewed conflict in Gaza and Lebanon soured a majority of Israelis on withdrawing from any territory, no matter how negligible or useless.

Now that the Israeli-Palestinian conflict appears stalemated once again, one might be justified in wondering whether the conflict will ever be resolved. There are plenty of reasons for skepticism. Perhaps the most convincing of all is the fact that the conflict has not only been defined by the antagonists, it has defined the antagonists.

Like all nationalisms, both Zionism and Palestinian nationalism defined themselves in relation to what they opposed. Early Zionist settlers saw their mission as establishing an outpost of civilization within a land inhabited by primitives. The Zionist settler—with rifle in one hand and plow in the other—became their heroic ideal and the center of a national cult. Palestinian nationalism reflects its "other" in like manner. After all, had it not been for Zionism, Palestinian nationalism would have evolved along the lines of Syrian or Iraqi nationalism—had it evolved at all. But more has been at stake than beliefs. The conflict has encouraged the emergence of the distinct institutions, social organization, and patterns of behavior within each community that have kept the conflict alive. Since the days of Ben Gurion, the Israeli state has depended on foreign aid and private contributions to maintain itself as a "national security state." On the other hand, the Great Revolt of 1936–1939 and the 1948 war decimated Palestinian society and opened up social cleavages within it. There were Palestinians who collaborated and those who did not, Palestinians who participated in armed gangs and those who were their victims, Palestinians who fled their homes and those who stayed, Palestinians in camps and those who were fortunate enough to live outside them.

The dispute has not just defined the Israeli and Palestinian communities, however. The Arab world has been defined to a certain extent by the Arab-Israeli dispute as well. Over the past fifty years, the conflict has militarized Arab political culture, coarsened politics so that even torture and terror could be rationalized, led to the destruction of centuries-old Arab Jewish communities, and reinforced the tendency for regimes to find military solutions to political problems. The conflict has encouraged regimes to replace political debate with nationalist sloganeering and has thus led to the banalities that pass for official political discourse. Arab countries have used the permanent state of war as an excuse to divert resources to bloated military budgets and to curtail civil and political freedoms. Currently, Arab states account for about 30 percent of the world's arms sales. Finally, there are the wasted lives. From 1948 to the present, Arab states have experienced anywhere from fifty thousand to 125,000 military casualties (there have been about twenty-one thousand Israeli military casualties). Egypt leads the list by far, lending credence to a modern Egyptian proverb: "Iraq is willing to fight for the liberation of Palestine to the last drop of (Egyptian) blood."

In all fairness, one should not lose sight of the fact that the terms of the dispute have evolved over time and so it is possible that a solution may yet be found. The dispute, after all, began as a conflict between Zionist settlers and the indigenous inhabitants of Palestine. After Israel declared its independence and the neighboring Arab states invaded in the spring of 1948, it was transformed from a Zionist-Palestinian dispute to an Arab-Israeli dispute. The definition of the dispute as one between the Arab states and the Israeli state was confirmed by the 1967 war, when the dispute focused on the "land for peace" equation. Only after the Oslo Accord did the dispute come around full circle, from a conflict between two peoples, to a conflict among states, and finally once again to a conflict between two peoples.

All this means that a final resolution of the conflict may take a form that is presently impossible to visualize. Who could have imagined the Camp David treaty between Israel and Egypt before Anwar al-Sadat's announcement that, "I am ready to go to their house, the *knesset*, to discuss peace with the Israeli leaders"? Or who could have anticipated that a century after Zionists invented the slogan, "a land without a people for a people without a land," a former Israeli prime minister, Ehud Barak, would describe the Palestinian *nakba* as the "shattering and exile of a whole society, accompanied by thousands of deaths and the wholesale destruction of hundreds of villages." Although it may appear to be grasping at straws, it must be remembered that the dispute is one between two rival nationalist movements and that nationalist movements are flexible. The very demands that are held as unconditional today—the ownership of Jerusalem, the Palestinian right of return, maintaining Israeli settlements—may recede in importance tomorrow as shifts in international and regional conditions extend the realm of the possible.

Nineteen

The Iranian Revolution

The Iranian Revolution overthrew the Pahlavi Dynasty, which had ruled Iran from 1926 to 1979. "Dynasty" is perhaps too grand a name for it, inasmuch as there were only two shahs from the Pahlavi family. The first was Reza Shah and the last was his son and successor, Muhammad Reza Shah. As discussed in Chapter 12, Reza Shah had been the leader of an elite cavalry unit, the Cossack Brigade. With an unknown amount of British assistance, he took control of Persia in the wake of famine, foreign occupation, and the chaos of World War I. Although he expanded the role of the state and attempted to impose a policy of Westernization from the top-down during this period, Reza Shah's legacy was far from assured. Indeed, during the latter days of his reign the state increasingly had to resort to violence to repress tribal and social conflicts that were simmering just below the surface.

The end of Reza Shah's rule came during World War II. Because Reza Shah's tilt toward the Nazis threatened Allied supply lines to Russia, the British and the Russians invaded Iran early in the war and forced Reza Shah to abdicate. They then engineered his replacement by his Swiss-educated son, Muhammad Reza. To prevent the new shah from following his father's independent course, the Allies made sure to limit his power. They reestablished the *majlis* as an independent power center and allowed the organization of trade unions and political parties. Much to the chagrin of the British and Americans, the most popular party proved to be the Communist Party (Tudeh), which soon included over one hundred thousand members.

The shah's authority was further eroded by the events of the early 1950s. The last foreign troops left Iran in 1946. In May of 1951, Muhammad Mossadegh became prime minister on a platform that advocated nationalizing the oil industry and restricting the shah's power. Mossadegh was a Swiss-educated politician who had been a prominent opponent of Reza Shah in the 1920s. Arrested by Reza Shah, he had returned to politics in the 1940s and became one of the founders of the National Front. The front was a coalition of politicians united on the issues of nationalization of Iran's natural resources, the expansion of parliamentary democracy, and economic development.

In many ways Mossadegh was typical of a generation of Third World leaders that included, among many others, Gamal 'Abd al-Nasser. Like his contemporaries, Mossadegh believed that modernization and nation-building were the tickets to success. Only through modernization, they believed, could their nations preserve their independence and realize their national destiny. Only through nation-building could their nations shake off the colonial past that inhibited modernization, allowing them to join the "civilized" world. Like his contemporaries, Mossadegh sought to end the dependency of his state on the export of raw materials and the import of finished goods from more advanced nations. As a matter of fact, Mossadegh took Reza Shah's program of industrialization to its extreme, advocating the eventual establishment of an "oilless" economy. Like his contemporaries, Mossadegh attempted to finance a crash industrialization program by seizing control of foreign assets in his country and using the revenues from those assets to foster development. Like his contemporaries, Mossadegh refused to take sides in the cold war and instead adopted a policy of nonalignment. Mossadegh spoke of something called "negative equilibrium" to distinguish his foreign policy from that of the Qajars. The Qajars had attempted to balance the Russians and British off against each other, often by granting them equal concessions. Mossadegh rejected the granting of concessions on principle. Overall, the policy of negative equilibrium alienated the United States, which was engaged in what it considered to be a life-and-death struggle with international communism.

In the beginning, Mossadegh's program received the support of both the so-called "traditional middle class" (artisans, merchants, ulama, and the like) and the "modern middle class" (students, industrial workers, professionals, and so on). When the shah attempted to oust Mossadegh, many from these groups held huge demonstrations in support of the prime minister's policies. These demonstrations so frightened the shah that he fled to Rome. In the wake of the shah's flight, Mossadegh dissolved parliament and assumed extraordinary powers. These actions fragmented the coalition that had supported him. They also encouraged the emergence of a broad anti-Mossadegh coalition made up of conservative elements of society, such as army officers, government officials, ulama, tribal chiefs, large merchants, and landlords who feared the expropriation of their property. With the help of British intelligence and one hundred thousand dollars from the American CIA, which claimed that Mossadegh's movement was being manipulated by communists, anti-Mossadegh fervor grew. The army seized control and restored the shah. Thus, unlike his father, who was invested by a foreign power but once, Muhammad Reza Shah was invested by a foreign power twice. In the eyes of many Iranians, this was more than enough to call his legitimacy into question. Once reinstated, the shah sentenced Mossadegh to house arrest, where he died in 1967.

The Mossadegh period was a key period in the history of modern Iran for a number of reasons. With the failure of the "oilless" economy and "negative equilibrium," Iran became more dependent than ever on oil exports and became firmly aligned with the West against the Soviet Union. Just as important, the political struggles of this period created a mythology. The Mossadegh period came to be viewed by many Iranians as a period of relative freedom and national reassertion. It has also become the subject of an enormous amount of "what might have been" speculation. The story of the

U.S. "sponsorship" of the coup against Mossadegh has become something of an urban legend among Iranians. The students who took over the United States embassy in 1979 reportedly had copies of Kermit Roosevelt's self-serving memoirs of the period, *Countercoup*, with them. Roosevelt, the CIA station-chief in Tehran, ignores the genuine fear that Mossadegh's policies inspired among many Iranians. Instead, he claims inordinate responsibility for the restoration of the shah, and even quotes a grateful shah as saying, "I owe my throne to God, my people, and to you." Unfortunately, little of Roosevelt's account can be verified. The CIA's own records of the episode are "missing."

Once restored to power, the shah continued his father's programs, intending that Iran become the fifth great industrial power. Like Mossadegh, he proposed using revenues from oil to finance rapid development. For example, the shah used revenues from oil to support his White Revolution, discussed in Chapter 15. In many ways, however, the White Revolution proved counterproductive. The attempt to make Iran a great industrial power floundered, in part because of the collapse of oil prices, in part because of inefficiency, domestic resistance, and corruption. As in most other places, the land reform provisions of the White Revolution were at best a partial success. Landowners found ways of getting around restrictions on landownership, more often than not peasants received low-quality land, peasants who had no formal sharecropping agreements received nothing, and the large-scale commercialization of agriculture was inefficient. As agriculture became increasingly commercialized, however, fewer and fewer peasants were needed to work the land. Peasants emigrated from the countryside to the cities, particularly Tehran. In 1940, 22 percent of the Iranian population had lived in cities. By 1976, almost half the Iranian population lived in cities. Tehran doubled in size from 1970 to 1977 alone, reaching a population of five million. Many of those who migrated were unskilled. They thus could not find permanent work and became either day laborers or members of an urban underclass.

On the other hand, revenue from oil did enable the shah to concentrate a vast amount of power in the hands of the state. The government attempted to regiment the peasantry by inundating the countryside with a host of agencies and programs. The shah's government sponsored a Literacy Corps, a Health Corps, an Extension and Development Corps, government-run cooperatives, credit unions, and special rural courts. Using revenue from oil, the government also tried to break the back of potentially subversive urban groups. To keep urban shopkeepers (bazaaris) in line, the government abolished the old guilds and replaced them with compliant new ones, bulldozed the central bazaars in some cities (such as Tehran), and conducted antiprofiteering campaigns. These campaigns resulted in the exile of more than twenty-three thousand shopkeepers. To keep the ulama in line, the state created a "religious corps" to spread its own brand of Islam, closed religious publishing houses, asserted its control over religious endowments, and passed a family law that took precedence over, and frequently contravened, the shari'a. These measures did little to prevent shopkeepers and ulama from playing a central role in the revolution.

Just as his father had done before him, Muhammad Reza Shah resorted to repression to eliminate dissent. He banned the independent political parties that had emerged during the 1940s and 1950s. At first, he constructed two parties in the *majlis*, commonly referred to as the "yes" and the "yes, sir" parties. Then, in 1975, he combined them into a single party, the "National Resurgence Party," made up of "all loyal Iranians." He built a security apparatus that was one of the most repressive in the world. In 1976, Amnesty International reported that "no country in the world has a worse record in human rights than Iran."

Many Iranians were also angered by the fact that the shah's family was the foremost beneficiary of the income generated by oil, and the line between state earnings and family earnings blurred. By 1976, the shah had accumulated upward of one billion dollars from oil revenue; his family—including sixty-three princes and princesses—had accumulated between five and twenty billion dollars; and the family foundation controlled approximately three billion dollars. The foundation used its money for patronage and investment in agriculture, real estate, construction, insurance, hotels, publishing, automobile manufacture, food-processing, and textile factories. In all, the Pahlavi Foundation controlled more than two hundred companies. This, of course, made the shah open to the charges of corruption and nepotism.

During the 1960s, the shah's policies began to spark resistance. Armed groups, modeling themselves on the Algerian and Palestinian resistance, undertook a guerilla war against the state. Some in those groups borrowed their ideas from such celebrity-revolutionaries as Che Guevara of Cuba and Ho Chi Minh of Vietnam. Others borrowed their ideas from an Iranian writer and political activist, 'Ali Shari'ati, who promoted a doctrine that combined elements of Islamic modernism and Marxist analysis. Shari'ati's ideas influenced a wide spectrum of Iranians, from university students to ulama. Little wonder. His denunciation of those who slavishly imitate the West, his advocacy of cultural authenticity, his division of individual societies and whole nations into the categories of oppressor and oppressed, and his belief that the principal function of the state is to promote social justice contained many of the elements of Third Worldism popular at the time.

While the war waged by the guerilla groups against the regime was debilitating, it was not nearly as threatening as the agitation against the White Revolution in which ulama played a leading role. Because many ulama were landowners, they were not particularly enamored by the shah's land reform measures. Ulama also objected to the expansion of the right of Americans to be tried in their own courts (the right of extraterritoriality) and a new electoral law guaranteeing women's suffrage. It was during this uprising that a then little-known cleric, Ayatollah Khomeini, first came to public attention by calling for the shah's resignation. (Ayatollah is a title granted to prominent teaching *mujtahids*.) In the wake of the anti–White Revolution agitation, the shah forced Khomeini into exile.

In December 1977, U.S. president Jimmy Carter visited the shah and proclaimed Iran to be "an island of tranquility in a sea of turbulence." This show of support emboldened the shah to begin a new round of repression. Early in 1978, the official newspaper published an attack on Ayatollah Khomeini, then in exile in France. The attack on Khomeini was the spark that set off the revolution. Theological students in the city of Qom staged a protest which the government broke up at the cost of seventy lives. In accordance with Shi'i ritual, memorial demonstrations were held after forty days. The government broke these up as well, again with loss of life. Thus a cycle was initiated: a demonstration, a massacre, a memorial demonstration, another massacre, and so on. The demonstrations grew larger and larger with greater and greater loss of life. Khomeini, using widely distributed cassettes, telephone lines, and networks of ulama, kept in touch with and helped coordinate these demonstrations from France. In January 1979, the shah went into exile. He died the next year.

Khomeini was not the only opponent of the regime, nor were ulama the only segment of society to rebel. The revolution succeeded in part because of strikes among oil field workers. These strikes limited the access of the government to revenues that, in turn, frustrated the government's ability to suppress the revolution. Students, leftist guerrillas, members of the Tudeh party, even women's groups all mobilized to get rid of the shah. Nevertheless, the ulama emerged on top for two reasons. First, many ulama were able to speak a language that had broad appeal. They were able to counterpose their own brand of "cultural authenticity," as represented by Islam, to the secular nationalism of the shah's regime or the communism of the Tudeh party. Secular nationalism, they argued, was inauthentic because it had been imported from the West. Furthermore, it had brought economic disaster (as represented in the economic downturn of 1975–1977) and repression to Iran. The second reason the ulama emerged on top was that this group was linked to the urban masses, particularly the bazaaris, that fought the revolution. Many ulama themselves came from the urban lower middle and middle classes. Furthermore, since the Qajar state had been weak, many activities normally associated with governments, such as witnessing contracts, were still handled by ulama. The participation of ulama was thus essential to many activities essential to day-to-day life. While the Pahlavi Dynasty had sought to break the power of the ulama, its success was limited.

Revolutions are rare occurrences in world history. After the big two—the French Revolution and the Russian Revolution—social scientists find it hard to agree on others. Why would a list of revolutions include the Chinese Revolution and not the Cuban? Why the American Revolution and not the British Glorious Revolution of 1688? Did the Free Officers of Egypt pull off a revolution in 1952? 1956? At all? Even those social scientists who swear by the concept of revolution cannot agree on how to assess their causes. Accordingly, there have been a number of theories about the causes of the Iranian Revolution. Some social scientists have offered religious or cultural explanations, stressing the role played by Shi'ism. They argue that Shi'ism was

Khomeini sends the shah packing. Poster from the Iranian Revolution, 1978–1979. (From: Barry M. Rosen, ed., Iran Since the Revolution: Internal Dynamics, Regional Conflicts, and the Superpowers (Boulder, Colo.: Social Science Monographs, 1985), p. 43.)

born as an opposition movement and that this gave Shi'ism a unique ability to function as a basis for revolutionary activity. Hence, the role played by Shi'i ulama in Iranian politics from the 1891 protests against the Tobacco Concession to the Iranian Revolution of 1978–1979. Unfortunately, this explanation fails on three grounds. First, Shi'ism has been the religion of a majority of Iranians since the sixteenth century. Religious and cultural explanations fail to account for the timing of the revolution. As a matter of fact, before the Iranian Revolution, Shi'ism was considered by many experts to promote "quietism"—the passive acceptance of any political order. Citing Shi'ism as the cause of the revolution also overemphasizes the role played by the ulama in the revolution and discounts the role played by other groups in bringing down the shah. Furthermore, religious and cultural explanations fail to account for the fact that the Iranian Revolution took place during a period of widespread revolutionary activity, from eastern and central Europe (for example, the "Velvet Revolution" in Czechoslovakia) and the Philippines (the "people power" revolution), to Nicaragua and Palestine (the *intifada*). None of these states was predominantly Shi'i. None of this revolutionary activity was led by Shi'i clerics.

Other social scientists use economic or structural explanations to account for the Iranian Revolution. Those who argue for economic explanations point to the downturn in the economy in 1975–1977. Iranians rebelled, they claim,

The Making of a Revolutionary Symbol

In successful revolutions, a broad coalition of groups unites around common slogans and common symbols. Hence, the "bread, peace, land" of the Russian Revolution and the tricolor of the French. The participants in the Iranian Revolution united around a single demand—the shah had to go. They also adopted symbols from Shiᶜi lore.

The central event in the Shiᶜi calendar is the commemoration of the killing of Husayn, the third imam and grandson of Muhammad, at the Battle of Karbala in A.D. 680. Husayn was killed on his way to the city of Kufa, in present-day Iraq, where the population had proclaimed him the rightful caliph. When the governor of Kufa sent out an army to meet Husayn's challenge, most of Husayn's army melted away, leaving only about seventy men, women, and children to do battle. The results were as one might expect. As recorded in a ninth-century chronicle, a soldier in the governor's army described the battle in the following manner:

> We attacked them as the sun rose and surrounded them on every side. Eventually, our swords took their toll of the heads of the people; they began to flee without having any refuge; they sought refuge from us on the hills and in the hollows as doves seek refuge from a hawk. By God! . . . It was only a time for the slaughtering of animals, or for a man to take his siesta before we had come upon the last of them. There were their naked bodies, their bloodstained clothes, their faces thrown in the dust. The sun burst down on them; the wind scattered dust over them; their visitors in this deserted place were eagles and vultures.

Every year, in the month of Muharram, Shiᶜis recall the Battle of Karbala in ritual and pageant. As a penance for the abandonment of their imam in his

simply as a result of economic privation. Those who cite structural reasons usually point to the fact that Iran was a rentier state. In rentier states, they assert, the government's relationship with its population is one of a patron to a client. When the government can no longer distribute the goodies to which the population feels entitled, that population withdraws its allegiance. The Iranian government, they argue, faced such a crisis in the second half of the 1970s. Once again, neither the economic nor the structural explanations are persuasive. In terms of the former, even if revolutions were nothing more than glorified bread riots (a good reason to get rid of the concept of revolution in the first place) there is no evidence that hungry people are more likely to rebel than well-fed people. Furthermore, while economic downturns occur all the time, revolutions are a rare occurrence. If it is economic privation that causes revolutions, why was there no revolution in the United States during the 1930s? Social scientists who argue for structural hour of need, Shi'i men march in processions, whipping themselves and chanting, "Oh Husayn, we were not there."

Commemorations of acts of cowardice do not, of course, contribute to revolutionary fervor. Enter Ayatollah Khomeini, who, on the eve of the Iranian Revolution, offered his followers a different reading of the Battle of Karbala. Khomeini counseled his followers not to fixate on the community's abandonment of their imam. Rather, he advised, Iranians should take heart from the courage displayed by Husayn and his handful of followers who stood up to tyranny in the face of overwhelming odds. According to Khomeini:

> I tell you plainly that a dark, dangerous future lies ahead and that it is your duty to resist and to serve Islam and the Muslim peoples. Protest against the pressure exerted upon our oppressed people every day. Purge yourselves of your apathy and selfishness; stop seeking excuses and inventing pretexts for evading your responsibility. You have more forces at your disposal than the Lord of Martyrs (upon whom be peace) did, who resisted and struggled with his limited forces until he was killed. If (God forbid) he had been a weak, apathetic, and selfish person, he could have come up with some excuse for himself and remained silent. His enemies would have been only too happy for him to remain silent so that they could attain their vile goals, and they were afraid of his rebelling. But he dispatched [a messenger] to procure the people's allegiance to him so that he might overthrow that corrupt government and set up an Islamic government. If he had sat in some corner in Medina and had nothing to do with anyone, everyone would have respected him and come to kiss his hand. And if you sit silently by, you too will be respected, but it will be the kind of respect that is given a dead saint. A dead saint is respected by everyone, but a living saint or Imam has his head cut off.

causes also have to explain why other rentier states, such as Saudi Arabia and Kuwait, did not undergo revolutions in the late 1970s while nonrentier states, such as the Philippines and Nicaragua, did. Last, as we saw in Chapter 15, all states in the Middle East are, to some extent or another, rentier states, and the political structures of all states in the region are fundamentally similar. So, again, why Iran and not, for example, Egypt?

Finally, there are those who argue for what are called "conjunctural/multicausal theories." According to these theories, revolutions occur when a variety of factors—none of which is sufficient to spark a revolution by itself—converge. According to one scholar, for example, the Iranian Revolution might be traced to the simultaneous occurrence of rapid and uneven capitalist development, political weakness of the monarchy (prior to Jimmy Carter's visit, the shah had temporarily eased repression), the development of a broad oppositional coalition, the unification of that coalition around a set of key symbols, and the right international context. The main problem with conjunctural/multicausal theories is that they are inelegant. They violate that fundamental rule of the natural and social sciences, Ockham's razor, which states *"entia non sunt multiplicanda praeter necessitatem"* (simpler is better). In addition, because every revolution might be attributed to a different set of causes, conjunctural/multicausal theories lack universal applicability. They also appear to rely on that bane of historians, *post hoc, ergo propter hoc* (after this, therefore because of this) reasoning. Unfortunately, for the time being, they are the best theories we have.

Determining the causes of the revolution is not the only problem that has proven to be contentious. There is also the problem of the revolution's significance. Some social scientists consider the Iranian Revolution to be one of the most significant events in the history of the modern Middle East. They believe this for two reasons. First, they argue that the Iranian Revolution established a new model for government—one not borrowed from the West. This model has inspired social movements from Algeria and Egypt to Palestine and Afghanistan. Second, they argue that the doctrines of the dominant group of revolutionaries were exceptional in the history of revolutions.

Iran is, at least on paper, a theocracy. According to the Iranian constitution, adopted in 1979, all laws of the Islamic republic were to be based on "Islamic principles." It was up to the ulama to ensure these principles were met. The primary political, military, and judicial figure in the Islamic republic was to be a *vali-e faqih*, defined by the Iranian constitution as a "just and pious *faqih* [a legal expert qualified to rule on matters pertaining to Islamic law] who is acquainted with the circumstances of his age; courageous, resourceful, and possessed of administrative ability; and recognized and accepted as leader by the majority of the people." The first *vali-e faqih* was Ayatollah Khomeini, who dubbed this type of government a *velayat-e faqih*—that is, a government of the *faqih*. The supreme court of the Islamic republic, the Supreme Judicial Council, was also to be composed of ulama, as was the Council of Guardians, whose job it is to ensure that laws passed by the *majlis* are compatible with Islam.

The second reason some scholars believe that the Iranian Revolution marks an epochal shift in the history of the modern Middle East is the doctrinal foundation for the new governing structures. One historian has argued it this way: Since the French Revolution, revolutionary movements had sought power in order to establish some utopian vision of a new society based on one or another modernizing ideology. The French had their "republic of reason," the Bolsheviks of Russia had their Marxism-Leninism. The leaders of the Iranian Revolution, on the other hand, rejected utopian models for the future in favor of an ancient one. Theirs would be a society that gave pride of place to purity rather than modernity—a society in which its members abided by the shari'a. This means that the values promoted by the Islamic revolution differ from those of other revolutions. This also means that the Islamic republic represents a system detached from Western notions of individual rights, women's rights, popular sovereignty, and so on.

Other scholars are more leery about attributing special significance to either the structure of the Islamic republic or its doctrines. When Ayatollah Khomeini returned from exile in 1979, he gave a speech in which he outlined the reasons for the revolution. According to Khomeini,

> Muhammad Reza Pahlavi is gone. . . . He fled after destroying everything. He ruined our country and made our cemetaries flourish. . . . Our agriculture is wiped out. . . . He kept our culture in a backward state. . . . We have had universities for more than fifty years. . . . Due to treason committed against us, however, there has been no human development. . . . As regards oil, it has been given totally over to foreigners, whether to Americans or other countries. . . . If, God forbid, that man had remained on the throne for several more years, our oil reserves would have been exhausted. . . . The blood of our young has been shed for these same causes and for freedom. . . . We want a strong country with a stable and powerful system. We do not seek to reverse the system totally. In fact, we want to maintain it, only let it be based on—and in service to—the people.

The same speech might have been given by Muhammad Mossadegh or ʿAli Shariʿati.

Lest it be thought that Khomeini was only playing to the crowd, the record of the Islamic republic seems to indicate otherwise. In spite of its discourse, the Iranian revolutionary model of government *is*, in many ways, borrowed from the West. Where in the Qur'an or hadith is there mention of an Islamic *republic*? Where is there mention of elections, parliaments, or constitutions? The Islamic Republic of Iran has all three. Indeed, the constitution seems to waffle on the idea of popular sovereignty. While the constitution proclaims sovereignty belongs to God, it also stipulates that God "has placed man in charge of his social destiny." Nor has the Islamic republic rejected the ideology of nationalism. The president of the Islamic republic must be Iranian, and Khomeini himself spoke of the "Iranian fatherland." Rather than Islamizing the nation, it might be argued that the revolution nationalized religion.

As for establishing an "Islamic third way" in economics, the record of the Islamic republic has been equally dismal. From 1982 to 1988, the government of the Islamic republic advocated public ownership of industry, price controls, industrial regulation, and import substitution industrialization. While these statist economic policies may have been necessary for mobilizing Iran's economy during its eight-year war with Iraq, the Iranian leadership also argued that they would enable Iran to achieve economic self-sufficiency after hostilities had ended. As a result, the economy of Iran during this period resembled that of Egypt under Gamal ʿAbd al-Nasser or Syria or Iraq in the early days of Baʿth Party rule. After 1988, however, the Islamic republic reversed economic course. It not only looked favorably on the reemergence of the private sector, it cut government subsidies on everyday goods and promoted the establishment of offshore free trade zones, foreign investment, privatization, and deregulation. The government even brought in consultants from the International Monetary Fund to advise it on its change of course. Anwar al-Sadat would have felt quite at home.

While social purity has pride of place in official doctrine, skeptics argue that the revolution has had little effect in most areas of daily life. True, women's clothing has been tightly regulated, but girls are still educated and women still vote. In fact, the revolution's quest for social purity might be put in the same category as the French revolutionaries' quest for a society built on "republican virtues" and even the Third Worldist quest for social justice. And even though the Islamic revolution claimed as a model the first Islamic community, what revolution has not looked backward to a more pristine time? As Karl Marx put it more than a hundred years before the Iranian Revolution,

> At the very time when men appear engaged in revolutionizing things and themselves . . . they conjure up into their service the spirits of the past, assume their names, their battle cries, their costumes to enact a new historic scene in such time-honored disguise and with such borrowed language. Thus did Luther masquerade as the Apostle Paul; thus did the revolution of 1789–1814 drape itself alternatively as the Roman Republic and the Roman Empire.

And, lest anyone forget, the very rejection of Westernization and the embrace of "cultural authenticity" is itself part of the Western cultural tradition— nineteenth-century Romanticism.

There is another way in which the Iranian Revolution may have borrowed from the revolutionary model of the West. After the reign of terror of the French Revolution, moderates took over and put an end to the revolutionary excesses of the radicals. Since this took place in the revolutionary month of Thermidor, historians call the period of relative calm and reconstruction that usually follows a revolutionary upsurge a revolution's Thermidor. Toward the end of the 1990s, some analysts argued that Iran was entering its Thermidorean period. In 1997, Muhammad Khatami won the presidency on a reformist platform that called for greater openness in the Islamic republic. That same year, his party swept local elections nationwide, and in 1998 it won two-thirds of the seats in the *majlis*. Many Iranians appeared fed up with the repression, corruption, economic stagnation, and ideologically inspired excesses of the revolutionary regime. Ironically, these were the same charges that the revolutionaries had lodged against the shah in 1978–1979. And little wonder: At the time of Khatami's ascendancy, most Iranians were too young to remember the shah or the revolution. In 2000, it was estimated that 70 percent of Iranians were under the age of thirty. Two years after Khatami's accession, their accumulated grievances and anger at the slow pace of reform found expression in student riots that sparked a nationwide uprising. It took the government a week to suppress the disturbances. Similar student riots occurred in 2003.

Without a doubt, the election of the radical populist Mahmoud Ahmadinejad as Khatami's successor as president of Iran has seemed to cast doubt on the idea of an "Iranian Thermidor." As president, Khatami had called for a "dialogue among civilizations" (in contrast to the view, popularized by Samuel P. Huntington and described in the Introduction, that the *clash* of civilizations would spark future wars). In place of Khatami's conciliatory rhetoric, Ahmadinejad's seemed deliberately provocative (he once called Israel "a disgraceful blot . . . [that should be] wiped off the map"). And Iran's pursuit of nuclear weapons hardly demonstrates the winding down of revolutionary passions. But a number of analysts have argued that this is exactly how we should read Ahmadinejad's rhetoric and actions. For them, every policy and rhetorical flourish articulated by Ahmadinejad should be understood as a desperate effort to rally frustrated Iranians around the regime and restore the standing of a government in which all too many had lost faith.

As president, Ahmadinejad has attempted to keep the increasingly unpopular clerics in the background, diminish their role in day-to-day governance, and expand the power and popular base of the presidency. His high-risk pursuit of nuclear weapons, some analysts contend, is part of a strategy to expand Iranian prestige and influence abroad, humiliate the "Great Satan," and thus energize domestic support for the regime—just as the seizure of the American embassy in Tehran had energized an earlier generation of revolutionaries. Ahmadinejad has also resurrected Khomeini's economic populism (a sop to the urban poor) while abandoning some of the most divisive policies handed down from the revolutionary era (a sop to cultural critics of the regime). Thus, alongside promises of social justice and pledges to recommit the government to social welfare programs and economic development, he has reportedly eased the enforcement of women's dress codes and the censorship of music and certain periodicals. Ahmadinejad even tried to overturn a ban on women's right to attend sports events in arenas where men are present (even if it is only to watch soccer). This proved, however, too much for the clerics to swallow.

Whatever the rhetoric and policies of one or another Iranian government, it might be argued that the domestication of the revolutionary fervor that had once engulfed Iran and terrified its neighbors had been guaranteed from the start. This is because of the strength and resiliency of the international economic and state systems, because Iran cannot simply opt out of those systems, and because, in the end, Iran must play by the rules of those systems. Iran still depends on the export of oil for over 80 percent of its revenue. Most of this oil goes to states in Asia and Europe, particularly Japan and Italy, with whom Iran must maintain friendly commercial relations. Furthermore, for all its early identification as the spearhead of an international Islamic movement, Iran has been forced to conform to the dictates of the international state system. When the United States froze Iranian assets in the aftermath of the takeover of its embassy in Tehran, the government of the Islamic republic took the dispute to the World Court. The World Court only recognizes states that conform to international norms as litigants. For Iranians to take a commercial airliner abroad, for them to send a letter abroad, Iran must adhere to international civil aviation and postal conventions. Only states that conform to international norms participate in these conventions. Overall, then, the modern economic and state systems gave the revolutionaries of the Islamic republic little leeway for accomplishing or even envisaging a new order that lay outside those systems.

Twenty

Islamic Political Movements

Granted, the Iranian Revolution may not have provided the world with an alternative model for organizing political and economic relations. And, bluster aside, the Islamic Republic of Iran may well have found its niche in the international state and economic systems rather than challenging those systems. Nevertheless, the Iranian Revolution certainly provided a model for political mobilization that has been embraced by many in the Middle East and beyond. Although in the aftermath of 9/11 much of the world's attention has focused on the outrages perpetrated by fringe jihadi groups like al-Qaeda, it has been mass-based Islamic movements—many of which drew inspiration from their reading of events in Iran—that truly have been transforming the political landscape of the Middle East in recent decades.

Soon after the Iranian Revolution (the exact year is disputed), Islamic activists in Leabanon founded Hizbullah to provide assistance and protection for that country's disadvantaged and underrepresented Shi'i community. After the Israeli invasion of Lebanon in 1982, Hizbullah waged a successful guerrilla war against the invaders, eventually forcing them out. In 1987, another Islamic movement, Hamas, emerged in the occupied Palestinian territories. Drawing from the social service and mosque networks its members had established throughout the territories, Hamas coalesced into a formidable political machine capable of challenging both the Israeli occupation and the dominance of the secular Palestine Liberation Organization. By conducting a campaign of terror against Israeli civilians, Hamas played a critical role in derailing the Oslo process. Islamic groups have used violence in their attempts to destabilize the Egyptian and Syrian governments, and Islamic political parties have won elections in Jordan, Turkey, and Algeria. In the last case, the government nullified the results, precipitating a civil war which claimed the lives of anywhere between forty thousand and one hundred thousand Algerians. And on the periphery of the Middle East, Islamic movements have taken power in the Sudan and Afghanistan, and a group calling itself the Council of Islamic Courts was on the verge of doing the same in Somalia before being ousted by troops from neighboring Ethiopia.

Not all Islamic groups that emerged during this period had political aspirations. Many limited their activities to providing services for their communities. After an earthquake devastated parts of Cairo in 1992, for example, Islamic groups delivered medical aid, food, and drinking water to the stricken areas of the city far more quickly and more efficiently than did the government. Others devoted themselves to "re-Islamizing" their societies through missionary work, arguing that Islamic governance could not be imposed from the top on a nation unprepared and undeserving of it. Still other Islamic groups attempted to avoid as much contact with mainstream society as possible, preferring withdrawal from an impious world to contamination by it. Nor were all Islamic political groups that emerged during this period committed to the same tactics to achieve their goals. As we have seen, some resorted to revolutionary violence or wars of national liberation, others to pressure-group tactics or electoral politics. Nevertheless, over the course of the past quarter century the secular nationalisms which had dominated the politics of the region since the end of World War I and had appeared so alluring to the generation of the 1950s and 1960s—the generation of Gamal ʿAbd al-Nasser and the pre-Saddam Hussein, pre-Hafiz al-Assad Baʿth Party, for example—have been placed on the defensive in many parts of the Middle East. The political sphere, which had once pushed Islamic political groups to its fringes, now includes them as a matter of course.

Although Islamic political movements differ from each other on a host of issues, they all promote a common agenda. Islamic political movements are dedicated to expanding the realm of Islamic law and imposing "Islamic values" and "Islamic norms" (dress codes and the segregation of men and women, for example) on society. They all profess doctrines in which social justice plays a prominent role. They all seek to influence or take over the reins of government. This, of course, raises an interesting question. Since nationalist movements also seek to establish a new set of norms on society ("republican virtues"), promote the common interest, and take over the reins of government, just how do Islamic political movements differ from nationalist movements?

The relationship between Islamism (as it is often called) and nationalism is a complex one. Take, for example, the following excerpts from a document called the "Charter of God: The Platform of the Islamic Resistance Movement." The Islamic Resistance Movement is better known by its Arabic acronym, Hamas. After a preamble, the charter includes the following sentences:

> The basis of the Islamic Resistance Movement is Islam. From Islam it derives its ideas and its fundamental precepts and view of life, the universe, and humanity; and it judges all its actions according to Islam and is inspired by Islam to correct its errors. . . .
>
> Because the Islamic Resistance Movement adopts Islam as its way of life, its historical conception extends back as far as the birth of the Islamic message, of the Righteous Ancestors (*al-salaf al-salih*). [Therefore] Allah is its goal, the Prophet is its model, and the Qurʾan is its constitution. Its spatial conception extends wherever Muslims—who adopt Islam as their way of life—are found, in any place on the face of the earth. Thus it reaches both the depths of the earth and the highest spheres of the heavens. . . . [T]he movement is a universal one.

This is, of course, the sort of boilerplate that one naturally associates with an Islamic political movement. In this portion of its charter, Hamas confirms its foundation in Islam, which the charter regards as having a message that is bounded by neither time nor territory. But in several of the passages that follow there appears to be a bit of a contradiction. For example, the charter goes on to stipulate the following:

> According to the Islamic Resistance Movement, nationalism is part and parcel of its religious creed. Nothing is loftier or deeper in nationalism than waging jihad against the enemy and confronting him when he sets foot on the land of the Muslims. . . . All nationalist currents operating in the Palestinian arena for the liberation of Palestine may rest assured that [Hamas] is definitely and irrevocably [a source] of support and assistance to them, in both speech and action, at the present and in the future.

Now it might be argued that this second group of passages does not really contradict the eternal and universal message of Islam and Islamic movements at all—that all these passages are saying is that Muslims must, in the words of the Green Party slogan, "think globally and act locally." But while the first set of passages claims religion as the sole foundation for Hamas, the other acknowledges a second source of authority as well: the ideology of nationalism. Because nationalism is one of the hallmarks of the modern age, it thus seems strange that movements that claim adherence to a message that is timeless, divinely inspired, and universal should acknowledge nationalism as one of the supports upon which they rest.

As we saw in Chapter 13, nationalism might be defined in two ways: as the principle that guides the organization of political communities in the modern world, and as the specific incarnations of that principle (Arab or Palestinian nationalism, for example). Nationalism in the first sense is a set of assumptions about the nature of human society. All nationalist movements assert that humanity is naturally divided into nations that have their own identities and homeland, that nations can be identified by certain characteristics that all members of the nation hold in common, that nations retain their essential characteristics even as they travel through time, and that there is something called a "common interest" and it is the role of the state to promote it.

Islamism shares with the ideology of nationalism the same set of assumptions. In their writings and proclamations, Islamic political activists constantly refer to Islam as the true and unalterable essence of the nation which has defined their nation throughout its history. Like nationalists, Islamists see their role as recovering that essence from decay and safeguarding it in its home territory. In a manner reminiscent of nationalists, they believe that recovering the Islamic essence of their societies will bind their societies together and allow each of the members of the society to contribute to the "common interest." According to the "Charter of God,"

> Islamic society is a society of solidarity. The Messenger—may [God's] prayers and peace be with him—said, "How wonderful people are the Ash'aris! When

they were under stress, either in residence or in travel, they would gather all their possessions and divide [them] up equally among themselves." It is this Islamic spirit that should prevail in every Muslim society.

It should not be surprising that Islamism and nationalism share assumptions. As we have seen, the doctrines and institutions associated with Islam or any other religion are not frozen in time. They exist within history, not outside history. And while there are continuities of religious doctrines and institutions, the meaning those doctrines and institutions hold for society, and the function they play in society, evolve through time. Or, to turn the old adage on its head, the more things stay the same the more they change. Thus, during the nineteenth century, as Middle Eastern rulers and commoners alike confronted the new social, economic, and political conditions created by the expansion of the modern world economic and state systems, they began to adapt Islam to meet these new conditions. Ironically, then, Islamism holds a lot in common with Zionism. Both arose in response to the same conditions and responded by "nationalizing" religion. That is, both Zionism and Islamism transformed a religion into the distinctive characteristic of their nation. By so doing, they transformed religious communities into national communities.

The fact that Islamic political movements partake of assumptions associated with the ideology of nationalism explains two peculiar aspects of these movements. First, Islamic political movements have adapted themselves quite readily to the regional state system as it is currently constituted. While Islamic political movements pay lip-service to the universal message of Islam or jihad or whatever, they are organized on a state-by-state basis and address the specific concerns of the national community in which they operate. Hamas fights for the liberation of Palestine, for example, Hizbullah for the liberation of Lebanon, and the Syrian Muslim Brotherhood used to be notorious for betraying members of the Jordanian Muslim Brotherhood to the Jordanian government—a favor that the Jordanian Muslim Brotherhood returned in spades. In the cases of Iran, Afghanistan, and the Sudan, where Islamic political movements have taken power, little change has taken place either in the boundaries of those states or in their methods of dealing with the outside world. While this is, in part, a result of the strength of the international state system that forces compliance with its standards, it is also a result of the fact that Islamic political movements are designed to work within, not against, those standards.

In addition, the fact that Islamism shares assumptions with the ideology of nationalism has made it easy for adherents of one or another secular nationalist movement to switch to the Islamist camp with ease. For example, as a number of scholars have pointed out, many of the Shi'i inhabitants of the slums of Baghdad who were secular nationalists (or communists) in the 1950s and 1960s became Islamists in the 1970s and 1980s. All too often, observers have attributed this transfer of allegiance to one of two causes: Either the inhabitants of the Middle East are hopelessly fickle, inasmuch as they are nationalist one day and Islamist the next, or they are hopelessly

Islamism—or Fundamentalism?

This book uses the terms "Islamic movements" and "Islamist" to refer to those groups that use Islamic symbols and rhetoric and advocate the return to Islamic law and "Islamic values." These terms are not the only ones that have been applied to those groups. Indeed, finding an agreed-upon term in English for those groups has not been easy for scholars and commentators. It is not simply a question of taking the Arabic term and translating it into English—there is, after all, no agreed-upon Arabic term for them either.

One term that has commonly been applied to these groups is "fundamentalist," as in Islamic fundamentalist or Muslim fundamentalist. Many scholars of the Middle East have found this term inappropriate because it so obviously borrows from the Western—particularly American—experience. The word "fundamentalism" emerged in the United States at the end of the nineteenth century to describe a school of theology that advocated a return to the fundamentals of Christianity. While this school was particularly strong among American Protestants, it affected American Catholics as well.

The desire to return to Christian fundamentals arose in response to two movements in American Christianity: modernism and the social gospel movement. Protestant and Catholic modernists, like Islamic modernists, sought to make religion compatible with the findings of modern science, social theory, and social practice. Those who preached the doctrine of the social gospel sought to apply Christian principles to solve social problems—the sort of problems (poverty, crime) sparked by the industrialization and urbanization of America. Many American Christians thought that the advocates of modernism and the social gospel doctrine had lost touch with their theological roots. In particular, they felt that any attempt to use Christianity to create a "heaven on earth" ignored two fundamental precepts of Christianity: original sin, which made the effort sacrilegious, and the imminent return of Christ, which made the effort superfluous.

Beginning in 1878, those associated with the attempt to return to Christian orthodoxy began holding meetings in upstate New York, an annual event called the Niagara Falls Bible Conference. At the same time, conservative

backward, inasmuch as Islam is presented as the invariable ideological default setting and the commitment of the inhabitants of the region to nationalism has been, at best, superficial. There is, however, a third, less patronizing way to read this phenomenon. The fact that the Shi'is of Baghdad might transfer their loyalties from some variety of secular nationalism (or communism) to Islamism with such ease should alert us to the similarities, born of common roots, that link these various movements.

This being the case, it should come as no surprise that the same factors that contributed to the expansion of the domain of nationalism and the mul-

Protestant theologians associated with the Princeton Theological Seminary began to weigh in on the issue. Believing in the literal truth of the Bible, these theologians founded a school of theology called the "Princeton School" or the "Princeton Theology." A marriage of these two groups took place in 1895 when the organizers of the Niagara Falls Bible Conference drew up a list of five principles in which, they maintained, all real Christians believed: the literal truth of the original Bible, the virgin birth and deity of Christ, the redemption of mankind through Christ's death, the bodily resurrection of Christ, and the imminent return of Christ. To make these principles widely known, two brothers, Milton and Lyman Steward, published a twelve-tract series called "The Fundamentals." Because they were wealthy—the brothers were founders of the Union Oil Company—they were able to print and distribute over three million copies of their tracts. By the early 1920s, those who held to the principles of "The Fundamentals" began to be labeled "fundamentalists" by their modernist adversaries.

If Christian fundamentalists advocated a return to the original sources of Christianity, why can't the term fundamentalism be used to describe Muslims who also advocate a return to the original sources? Many Middle Eastern scholars believe that the circumstances surrounding the emergence and growth of the two movements are so different that calling them both "fundamentalism" does more to obscure than enlighten. They assert that applying a term originally coined to denote a Western phenomenon demonstrates cultural arrogance—once again, it appears, the West has provided a model whereas the Middle East has only a cheap knock-off. They also point out that the social composition of the American movement is different from that of the Middle Eastern movement: Whereas contemporary Islamist movements have a particularly strong following among better educated urban dwellers, Protestant fundamentalism is a doctrine of choice among lesser educated Americans living in rural areas. Interestingly, this was not always the case. American fundamentalism began as a predominantly urban movement and found strong support in such cities as Philadelphia, Minneapolis, and Los Angeles. In the beginning, the movement also attracted the well educated, as one would expect with a movement that was expounded by theologians at the Princeton Theological Seminary.

tiplication of nationalist movements in the Middle East also contributed to the multiplication of Islamic political movements. These factors should be familiar by now. There were the effects of the great nineteenth-century transformation: the standardization of cultural norms, the emergence and enlargement of a modern public sphere, and the expansion of the role of the state and the public's expectations from it. As we have seen, this was also the period in which a number of Muslim intellectuals, and the Ottoman government of Abdulhamid II, formulated the intellectual foundations for modern Islamic political movements and spread their ideas. There was World

War I, which destroyed the Ottoman Empire and opened up the Arab Middle East to a variety of political currents that had previously been held in check. As a matter of fact, the period of World War I was bracketed by the 1911 call of Syrian ulama for the formation of an Islamic party, on the one hand, and the 1928 founding of the Muslim Brotherhood of Egypt—the largest, most effective, and most influential Islamic political party for the next half century—on the other. There was the period of the 1930s and 1940s, which was marked by expanded urbanization, the proliferation of urban-based popular political movements, and the further intrusion of the state into the economic and social spheres. There was the 1950s and 1960s, when Third Worldism was at its peak and governments promoted anti-imperialism and based their right to rule on their ability to deliver development and social justice.

Thus, from the nineteenth century through the 1960s, as the numbers of those inhabitants of the Middle East willing and able to engage in political activity expanded, many joined one or another political movement that shared the same fundamental assumptions and expectations. Of course, by the mid-twentieth century a preponderance of power resided in the hands of the nationalist movements that held the reins of government. Like their European counterparts, most of these nationalist movements were secular. The smug self-assurance of nationalists that nationalism, not religion, was on the side of history is reflected in a statement that was published in a Syrian newspaper at the beginning of the nationalist era: "I proclaim a new religion above all others. It is the religion of Arab unity which gathers together the children of the nation regardless of their faith."

By the 1970s, however, the states of the region were in deep crisis. More often than not, the accomplishments of Middle Eastern governments did not match the commitments to development and social justice they had made. None was able to bring about the economic miracles they had promised, none brought about the expected social transformation, none ended imperialism or, later, defeated Israel in battle. But what is important here is precisely those commitments, for in the commitments to social justice, true political and economic independence, true democracy, and so on, we find the aspirations of so many in the region. These commitments ran afoul of pressure from the West, the authoritarian tendencies of the regimes in the region, and the inefficiency of centralized economic planning. As a result, governments began to back away from the commitments they had made, leaving the playing field open to those who still took those commitments seriously and who had not been tarnished by failure. Among those groups that still took those commitments seriously were Islamic groups.

Islamic political groups had an added advantage in their battle with official nationalisms: They were able to counterpose their own brand of "cultural authenticity," as represented by Islam, to the "imported" secular nationalist creeds, which, they argued, brought nothing but oppression, economic stagnation, and defeat to the region. But it has not only been the failures of secular nationalisms that have fueled Islamist polemics or bolstered their claims to authenticity. In Saudi Arabia, the Islamic opposition has taken a "holier than thou" stance against a monarchy that claims to promote a strict puritanical interpretation of Islam while, according to the opposition, it is mired in corruption, "un-Islamic" practices, and servility to the West. Both Hamas in Palestine and Hizbullah in Lebanon have not only confronted the non-Islamic "Zionist enemy," they have challenged their own secular or sectarian political elites at home. The Ba'th party rulers of Syria and Iraq have come from minority communities, as did their most trustworthy associates: Alawites from the city of Latakia in the case of Syria, Sunni Muslims from the village of Tikrit in the case of Iraq. This, of course, enabled Islamists in those countries to define themselves as the true representatives of the nation in opposition to a sectarian "other."

Middle Eastern regimes certainly have done all they could to repress all opposition, including their Islamic opposition. And they have certainly been successful in repressing individual Islamic groups, just as they have been in repressing secular opponents such as communists and supporters of rival nationalist creeds. Nevertheless, Middle Eastern regimes have been relatively ineffective in suppressing the impulse behind Islamic groups. Islamic movements could not but thrive underground in an atmosphere in which the state not only broadcast its commitment to social justice, but made that commitment the foundation for political legitimacy. Beginning in the mid-1970s, financially strapped regimes began to heed the dictates of the American government and the international economic institutions it dominated by withdrawing from responsibilities they had assumed earlier. The appeal of Islamic movements touched those who were hardest hit by that withdrawal, as well as those who simply viewed the state's attempted retreat as a betrayal of its responsibilities.

The appeal of Islamic political parties has been demonstrated time and again across the region. In November 2003, George W. Bush gave a speech celebrating the twentieth anniversary of the National Endowment for Democracy. In the speech he proclaimed, "Many Middle Eastern governments now understand that military dictatorship and theocratic rule are a straight, smooth highway to nowhere," and hailed the steps toward democracy taken in Morocco, Bahrain, Oman, Qatar, Yemen, Kuwait, Jordan, the Palestinian Authority, Afghanistan, and Iraq. Interestingly, however, practically every example cited by Bush—and some that went unmentioned—only serves to underscore the popularity of Islamist parties. Although governments have repressed Islamists, banned their political parties, restricted Islamist fundraising and media access, and gerrymandered districts and fixed electoral lists, Islamists still managed to score significant successes in parliamentary elections in Morocco, Bahrain, Kuwait, Yemen, Jordan, Egypt, Lebanon, and the Palestinian Authority during the period stretching from 2002–2006. What all this bodes for political developments in those countries is unpredictable. In spite of dire predictions, participation in electoral politics and governance seems to have kept Turkey's Justice and Development Party and Jordan's Islamic Action Front on the straight and narow. In Lebanon and Palestine, on the other hand, where Hizbullah and Hamas have competed quite successfully in electoral campaigns, neither party seems prepared to abandon a military wing that remains independent of the government. The same might be said for practically every major party active in Iraq since the American-led invasion.

In spite of it all, the inability of regimes to suppress the impulse behind their Islamic opposition does not necessarily mean that those regimes will eventually succumb to that (or any other) opposition. Middle Eastern states have been able to concentrate into their hands an inordinate amount of power, particularly repressive power. Although political scientists may talk about populations "bargaining" with their governments to obtain rights or preserve pockets of freedom unfettered by state control, it must be remembered that Middle Eastern states are maintained by seemingly pervasive intelligence services and militaries designed as much to preserve internal order as to make war on external enemies. Bargaining under such conditions cannot be but one-sided. When pushed against a wall, regimes have responded with a unrestrained viciousness. As we noted before, the Syrian government suppressed an Islamist rebellion in the city of Hama in 1982 by shelling the city center at an estimated cost of ten to twenty thousand lives. Saddam Hussein's repression of Shi'i revolts that broke out in Iraq in the aftermath of the 1990–1991 Gulf War was even more savage. The tanks that entered towns controlled by the rebels bore the legend, "After today, no more Shi'is," and after rebels fled to the expansive marshlands of southern Iraq the Iraqi government had the marshes drained. In the process, it displaced as many as a quarter of a million "Marsh Arabs" and created what the United Nations has called an "ecological disaster."

But while all states in the region have not been afraid to use their coercive power, they have also learned not to test its limits unnecessarily. Even under the most adverse economic and political conditions, states have been reluctant to redefine their missions radically. As we have seen, after Anwar al-Sadat—at the insistence of the International Monetary Fund—attempted to withdraw price supports from basic commodities in 1977, rioting broke out throughout Egypt. The government backed down. When it comes to tampering with the social safety net, the Egyptian government has avoided direct confrontation with its population by acting more deliberately and furtively. By maintaining at least the illusion that they are committed to social welfare, Egypt and the other states of the region have been able to take some of the wind out of the sails of Islamic political groups.

Furthermore, since the mid-twentieth century, governments in the region have been able to refashion society and bind their populations to them through an elaborate system of patronage. Governments have undercut the power of potential opponents, such as wealthy landowners, independent capitalists, and former political elites, and have bound favored social classes to the regime with economic and political rewards. This has made large segments of the population complicit in the regimes that govern them. Too many people count on too many things from the governments of the Middle East—price supports, jobs, official recognition, and so on—to gamble on new regimes.

There are other reasons as well why regimes in the region may be able to weather the Islamist storm. Many in the region consider the Islamist cure more dangerous than the authoritarian disease. Among them are secularists, religious minorities, liberals, and advocates of women's rights. This "better the devil you know" attitude can be seen by once again taking a look at the Hama revolt of 1982. While most commentators have viewed the entire incident as a morality tale underscoring the ruthlessness of the regime, there is another lesson to be learned as well: The population outside Hama remained quiet in spite of attempts by Islamic organizations to spark revolts in Damascus and Aleppo. Fear and repression certainly played a role, but so did the fact that non-Sunni Muslims make up a quarter of the population of Syria, that some layers of the population (such as those who live in rural areas of Syria) had been neglected before the Ba'th Party took power and have benefited greatly from regime policies, that there are still many secular nationalist true believers, and that many are just plain skeptical of the promises of Islamic groups, whatever the sins of the regime.

Finally, governments may be able to meet the Islamic challenge because of the nature of the relationship between nationalism and Islamism. Nationalism and Islamism grew in tandem because, at heart, they are roughly equivalent. Both emerged as a result of the same historical conditions, both address similar concerns, both draw their legitimacy from the same assumptions. But the relationship between nationalism and Islamism is an ironic one: While the strengthening of one has led to the strengthening of the other, the failure of one has led to a surge in popularity of the other. Again, in the first instance we are dealing with an ideology nationalists and Islamists hold in common, in the second with specific manifestations of that ideology. Although it may be true that the failure of the state with its nationalist doctrines led to the efflorescence of Islamist movements in the region, the reverse is true as well. Islamic movements have either failed to provide an alternative to the state and have been drenched in blood (as in Algeria and Egypt) or have been coopted by the state (as in Jordan) and, as a result, have come to share responsibility for its failings.

The Middle East in the "Age of Globalization"

socialism
welfare state
globalization

At the end of the twentieth century, historians began to look back and assess what had taken place and what was the meaning of it all. One of the questions they raised concerned the problem of periodicization, that is, where to put the historical boundaries of the twentieth century.

Chronologically, of course, the twentieth century began in 1900 (or 1901, if you are a stickler for details), just as the nineteenth century had begun in 1800 (or, again, 1801). But most historians do not plot history simply by referring to a calendar. In the case of the nineteenth century, for example, many historians use a periodicization that places the beginning of the century in 1789—the year of the French Revolution—and the end of the century in 1914—the year World War I broke out. Historians call this the "long nineteenth century." According to their accounts, the long nineteenth century was distinguished by a number of characteristics. During the long nineteenth century the modern world economic system reached the far corners of the globe as workers and farmers on every continent came to participate in a worldwide division of labor. The nation-state replaced the empire as the prototypical political unit and spread throughout the world. Certain dogmas, such as a belief in progress, standards of civilization, popular sovereignty, and nationalism, gained almost universal currency as a result of European global dominance, also a hallmark of the long nineteenth century. Finally, new social classes—the bourgeoisie, the working class—appeared on the world stage for the first time as a result of the twin processes of urbanization and industrialization.

If all or some of these phenomena have come to mark the long nineteenth century, what phenomena mark the century that followed? Some historians have placed a "short twentieth century" alongside the long nineteenth century. The great British historian Eric Hobsbawm, for example, begins his twentieth century with World War I and ends it in 1991. His timing of the twentieth century coincides with the establishment of the first great "socialist experiment" in Russia, which divided the world into rival socialist and capitalist camps. According to Hobsbawm, the rise of Soviet communism not only created a socialist state, it affected the entire world. To save capitalism, he argues, nonsocialist states had to undertake reforms. These reforms led to the emergence of the welfare state in the West and to the rescue of liberal capitalism. Hobsbawm ends his periodicization of the twentieth century with the demise of the Soviet Union, the end of the cold war, and the emergence of the United States as the world's only superpower.

As we have seen, the welfare state idea did leave a lasting impression on the states and citizens of the Middle East. In other ways, however, this periodicization ill suits the Middle East or other regions outside Europe. It is likely that states in the Middle East would have gone down the road of state-directed development and would have assumed many of the attributes of welfare states no matter what was going on in Europe. As a matter of fact, some historians and political scientists, following in the footsteps of economist Alexander Gerschenkron, have proposed a model of "late development" for nations that emerged in the wake of the industrial revolution. According to Gerschenkron and his followers, nations as diverse as nineteenth-century Germany and twentieth-century India commonly found market forces an insufficient basis for industrial development. Instead, there had to be some central mechanism—a state or a group of industrial elites—that had to take charge of industrial development and that had to win over various classes to its endeavors by extending promises to them. None of this can be attributed to the rise of the socialist bloc. And while the superpower rivalry between the United States and the Soviet Union did leave an imprint on the region and did aggravate regional conflicts, it hardly provides the hallmarks of an epoch. Instead, as we have seen, American-Soviet competition in the region was more akin to "new wine in old bottles."

Like Hobsbawm, other historians and political scientists have tried their hand at defining the twentieth century. Some have opined that Hobsbawm's notion of the short twentieth century should be replaced by a long twentieth century. Historian Charles S. Maier, for example, has proposed a twentieth century that stretches from 1850 to 1970. His twentieth century coincides with the rise and fall of the territorial state. How this periodicization would deal with the problem of defining the boundaries of the nineteenth century is not clear. Nor is it clear whether the highly touted weakening of the territorial state in the wake of an increasingly globalized world economy marks an irreversible trend or a shortsighted infatuation on the part of social scientists.

These bold attempts to figure out the central theme of twentieth-century history illustrate the principal problem historians confront when they attempt to divide history into bite-size pieces. For historical periods to have any meaning, historians assign to them certain attributes that distinguish each one from earlier and later periods. This means that historians must make choices and stress certain events or phenomena at the expense of others. We all know that the Renaissance was a period of great artistic achievement in Europe, but just how much did social or economic life during this period differ from daily life in the Medieval period that preceded it or in the Reformation period that followed it? The division of history into periods is thus both helpful and deceptive. On the one hand, it enables historians to highlight elements of change. On the other, it compels historians to privilege some types of change over others and to lose sight of historical continuities.

Take, for example, the common practice of using World War I as the dividing line between two historical eras. Part III of this book argued that World War I was perhaps the most important political event in the history of the modern Middle East for four reasons: the creation of the state system, the emergence of the Israeli-Palestinian conflict, the spread of a variety of nationalist sentiments throughout the region, many of which were embodied in states, and the consolidation of Iran as a modern nation-state under the guidance of Reza Shah. These are certainly important developments, but there are two things that are worthy of note. First of all, the roots of all these post–World War I developments might be traced to developments in the second half of the nineteenth century. It would have been impossible for nationalist movements to spread in the region had the Ottomans not already introduced modern institutions and structures of governance into the region, the Zionists who came to Palestine put themselves squarely within the tradition of European colonialism and the imperative to spread "civilization," and recent scholarship has demonstrated that many of the innovations attributed to the Reza Shah period—nationalism and defensive developmentalism, for example—also had their roots in late nineteenth-century Qajar rule. In addition, while World War I may have been the most important political event in the history of the modern Middle East, the war did not substantially change the social and economic history of the region. As we have seen, the region remained locked in a colonial relationship with the industrialized world, and the social and economic structures that had defined Middle Eastern society during the nineteenth century remained pretty much intact until they were disrupted in the 1930s and 1940s and reconstituted in the 1950s and 1960s.

So if World War I did not mark the beginning of a new twentieth-century dispensation, what did? Perhaps nothing. Turning Maier on his head, it is possible to argue that there was no twentieth century in the Middle East. This does not mean that the Middle East is backward in some way. Rather, it means that after the twin Middle Eastern revolutions of the nineteenth century—the integration of the region into the modern world economy and international state system—historians have not been able to come up with a yardstick for historical periodicization that has any true meaning for the region. The current Middle East—the Middle East of strong, authoritarian governments, of Islamic movements, of the Iranian and oil revolutions, of the unsolvable Israeli-Palestinian conflict—is a product of these twin processes. And, for better or worse, it is the Middle East of the foreseeable future.

Thus, dividing the history of the Middle East into centennial units may not be particularly useful. Nevertheless, there are some historians, like Charles S. Maier, who argue that even if we chose to privilege the continuities of modern Middle Eastern history over discontinuities, the region is on the verge of an epochal shift. Some attribute this epochal shift to globalization. Others attribute it to new electronic media such as the Internet and satellite television or to the global impact of newly established international principles of human rights and democracy. Still others argue that this epochal shift is coming as a result of some combination of the aforementioned three. Let us take a look at each of these forces in turn.

First, globalization. Globalization enthusiasts claim that the current trend toward free trade will have revolutionary effects. They predict that this trend will break down international boundaries, making the world a smaller place and, in the eyes of the most optimistic among them, a more tolerant and peaceful one. Or, to put it in the glib words of the journalist Thomas Friedman, no two countries that have McDonald's have ever engaged in war (forgetting for a moment that while the United States was bombing Belgrade, Yugoslavia, local McDonald's franchises were handing out free hamburgers to crowds at anti-NATO rallies).

If we look at globalization historically, however, the prediction that globalization will bring about an era in which states and conflicts between them will disappear appears a bit overly optimistic. The first great period of globalization took place during the nineteenth century, meaning, in this case, the period between 1815 and 1914. According to a number of indicators, globalization during this period was even more successful than during the so-called second period of globalization that began in 1950 or 1970, depending on your point of view, and continues to this day. During the first period of globalization labor was more mobile than it is today. There were no passports and people could and did move freely from continent to continent to find work. In 1900, about 14 percent of Americans were foreign born. Now, the figure is about 8 percent. Free trade ruled during much of the nineteenth century and exports boomed. But, at that time, exports provided only 7 percent of the gross national product of the United States—a figure that, at the turn of the twenty-first century, only increased one percentage point. According to the International Monetary Fund, capital flow across national lines still has not reached the same level as it did in the 1880s. This was, of course, the golden age of imperialism, which was also the golden age of foreign investment.

If the current period of globalization is to be considered successful then, so must the first period. But the first period of globalization hardly broke down international borders and made the world a smaller, more tolerant place. To the contrary. The first period of globalization ended with the onset of World War I, the bloodiest inter-national conflict until that time. There is no reason to think that the current impulse toward globalization, if it continues, would not produce a similar countercurrent. Indeed, as we saw in the Introduction, that countercurrent—expressed in movements as varied as neopopulist and anarchist movements—is already at work today. Furthermore, the end of multilateralism as a central plank of American foreign policy, the defeat of the European constitution, and so on, hardly point to a new era of international cooperation or the emergence of a new, non-national future.

Even if globalization were somehow to have the miraculous effects that enthusiasts predict that it will, it is not likely to be embraced either by gov-

Wave of the future? Flyer distributed by McDonald's Corporation urging the citizens of Beirut to break their daily Ramadan fast with a "Mac Combo."

ernments or populations of the Middle East. The push by the United States and international financial institutions like the International Monetary Fund (IMF) to win acceptance for the principles upon which globalization rests—particularly the principle of limiting government intervention into national economies—has already met with stiff resistance in the region. Since 1980, the International Monetary Fund has struck deals with governments from Morocco to Turkey to Jordan whose economies have fallen on hard times on close to a dozen occasions. In return for emergency loans, the IMF has required those governments to restructure their economies by privatizing government-run industries, ending government subsidies on consumer goods, eliminating tariffs, and the like. The IMF also supervised the voluntary restructuring of the Iranian economy. On each occasion, the governments met with resistance, and in some cases that resistance was regime-threatening.

No wonder the president of Egypt, Hosni Mubarak, has tried to tap into the popular mood by referring to the IMF as the "Fund of Misery." For all too many in the Middle East, globalization represents a return to old-fashioned imperialism and the end of the protective, welfare-oriented state that still provides legitimacy for states in the region, whatever the realities.

If globalization does not bring about an epochal shift in the history of the Middle East, perhaps new technologies, such as the Internet or satellite dishes, will. After 9/11, many in the West became aware of the explosion of new technologies in the region by watching images originally broadcast by the al-Jazeera television station based in Qatar. Some technology enthusiasts argue that access to international television stations like al-Jazeera or the Internet will render international borders ineffective and hasten the end of the nation-state, in the Middle East as elsewhere. This argument is not a new one. According to sociologist Claude Fischer, the prediction that new technologies will break down international boundaries was foreshadowed by a similar prediction made in the 1940s, when it was prophesied that the invention of the telephone and access to long-distance calling would weaken local ties and hasten the emergence of a borderless international community. Hope for a peaceful international order based on a global public sphere, it seems, springs eternal.

What technology enthusiasts fail to note is that the Internet and satellite television cannot break the monopoly over information that governments in the region hold today because governments in the region have never held such a monopoly. For example, during the invasion of Iraq in 2003, residents of Baghdad were able to keep abreast of the news by reading local newspapers, listening to local radio, and (for a time) local television broadcasts. But they also supplemented these sources of information with sources outside the country. Not only did they tune into the relatively new al-Jazeera, they relied on the same news sources—the B.B.C., Radio Monte Carlo, and the American Armed Forces Radio—that their parents had during previous crises. This did not make the job of the "coalition of the willing" any easier. Likewise, strong states emerged in the Middle East in spite of the public's access to alternative sources of news. After all, getting to know one's neighbors and hearing their viewpoints does not necessarily mean accepting those neighbors and adopting those viewpoints.

It would, of course, be foolish to discount the arguments of technology enthusiasts out of hand. There *have* been technologies in history that have provided the wherewithal for epochal social or political or economic change. As we have seen, harnessing gunpowder allowed for the emergence of large-scale, long-lived empires throughout the Eurasian continent. Along the same lines, historians have cited the epoch-making significance of the stirrup, the compass, the printing press, and the steam engine. But even if these inventions have had the power to transform history, as some historians claim, more often than not technological change merely reinforces already existing social, economic, and political relationships. From the inception of al-Jazeera, for example, the U.S. government has argued that images of Israeli tanks attacking Palestinian towns or injured Iraqi civilians were amplifying existing nationalist passions that the U.S. government was desperately trying to dampen. The Internet has already been used by nationalist movements such as the Kosovar Liberation Organization and the Zapatista Army for National Liberation (EZLN) in Mexico to garner international support and create a national public space in cyberspace, which would have been impossible to achieve in real space. Hence, rather than breaking down national boundaries, the Internet can and has been used to reinforce national allegiances and movements. Or, in the words of anthropologist Benedict Anderson, the Internet has made it possible for people to become "long-distance nationalists."

Finally, democratization. In the immediate aftermath of the cold war, Francis Fukuyama, a neoconservative who has since renounced the faith, wrote an influential article titled "The End of History?" According to Fukuyama, the collapse of the Soviet Union brought to an end the threat to liberal democracy posed by the second great "ism" of the twentieth century—communism (the other "ism" was fascism). Although the new order may take a while to sort itself out, he wrote, we should nevertheless expect the eventual emergence of an international system in which democratic principles reign supreme and uncontested. For Fukuyama, this meant that history will have reached its final destination (hence the title of the article), and while life may be a bit duller, it will certainly be more tranquil.

Although Fukuyama's optimistic prediction faced a number of harsh critiques, his article captures well the spirit of the time. Even some scholars of the Middle East joined the democratization bandwagon. They pointed out that the ardor with which broad segments of the Middle Eastern population had first greeted the revolutionary regimes in the early Third Worldist period has long since dissipated. They attributed this to chronic repression and unfulfilled promises. The time will come, democratization theorists argued, when long-awaited democratization movements would emerge in the region and effectively challenge authoritarian governments and their equally authoritarian (mostly Islamist) opponents. When this did not occur and 9/11 did, the Bush administration and its supporters linked those two phenomena. They also added a new twist to democratization theory: Sometimes, they asserted, it might be necessary for the United States to force the hand of history. Although many observers are skeptical about America's commitment to transforming the authoritarian regimes it had aided and abetted for years, democratizing the Middle East remains the stated goal of American policy.

Thus, some have argued that democratization in the Middle East will occur by natural evolution. For others, it will be, as a recent essayist has put it, "a gift of the foreigners." Let's look at each in turn.

First, democratization-as-evolutionary-process. As political scientist Lisa Anderson has argued, democratization enthusiasts assume that democracy is in some way preordained and that a "country's failure to embrace it is evidence of political perversity or moral obtuseness on the part of its citizenry." Such assumptions are not new to the social sciences. Democratization enthusiasts are following in the footsteps of their nineteenth-century predecessors who predicted the inevitable triumph of liberal values or communism or whatever. Wishful thinking, as reflected in theories of inevitable progress, was not borne out by events then and is unlikely to be borne out by events now. The power of states in the Middle East still remains far greater than the power of those seeking expanded democratic rights. Governments in the region have been quite successful not only in increasing their own power but in diminishing the power of their opponents. For example, states in the region have been able to divide their populations into competing groups, pitting cities against the countryside, religious sect against religious sect, ethnic group against ethnic group, province against province. They are certainly not likely to relinquish any of their hard-earned power voluntarily.

That seems to leave it up to the United States or even a concert of nations to impose democratic structures in the Middle East. So far the United States has applied a number of tactics in its democratization campaign. It invaded and occupied Iraq. It encouraged the "Cedar Revolution" in Lebanon in 2005. It coerced the regime in Egypt to hold elections. And it midwifed the Oslo process which led to democratic elections in Palestine. And, so far, American democratization efforts have borne unanticipated consequences at every turn. The case of Iraq is too well-known to merit further comment. In Lebanon, the spirit of the Cedar Revolution soon dissipated and politics returned to business as usual, with one exception: A reinvigorated Hizbullah entered the Lebanese government for the first time. In December 2005, the Egyptian government held what President Hosni Mubarak bragged were the freest elections in modern Egyptian history (Mubarak himself won only 88.6% of the vote). In spite of widespread intimidation of opposition candidates, ballot-stuffing and vote suppression, and government control over the media, candidates affiliated with the banned Muslim Brotherhood won close to 20 percent of the seats in the Egyptian parliament. Were it allowed to organize itself as a political party, the Muslim Brotherhood would represent the largest opposition party in that body. And as we have seen, elections in Palestine handed a resounding victory to Hamas, although this was probably more an indication of Palestinian anger at PLO corruption and inefficiency—and a flawed electoral strategy on the part of the PLO—than of support for Hamas's program (at the time of the election, polls indicated that only 2 percent of the population of the territories wanted to see Islamic law applied there).

Overall, even if America's commitment to democratic change in the region is genuine and not mere window dressing, it faces daunting challenges: the unanticipated popularity of Islamic political parties, the tenacity of governments in the region, America's fear of offending or destabilizing its allies in the war on terror, and fatigue felt by many Americans facing the prospect of further foreign adventures.

What all this portends for the future of the Middle East is unclear. What is clear is that one should be wary of those who claim that all it will take to transform the region is the application of the right magic formula—whether the ingredients of that formula are to be found in globalization, new technologies, or elections. And whatever policies the states of the region pursue, one other thing is clear as well: If modernity is defined by the dominance of the world economic and nation-state systems, the Middle East is firmly entrenched in its modern moment and there it is likely to stay. There does not appear to be a postmodern moment yet on the Middle Eastern horizon.

DOCUMENTS

Speech Delivered by President Gamal ʿAbd al-Nasser at Port-Said on the Occasion of Victory Day on 23 December 1961

President Gamal ʿAbd al-Nasser delivered the following speech at Port Said on 23 December 1961.

In 1956, the people sacrificed—they gave their blood and there were martyrs—we did not grudge this blood or these martyrs—the people were not frightened by brute force, they were not frightened by the great powers; Britain, France and Israel did not frighten them. . . .

I am confident, fellow-brethren, that it was the great struggle that you undertook in 1956 which has opened for us the way to build the new society. I am also confident that the whole of the people of the U.A.R. have taken the same stand and fought and struggled as you did for the sake of its freedom and its independence throughout all those long years which have passed. We have fought and we have struggled. We were undaunted by imperialism and all its methods, and we were not intimidated by the tyrannical powers; neither was imperialism, with its policy which is based on sowing the seeds of dissension amongst us, able to overpower us. The proof of this is that today we are living in freedom. We are neither dominated by open imperialism nor by disguised imperialism, but we are enjoying political freedom because we have struggled to gain our political freedom. We are enjoying this political freedom because we have taken it upon ourselves to put an end to political domination. The people have risen and struggled throughout all those long years during which we suffered from imperialism, foreign domination and occupation in order that we might be liberated. We thank God, fellow-brethren, that we are able to enjoy this freedom today. Our struggle has borne its fruits. We, our fathers and our forefathers before them, have long struggled for the sake of this freedom. We have always stood face to face with the foreign exploiting domination, and we have never wavered from our stand in any way whatsoever. . . .

Today, brethren, after this long struggle, the way has been paved for the re-alisation of our hopes to build the society we desire, the society in which prosperity and welfare reign supreme, the society in which class differences disappear, no masters, no slaves, but all are the sons of one nation working for the Mother-country and everyone feeling himself on an equal footing with his fellow-citizens and fellow beings. . . .

This second revolution is the people's revolution, a revolution, for every son of this nation, a revolution for social justice, a revolution for the removal of class differences. By this I mean that we aim, while forging ahead with our revolution, that the society we desire, the society everyone of us desires for himself and for his children, the society in which prosperity and welfare shall reign supreme, shall be no capitalistic nor feudalistic dictatorship, no exploitation, no monopoly, but only social justice and equality of opportunity for every able-bodied son of the nation—no exploitation in any circumstances or under any condition of man by man. . . .

We say sufficiency and justice—justice is equality of distinction and not dictatorship of capital, not dictatorship of feudalism, not political nor economical nor social exploitation. Justice is that the wealth of this country be justly and equally owned by all the sons of this country each according to his work. This is justice. As to sufficiency, it is to work, strive, sweat, and build in order that we increase our national income. In order to increase our share of the wealth of this country, we nationalized the banks, the insurance companies and a number of factories and trading companies. We also nationalized all foreign trade, fifty per cent of the Anglo-Egyptian Petroleum Company, and some other companies. We also nationalized what is over L.E. 10,000 in some other industries. In this way, rights were restored. Means were restored to its owners, means of production in which they employed the worker. What does the worker have? He has his work. The capitalist? He has his money. The capitalist employs the workers. The wages of the workers were 25% of the profits whereas the few capitalists gained 75%. Is this justice? Is this the law of right, the law of God? Is this the law of justice, the law of God? Is this Islam? Is this religion? Is this Christianity in any way? This is exploitation and imperialism. This is the co-operation between imperialism, reactionism and exploitation. Who can accept this? All the profits went to a small group, while one million workers received the wages of five thousand persons, and five thousand persons got thrice as much as one million workers. This means that the capitalists, the five thousand capitalists, took thrice as much as the pay of one million workers, as profits. Is this the law of God? Can any one accept this?

President Gamal Abdel-Nasser's Speeches and Press-Interviews, January–December 1961
(Cairo: Information Department, United Arab Republic, 1962), pp. 332–43.

Zakaria Tamer: Tigers on the Tenth Day

In his speeches, Gamal 'Abd al-Nasser presented one side of the story of the post-revolutionary Middle Eastern state. In his short story, "Tigers on the Tenth Day," Syrian writer Zakaria Tamer presents another.

The jungles had journeyed far from the tiger imprisoned in his cage, yet he was unable to forget them. He would stare angrily at men who gathered round his cage, their eyes regarding him with curiosity and without fear.

One of them would talk to him, in a voice that was quiet and yet had a commanding ring about it: 'If you really want to learn my profession, the profession of being a trainer, you must not for an instant forget that the stomach of your adversary is your first target, and you will see that the profession is both hard and easy at one and the same time.

'Look now at this tiger. He is a fierce and haughty tiger, exceedingly proud of his freedom, his strength and his courage, but he will change and become as gentle, mild and obedient as a small child. Watch what will occur between him who possesses food and him who does not, and learn.'

The men promptly said that they would be devoted students of the profession of animal training, and the trainer smiled delightedly, then addressed the tiger, enquiring of him in a sarcastic tone: 'And how is our dear guest?'

'Bring me what I eat,' said the tiger, 'for my mealtime has come.'

With feigned surprise the trainer said: 'Are you ordering me about when you are my prisoner? What an amusing tiger you are! You must realize that I am the only one here who has the right to issue orders.'

'No one gives orders to tigers,' said the tiger.

'But now you're not a tiger,' said the trainer. 'In the jungles you're a tiger, but now you're in a cage, you're just a slave who obeys orders and does what I want.'

'I shan't be anyone's slave,' said the tiger impetuously.

'You're compelled to obey me because it is I who possess the food, said the trainer.

'I don't want your food,' said the tiger.

'Then go hungry as you wish,' said the trainer, 'for I shall not force you to do what you don't want to.'

And, addressing his pupils, he added: 'You will see how he will change, for a head held high does not gratify a hungry stomach.'

The tiger went hungry and remembered sadly the days when he would rush about, as free as the wind in pursuit of his prey.

On the second day the trainer and his pupils stood around the tiger's cage and the trainer said: 'Aren't you hungry? You're for certain so hungry it's a pain and a torture to you. Say you're hungry and you'll get what meat you want.'

The tiger remained silent, so the trainer said to him: 'Do what I say and don't be stupid. Admit you're hungry and you'll eat your fill immediately.'

'I'm hungry,' said the tiger.

The trainer laughed and said to his pupils: 'Here he is, he's fallen into a trap from which he won't escape.'

He gave orders and the tiger got a lot of meat.

On the third day, the trainer said to the tiger: 'If you want to have any food today, carry out what I ask of you.'

'I shall not obey you,' said the tiger.

'Don't be so hasty, for what I ask is very simple. You are now pacing up and down your cage; when I say to you: "Stop", you must stop.'

'That's really a trivial request,' said the tiger to himself, 'and it's not worth my being stubborn and going hungry.'

In a stern, commanding tone the trainer called out: 'Stop.'

The tiger immediately froze and the trainer said in a joyful voice, 'Well done.'

The tiger was pleased and ate greedily. Meanwhile, the trainer was saying to his pupils: 'After some days he'll become a paper tiger.'

On the fourth day the tiger said to the trainer: 'I'm hungry, so ask of me to stand still.'

The trainer said to his pupils: 'He has now begun to like my orders.'

Then, directing his words to the tiger, he said: 'You won't eat today unless you imitate the mewing of a cat.'

The tiger suppressed his anger and said to himself: 'I'll amuse myself with imitating the mewing of a cat.'

He imitated the mewing of a cat, but the trainer frowned and said disapprovingly: 'Your imitation's no good. Do you count roaring as mewing?'

So the tiger again imitated the mewing of a cat, but the trainer continued to glower and said scornfully: 'Shut up. Shut up. Your imitation is still no good. I shall leave you today to practise mewing and tomorrow I shall examine you. If you are successful you'll eat; if you're not successful you won't eat.'

The trainer moved away from the tiger's cage, walking with slow steps and followed by his pupils who were whispering among themselves and laughing. The tiger called imploringly to the jungles, but they were far distant.

On the fifth day the trainer said to the tiger: 'Come on, if you successfully imitate the mewing of a cat you'll get a large piece of fresh meat.'

The tiger imitated the mewing of a cat and the trainer clapped in applause and said joyfully: 'You're great—you mew like a cat in February,' and he threw him a large piece of meat.

On the sixth day the trainer no sooner came near the tiger than he quickly gave an imitation of a cat mewing. The trainer, however, remained silent, frowning.

'There, I've imitated a cat mewing,' said the tiger.

'Imitate the braying of a donkey,' said the trainer.

'I, the tiger who is feared by the animals of the jungles, imitate a donkey?' said the tiger indignantly. 'I'd die rather than carry out what you ask.'

The trainer moved away from the tiger's cage without uttering a word. On the seventh day he came towards the tiger's cage, with smiling face. 'Don't you want to eat?' he said to the tiger.

'I want to eat,' said the tiger.

Said the trainer: 'The meat you'll eat has a price—bray like a donkey and you'll get food.'

The tiger endeavoured to remember the jungles but failed. With closed eyes he burst forth braying. 'Your braying isn't a success,' said the trainer, 'but out of pity for you I'll give you a piece of meat.'

On the eighth day the trainer said to the tiger: 'I'll deliver a speech; when I've finished, you must clap in acclaim.'

So the trainer began to deliver his speech. 'Compatriots,' he said, 'we have previously on numerous occasions propounded our stand in relation to issues affecting our destiny, and this resolute and unequivocal stand will not change whatever hostile forces may conspire against us. With faith we shall triumph.'

'I didn't understand what you said,' said the tiger.

'It's for you to admire everything I say and to clap in acclaim,' said the trainer.

'Forgive me,' said the tiger. 'I'm ignorant and illiterate. What you say is wonderful and I shall, as you would like, clap.'

The tiger clapped and the trainer said: 'I don't like hypocrisy and hypocrites—as a punishment you will today be deprived of food.'

On the ninth day the trainer came along carrying a bundle of grass and threw it down to the tiger. 'Eat,' he said.

'What's this?' said the tiger. 'I'm a carnivore.'

'From today,' said the trainer, 'you'll eat nothing but grass.'

When the tiger's hunger became unbearable he tried to eat the grass, but he was shocked by its taste and moved away from it in disgust. However, the tiger returned to it and very gradually began to find its taste pleasant.

On the tenth day the trainer, the pupils, the tiger and the cage disappeared: the tiger became a citizen and the cage a city.

Zakaria Tamer, *Tigers on the Tenth Day and Other Stories*, trans. Denys Johnson-Davies (London: Quartet Books, 1985), pp. 13–17.

U.N. Security Council Resolution 242

United Nations Security Council Resolution 242, adopted in the aftermath of the 1967 war, became the basis for all subsequent peace negotiations between Israel and its neighbors.

The Security Council,

Expressing its continuing concern with the grave situation in the Middle East,

Emphasizing the inadmissibility of the acquisition of territory by war and the need to work for a just and lasting peace in which every State in the area can live in security,

Emphasizing further that all Member States in their acceptance of the Charter of the United Nations have undertaken a commitment to act in accordance with Article 2 of the Charter,

1. Affirms that the fulfilment of Charter principles requires the establishment of a just and lasting peace in the Middle East which should include the application of both the following principles:
    (i) Withdrawal of Israel armed forces from territories occupied in the recent conflict;
    (ii) Termination of all claims or states of belligerency and respect for and acknowledgment of the sovereignty, territorial integrity and political independence of every State in the area and their right to live in peace within secure and recognized boundaries free from threats or acts of force;

2. Affirms further the necessity
    (a) For guaranteeing freedom of navigation through international waterways in the area;

(b) For achieving a just settlement of the refugee problem;

(c) For guaranteeing the territorial inviolability and political independence of every State in the area, through measures including the establishment of demilitarized zones;

3. Requests the Secretary-General to designate a Special Representative to proceed to the Middle East to establish and maintain contacts with the States concerned in order to promote agreement and assist efforts to achieve a peaceful and accepted settlement in accordance with the provisions and principles in this resolution;

4. Requests the Secretary-General to report to the Security Council on the progress of the efforts of the Special Representative as soon as possible.

Adopted unanimously at the 1382nd meeting

'Ali Shari'ati: The Philosophy of History: The Story of Cain and Abel

'Ali Shari'ati (1933–1977) received training as a sociologist at the Sorbonne and the University of Mashhad in Iran. His ideas, which drew from Islamic modernism and Marxism, gained a wide following in Iran in the decades before the revolution. In this selection, he reinterprets the story of Cain and Abel.

Now the commentators on the Qur'an and other religious scholars have said in explanation of the narrative concerning Cain and Abel that the purpose for its revelation was the condemnation of murder. But this is very superficial and oversimplifies the matter. Even if my theory is not correct, the narrative of the two brothers cannot be as slight in meaning and purpose as they hold it to be. The Abrahamic religions, especially Islam, depict this story as the first great event that occurs on the threshold of human life in this world. It is not credible that their only purpose in so doing should be the mere condemnation of murder. Whatever may be the underlying sense of the narrative, it is surely far more than a simple ethical tale, yielding the conclusion, "It has thus become clear to us now that murder is an evil deed, so we must try never to commit this shameful act. Let us avoid doing it, particularly to our brothers!"

In my opinion, the murder of Abel at the hands of Cain represents a great development, a sudden swerve in the course of history, the most important event to have occurred in all human life. It interprets and explains that event in a most profound fashion—scientifically, sociologically, and with reference to class. The story concerns the end of primitive communism, the disappearance of man's original system of equality and brotherhood, expressed in the hunting and fishing system of productivity (equated with Abel), and its replacement by agricultural production, the creation of private ownership, the formation of the first class society, the system of discrimination and exploitation, the worship of wealth and lack of true faith, the beginning of enmity, rivalry, greed, plunder, slavery and fratricide (equated with Cain). The death of Abel and the survival of Cain are objective, historical realities, and the fact that henceforth religion, life, economy, government and the fate of men were all in the hands of Cain represents a realistic, critical and progressive analysis of what happened. Similarly, the fact that Abel died without issue and mankind today consists of the heirs of Cain[1] also means that the society, government, religion, ethics, world-view and conduct of Cain have become universal, so that the disequilibrium and instability of thought and morality that prevail in every society and every age derive from this fact.

The story of Cain and Abel depicts the first day in the life of the sons of Adam on this earth (their marriage with their sisters)[2] as being identical with the beginning of contradiction, conflict and ultimately warfare and fratricide. This confirms the scientific fact that life, society and history are based on contradiction and struggle, and that contrary to the belief of the idealists, the fundamental factors in all three are economics and sexuality, which come to predominate over religious faith, brotherly ties, truth and morality. . . .

My purpose in examining the story in such detail has been first, to refute the idea that it is exclusively ethical in purpose, for it treats of something far more serious than the topic for a mere essay, and secondly, to make clear that it is not the story of a dispute between two brothers. Instead, it treats two wings of human society, two modes of production; it is the story of history, the tale of bifurcated humanity in all ages, the beginning of a war that is still not concluded.

The wing represented by Abel is that of the subject and the oppressed; i.e., the people, those who throughout history have been slaughtered and enslaved by the system of Cain, the system of private ownership which has gained ascendancy over human society. The war between Cain and Abel is the permanent war of history which has been waged by every generation. The banner of Cain has always been held high by the ruling classes, and the desire to avenge the blood of Abel has been inherited by succeeding generations of his descendants—the subjected people who have fought for justice, freedom and true faith in a struggle that has continued, one way or another, in every age. The weapon of Cain has been religion, and the weapon of Abel has also been religion.

It is for this reason that the war of religion against religion has also been a constant of human history. On the one hand is the religion of *shirk*, of assigning partners to God, a religion that furnishes the justification for *shirk* in society and class discrimination. On the other hand is the religion of *tauhid*, of the oneness of God, which furnishes the justification for the unity of all classes and races. The transhistorical struggle between Abel and Cain is also the struggle between *tauhid* and *shirk*, between justice and human unity on the one hand, and social and racial discrimination on the other. There has existed throughout human history, and there will continue to exist until the last day, a struggle between the religion of deceit, stupefaction and justification of the status quo and the religion of awareness, activism and revolution. The end of time will come when Cain dies and the "system of Abel" is established anew. That inevitable revolution will mean the end of the history of Cain; equality will be realized throughout the world, and human unity and broth-

---

[1]We mean heirs in a typological sense, not a genealogical one.

[2]Certain pious believers have invented various devices for legitimizing the marriages of Cain and Abel in order to free mankind of the blemish of bastardy. However, it is a little late for that!

erhood will be established, through equity and justice. This is the inevitable direction of history. A universal revolution will take place in all areas of human life; the oppressed classes of history will take their revenge. The glad tidings of God will be realized: "We have willed that We should place under obligation those who have been weakened and oppressed on the earth, by making them the leaders of men and heirs to the earth" (Qur'an, 28:5).

This inevitable revolution of the future will be the culmination of the dialectical contradiction that began with the battle of Cain and Abel and has continued to exist in all human societies, between the ruler and the ruled. The inevitable outcome of history will be the triumph of justice, equity and truth.

'Ali Shari'ati, *On the Sociology of Islam*, trans. Hamid Algar (Berkeley, Calif.: Mizan Press, 1979), pp. 103–109.

Ayatollah Khomeini: Islamic Government

In 1970, Ayatollah Khomeini delivered a series of lectures entitled "Islamic Government" to religious students studying in Najaf, Iraq. In the lectures, he outlines the role he believes Islam should play in governance.

Islam is the religion of the strugglers who want right and justice, the religion of those demanding freedom and independence and those who do not want to allow the infidels to dominate the believers.

But the enemies have portrayed Islam in a different light. They have drawn from the minds of the ordinary people a distorted picture of Islam and implanted this picture even in the religious academies. The enemies' aim behind this was to extinguish the flame of Islam and to cause its vital revolutionary character to be lost so that the Moslems may not think of seeking to liberate themselves and to implement all the rules of their religion through the creation of a government that guarantees their happiness under the canopy of an honorable human life.

They have said that Islam has no relationship whatsoever with organizing life and society or with creating a government of any kind and that it only concerns itself with the rules of menstruation and childbirth. It may contain some ethics. But beyond this, it has no bearing on issues of life and of organizing society. It is regrettable that all this has had its bad effect not only on the ordinary people but also among college people and the students of theology. They misunderstand Islam and are ignorant of it. Islam has become as strange to them as alien people. It has become difficult for the Moslem missionary to familiarize people with Islam. On the other hand, there stands a line of the agents of colonialism to drown Islam with clamor and noise. . . .

What we are suffering from currently is the consequence of that misleading propaganda whose perpetrators got what they wanted and which has required us to exert big efforts to prove that Islam contains principles and rules for the formation of government.

This is our situation. The enemies have implanted these falsehoods in the minds of people in cooperation with their agents, have ousted Islam's judiciary and political laws from the sphere of application and have replaced them by European laws in contempt of Islam for the purpose of driving it away from society. They have exploited every available opportunity for this end. . . .

We believe in government and we believe in the need for the prophet to appoint a caliph [successor] after him, and he did. What does the appointment of a successor mean? Does it mean a mere explanation of the laws? The mere explaining of laws does not require a successor. It would have been enough for the prophet, God's prayers be upon him, to disseminate the laws among the people and then lodge them in a book and leave it with the people to consult after him. The need for a successor is for the implementation of the laws because no law without an executor is respected. In the entire world, legislation alone is not enough and cannot secure the happiness of people. There must be an executive authority and the absence of such an authority in any nation is a factor of deficiency and weakness. This is why Islam decided to establish an executive power to implement God's laws. The prophet, may God's prayers be upon him, did. Had he not done so, he would not have conveyed his message. The appointment of a successor after him to implement and uphold the laws and to spread justice among the people was an element complementing and completing the prophet's message. In his days, the prophet, may God's prayers be upon him, was not content with explaining and conveying the laws. He also implemented them. God's prophet, may God's prayers be upon him, was the executor of the law. He punished, cut off the thief's hand, lashed and stoned and ruled justly. A successor is needed for such acts. A successor is not the conveyor of laws and not a legislator. A successor is needed for implementation. Here is where the importance of forming government and of creating and organizing executive agencies emerges. The belief is the need for forming government and for creating such agencies is an indivisible part of the belief in governance. Exerting efforts for and seeking this goal are an aspect of the belief in governance. . . .

In view of the fact that the Islamic government is a government of law, it is a must that the ruler of the Moslems be knowledgeable in the law, as the Hadith says.

The ruler must have the highest degree of faith in the creed, good ethics, the sense of justice and freedom from sins because whoever undertakes to set the strictures, to achieve the rights and to organize the revenues and expenditures of the treasury houses must not be unjust. God says in his precious book: "The unjust shall not have my support." Thus, if the ruler is not just, he cannot be trusted not to betray the trust and not to favor himself, his family and his relatives over the people.

Ayatollah Khomeini, "Islamic Government," trans. Joint Publications Research Service (Arlington, Va: 19 January 1979).

Sayyid Qutb: Milestones

Sayyid Qutb (1906–1966) was one of Islamism's most influential theorists. A member of the Muslim Brotherhood of Egypt, Qutb was imprisoned, then executed, by the government of Gamal ʿAbd al-Nasser. In this selection, Qutb discusses *jahiliyya*, a term that originally referred to the "period of ignorance" before Islam.

Qutb redefined *jahiliyya* to mean the state of ignorance that exists wherever Muslims do not or cannot live their lives according to Islamic principles.

If we look at the sources and foundations of modern ways of living, it becomes clear that the whole world is steeped in **Jahiliyyah,** and all the marvellous material comforts and high-level inventions do not diminish this ignorance. This **Jahiliyyah** is based on rebellion against God's sovereignty on earth. It transfers to man one of the greatest attributes of God, namely sovereignty, and makes some men lords over others. It is now not in that simple and primitive form of the ancient **Jahiliyyah,** but takes the form of claiming that the right to create values, to legislate rules of collective behavior, and to choose any way of life rests with men, without regard to what God has prescribed. The result of this rebellion against the authority of God is the oppression of His creatures. . . . Only in the Islamic way of life do all men become free from the servitude of some men to others and devote themselves to the worship of God alone, deriving guidance from Him alone, and bowing before Him alone. . . .

When a person embraced Islam during the time of the Prophet—peace be on him—he would immediately cut himself off from **Jahiliyyah**. When he stepped into the circle of Islam, he would start a new life, separating himself completely from his past life under ignorance of the Divine Law. He would look upon the deeds during his life of ignorance with mistrust and fear, with a feeling that these were impure and could not be tolerated in Islam! With this feeling, he would turn toward Islam for new guidance; and if at any time temptations overpowered him, or the old habits attracted him, or if he became lax in carrying out the injunctions of Islam, he would become restless with a sense of guilt and would feel the need to purify himself of what had happened, and would turn to the Qur'an to mold himself according to its guidance.

Thus, there would be a break between the Muslim's present Islam and his past **Jahiliyyah,** and this after a well thought out decision, as a result of which all his relationships with **Jahiliyyah** would be cut off and he would be joined completely to Islam, although there would be some give-and-take with the polytheists in commercial activity and daily business; yet relationships of understanding are one thing and daily business is something else.

This renunciation of the **jahili** environment, its customs and traditions, its ideas and concepts, proceeded from the replacement of polytheism by the concept of the Oneness of God, of the **jahili** view of life and the world by that of the Islamic view, and from absorption into the new Islamic community under a new leadership and dedication of all loyalties and commitments to this new society and new leadership.

This was the parting of the ways and the starting of a new journey, a journey free from the pressures of the values, concepts and traditions of the **jahili** society. The Muslim encountered nothing burdensome except the torture and oppression; but he had already decided in the depths of his heart that he would face it with equanimity, and hence no pressure from the **jahili** society would have any effect on his continuing steadfastness.

We are also surrounded by **Jahiliyyah** today, which is of the same nature as it was during the first period of Islam, perhaps a little deeper. Our whole environment, people's beliefs and ideas, habits and art, rules and laws—is **Jahiliyyah,** even to the extent that what we consider to be Islamic culture, Islamic sources, Islamic philosophy and Islamic thought are also constructs of **Jahiliyyh!**

This is why the true Islamic values never enter our hearts, why our minds are never illuminated by Islamic concepts, and why no group of people arises among us who are of the calibre of the first generation of Islam.

It is therefore necessary—in the way of the Islamic movement—that in the early stages of our training and education we should remove ourselves from all the influences of the **Jahiliyyah** in which we live and from which we derive benefits. We must return to that pure source from which those people derived their guidance, the source which is free from any mixing or pollution. We must return to it to derive from it our concepts of the nature of the universe, the nature of human existence, and the relationship of these two with the Perfect, the Real Being, God Most High. From it we must also derive our concepts of life, our principles of government, politics, economics and all other aspects of life.

We must return to it with a sense of instruction for obedience and action, and not for academic discussion and enjoyment. We should return to it to find out what kind of person it asks us to be, and then be like that. During this process, we will also discover the artistic beauty in the Qur'an, the marvellous tales in the Qur'an, the scenes of the Day of Judgment in the Qur'an, the intuitive logic the Qur'an, and all other such benefits which are sought in the Qur'an by academic and literary people. We will enjoy all these other aspects, but these are not the main object of our study. Our primary purpose is to know what way of life is demanded of us by the Qur'an, the total view of the universe which the Qur'an wants us to have, what is the nature of our knowledge of God taught to us by the Qur'an, the kind of morals and manners which are enjoined by it, and the kind of legal and constitutional system it asks us to establish in the world.

We must also free ourselves from the clutches of **jahili** society, **jahili** concepts, **jahili** traditions and **jahili** leadership. Our mission is not to compromise with the practices of **jahili** society, nor can we be loyal to it. **Jahili** society, because of its **jahili** characteristics, is not worthy to be compromised with. Our aim is first to change ourselves so that we may later change the society.

Our foremost objective is to change the practices of this society. Our aim is to change the **jahili** system at its very roots—this system which is fundamentally at variance with Islam and which, with the help of force and oppression, is keeping us from living the sort of life which is demanded by our Creator.

Our first step will be to raise ourselves above the **jahili** society and all its values and concepts. We will not change our own values and concepts either more or less to make a bargain with this **jahili** society. Never! We and it are on different roads, and if we take even one step in its company, we will lose our goal entirely and lose our way as well.

We know that in this we will have difficulties and trials, and we will have to make great sacrifices. But if we are to walk in the footsteps of the first generation of Muslims, through whom God established His system and gave it victory over **Jahiliyyah,** then we will not be masters of our own wills.

It is therefore desirable that we should be aware at all times of the nature of our course of action, of the nature of our position, and the nature of the road which we must traverse to come out of ignorance, as the distinguished and unique generation of the Companions of the Prophet—peace be on him—came out of it.

Sayyid Qutb, *Milestones* (Cedar Rapids, Iowa: The Mother Mosque Foundation, n.d.), pp. 10–11, 19–22.

SUGGESTED READINGS

Abrahamian, Ervand. *Khomeinism: Essays on the Islamic Republic.* Berkeley: University of California Press, 1993. Wonderful collection of essays that examine just how the revolution of 1978–1979 affected Iranian politics and society.

Beblawi, Hazem, and Luciani, Giacomo, eds. *The Rentier State.* London: Croon Helm, 1987. Wide-ranging collection of essays discussing the economic, political, and social changes brought about by oil wealth, remittances, and foreign aid in the Middle East.

Beinin, Joel, and Stork, Joe. *Political Islam: Essays from Middle East Report.* Berkeley: University of California Press, 1997. Updated and more empirically inclined version of *The Islamic Impulse.*

Brynen, Rex, et al., eds. *Political Liberalization and Democratization in the Arab World.* Vol. 1: *Theoretical Perspectives.* Boulder, Colo.: Lynne Rienner, 1995. Collection of essays describing democratization theory and prospects for democratization in the Arab Middle East.

Cattan, Henry. *The Evolution of Oil Concessions in the Middle East and North Africa.* Dobbs Ferry, N.Y.: Oceana Publishers, 1967. Useful, if dated, history of Western exploitation of oil in the first half of the twentieth century.

Farouk-Sluglett, Marion, and Sluglett, Peter. *Iraq Since 1958: From Revolution to Dictatorship.* London: Routledge Kegan & Paul, 1987. Traces the political and economic history of Iraq from the beginnings of the republican period through Saddam Hussein.

Goldberg, Ellis, et al. *Rules and Rights in the Middle East: Democracy, Law, and Society.* Seattle: University of Washington Press, 1993. Critical perspectives on the evolution of the authoritarian state in the region and prospects for its transformation.

Gordon, Joel. *Nasser's Blessed Movement: Egypt's Free Officers and the July Revolution.* New York: Oxford University Press, 1992. Clearly written study of the political origins of the 1952 Egyptian Revolution.

Halliday, Fred. *Islam and the Myth of Confrontation: Religion and Politics in the Middle East.* London: I. B. Tauris, 1996. Critical assessment of West's attitudes and approaches to the Middle East.

Heydemann, Steven, ed. *War, Institutions, and Social Change in the Middle East.* Berkeley: University of California Press, 2000. Excellent collection of essays on the role of war in state formation and social transformation in the Middle East in the modern period.

Khomeini, Ayatollah Ruhullah Musawi. *Islam and Revolution: Writings and Declarations.* Translated by Hamid Algar. London: Routledge and Kegan Paul, 1985. Annotated collection of Khomeini's writings selected by a preeminent scholar of Iran.

Khoury, Philip S. "Islamic Revivalism and the Crisis of the Secular State in the Arab World: An Historical Appraisal." In *Arab Resources: The Transformation of a Society.* Edited by Ibrahim, 213–36. Ibrahim. Washington, D.C.: Center for Contemporary Arab, Studies, 1983. After all these years, still the best introduction to the contemporary "turn to Islam."

Lesch, David W. *The Middle East and the United States: A Historical and Political Reassessment.* Boulder, Colo.: Westview Press, 1999. A strong collection of essays tracing U.S. policy in the region from the King-Crane Commission in 1919 to the present day.

Lockman, Zachary, and Beinin, Joel, eds. *Intifada: The Palestinian Uprising against Is-raeli Occupation*. Boston: South End Press, 1989. Selection of articles about the Palestinian uprising collected from the periodical *MERIP Reports*, along with supplementary materials.

Louis, William Roger. *The British Empire in the Middle East: 1945–1951: Arab Nationalism, the United States, and Postwar Imperialism*. Oxford: Clarendon Press, 1984. Narrative of postwar British diplomacy and British-American rivalry in the region.

Makovsky, David. *Making Peace with the P.L.O.: The Rabin Government's Road to the Oslo Accord*. Boulder, Colo.: Westview Press, 1999. A detailed account of Israeli motivations for entering into the Oslo process.

Malley, Robert. *The Call from Algeria: Third Worldism, Revolution, and the Turn to Islam*. Berkeley: University of California Press, 1996. Readable intellectual history of the rise and fall of Third World movements.

Mann, James. *Rise of the Vulcans: The History of Bush's War Cabinet*. New York: Penguin, 2004. Readable account of the careers, ideas, and decisions of those who set foreign policy under George W. Bush.

Migdal, Joel S. *Strong Societies and Weak States: State-Society Relations and State Capabilities in the Third World*. Princeton, N.J.: Princeton University Press, 1988. An alternative view of the Nasser regime that stresses the regime's inefficiencies, not its power.

Najmabadeh, Afsaneh. "Iran's Turn to Islam: From Modernism to a Moral Order." *The Middle East Journal*, 41 (1987): 202–17. Did the Iranian Revolution have epochal significance? The author argues that it did.

Owen, Roger, and Pamuk, Sevket. *A History of Middle East Economies in the Twentieth Century*. Cambridge, Mass.: Harvard University Press, 1999. Chronological supplement to *The Middle East in the World Economy*; uses a "national economy" approach to post–World War I economic history of the region.

Richards, Alan, and Waterbury, John. *A Political Economy of the Middle East*. Boulder, Colo.: Westview Press, 1998. Covers territory similar to Owen and Pamuk, but organizes material along conceptual, not chronological or national, lines.

Rogan, Eugene L., and Shlaim, Avi. *The War for Palestine: Rewriting the History of 1948*. Cambridge: Cambridge University Press, 2001. Essays on the war, including those of some of the leading revisionist scholars.

Said, Edward W. "Cry Palestine." *New Statesman and Society* 8 (10 November 10 1995): 378. Why the foremost Palestinian intellectual of his time regarded Oslo as a bad deal.

Silberstein, Laurence J., ed. *New Perspectives on Israeli History: The Early Years of the State*. New York: New York University Press, 1991. Wide-ranging collection that runs the gamut from institutional history to analyses of national symbols.

Stowasser, Barbara Freyer, ed. *The Islamic Impulse*. Washington, D.C.: Center for Contemporary Arab Studies, 1989. A wide-ranging collection of essays written when scholars had just begun thinking about the historic implications of the "turn to Islam."

Wedeen, Lisa. *The Ambiguities of Domination: Politics, Rhetoric, and Symbols in Contemporary Syria*. Chicago: University of Chicago Press, 1999. Examines jokes, spectacles, and political discourse to analyze the nature of the bargain made between Hafiz al-Assad's government and the population of Syria.

Zubaida, Sami. *Islam, the People, and the State: Political Ideas and Movements in the Middle East*. London: I.B. Tauris, 1993. A collection of some of the best essays to date on politics and political developments in the region.

Timeline

1453	Ottomans conquer Constantinople, effectively ending the fifteen-hundred-year-old Roman Empire.
1497	Vasco Da Gama discovers Cape Route, enabling European merchants to bypass overland route through the Middle East.
1501	Shah Isma'il enters city of Tabriz, establishing the Safavid Empire.
1517	Traditional date for the founding of the Ottoman Empire.
1517	Martin Luther tacks his 95 Theses on door of Wittenburg Cathedral; traditional date for the beginning of the Protestant Reformation.
1519	Conquest of Mexico by Hernando Cortes; five years later, Francisco Pizarro conquers Peru.
1526	Founding of Mughul Empire.
1569	Ottoman Empire grants first successful capitulations to a European power.
1722	Collapse of Safavid Empire.
1756–1763	Seven Years' War; Britain eclipses France in the Atlantic economy.
1774	Treaty of Kuchuk Kaynarja between Ottoman Empire and Russia gives Russia foothold on the Black Sea.
1796	Founding of Qajar Empire.
1798	Napoleon invades Egypt.
1801	Mehmet Ali (Muhammad 'Ali) seizes control over Egypt and establishes a dynasty that will last until 1953.
1803	Muhammad ibn Sa'ud conquers Mecca and establishes the "first Saudi state."
1817	Serbian rebellion ushers in era of Balkan nationalism.
1830	French begin conquest of Algeria.
1831–1840	Egyptian occupation of Levant.
1838	Treaty of Balta Liman opens the market of the Ottoman Empire to Great Britain.
1839	Ottoman sultan issues the *Hatt-i Sharif* of Gulhane, ushering in the *tanzimat* "reform" period.
1851	Dar al-Funun, a school established to train military officers and bureaucrats, established in Persia.

1856	The *Islahat Fermani* reaffirms the principles first enunciated in the *Hatt-i Sharif* of Gulhane.
1861–1865	American Civil War leads to the expansion of cotton cultivation in Egypt and Levant.
1869	Suez Canal opened, reducing distance ships have to travel between Britain and India by half.
1872	Persians grant Julius de Reuter concession to oversee wide range of economic activities.
1873	Onset of the first truly worldwide depression.
1876	Ottoman and Egyptian bankruptcies lead to European control over finances.
1876	Promulgation of Ottoman Constitution.
1878–1908	Hamidian period ends *tanzimat*: Sultan Abdulhamid II rules Ottoman Empire without constitution or parliament.
1881–1882	ʿUrabi Revolt in Egypt ends with British occupation.
1882	Beginning of the first wave of Jewish immigration to Palestine.
1901	Persian government grants William Knox d'Arcy first oil concession in Middle East.
1904–1905	Russo-Japanese War, followed by Russian Constitutional Revolution.
1905	Beginning of Persian Constitutional Revolution.
1907	First nationalist party in Arab world founded in Egypt.
1908	Young Turk Revolution in Ottoman Empire restores constitution.
1914–1918	World War I changes political map of the Middle East.
1915	Amir Faysal launches "Arab Revolt" against Ottomans.
1917	Bolshevik Revolution in Russia.
1917	Great Britain issues Balfour Declaration supporting the Zionist movement.
1919	Egyptian revolt against British occupation.
1919–1922	Turkish War of Independence.
1920	Treaty of Sèvres formally severs connection between Turkish and non-Turkish regions of the Ottoman Empire; mandates system imposed in Levant and Mesopotamia.
1921	British announce formation of Trans-Jordan (later Jordan) at Cairo Conference.
1922	Egypt granted conditional independence from Great Britain.
1924	Mustafa Kemal "Ataturk" abolishes caliphate.
1925	Last Qajar shah dethroned.
1926	Reza Khan proclaimed shah of Persia.

1928	Formation of Muslim Brotherhood in Egypt, an early example of a modern Islamic political movement.
1929	Traditional date marking the onset of the Great Depression.
1932	Iraq becomes first mandated territory to receive independence; Ibn Sa'ud announces creation of Saudi Arabia.
1936–1939	Palestinians launch revolt against Zionists and Great Britain.
1939–1945	World War II; under Middle East Supply Center, industrial production in Arab Middle East increases 50 percent.
1941	Allies invade Iran; replace Reza Shah with son, Muhammad Reza Shah.
1948	After First Palestine War, Israel proclaims independence.
1949	First postwar military *coup d'etat* in Arab world launched in Syria.
1952	Free Officers' coup in Egypt; Gamal 'Abd al-Nasser soon emerges as head of state.
1953	Iranians nationalize Anglo-Iranian Oil Company; the United States and Great Britain organize the overthrow of the Iranian government.
1954–1962	Algerian war of independence.
1955	International conference in Bandung, Indonesia, marks the beginning of the nonaligned movement.
1956	Great Britain, France, Israel launch Suez War against Egypt.
1958	Overthrow of monarchy in Iraq.
1958–1961	Unification of Egypt and Syria in United Arab Republic.
1960	Venezuela, Kuwait, Saudi Arabia, Iran, and Iraq form the Organization of Petroleum Exporting Countries (OPEC).
1967	June War between Israel and Arab states; Israel occupies Egyptian, Syrian, and Jordanian territory, along with East Jerusalem, the West Bank, and the Gaza Strip.
1969	Yassir Arafat takes control of the Palestine Liberation Organization.
1971	With the promulgation of the Nixon Doctrine, the United States expands support for the shah of Iran.
1971	Devaluation of United States dollar decreases revenue of oil-producing states.
1973	In wake of Arab-Israeli war, oil prices jump 380 percent.
1974	Arab states recognize Palestine Liberation Organization as the "sole, legitimate representative of the Palestinian people."
1978	Camp David Peace Accords negotiated between Egypt and Israel.
1978–1979	Iranian Revolution culminates with the establishment of an "Islamic republic."
1980–1988	Iran-Iraq war leaves 500,000 to one million dead and one to two million wounded.

1982   Israeli invasion of Lebanon.

1990   Iraqi invasion of Kuwait, followed by Gulf War in 1991.

1993   Oslo Accord extending mutual recognition between Israel and the Palestine Liberation Organization.

2001   Hijacked airliners crash into World Trade Center, Pentagon, and Pennsylvania woods; George W. Bush declares war on terrorism.

2003   The United States and allies invade Iraq and topple the government of Saddam Hussein.

Biographical Sketches

Shah Abbas (1571–1629) Ascending to the Safavid throne in 1588, the year of the Spanish Armada, Shah Abbas "bureaucratized" and strengthened the Persian Empire in a manner similar to his contemporaries, such as the Ottoman sultan Suleiman the Magnificent. Shah Abbas broke the power of the Qizilbash, established an army and bureaucracy under direct imperial control, and expanded the boundaries of the empire. To pay for his projects and conquests, he confiscated lands that had previously been granted to the Qizilbash, established monopolies over silk production and weaving, and attempted to supervise trade. While Shah Abbas was able to strengthen central control to an extent previously unheard of in early modern Persia, the Safavid Empire entered into a period of crisis soon after his death.

Gamal ʿAbd al-Nasser Born in 1918 in a town outside Alexandria, Nasser was the son of a postal clerk who rose in the Egyptian military to the rank of colonel. A member of a clandestine group known as the Free Officers, Nasser participated in the overthrow of the Egyptian monarchy and emerged as the leader of the Free Officers and Egypt shortly thereafter. With the rise of Third Worldism and the Suez War of 1956—known in Egypt as the Tripartite Aggression—Nasser became a leader of the nonaligned movement and put in place a populist, state-directed economic development program that became the model for much of the Middle East and beyond. If Nasser's political star rose after 1956, it fell after the catastrophic 1967 war. Nasser died in 1970.

Abdulhamid II Ottoman sultan from 1876–1909. While commonly derided as a reactionary and religious zealot (he reasserted his right to the title of caliph, a title rarely adopted by Ottoman sultans), Abdulhamid II is better viewed as the last great modernizing sultan of the Ottoman Empire. Although he came to power promising to uphold the constitution, Abdulhamid II revoked it and prorogued parliament within two years of his accession to the throne. His efforts to strengthen the empire by centralizing power, promoting an Islamic/Ottoman identity, and undertaking public works (such as the Hijaz Railway which linked Istanbul with Medina) are reminiscent of the efforts of the Russian tsars and French emperors of the same period.

Jamal al-Din al-Afghani (1839–1897) In spite of his name, which signifies he came from Afghanistan, it is more than likely that Jamal al-Din al-Afghani was born in Persia. This would make sense: While Jamal al-Din's ideas betray their Usuli roots, he sought to spread them in the Sunni Turkish and Arab worlds. Jamal al-Din al-Afghani was a salafi whose ideology combined three elements: a fierce hatred of imperialism, particularly British imperialism; the belief that the battle against imperialism would be successful only if it involved all Muslims; and the conviction that Muslims would have to adopt both the technology and scientic method of the West to defeat their enemies. More important as a political activist than as a thinker, most of Jamal al-Din's influence came through his contacts: one associate (Muhammad 'Abduh) became mufti of Egypt, one of his students assassinated the shah of Iran, and his followers played an important role in the Persian Constituional Revolution of 1905.

Yasir Arafat (1929–2004) Born in either Jerusalem or Cairo to a well-to-do merchant family, Arafat received an engineering degree from King Fuad University in Egypt. He reached political maturity during the golden age of secular Arab nationalism, when anticolonialism was at its zenith internationally. Arafat founded Fatah, a Palestinian guerrilla group, in the late 1950s but kept his group outside the Palestine Liberation Organization until after the 1967 war, when it became evident to many Palestinians that neither the Arab states nor the PLO as it had been constituted could be trusted with the liberation of Palestine. Elected chairman of the PLO in 1969, he led the PLO for twenty-five years, and in 1996 he was elected the first president of the Palestinian Authority. His death in 2004 coincided with the death throes of the Oslo Accord.

Hassan al-Banna (1906–1949) The son of a watchmaker in the town of Mahmudiyya, Egypt, Hassan al-Banna founded what many scholars consider to be the first modern Islamic political organization, the Society of Muslim Brothers (the Muslim Brotherhood), in 1928. He attended the Teachers' Training Center, then Cairo University, before he became a teacher in 1927. He founded the Muslim Brotherhood in the Suez Canal city of Isma'iliyya, where he preached and recruited members in coffeehouses and similar public venues. By 1934, the Brotherhood reportedly had more than fifty branches throughout Egypt. The ideology of the brotherhood combined anti-imperialism and nationalism with a call for moral and religious reconstruction. The brotherhood participated in a guerrilla campaign against the British in the Suez Canal Zone and sent volunteers to fight in the 1948 war for Palestine. Hassan al-Banna was assassinated in 1949, probably in revenge for the assassination of the Egyptian prime minister, which the government attributed to his organization.

Theodor Herzl (1860–1904) Born in Budapest, Hungary, Theodor Herzl is commonly regarded as the founding father of Zionism. There was nothing in Herzl's upbringing and early career that would have indicated the path he eventually took: The son of a wealthy merchant, Herzl moved to Vienna with his family when he was 18. Herzl studied law and worked briefly as a civil servant before he became a journalist in the capital of the sprawling Austrian Empire. According to most accounts, it was in 1894, while covering the Dreyfus Affair for his newspaper, that Herzl reached the conclusion that the only way Jews would be secure was if they formed a majority in a territory of their own. Herzl went on to publicize his views through a variety of media, from newspapers to novels, and organized the first Zionist Congress in 1897 which, in turn, launched the World Zionist Organization.

Ibrahim Pasha (1789–1848) Son of Mehmet Ali (Muhammad 'Ali), Ibrahim Pasha was one of the great military leaders of the nineteenth century. Among his achievements was the defeat of the Wahhabi movement in Arabia and the restoration of Mecca and Medina to Ottoman control. Although he was unable successfully to defeat Greek separatism—his fleet was sunk by a combined British, French, and Russian fleet at the Battle of Navarino in 1827—he soon thereafter launched a campaign to bring Greater Syria under Egyptian control, where it would remain for approximately ten years. During that time, he imposed many of the same defensive developmentalist programs in the Levant that his father had pioneered in Egypt. His army was finally expelled from the region by a joint Ottoman-British campaign assisted by a local rebellion.

Shah Isma'il (reigned 1501–1520) Descendent of the Kurdish mystic Safi ad-Din (from whom the Safavid dynasty got its name), Isma'il was the leader of a group of Qizilbash ("red hatted") warriors who seized control of Persia in 1501. Isma'il was a charismatic leader who claimed to be a nearly divine being. Under his leadership, the Qizilbash conquered Azerbaijan, Western Iran, and the Tigris-Euphrates basin. They also attracted a wide following among the Turkish tribes of central and eastern Anatolia, thus posing a threat to the Ottomans in western Anatolia. At the Battle of Chaldiran in 1514, Isma'il engaged the Ottomans in battle, where he was decisively defeated. Nevertheless, he left an important legacy for the region: His conquests established the Ottoman-Persian boundary, which roughly coincides with the contemporary Turkish-Iranian boundary; he consolidated Safavid rule; and under his leadership Persia was converted to Shi'i Islam.

Mustafa Kemal "Ataturk" (1881–1938) Mustafa Kemal was the most successful Ottoman general in World War I, organizing the defense of Gallipoli against British and Commonwealth invaders. After the war, when entente nations occupied parts of Anatolia, committees of resistance sprang up throughout Anatolia. The government in Istanbul dispatched Mustafa Kemal to put down the committees. Instead, he took control over the uprising, expelled foreign forces from Anatolia, established Turkey as an independent republic, and took the name "Ataturk," the father of the Turks. Mustafa Kemal was an unabashed Westernizer and secularist: He abolished the sultanate and caliphate, "Latinized" the Turkish alphabet, granted women the right to vote, pursued a policy of state-directed economic development, and even regulated headgear. All this was done at a price, however: His government suppressed minorities, attempted to standardize culture, and engaged in political repression and one-party rule.

Ayatollah Ruhollah Khomeini (1899–1989) Before 1963, Ayatollah Khomeini had been a relatively unknown cleric who, trained in the city of Qom, specialized in the field of theology. But in 1963, after the shah had launched the White Revolution, had expanded women's rights, and had increased the legal privileges of Americans in Iran, Khomeini rose to fame as one of the most vociferous opponents of the shah and his American backers. For his efforts, Khomeini was sent into exile, first to Iraq, then to France. After the shah expanded his crackdown on the opposition in 1977 and the official newspaper of Iran published scurrilous attacks on Khomeini, theological students in Qom protested. The army fired on the protest, killing seventy and triggering the Iranian Revolution. Khomeini kept in touch with the revolutionaries, and his exhortations to rebellion, recorded on cassettes, received wide distribution. In 1979 he returned to Iran to establish the *velayat-e faqih*—a state under the guardianship of a jurisconsult, or, as it is more commonly known, an Islamic republic.

Muhammad Mossadegh (1882–1967) Swiss-educated Iranian politician and prime minister from 1951–1953. Mossadegh rose to power on a platform to nationalize the oil industry, restore parliamentary rule, and reform and develop the economy—a program with which Nasser and many other Third World leaders of the time had much agreement. At first Mossadegh's program received such widespread support that the shah feared for his life and fled the country. However, Mossadegh's domestic program alienated segments of the Iranian population and, spurred on by the United States and Great Britain, anti-Mossadegh fervor grew. After the army seized control and restored the shah, Mossadegh was sentenced to house arrest. He died in 1967 and has since become a central figure in the Iranian nationalist narrative.

Mehmet Ali (Muhammad ʿAli) (1770?–1849) Ruler of Egypt who seized control of the Ottoman province in the wake of the Napoleonic invasion and established a dynasty that would oversee Egypt until 1953. Mehmet Ali was the son of an Albanian pirate or merchant (depending on the source) who was a commander of a contingent of forces sent to Egypt by the Ottomans. As ruler, he attempted to restructure the military, the government, and economy of Egypt so that he and his family might maintain an autonomous dynasty within the Ottoman Empire. Mehmet Ali was a member of the first generation of leaders in the Middle East who realized that their survival depended upon their ability to "modernize" their domains and centralize their power. Ironically, the programs that had been intended to preserve Egyptian autonomy resulted in further integration of Egypt into the world economy, bankruptcy, and British occupation.

Osman (1259–1326) Legendary founder of the Ottoman Dynasty, Osman was a frontier warrior who waged incessant campaigns against Byzantine territory in western Anatolia. The Ottoman Empire emerged from the principality he established.

Reza Khan/Reza Shah (reigned 1926–1941) The leader of the Cossack Brigade—a unit in the Persian army that had been established by the Russians—Reza Khan seized power after the chaos, foreign intervention, warlordism, and famine of World War I, establishing a dynasty that ruled Iran until 1979. Reza Khan first toyed with the idea of establishing a republic in Persia, but after the Persian parliament deposed the last Qajar shah he took the title himself. Like Mustafa Kemal "Ataturk," upon whom he modeled himself, Reza Shah imposed a far-reaching program for centralization and modernization. Under his direction, the power of tribes was broken, education and law were taken out of the hands of the ulama, the state played a dominant role in economic development, and the government even regulated dress and religious ritual. Because of his pro-Nazi sympathies, the Allies had him deposed during World War II, replacing him with his son, Muhammad Reza, the last shah of Iran.

Suleiman the Magnificent (1494–1566) Also known as Suleiman the Lawgiver. Suleiman was sultan of the Ottoman Empire at the same time Elizabeth I ruled Britain and Philip II ruled the Spanish Empire. Like his contemporaries, Suleiman consolidated imperial power, expanded the central bureaucracy, patronized the arts, and undertook monumental building projects. Under his leadership, the Ottoman Empire became the preeminent Muslim state of its time.

Ahmad ʿUrabi (1841–1911) Ahmad ʿUrabi was a colonel in the Egyptian army who hailed from Egyptian peasant origins at a time when the ruling elites of Egypt were descendents of Turks, Albanians, and Circassians. By the time he became the leader of the so-called ʿUrabi Revolt (1881–1882), Egypt had declared bankruptcy and Egyptian finances had been placed under the control of European creditors. The Europeans forced the government to expand taxation and cut military spending. The latter stipulation, alongside rules that discriminated against native-born Egyptians, angered many in the military. The former stipulation ensured that the military was not alone in its dissatisfaction. Military-led demonstrations were thus joined by a host of other disaffected groups, and soon the khedive faced a full-scale revolt that demanded the end of foreign interference, a national "charter," and a curtailment of the khedive's power. The revolt had two lasting effects: The British, who invaded Egypt to put down the revolt, stayed for another three-quarters of a century, and the Egyptians got the first hero to place in their national pantheon.

Saʿd Zaghlul (1857–1927) Born into a mid-level peasant family in the Nile delta, Saʿd Zaghlul studied at the Islamic university, al-Azhar, in Cairo before attending the Egyptian School of Law. After his marriage to a daughter of an Egyptian prime minister, Zaghlul secured a number of ministerial positions in government. A moderate nationalist before World War I, Zaghlul was a member of the Umma Party, a party that sought to achieve Egyptian independence from the British by demonstrating that Egyptians were "civilized" enough to merit it. On the eve of World War I, Zaghlul adopted a more radical stance, and during the war he and his colleagues used their positions to construct nationalist committees throughout the country that would prove invaluable to Zaghlul and like-minded nationalists in the postwar period. In the immediate aftermath of the war, Zaghlul petitioned the British to represent Egyptian aspirations at the Paris peace conference. For his efforts, British exiled Zaghlul and a few of his associates, an event that sparked the Egyptian Revolution of 1919. After the British granted Egypt conditional independence in 1922, Zaghlul's party—the Wafd—won 90 percent of the seats in parliament and Zaghlul became Egypt's first post-"independence" prime minister.

Glossary

'**Abdallah** Son of Sharif Husayn; ruler of Trans-Jordan and later first king of Jordan.

Akhbari School of Shi'i thought that claimed that the ulama were limited in their legal and doctrinal decisions to the traditions of the prophet and the teachings of the twelve imams.

'**Alawi/'Alawite** Religious sect that holds Muhammad's son-in-law, 'Ali, in particularly high regard; the ruling group in Syria is 'Alawi.

aliya (pl.: *aliyot*) Literally, ascent; wave of Jewish settlement in Palestine.

Anatolia Asia Minor, the site of the present-day Republic of Turkey.

Anglo-Persian Oil Company Company created after the British government bought William Knox d'Arcy's oil concession. At its inception, the company controlled almost every aspect of the oil business in Persia; later, Anglo-Iranian Oil Company.

Anglo-Persian Treaty (1919) Treaty negotiated between the British and Persian governments in the wake of World War I that, if enacted, would have made Persia a virtual British protectorate.

anjuman (pl.: *anjumanha*) A club or secret society in Persia; *anjumanha* were particularly active in the Persian Constitutional Revolution of 1905.

Ashkenazim Jews from eastern and northern Europe or their descendents.

"Auspicious Incident" (1826) Massacre of janissaries ordered by Sultan Mahmud II.

ayatollah Literally, light of god; a prominent teaching *mujtahid*.

al-Azhar Islamic university in Cairo, regarded by many as the most prestigious in the Sunni world.

Baku Capital of Azerbaijan; site of oil boom in early twentieth century.

Balfour Declaration Statement issued by the British government in 1917 that stipulated, among other things, that the British government viewed "with favor" the establishment of a Jewish home in Palestine.

Baring, Evelyn (Earl of Cromer) First British consul general in Egypt.

bast Refuge; taking refuge in a mosque or government building was a common form of protest in Persia.

bay'a Literally, agreement; mutual pledge between ruler and ruled.

bazaari Merchant who works in markets (bazaars) of Iran.

bedouin Member of nomadic tribe.

berat Certificate; in the nineteenth-century Ottoman Empire, foreign consuls granted *berats* to Ottoman citizens, making them honorary citizens of foreign countries, entitled to privileges granted foreigners.

beratli The holder of a *berat*.

Cairo Conference (1921) Conference held in wake of World War I at which the British created Trans-Jordan.

Caisse de la Dette Institution created by the governments of European creditors to oversee the repayment of debts owed their citizens in the wake of the Egyptian bankruptcy of 1876.

caliph "Successor to Muhammad"; for Sunnis, the leader of the Islamic community.

Camp David Accords (1978) Agreement negotiated among Jimmy Carter, Menachim Begin, and Anwar al-Sadat in 1978 that included a framework for peace between Israel and Egypt and a stillborn framework for peace in the region.

Canning, Stratford British representative in Istanbul who reportedly dictated the terms of the *Islahat Fermani* to the sultan in 1856.

capitulations Clauses in treaties between European countries and empires in the Middle East granting representatives of the former privileges (trade, religious, and the like) in Middle Eastern domains.

caravansaray Resting place and trading center for caravans.

Circassian Member of a group of tribes in or from the Caucasus.

Cis-Jordan The territory between the Mediterranean Sea and the Jordan River; called Palestine after 1921.

"Commercial Revolution" Technological, institutional, and structural changes that took place in Europe during the sixteenth century and that expanded trade.

Committee of Union and Progress (C.U.P.) Secret society established in the military of Ottoman Empire in 1889; took full power in 1913.

Comstock Lode Source of huge quantities of silver discovered in Nevada in the nineteenth century; because Persia was a "silver zone," tapping the Comstock Lode had deleterious effects on the Persian economy.

concession Agreement between a government and an entrepreneur or company granting the latter exclusive rights to build infrastructure, exploit natural resources, establish institutions, and the like; granting concessions was a favored policy to foster economic growth in nineteenth-century Persia.

consortium A company of companies established to spread risk.

consul general Highest ranking British official in Egypt during the period of British occupation.

corvée Compulsory labor service.

Cossack Brigade Cavalry unit trained and equipped by the Russians but manned by Persians during the nineteenth and early twentieth centuries; Reza Khan was one of its leaders.

Crémieux Decree Decree issued by the French government in 1870 granting Algerian Jews the right to French citizenship.

Crimean War (1854–1856) War pitting the British, French, Piedmontese, and Ottomans against an expanding Russia.

Dar al-Funun School established in Persia in 1851 during a brief attempt at defensive developmentalism.

d'Arcy, William Knox British adventurer who was granted the first oil concession from the Persian government in 1901.

de Reuter, Julius Recipient of a wide-ranging concession from the Persian government in 1872.

defensive developmentalism Policy of centralization and "modernization" undertaken by governments in the Middle East to strengthen their power and promote economic activity.

département French province.

devshirme A levy exacted by the early Ottoman government on Balkan Christians to recruit for the imperial bureaucracy and janissary corps.

dey A locally chosen Ottoman governor of Algeria.

Druze A member of an esoteric religious sect, found most commonly in Lebanon and Palestine.

Eastern Question Eighteenth- and nineteenth-century competition over the fate of the Ottoman Empire and its provinces involving Britain, France, Russia, and later Germany.

entente powers/Central Powers Two main alliances in World War I; the entente consisted of, among others, Great Britain, France, Russia, and eventually the United States; the Central Powers included, among others, Germany, the Austro-Hungarian Empire, and the Ottoman Empire.

faqih Islamic legal expert qualified to rule on matters pertaining to the shariʿa.

Faysal Son of Sharif Husayn; leader of Arab Revolt; later king of Iraq.

feddan Unit of land measurement; one feddan approximately equals one acre.

fez A brimless, conical felt hat introduced into the Ottoman Empire in the nineteenth century as a sign of the empire's "modernity."

Fourteen Points American aims in World War I as enunciated by Woodrow Wilson; one of the points—the call for the self-determination of peoples—was taken seriously by many in the Middle East.

Gallipoli Peninsula off western Anatolia; site of battle for the Turkish straits involving mainly British and Commonwealth forces, on the one hand, and Ottoman forces, on the other; the battle made a hero of the successful Ottoman general, Mustafa Kemal.

ghazi Frontier warrior.

ghulam **(pl.: *ghilman*)** Slave brought into Persia to serve in the military or bureaucracy.

"Great Game" Term popularized by Rudyard Kipling to refer to nineteenth-century British-Russian competition in Central Asia.

Great Inflation Increase in prices throughout the Eurasian continent beginning in the sixteenth century. Determining the causes of the Great Inflation has resulted in great contention among historians.

Great (Palestine) Revolt (1936–1939) Palestine-wide rebellion against Zionist immigration and British control; put down harshly by the British.

guild An organization comprising all who participate in a given profession or trade.

hadith Account of the words and actions of Muhammad.

hajj Annual pilgrimage undertaken by Muslims.

Hamas Acronym for the Islamic Resistance Movement, founded during the *intifada* in the occupied territories.

Hatt-i Sharif of Gulhane (1839) Decree promising equality and rights to all Ottoman citizens; regarded as the opening salvo of the *tanzimat*.

Hemmat Persian affiliate of the Russian Social Democratic Workers Party; played a role in the Persian Constitutional Revolution of 1905.

Hijaz Western region of the Arabian peninsula; site of Mecca and Medina.

Hijazi, Salamah Influential participant in *nahda*; pioneered "neo-classicism" in Arabic music and theater.

Histadrut Trade union federation established in Palestine by Zionists during the early twentieth century.

Hizbullah Shiʻi political movement in Lebanon.

Husayn 1. Sharif Husayn: Descendent of the prophet and overseer of the two holy cities in Arabia; entered into agreement with the British during World War I to declare jihad against the Ottoman Empire in return for gold, weapons, and promises of postwar independence. 2. Imam Husayn: Son of ʻAli (Muhammad's son-in-law) and, according to Shiʻis, the third imam; led revolt against caliph but was defeated at the Battle of Karbala in A.D. 680.

ibn ʻAbd al-Wahhab, Muhammad Founder of a puritanical movement in central Arabia; Wahhabism is the official ideology of the contemporary Saudi government.

ibn Saʻud, ʻAbd al-ʻAziz Founder of modern Saudi state.

ibn Saʻud, Muhammad Tribal chieftain and follower of Muhammad ibn ʻAbd al-Wahhab; established state in Arabia that was demolished by Ibrahim Pasha in the early nineteenth century.

ijtihad The application of reason to supplement the foundational texts of Islam.

ikhwan Literally, brothers; nontribal levies and followers of ʻAbd al-ʻAziz ibn Saʻud; instrumental in his conquest of the Arabian peninsula.

imam In Sunni Islam, a prayer leader; in Shiʻi Islam, descendant of Muhammad's son-in-law, ʻAli, and rightful leader of the community.

Imperial Tobacco Company The recipient of a concession from the Persian government in 1889 that allowed the company to control the cultivation, sale, distribution, and export of all Persian tobacco and tobacco products; the concession was cancelled after protests.

infitah Literally, opening up; economic liberalization program initiated by Anwar al-Sadat.

integration and peripheralization The process whereby areas of the world are brought into a common economic system (integration) but as subsidiary units (that is, mostly raw materials suppliers) to the industrialized core (peripheralization).

intifada The Palestinian uprising against Israeli occupation that broke out in 1987 and lasted until 1993; a second intifada broke out in 2000.

Iraq Petroleum Company Consortium that controlled all aspects of the petroleum industry throughout all of Iraq.

Islahat Fermani (1856) Decree promulgated by the Ottoman government that reaffirmed the rights granted Ottoman citizens by the *Hatt-i Sharif* of Gulhane.

jihad Literally, struggle; the word has various meanings, sometimes connoting an "inner struggle" against bad behavior, sometimes connoting "holy war."

karakoz Shadow play; popular form of entertainment throughout Middle East.

Kemalism The doctrines introduced to Turkey by Mustafa Kemal "Ataturk."

khedive Ottoman viceroy of Egypt; title held by descendants of Mehmet Ali until 1914.

kibbutz (pl.: kibbutzim) Zionist/Israeli communal farm; the first kibbutz was established in 1909–1910.

Kurd Member of ethnic grouping inhabiting eastern Anatolia, western Iran, northern Iraq, and Syria.

Late Antiquity Period of history stretching from the fourth to the seventh centuries, A.D.

Law of Liquidation (1880) Law enacted by the Egyptian government that gave the Caisse de la Dette expanded powers for revenue extraction.

Lawrence, T. E. ("Lawrence of Arabia") British advisor to Arab Revolt.

Levant Region on eastern Mediterranean, usually considered to comprise present-day Syria, Lebanon, Israel, Palestine, Jordan, and western Iraq.

Lord Milner British government official who led inquiry into the 1919 Egyptian Revolution. At the Milner Commission's suggestion, Britain granted Egypt conditional independence in 1922.

majlis Parliament; term is used in both the Arab world and Iran.

mamluk Slave-soldiers, originally brought into the Middle East by Arab caliphs from amongst Turkic tribes; later established their own dynasties in the region.

mandates system An administrative system established by the League of Nations whereby more "advanced" states would supervise the development of less advanced peoples to prepare them to face "the strenuous conditions of the modern world."

mandatory powers Nations that assumed control over mandated territories.

market economy Economic system that is primarily based on production for exchange.

marketplace economy Economic system that is primarily based on production for subsistence.

Maronite Member of Christian sect, mainly in Lebanon.

megali idea Literally, grand idea; a doctrine associated with Greek nationalism that entailed the unification of all Greek-speaking, Orthodox peoples in the Balkans, Mediterranean, and Anatolia into a single (Greek) state.

mercantilism Seventeenth-century European economic doctrine that made the accumulation of gold the primary goal of national economic policy.

military-patronage state Any one of the Turco-Mongolian states established during and after the thirteenth century in which society was divided into a ruling military class and the remainder of the population; land belonged to the chief military family or families and was leased out in exchange for services rendered by the military class; and dynastic law supplemented local customs and Islamic law.

millet system Ottoman administrative practice allowing religious minorities control over many of their own affairs, including educational, charitable, and judicial affairs.

moral reconstruction The idea that social ills could be healed through individual pious acts.

moshav **(pl.:** *moshavim***)** Cooperative village first established in the Yishuv in 1921.

Mosul Northern province of Iraq.

mufti Muslim judicial official who interprets Islamic law.

mujtahid In Shi'i Islam, a religious scholar who can render legal opinions by use of informed reason.

Muslim Brotherhood Islamic political organization established by Hassan al-Banna in Egypt in 1928.

mutasarrifiya A special administrative district, established in Mount Lebanon in 1861, governed by a non-Lebanese Ottoman Christian and protected by the concert of European powers.

nahda Nineteenth-century Arabic literary renaissance.

Najd Region in the central and eastern Arabian peninsula.

nakba Literally, disaster; word used by Palestinians to refer to the 1948 war.

narghile Water pipe; hookah.

Nasir al-Din Shah Ruler of Persia during much of the late nineteenth century; assassinated in 1896.

National Pact An agreement reached among leading Lebanese politicians in 1943 dividing the political spoils available to each religious community residing in Lebanon proportionally.

National Resurgence Party Political party founded in 1975 by the shah of Iran for "all loyal Iranians."

Naus, Joseph Belgian national who was hired by the Persian government to oversee collection of customs; his policies were one of the triggers for the Persian Constitutional Revolution.

negative equilibrium Nonalignment policy advocated by Muhammad Mossadegh.

neo-sufism The redefinition of sufi movements, beginning in the eighteenth century, to reflect a more legalistic and scripturalist approach.

nonalignment Policy followed by Third World states that advocated a political stance independent of either the Western alliance or the Soviet bloc.

occultation State of being hidden; Shi'is believe that the last imam (either the seventh or twelfth in the line of descent, depending on the branch of Shi'ism) was hidden by God but will one day return to guide his community.

Organization of Petroleum Exporting Countries (OPEC) Organization founded in 1960 to coordinate petroleum policies of the major producers; OPEC became a producers' cartel in 1982.

Oslo Accord The 1993 Agreement reached between Israel and the Palestinians that included mutual recognition and established a framework for further negotiations.

osmanlilik An ideology that might loosely be called Ottoman nationalism.

Ottoman Public Debt Administration Institution created by the governments of European creditors to oversee the repayment of debts owed their citizens in the wake of the Ottoman bankruptcy of 1876.

Pahlavi Last ruling dynasty of Iran (1926–1979).

pan-Arabism The doctrine that Arabs constitute one people; pan-Arab nationalists believe they should be joined in a single state.

personal status law Laws related to marriage, divorce, registering births, and so on; in the Middle East, usually managed by religious community.

prebendalism System of Ottoman and Safavid land management wherein most land is worked by a free peasantry but belongs to the ruling dynasty; land thus cannot be bought and sold.

proletarianization The process of creating a class of people who sell their labor.

qadi Judge working in an Islamic law court.

Qizilbash Turcomen followers of Safi al-Din's teachings and their descendents.

remittances Money sent home by guest workers working in a foreign country.

rentier state A state dependent on money derived from sources other than taxation for a certain percentage of its income.

Russian Social Democratic Workers Party Russian socialist party that was influential in Baku and northern Persia at the beginning of the twentieth century.

al-Sadat, Anwar President of Egypt after Nasser (1970–1981); noteworthy for rolling back many of the populist policies of the Nasser era, his pro-American stance, and the Camp David Accords.

Safi al-Din Legendary founder of the Safavid Dynasty; leader of Turcomen sufi order.

al-salaf al-salih The "pious ancestors"; those who made up the first Islamic community and served as a source of emulation and chroniclers of the acts and sayings of Muhammad.

salafism Islamic intellectual movement that advocated a return to the foundational texts of Islam and the emulation of the first Islamic community.

al-Sanusi, Muhammad ibn ʿAli (1787–1859) Founder of puritanical sufi order (Sanusiyya) in North Africa that played an important role in fighting Italians in the early twentieth century.

SAVAK The often brutal intelligence agency in pre-revolutionary Iran.

Second Serfdom The reimposition of serfdom in Eastern Europe during the sixteenth and seventeenth centuries; in part, a response to the Great Inflation.

settler-plantation colony Form of colonial settlement in which agents of a colonial power establish and supervise the operation of largescale plantations worked by local labor.

shah Persian emperor.

shariʿa Islamic law.

Shiʿism One of the two main branches of Islam; predominant in Iran, Iraq, and Lebanon.

shura Literally, consultation; early Islamic practice cited by Islamic modernists as precedent for parliaments.

Suez War/Tripartite Aggression War launched against Nasser's Egypt in 1956 by the British, French, and Israelis.

sufism Popular religiosity, sometimes mystical, in which the followers of a pious founder group themselves into paths or *turuq*.

sultan Title adopted by rulers, such as the head of the Ottoman Empire, in much of the Middle East.

Sunnism Predominant branch of Islam in most of the world, including Turkey and most of the Arab world.

Tabriz City in northern Iran.

tanzimat Literally, regulations; refers to Ottoman "reform" period of the nineteenth century, during which the imperial government attempted to "modernize" and centralize its power.

tariqa **(pl.: *turuq*)** Sufi "path."

tawula Backgammon.

tax farmer Agent who pays taxes for a given territory or industry up front; in return, he is allowed to extract surplus from that territory or industry.

timar Land grant made to the commander of a cavalry unit in the early Ottoman Empire.

tiyul Persian equivalent of *timar*.

Trans-Jordan The territory to the east of the Jordan River; currently the Hashemite Kingdom of Jordan.

Treaty of Balta Liman (1838) Treaty between Britain and the Ottoman Empire in which the Ottomans agreed to abolish monopolies in their realms and lower customs duties; for signing the treaty, the Ottomans received British assistance in removing Egyptian troops from the Levant.

tribe A group of people who claim descent from a common ancestor, whether or not they are related to that common ancestor or even to each other.

Tudeh The Communist Party of Iran.

Turkish Petroleum Company The second great oil concession and the first one made to a consortium; controlled all aspects of the oil industry in Ottoman domains.

ulama (sing.: *'alim*) Muslim religious scholars.

United Nations Relief and Works Agency (UNRWA) United Nations agency entrusted with caring for Palestinian refugees after the 1948 war for Palestine.

U.N. Resolution 242 Resolution passed by the Security Council of the United Nations after the 1967 war establishing the "land for peace" formula.

U.N. Resolution 338 Resolution passed by the Security Council of the United Nations after the 1973 war that fundamentally reiterated U.N. Resolution 242.

United Nations Special Committee on Palestine (UNSCOP) Committee established in the General Assembly of the United Nations to determine the fate of the British mandate in Palestine; the majority report called for division of Palestine between Zionist and Arab communities.

'Urabi Revolt (1881–1882) Revolt initiated by the Egyptian military to end foreign interference, domestic autocracy, and discrimination against native Egyptians. The revolt received wide support, but was crushed by the British.

Usuli School of Shi'ism that asserted that select religious scholars could supplement the original sources of law through the use of reason (*ijtihad*).

vali-e faqih Head of state of the Islamic Republic of Iran.

velayat-e faqih Literally, government of the jurisconsult; form of government of the Islamic Republic of Iran in which the head of state is a legal expert qualified to rule on matters pertaining to the shari'a.

wafd/**Wafd** Literally, delegation; Egyptian political party founded by Sa'd Zaghlul.

Wahhabism Puritanical religious movement found by Muhammad ibn 'Abd al-Wahhab in the eighteenth century.

waqf Religious endowment.

World Zionist Organization Organization established in 1897 at the First Zionist Congress "to create for the Jewish people a home in Palestine secured by Public Law"; the W.Z.O. has been the central institutional expression of the international Zionist movement.

Young Ottomans Diffuse group of nineteenth-century intellectuals who advocated Islamic modernism and constitutional rule in the Ottoman Empire.

Young Turks Name given to an amalgam of groups opposed to Abdulhamid II; in 1908 the Young Turks staged a revolt and restored the Ottoman constitution.

Zaghlul, Sa'd Leader of a group of Egyptians that sought to represent Egypt at the Paris Peace Conference after World War I; his arrest and deportation led to the 1919 Revolution; founder of Wafd Party.

Zionism The belief that Jews are a national community entitled to their own independent state; most Zionists believe that such a state should be situated in Palestine.

Credits

Page 24: "Because of their distance from the circuit of the sun. . . ." Bernard Lewis, Islam from the Prophet Muhammad to the Capture of Constantinople, vol. 2: Religion and Society (New York: Oxford University Press, 1987), 122.

Page 25: "A moon arose from the holy man's breast. . . ." Cemal Kafadar, Between Two Worlds: The Construction of the Ottoman State (Berkeley: University of California Press, 1995), 8.

Page 28: "After a siege of forty days . . ." Edward Gibbon, The Decline and Fall of the Roman Empire, vol. 3 (New York: Modern Library, n.d.), 771.

Page 30: "Musitch Stefan." Helen Rootham, Kossovo: Heroic Songs of the Serbs, (Oxford: B.H. Blackwell, 1920), 59–60.

Page 45: "The sale of Bengal opium. . . ." A.J.H. Latham, The International Economy and the Undeveloped World, 1865-1914 (London: Croom Helm, 1978), 409–10.

Page 92: "The Algerians were revolutionists. . . ." http://www.americanrhetoric.com/speeches/malcolmxgrassroots.htm

Chapter 7: All quotes from Salim Tamari, "Jerusalem's Ottoman Modernity: The Times and Lives of Wasif Jawhariyyeh," Jerusalem Quarterly File 9 (2000), 5–34.

Page 140: "the word 'Constitution' was in every mouth. . . ." Bernard Lewis, The Emergence of Modern Turkey (New York: Oxford University Press, 2002), 161.

Page 146: "Imagine some five hundred illiterate young men. . . ." Elie Kedourie, Arabic Political Memoirs (London: Cass, 1974), 137.

Page 188: "The wave of civilization has come to us. . . ." Ibrahim Ibrahim, "Ahmad Amin and ʿAbbas Mahmud al-ʿAqqad between al-Qadim and al-Jadid: European Challenge and Islamic Response," in Arab Civilization: Challenges and Responses, ed. George N. Atiyeh and Ibrahim M. Oweiss (Albany: SUNY Press, 1988), 209.

Page 188: "The love for one's country. . . ." Robert P. Mitchell, The Society of the Muslim Brothers (New York: Oxford University Press, 1993), 265.

Page 232: "In the future Turks must possess. . . ." Ziya Gokalp, The Principles of Turkism, trans. Robert Devereaux (Leiden: EJ Brill, 1968), n.p.

Page 233: "Establishing industries is a delegated duty. . . ." Jacqueline S. Ismael and Tareq Y. Ismael, "Cultural Perspectives on Social Welfare in the Emergence of Modern Arab Social Thought," The Muslim World LXXXV:1–2 (January–April 1995), 95.

Page 236–37: "The aim of the Syrian Social Nationalist Party. . . ." Labib Zuwiyya Yamak, The Syrian Social Nationalist Party: An Ideological Analysis (Cambridge, MA: Harvard Middle Eastern Monograph Series, 1966), 98.

Page 277: "Yasser Arafat and I knew. . . ." Helena Cobban, The Palestinian Liberation Organisation: People, Power, and Politics (Cambridge, ENG: Cambridge University Press, 1984), 21–22.

Page 288: "We attacked them as the sun rose. . . ." F.E. Peters, A Reader on Classical Islam (Princeton: Princeton University Press, 1994), 130–31.

Page 289: "I tell you plainly. . . ." Ayatollah Khomeini, Islam and Revolution: Writings and Declarations of Imam Khomeini, trans. and annot. Hamid Algar (Berkeley: Mizan Press, 1981), 207.

Page 291: "Muhammad Reza Pahlavi is gone. . . ." http://www.irna.ir/occasion/ertehal/english/biog/(Iranian News Agency)

Page 295–97: Quotes from Hamas Charter found in Shaul Mishal and Avraham Sela, The Palestinian Hamas: Vision, Violence, and Coexistence (New York: Columbia University Press, 2000), 175–99.

Index